RAIN DANCING: SANCTIONS IN CANADIAN AND AUSTRALIAN FOREIGN POLICY

Since their success during the First World War, sanctions have become a popular tool of statecraft, used to deter, coerce, or punish regimes that violate international norms. For example, like other Western states, Canada has been an active sanctioner, imposing sanctions against some twenty-two countries during the 1980s. In this book, Kim Richard Nossal questions the usefulness, for middle powers such as Canada and Australia, of the theory that underpins international sanctions. He contends that because Canada and Australia lack the economic capabilities that give the sanctions of major powers their bite, the sanctions of these middle powers amount to no more than a rain dance: they accomplish little but make the public feel that something is being done about a serious problem.

Nossal presents six case studies of Canadian and Australian sanctions episodes from the late 1970s to the early 1990s, against China, Indonesia, Iraq, the former Soviet Union, South Africa, and Vietnam. He explores the conception and justification of sanctions within the political discourse surrounding each episode, and examines factors such as domestic, coalition, and symbolic politics. Nossal concludes that even though sanctions achieve few foreign-policy goals, they inflict harm on ordinary people and are therefore a foreign-policy tool of questionable morality.

KIM RICHARD NOSSAL is Professor in the Department of Political Science, McMaster University, Hamilton, Ontario.

KIM RICHARD NOSSAL

Rain Dancing: Sanctions in Canadian and Australian Foreign Policy

UNIVERSITY OF TORONTO PRESS
Toronto Buffalo London

© University of Toronto Press Incorporated 1994
Toronto Buffalo London
Printed in Canada

ISBN 0-8020-0472-5 (cloth)
ISBN 0-8020-7571-1 (paper)

∞

Printed on acid-free paper

Canadian Cataloguing in Publication Data

Nossal, Kim Richard
  Rain dancing : sanctions in Canadian and Australian
  foreign policy

  Includes index.
  ISBN 0-8020-0472-5 (bound)   ISBN 0-8020-7571-1 (pbk.)

  1. Sanctions (International law). 2. Economic
  sanctions, Canadian. 3. Canada – Foreign relations –
  1945–   . 4. Economic sanctions, Australian.
  5. Australia – Foreign relations – 1945–   .
  I. Title.

  FC602.N67 1994   327.71   C94-930334-8
  F1034.2.N67 1994

University of Toronto Press acknowledges the financial assistance to its
publishing program of the Canada Council and the Ontario Arts Council.

This book has been published with the help of a contribution from the
Department of Foreign Affairs and International Trade.

For Renée and Margot

Contents

Preface

As a tool of statecraft, sanctions have enjoyed a persistent popularity over the course of the twentieth century. Following the First World War, when economic statecraft against the Central Powers in Europe was widely believed to have contributed to the eventual victory of the Western allies, sanctions became the instrument of choice for the new system being put into place by the victors at the Versailles peace conference. Sanctions were widely regarded as the preferred and peaceful alternative to war that would undergird the new world order to be created by the League of Nations.

Not even the collapse of the League system caused sanctions to fall from favour: instead, in the 1950s and 1960s, sanctions proved to be an integral part of the American-led Western statecraft against the Soviet Union and China, as well as their smaller allies such as North Korea, Cuba, and North Vietnam. By the 1970s, sanctions had been established as the premier diplomatic instrument for dealing with wrong-doing in the international system: between the late 1970s and the early 1990s, sanctions were employed against numerous states in the international system.

Even with the radical transformation of the system that came with the disappearance of the Soviet Union in December 1991, sanctions remain a popular tool of statecraft at century's end. They are eagerly advocated when some cruelty is committed by a government – consider Western reactions to the Tiananmen massacre in June 1989; or the murder of East Timorese protestors by Indonesian forces in Dili in November 1991; or the attacks by Serbian forces on other groups in the former Yugoslavia in the years after 1991; or the assassinations in Haiti in 1993. Sanctions tend to be the response of choice when there is a coup, as Western reactions in the cases of the coups in Haiti, the former Soviet Union, and Algeria in 1991, or Thailand in 1992, suggest. Sanctions remain the favoured policy instrument against regimes that systematically violate human rights on an on-going basis, as the cases of Burma (or Myanmar) and South Africa have persistently demonstrated.

Not surprisingly, sanctions enjoyed the same kind of popularity in Canada as in other Western states. And, on numerous occasions, the Canadian government, as a member of the Western alliance, was an active sanctioner. Over the course of the 1980s, the Canadian government imposed sanctions against some twenty-two countries: Afghanistan, Angola, Argentina, Burma (Myanmar), China, Cuba, El Salvador, Fiji, Guatemala, Haiti, Iran, Iraq, Kenya, Kuwait, Libya, Poland, South Africa, the Soviet Union, Sri Lanka, Yugoslavia, Vietnam, and Zaire.

To be sure, the government in Ottawa was not always an eager sanctioner. At times the government was clearly reluctant, and in at least one case – the American-sponsored sanctions against the Sandinista government of Nicaragua in the mid-1980s – Canadian policy sharply diverged from the sanctionist enthusiasms of the United States administration of Ronald Reagan. On the whole, however, the Canadian government proved no less willing than other Western governments to embrace this particular tool of statecraft.

It can be argued that one of the most striking aspects of Canada's use of sanctions in the 1980s was not that they were employed, but rather how these sanctions were conceived and justified in political discourse within Canada. For the terms of the public and governmental debate in Canada about sanctions, applied to the case of a specific country, such as South Africa, or the Soviet Union, or China, closely mirrored the debates being carried on in the United States and major European powers about how to deter or coerce states accused of wrong-doing. Indeed, so close were the terms of the debate that they tended to blur completely the fact that there is one basic difference between Canada and such great powers as the United States, Japan, or the major European states – Britain, France, or Germany: while these larger states possess the capabilities to produce considerable and concrete harms on the targets of their sanctions, Canada's capabilities are simply not at all commensurate with the attributes of the major powers. On the contrary, the ability of the Canadian government to inflict significant and sufficient harm on other states in the international system is quite limited.

In other words, despite the *heterogeneity* of the states employing sanctions, there tends to be an essential *homogeneity* to the public discussions and political justifications about the usefulness (or lack thereof) of sanctions; about the effectiveness (or inefficacy) of this tool of statecraft; or about their positive (or negative) aspects in a particular country-specific context. In particular, the justificatory arguments about the utilities (or 'useful purposes') of sanctions being offered by policymakers in Ottawa (and by those advocates pressing their pro- or anti-sanctions perspective on the government) were informed by theoretical perspectives on the utilities of international sanctions being advanced by scholars in both the United States and Europe.

These theoretical perspectives, which taken together can loosely be called an orthodox 'theory' of international sanctions, conceive of this tool of statecraft in largely generic terms. Sanctions always have a set of 'purposes,' the generic theory suggests, and it does not matter whether the sanctions are being embraced by a global and hegemonic superpower or a microstate: foreign policy decision-makers will seek to advance a generic set of purposes through their embrace of sanctions. When a state imposes sanctions on another state – the 'target,' as it is called in the literature – the sanctioning state (or the 'sender') does so for instrumental purposes: to deter or compel the target into changing its behaviour; or to subvert the government of the target state through economic deprivation; or to express a policy position symbolically to one's own public or to other states in the international system. These are the generic utilities of sanctions.

It is true that, at one level, the similarities in political discourse about sanctions between the greater and the smaller powers are hardly surprising. After all, imitative behaviour that crosses political boundaries is a phenomenon in world politics that is not new; nor is the general direction of the copying observed in the Canadian case unusual. Transnational copycatting has a long pedigree: societies have always borrowed, copied, and adopted from other societies. Moreover, the tendency has generally been for societies on the periphery to look to those of the centre as the standard-bearer, whether it be in haute couture or the terms of political discourse. In short, it is not at all remarkable that debates in Canada over international sanctions against South Africa, the Soviet Union, China, Iraq, or Vietnam should be conducted in terms that would be instantly recognizable to Americans or Britons.

While it is understandable that the terms of the sanctions debate in Canada should mirror so closely the debates being carried on elsewhere, it is none the less remarkable that there has been so little questioning in a middle power like Canada of the purposes of international sanctions, which are tools of statecraft by and for great powers. For the purposes of these sanctions are closely bound to the political purposes of the governments of the great powers. Likewise, the logic that drives the generic 'theory of sanctions' – as it has been explicated in English, at least – is the logic proposed by political scientists from the hegemonic centre.

As a student of Canadian foreign policy, I have been particularly interested in Canada's involvement in these sanctions 'episodes' (as the particular case studies of sanctions tend to be referred to in the academic literature). The more I examined Canada's sanctions policy, however, the more I came to believe that the generic 'theory of sanctions' was not very useful in the Canadian context. For while the generic theory might provide a useful theoretical framework to analyse – or debate – the use of sanctions by states that are great powers, the same cannot be said when this theory is applied in the case of states that do not have great resources and capabilities to give their sanctions concrete effectiveness.

In my previous writing on sanctions, I tried to test this belief. My initial work in this area – a 1987 study of Canadian sanctions against Vietnam after its invasion of Cambodia in 1978 – suggested that the generic theory of sanctions did not account at all clearly for the imposition of sanctions against Vietnam by the Canadian government. It suggested that if one did not go beyond the 'utilities' outlined by the generic theory, one would be left with a most incomplete view of what drove Canadian sanctions against Hanoi in the 1980s.

But the case of Canada's punishment of Vietnam also demonstrated one of the serious shortcomings of using a single country as the basis for a test of generic sanctions theory. It would not be clear from a single case alone whether the generic theory could provide a nuanced analysis of the sanctions experience. Rather, a stronger test of the viability of the generic theory would be to also apply it to another state that was also not a great power.

The choice of Australia as a comparison for the Canadian experience was in many respects natural. Australia, like Canada, was an active sanctioner in the 1980s, and the two states frequently found themselves sanctioning the same wrong-doer. Most important for our purposes here, both states share numerous structural similarities in world politics. While the term is admittedly problematic, both states are 'middle powers' in contemporary international politics. They have similar politico-historical roots, and comparable historical places in the contemporary international system. Since their transformation in the nineteenth century into relatively independent (if not always autonomous) communities in the modern states-system, both states have always been tightly aligned to the hegemonic power of the era – first Britain, and then the United States. Likewise, both states have industrialized economies, with a large service sector, but also a fair reliance on exportable primary products; and both are heavily dependent on trade with the other industrialized powers (the United States, Japan, and the European Community) for their wealth. As dependent states, therefore, both are comparably located in the contemporary international political economy (although their dependencies differ considerably). In short, both states are well placed to test the assumptions of the generic theory of sanctions.

This book begins with an exploration into the generic theory of sanctions. It outlines the main tenets of that theory, and demonstrates its usefulness when applied to states in the international system that have superordinate resources and capabilities. This introductory chapter also shows what nuances the generic theory fails to expose, particularly for non-great powers like Australia and Canada. Instead, it seeks to elaborate a different set of 'utilities' that smaller powers are likely to have as they consider embracing the sanctions option.

Smaller powers, I argue, have reasons for embracing sanctions that are fundamentally different from the reasons that underwrite the sanctions policies of larger states. Rather than being primarily moved by instrumentality, non-great powers like Australia and Canada embrace sanctions for largely symbolic reasons. Indeed, I suggest that the sanctions policies of middle powers tend to have all the attributes of what a witness, testifying before a United States Senate foreign relations committee panel in 1982, called a 'rain dance' – in other words, an activity that actually accomplishes very little, but that makes the participants feel good because something is being done about a serious problem.

The chapters that follow seek to provide confirming evidence for the general proposition that the generic theory of sanctions does not provide a sound basis for understanding the sanctions policies of middle powers such as Australia and Canada. It should be noted that this book does not aim to provide a comprehensive history of all the sanctions episodes engaged in by these two middle powers. Rather, the confirmation is offered in a series of illustrative case studies, five of which focus primarily on the Canadian experience with sanctions in the 1980s, and three of which offer explicit comparisons of the Australian and Canadian experiences.

Part One begins with an examination of the case of Indonesia and of the responses of the Canadian government to large-scale human rights violations by Indonesia in the 1970s, and in particular to the Indonesian invasion of Timor in 1975. This was a case in which sanctions were actively avoided by Ottawa for many years. This chapter contrasts – and explains – Canada's silence on these issues in the 1970s and 1980s with its willingness to embrace sanctions in the aftermath of the Dili massacre in November 1991, arguing that we cannot understand a middle power's sanctions unless we put them into a wider geopolitical context.

The two chapters that follow focus on Canada's sanctions against Vietnam in response to that country's invasion of Cambodia: chapter 3 examines the factors that led to the imposition of sanctions against the government in Hanoi in early 1979, and the factors that led to their continued imposition throughout the 1980s. Chapter 4 examines the complex dynamic of ending Canada's sanctions against Vietnam in 1990 following the Vietnamese troop withdrawal from Cambodia.

Two chapters focus on Canadian sanctions against South Africa, imposed in response to the institutionalized racism of apartheid. Chapter 5 examines how a change of leadership may affect a state's approach to sanctions, and explores the impact that Brian Mulroney and his senior policy-makers had on Canadian sanctions against South Africa. Chapter 6 focuses on the effect of federalism on the sanctions experience. Using the case of the Ontario government's sanctions against South Africa in the mid-1980s, this chapter explores how the federal dynamic can alter the sanctions policy of states.

In order to demonstrate the degree to which Canadian sanctions policy was by no means unique, Part Two presents three case studies that are explicitly comparative – the case of Australian and Canadian sanctions against the Soviet Union following the invasion of Afghanistan in December 1979 (chapter 7); the sanctions both countries imposed against China after the Tiananmen massacre of June 1989 (chapter 8); and those against Iraq following its invasion of Kuwait in August 1990 (chapter 9). These chapters seek to illustrate both the Australian and Canadian experiences within each case, and highlight important similarities and differences.

The third part of the book examines the implications for theory and policy of these case studies. Canada's use of sanctions against both the Soviet Union and China provides the backdrop for an examination of one of the key problems of sanctions: knowing when to lift them. For sanctions are kept in place because policy-makers frequently cannot find an appropriate time to lift them. Chapter 10 explores what I have termed the 'termination trap' in international sanctions, contrasting Canadian experience with the Australian sanctions imposed in the wake of the Tiananmen massacre. Chapter 11 looks at the issue of the impact of rhetoric on a state's sanctions policy, and in particular how rhetoric affected the Canadian government's sanctions against South Africa in the years following the Mulroney government's activism of 1985–6.

Finally, the conclusion (chapter 12) attempts to draw together briefly the evidence of the case studies in support of the argument that the generic theory of sanctions does not provide an adequate basis for analysis of why smaller states employ sanctions in international politics. And if the generic theory is found wanting at the analytical level, then, by implication, it should also be inadequate as the basis for policy.

The conclusion is an excursus into an explicitly normative discussion of the implications of the findings of this book for the policy debate about sanctions in Canada – but it also has relevance for other non-great powers such as Australia. It concludes that the terms of the sanctions debate, borrowed so liberally from the great powers, are either inadequate or downright misleading when applied in the Australian or Canadian context. The case studies in this book might suggest that in future instances of wrong-doing by other states, the debate over sanctions in the non-great powers should embrace greater realism; that advocates of a sanctionist approach, both within and outside government, should adopt more moderate expectations; that policy-makers, for their part, should employ more nuanced and balanced justifications that more accurately reflect why this tool of statecraft is as attractive to non-great powers as it is to the great powers. But the conclusion also examines why the sanctions debate in countries like Canada and Australia will remain largely unaffected by such analytical considerations, and why therefore the sanctions debate will continue to have many of the attributes of a rain dance.

But if a rain dance is basically benign, international sanctions are not. For while they may not prove effective in making governments 'mend their ways,' sanctions none the less are quite effective in producing deprivations within target states. Because of the effects that sanctions do produce – notably hurting the wrong people in the target state – I conclude that for all their popularity, sanctions are a notoriously poor tool of statecraft.

The research for this book was supported by grants from several organizations. Most of the work – on some of the Canadian cases and all the Australian cases – was aided by a research grant from the Social

Sciences and Humanities Research Council of Canada, and so it is to the Council that I owe my most considerable debt of gratitude for its continued support of my research and writing. This grant also enabled me to present the results of my research to colleagues on both sides of the Pacific, and to benefit from their comments and criticisms. For assistance in the publication of this work, I am particularly grateful to the Department of Foreign Affairs and International Trade.

My research on Vietnam was aided by grants from both the now-defunct Canadian Institute for International Peace and Security and the Arts Research Board of McMaster University. These grants allowed me to join a group of Canadian academics, under the leadership of Professor David Wurfel of the University of Windsor, who travelled to Thailand and Vietnam in April and May 1988 on a research trip focusing on Canadian relations with the states of Indochina. (The results of that visit were published in Richard Stubbs, comp., *Vietnam: Facing the 1990s*, Asia Papers 1 [Toronto 1989].)

Much of the case-study material in this book is drawn from articles and book chapters I have published over the last six years. In particular, material has been drawn from the following sources: 'Les droits de la personne et la politique étrangère canadienne: Le cas de l'Indonésie,' *Etudes internationales* 11 (juin 1980), 223–38; 'Les sanctions économiques et les petits états: Le cas de la "punition" du Vietnam par le Canada,' *Etudes internationales* 18 (septembre 1987), 523–44; 'Necessary and Sufficient Conditions: The Inertial Factor in Canadian Sanctions against Vietnam,' in Richard Stubbs, comp., *Vietnam: Facing the 1990s*, Asia Papers 1 (Toronto: Joint Centre for Asia Pacific Studies 1989), 61–79; 'Canadian Sanctions against South Africa: Explaining the Mulroney Initiatives, 1985–86,' *Journal of Canadian Studies* 25 (Winter 1990–1), 17–33; ' "Microdiplomacy": The Case of Ontario and Economic Sanctions against South Africa,' in William M. Chandler and Christian W. Zöllner, eds, *Challenges to Federalism: Policy-Making in Canada and the Federal Republic of Germany* (Kingston: Institute of Intergovernmental Relations, Queen's University 1989), 235–50; 'The Symbolic Purposes of Sanctions: Australian and Canadian Reactions to Afghanistan,' *Australian Journal of Political Science* 26 (March 1991), 29–50; Andrew F. Cooper, Richard A. Higgott, and Kim Richard Nossal, *Relocating Middle Powers: Australia and Canada in a Changing World Order* (Vancouver: University of British Columbia Press 1993), 116–43; 'Knowing When to Fold: Western Sanctions against the USSR 1980–1983,' *International Journal* 44 (Summer 1989), 698–724; and 'Out of Steam? Mulroney and Sanctions,' *Interna-

tional Perspectives 17 (November/December 1988), 13–15. I am most grateful to the following for their permission to use material from those publications here: the Centre québécois de relations internationales; Joint Centre for Asia-Pacific Studies, York University–University of Toronto; *Journal of Canadian Studies*; Institute of Intergovernmental Relations, Queen's University; Australasian Political Studies Association; University of British Columbia Press; and the Canadian Institute of International Affairs.

This book would not have been possible without the help of numerous people. First, I owe a debt of gratitude to all those students at McMaster University who were my research assistants over the course of this project. The labours of Luc Baudouin St-Cyr, Robert Crawford, Heather McTavish, Christopher LeClair, and Dave Collins made my own tasks so much easier, and for that I thank them sincerely.

Research on contemporary foreign policy inevitably depends heavily on officials and policy-makers who are willing to share with members of the academic community their perceptions of the decision-making process. I am grateful to the Canadian and Australian officials in Canberra and Ottawa whose interviews and meetings provided much of the information on which these case studies are based. Comparable thanks are owed to those numerous officials, governmental and non-governmental, from Australia, Cambodia, Canada, and Vietnam who gave our delegation lengthy and informative briefings and interviews in Bangkok and Hanoi.

A number of colleagues commented on different chapters of this book: my thanks to Howard Balloch, Earl Drake, Paul Evans, Richard Leaver, Peter Van Ness, and Jing-Dong Yuan for reading drafts so promptly – and offering such useful advice. I am also grateful to the anonymous reviewers engaged by the University of Toronto Press, both of whom offered helpful comments and suggestions. Special thanks are due to my editor, John St James, whose careful eye caught innumerable errors and inelegancies in the original manuscript.

I am also grateful to my Australian colleagues for their contribution to the comparative element of this book. The SSHRCC grant allowed me to spend two months as a visiting fellow in the Department of International Relations at the Australian National University in 1989, and to visit the Department in the years following. The members of the Department of International Relations and the Peace Studies Centre at the ANU not only extended to me a warm welcome; they were also unstinting in offering sorely needed assistance to a novice in Australian politics and foreign policy. In particular, I would like to thank Graeme Cheeseman, Trevor Finlay, Andrew Mack, Michael McKinley, J.L. Richardson, and Peter Van Ness. And special thanks are owed to Richard Leaver, whose own work on sanctions has influenced me considerably, and to Andrew F. Cooper and Richard A. Higgott, my collaborators on other trans-Pacific projects, for having helped sharpen my thinking on middle-power foreign policy.

KRN
Hamilton, Ontario
November 1993

RAIN DANCING

1

The 'Generic' Theory of Sanctions Reconsidered: A Non–Great Power Perspective

International sanctions remain one of the most popular tools of state-craft in contemporary international politics. They tend to be the favoured response for ordinary citizens who are outraged by what they regard as wrongful behaviour by other governments. They are widely seen to be a non-violent and non-lethal way of punishing such wrong-doing, or in Jean Prévost's words, bringing a country to 'mend its ways.'[1] Because they involve non-violent measures, sanctions are also seen as a superior alternative to other tools of statecraft, such as the use of force or assassination; because they involve concrete measures, sanctions are regarded as more effective than verbal condemnation.

For their part, policy-makers also find sanctions an attractive response to international wrong-doing. Not only do sanctions demonstrate that policy-makers are actually doing something in response to wrong-doing by another government, but this tool of statecraft allows political leaders to avoid having to use the more violent, and thus more unpredictable, tools in their repertoire. Moreover, governments seeking to sanction other governments have a wide variety of measures from which to select. Margaret Doxey enumerates thirty-eight different sanctions that a government can embrace. These include *diplomatic and political measures* (such as cancelling negotiations, reducing diplomatic represen-tation, or severing diplomatic relations); *cultural and communications measures* (such as cancelling exchanges, banning tourism, or suspending communications links); *economic measures* (such as cancelling aid, freez-ing assets, or banning the movement of goods, services, or capital); and *organizational penalties* (such as suspension or expulsion from interna-tional organizations).[2]

Much of the thinking of governors and governed alike about international sanctions as a tool of statecraft has been shaped by a large scholarly literature that has grown up over the course of the twentieth century.[3] This literature addresses two broad theoretical and practical issues. First, scholars have sought to uncover the 'utilities,' or useful purposes, of international sanctions, exploring what states are seeking to achieve when they embrace sanctions. Generally, as we will see below, scholars argue that sanctions are designed to meet a number of instrumental and expressive purposes: deterrence, compellence, subversion, and domestic and international symbolism.

Second, scholars have sought to know what effects sanctions have as a tool of statecraft – in particular whether they 'work' or not, and under what conditions international sanctions will produce the desired effects identified by sanctions theory. Disagreements on these general issues have generated much of the debate in the literature, a debate, it should be noted, that tends to be echoed in the political realm by both governors and the governed.

THE DEBATE OVER SANCTIONS

The broad contours of this academic and political debate over the use and effectiveness of international sanctions have remained remarkably constant over the course of the century: the same kind of arguments have been persistently used regarding the effectiveness of sanctions as a proper response against aggression, or human rights violations, or other wrong-doing by states in international politics. The advocacy for – and against – sanctions as a response to Japanese human rights violations in China, or Italian aggression in Ethiopia during the interwar years, could be heard echoing in debates about sanctions as an appropriate response to Serbian aggression against Croats and Bosnian Muslims at the century's end. The same arguments have resurfaced over the many cases of human rights violations in the post-1945 period, such as apartheid in South Africa during the 1970s and 1980s or the killing of pro-reform demonstrators in China during the massacre in and around Tiananmen Square in June 1989.

Likewise, the same positions tended to be articulated when one state invaded another country and overthrew the legitimate government there, either extinguishing its sovereignty outright or replacing it with a new government more to its liking. The equally lengthy litany of cases in the last quarter of the century would include the Indonesian invasion of East Timor in December 1975; the Vietnamese invasion of Cambodia (or Kampuchea, as it was known then) in December 1978; the Tanzanian invasion of Uganda in April 1979; the Soviet invasion of Afghanistan in December 1979; the Argentinean invasion of the Falkland Islands in April 1982; the American invasions of Grenada in October 1983 and of Panama in December 1989; the Iraqi invasion of Kuwait in August 1990; and the Serbian incursions into Croatia and Bosnia in the years after 1991.

That the debate over sanctions as a response to international wrong-doing should be so unchanging over the course of a single century is hardly remarkable. David A. Baldwin, for one, has shown that twenti-eth-century debates about the appropriateness and effectiveness of sanctions as a tool of statecraft find their own echoes in debates that Greeks were engaging in 2500 years ago about how best to respond to Megaran impieties.[4] The essential sameness in the terms of the debate over wrong-doing in international society mirrors the debate within civil society over how best to respond to rule-breaking domestically, and what punishments should be meted out to wrong-doers for their wrongs.

However, what is remarkable about the homogeneity of the debate about international sanctions and their effectiveness is that the states that employ these measures are so heterogeneous. All types of states – large and small, powerful and weak, rich and poor, from both the metropole and the periphery – have been prone to embrace sanctions in their statecraft. Yet both theoretical and political discussions about international sanctions tend to be derived from the experience of the great powers alone; there is little in the literature about the sanctions experience of what German scholars in the interwar period used to categorize simply as the 'non-great powers' – the *Nichtgrossmachten*. Instead, there is an underlying assumption that the orthodox 'theory'[5] of sanctions provides a satisfactory *generic* account of state behaviour: the theoretical perspectives on the useful purposes and the effectiveness of sanctions will hold true for any state employing sanctions, regardless of its attributes or characteristics.

Such an assumption, however, does not sit easily with another wide-spread assumption in international politics: that size and power are critical determinants of foreign policy behaviour. Just as a state will be inclined in particular directions by the very fact of its great power, so too will being a middle (or small) power incline a state in quite differ-ent directions, as Carsten Holbraad, among others, has demonstrated so persuasively.[6] Indeed, the assumption that size and power are key determinants of behaviour is so pervasive – and so commonsensical – that it strongly suggests that generic sanctions theory, which does not predict any variations on the basis of such attributes, should be examined more closely.

It is true that there is an obvious analytical rejoinder to the issue of size and power: that there is implicit allowance made in the generic theory for all those states that lack the superordinate resources and capabilities of the international system's major powers. Such states, it can be argued, use sanctions not for the *instrumental* purposes identified by the generic theory (that is, to elicit concrete results from the target), but only for the purely *symbolic* purposes (that is, to take a political position, regardless of whether that expression of policy actually had a concrete effect on the target). But one would not want to embrace this argument too readily or uncritically. For, as Makio Miyagawa, using the case of Japan, has argued,[7] there are some states in the international system that, although they are not great powers, none the less have sufficient resources and capabilities to design sanctions that could have an instrumental effect on targets.

The purpose of this book is to question whether the orthodox theory of sanctions offers us an adequate and sufficiently nuanced explanation of the sanctions policies of states other than those great powers that are the usual focus of sanctions theory. To this end, this book explores the sanctions policies of two 'non-great powers,' Australia and Canada.

Australia and Canada are usually considered middle powers in contemporary international politics. To be sure, the very notion of 'middle power' is problematic, for there is little agreement on what constitutes a middle power.[8] However, the terminology none the less provides a useful means of distinguishing between those larger powers endowed with considerable capabilities and smaller political communities with few power capabilities.

Despite the ambiguity of the term, middle powers do provide a useful focus for an investigation of the utilities of international sanctions precisely because of their middling capabilities. On the one hand, middle powers do not have the capabilities of the large powers that would give their sanctions effective and instrumental impact. Unlike the great powers, middle powers simply do not have the ability to inflict serious harm on other states with sanctions. On the other hand, middle powers have relatively greater capabilities than small states or microstates. While it is possible to explain the sanctions policies of a microstate as pure symbolism – in other words, sanctions not designed to have any instrumental impact on the target – middle powers are not so small that one could simply explain their sanctions policies in symbolic terms.

Australia and Canada are two middle powers that provide a good test of the orthodox generic theory. While Australia and Canada have frequently exhibited contrasting diplomatic styles,[9] the governments in Canberra and Ottawa tended to be like-minded and active sanctioners in the 1980s and 1990s. Since the late 1970s, Canberra and Ottawa have imposed sanctions against an array of other states, including Afghanistan, Argentina, China, Iran, Iraq, Libya, Poland, South Africa, the Soviet Union, and Vietnam. Both states have a fair degree of economic strength and, given the goods they trade in, not inconsiderable power resources: unlike small or micro states, both Australia and Canada have some capacity to inflict serious harm on a range of other states in the international system. Thus, the sanctions adopted by either state cannot be easily explained away as mere symbolism.

I begin by briefly outlining orthodox sanctions theory and the 'useful purposes' usually associated with sanctions in international affairs. However, I will suggest that these generic purposes of sanctions – purposes that ironically dominate so much of the contemporary debate over international sanctions in both Australia and Canada – actually have little connection to Australian or Canadian practice. Instead, I will argue that the orthodox theory tends to hide a more complex political dynamic that drives the sanctions process in smaller states, a process in which rather different utilities figure more prominently.

Such a finding, it should be stressed, is of more than merely academic interest. Leaders of non-great powers find sanctions just as attractive a tool of statecraft as their great-power counterparts. The difficulty is that non–great power leaders tend to use orthodox assumptions about sanctions, with the result that orthodox theory, which is reflective of great-power practice, also tends to drive political debates in middle powers like Australia and Canada. Thus, policy discussions over sanctions and their putative effects on the targets tend to become distorted in these smaller states. In particular, political leaders in middle powers tend to embrace the same rhetoric about the effectiveness of sanctions as that employed by their great-power counterparts, thus creating expectations, both domestically and internationally, that cannot possibly be fulfilled, as we will see in the final part of this book.

SANCTIONS IN THEORY

Much of our thinking about international sanctions, in both the academic literature and the political arena, is informed by a bundle of essentially liberal assumptions about political behaviour.[10] These include, first, the assumption that individuals are rational value-maximizers: they seek to embrace pleasure and avoid pain; and we can best understand (and predict) their political behaviour in these terms. Second, the theory assumes that states (or, more properly, government leaders) are essentially just like individuals in this respect: they, too, are rational value-maximizers, and will seek to avoid pain inflicted on them or their state, and instead will strive to embrace 'pleasure,' or the assumed benefits of transactions of all sorts with the international community at large. Third, it is assumed that just as individuals can be made to change their behaviour (if not their values or their preferences) by the threat, or imposition, of non-violent harms that cause pain or deprivation, so too can governments.

Thus armed with these key assumptions, sanctions theory focuses on the ways in which a government (in the literature commonly called 'the sender') can, by using the threat or imposition of non-violent hurts, alter the behaviour of another government (in the argot, the 'target') that the sender finds objectionable or 'wrong.'[11] In addition to these instrumental purposes, however, generic sanctions theory focuses on the 'symbolic' purposes of sanctions: the effects that using this tool of statecraft will have on those besides the wrong-doer. These purposes, instrumental and symbolic, are generally held to include the following.[12]

Deterrence

It is often argued that the principal purpose of sanctions is to deter a target from engaging in wrongful behaviour. More properly, deterrent sanctions are those harms that are *threatened* rather than actually *imposed*. The sender threatens that future harm will come if the target engages in wrong-doing. Should the deterrent fail, however, and should the target actually engage in wrong-doing, it is often said that sanctions can be imposed against the wrong-doer to deter *further* comparable acts. Some, like David A. Baldwin, have argued that this purpose seems highly problematic. For example, it is commonly asserted that one of the purposes of the Western sanctions imposed on the Soviet Union following its invasion of Afghanistan was to deter the Soviet leadership from making further expansionist moves in the Gulf. However, as Baldwin correctly notes, if the threat of sanctions did not forestall one act of wrongful behaviour by the target, it is unlikely that harms imposed would deter further wrongful behaviour. As he puts it, in the case of Afghanistan, a more powerful deterrent to the putative expansionism of the Soviet Union was the military threat contained in President Jimmy Carter's State of the Union address delivered in January 1980.[13]

A more logical aspect of the argument about deterrence is the classic position attached to systems of punishment domestically. In some philosophical defences of punishment *within* political communities, it is argued that harms should be imposed on individuals for one reason alone: to deter others from doing wrong. In other words, the purpose of punishment should not be the reform or rehabilitation of the wrongdoer, but the deterrence of all others. Applying this philosophy to the international system, it could be argued that sanctions imposed on a wrong-doer are designed to 'send a signal' – deter other potential wrong-doing states from engaging in comparable behaviour. Potential wrong-doers, perceiving the harm that is being visited on actual wrong-doers, recalculate the costs and benefits attached to a policy deemed wrongful, and decide to avoid doing wrong.

Compellence[14]

Sanctions may be designed for the instrumental purpose of compelling an offending state to abandon or cease behaviour that the sanctioner considers wrongful. Like a punishment imposed on a recalcitrant witness who refuses to answer a judge's question, a compellent harm is always contingent on behaviour: the punishment stops when the wrongful behaviour ceases. In a domestic juridical context, examples of compellent punishments would include sanctions imposed under back-to-work legislation that punishes strikers until they return to work or the imprisonment of a witness who refuses to answer a judge's question. In the international sphere, instances of compellent sanctions would include Western sanctions against the Soviet Union in the early 1980s for its occupation of Afghanistan; against Iran in 1980 for its holding of American diplomats as hostages; against Vietnam throughout the 1980s for its occupation of Cambodia; against South Africa for its continuing attachment to apartheid; against Libya for its support of international terrorist activity; against Iraq in 1990–1 for its occupation and annexation of Kuwait; or against the military leaders who seized power in Haiti after the 1991 elections. In each of these cases, the continued imposition of the sanctions was justified by senders in compellent terms: 'Our harms are intended to stop a wrongful act; as long as you continue to act wrongfully, our harms will continue. When you cease your wrong-doing, we will cease our harms.'

Symbolism

Sanctions may be designed not so much to have an *instrumental* purpose – that is, a concrete impact on the wrong-doer – as an *expressive*, or symbolic, purpose.[15] In other words, sanctions may be meant to express to targets other than the wrong-doing state the sender's abhorrence of the wrong-doer's actions. Sanctions with such a symbolic purpose can have both an internal and an external dimension. On the one hand, it is possible that the actual 'target' of these international sanctions may be the government's own domestic environment: sanctions can be used by government leaders to demonstrate to their publics that they are responding vigorously to an act of wrong-doing by another state, or to dampen demands from domestic groups for punitive action against other states.

On the other hand, the target of this symbolism may be other governments. Just as punishment within states is used to demonstrate the community's abhorrence of a particular act, or to uphold or reinforce commonly held norms in the community, so too in the international community sanctions may be used to underscore the importance of particular norms, to entrench the notion that certain behaviours (such as invading other states) are 'evil' within the broader community of states.[16]

Such symbolic sanctions can paradoxically have instrumental effects. As Baldwin reminds us,[17] governments watch what other governments do: to the extent that other states are convinced by a sender's display of symbolic commitment to a particular norm or rule, and are thus deterred from violating that norm, symbolic sanctions can have manifestly concrete results.

Subversion

Sanctions may be designed to alter the target state's behaviour by subverting, and eventually causing the overthrow of, its authorities in favour of a new government that will abandon the wrong-doing that provoked the sanctions in the first place. Briefly, this line of argument, dubbed by Johann Galtung as the 'naive' theory of sanctions,[18] runs as follows: as international sanctions begin to take effect (or 'bite,' in sanctions jargon) they will make life progressively more difficult for the citizens of the target state. These citizens (or, more commonly, their élites), being pain-avoiding value-maximizers, will seek to eradicate their pain by eliminating the proximate source of it – that is, they will seek to overthrow the existing authorities in favour of new governors who will abandon the state's wrong-doing, thus causing the sender to withdraw its sanctions, and thus restoring normalcy.

The 'naive' theory of sanctions has been exceedingly popular among foreign policy makers – and their publics. It continues to make an appearance in virtually all sanctions debates. For example, in the international response to the Iraqi invasion of Kuwait, it was commonly hoped that the tight and comprehensive sanctions net around Iraq would push Iraqis (particularly in the armed forces) into overthrowing the regime of Saddam Hussein.

What is puzzling about the continued popularity of the naive theory is that there is virtually no empirical support for its tenets. Indeed, Galtung's article in the 1960s argued that in the case of Rhodesia sanctions produced exactly the *opposite* reaction to the one predicted by the naive theory. Far from producing a virulent anger that swells to an overthrowing revolution, sanctions produce exactly the opposite effect. Because they are a punishment imposed against an entire society, these measures may deeply offend the community as a whole, and frequently cause the citizenry to rally around their leaders.

But proponents of the naive theory appear to suffer from a curious ethnocentric astigmatism here. On the one hand, they will readily assert that the naive theory will work when applied to other countries; they have great assurance that political support for the regime will diminish – and certainly not increase. But would they be willing to argue that such tactics would work in the case of *their* country? Consider if one were to ask American proponents of the naive theory how Americans would have reacted had the international community imposed sanctions against the United States in response to the invasion of Grenada in 1983 or Panama in 1989. One would be hard-pressed to imagine that popular support in the United States for the administrations of Ronald Reagan or George Bush would have *fallen* in the face of international sanctions in those cases; on the contrary, it is likely that domestic support for these administrations would have increased in the face of external criticism or punishment.

The 'rally-round-the-flag' phenomenon seems to be so pervasive that there are exceedingly few cases one can point to in which this phenomenon did not make an appearance, and in which international sanctions worked precisely as the naive theory predicts. Indeed, the only case where subversion has worked clearly is in the case of South African sanctions against Lesotho in 1985 over the issue of sanctuary for liberation-movement fighters. The South African measures took very little time to 'bite': they quickly produced a coup d'état – and a new government more responsive to South African interests. But the case of Lesotho is hardly representative: a poor and hugely dependent state, it is entirely surrounded by South Africa, and thus easily coerced. The cases of Iraq and Haiti are perhaps more illustrative of the fate of sanctions with subversive pretensions: in the case of Iraq, Saddam Hussein remained in power despite a tight blockade (not to mention a crushing military attack); in Haiti, the military junta might have been brought to the table to negotiate a return to power of the properly elected president, Jean-Bertrand Aristide, but they did not stop brutalizing and assassinating opponents of the regime, sometimes with astonishing boldness. One could also point to those subversive sanctions that have lingered long, sometimes for more than a generation – as American sanctions against Cuba, North Korea, and Vietnam have lingered – patiently waiting for the naive theory's subversive magic to work.

Retribution

Finally, sanctions may have an exclusively retributive purpose. Instead of seeking to use harms to alter anyone's behaviour (or to impress others), a sender imposes hurtful sanctions on a target for the oldest of reasons of punishment. In other words, one punishes a wrong-doer out of a simple desire to hurt that wrong-doer for having done wrong – and for no other purpose.[19] It is admittedly difficult to ascertain empirically, but it would appear that human beings feel a compulsion to ensure that a wrong-doer 'pays a price' for having done evil – by imposing some evil on the wrong-doer.

There is both an instrumental and a symbolic aspect to retributive punishment. On the one hand, retribution is always a purely symbolic act in the sense that one punishes to do no more than hurt the wrong-doer. That is the limited aim of the punishment. If the punishment happens to have other instrumental effects – if it happens to rehabilitate the wrong-doer or deter other potential wrong-doers, for example – that may be all well and good, but it is incidental to the most important reason for hurting the wrong-doer. On the other hand, retributive punishments also have an instrumental side. The 'price' exacted from wrong-doers will always hurt the target to some degree, and to that extent these sanctions always 'work': the target is punished; it pays a price for its wrong-doing.

To be sure, these five purposes are assumed to work with one another interactively: mixed motives underlie most foreign policy decision-making, and thus the generic sanctions theory readily admits that there may be more than one 'purpose' at work. Therefore, sanctions imposed after an invasion may be designed to 'satisfy domestic public opinion' as well as 'demonstrate abhorrence to other governments,' 'demonstrate resolve to allies,' 'deter further expansion,' and perhaps even 'force the invader to withdraw.' But the instrumental goals implicit in the mixed-motives formulation remain clear.

MIDDLE-POWER SANCTIONS IN PRACTICE: A MAGNETIC DYNAMIC

How useful is orthodox sanctions theory in explaining the various cases of middle-power sanctions explored in this book? If one were to judge by the justificatory rhetoric of political leaders in Canberra and Ottawa alone, it would appear that generic theories do reasonably well in accounting for the sanctions policies of these two middle powers. For the terms of the sanctions debates in both countries, the rhetoric employed by political leaders, and the justifications offered for the use of sanctions all tend to be framed within the rubric of the generic theory of sanctions. That is, the justifications offered for the sanctions embraced by both governments tended to stress the instrumental effects that these measures would have on the target state: they were, it was suggested, hurts designed to deter or compel others by invoking the dynamic of pain-avoidance. In this, the purposes of middle-power sanctions have tended to be conceived, at least in public rhetoric, as indistinguishable from the purposes of great-power sanctions, even though there might have been a passing recognition of the relative smallness of the sanctioning state and the importance of working in cooperation with other states. In short, much of the rhetoric has made it appear that the behaviour of the Australian or Canadian governments mattered – that is, that their sanctions could have an instrumental effect on the international political environment. In this, the rhetoric has implied a certain universality of purpose and motive at work, suggesting the appropriateness of orthodox theory.

On closer examination, however, the orthodox utilities of the generic theory do not seem to provide a very nuanced explanation for the sanctions policies of Australia and Canada in the 1980s. Indeed, the case studies presented in this book suggest that other factors, and other purposes, seemed to be more important in explaining the sanctions policies of these middle powers.

Thus, instead of the instrumentality suggested by the public rhetoric of Australian and Canadian politicians, the sanctions of these middle powers seem to have been driven by largely non-instrumental considerations, some not even mentioned in the generic theory. Instead of displaying ends and means that were more or less clearly conceived, actual policy behaviour by the governments in Canberra and Ottawa frequently appeared to be inconsistent, and often confused about ends and means. Instead of demonstrating a tidy pigeon-holing of motives according to five abstract and theoretical utilities (deterrence, compellence, symbolism, subversion, and punishment), the actual policy behaviour of the Australian and Canadian governments revealed a much messier mix of motivations at work.

What follows is an attempt to lay out, in an exploratory and heuristic fashion, how this dynamic operated, and what factors better explain the sanctions policies of Australia and Canada. For these middle powers, sanctions can best be conceived of as a policy instrument that had all the properties of a bag of magnets: at once attractive and repellent to the governments in Canberra and Ottawa, with different factors frequently pulling and pushing political leaders in opposing directions, in often seemingly haphazard and unpredictable fashion. I would argue that four factors are important for providing the 'push and pull' on sanctions policies: (1) the punitive calculus; (2) coalition politics; (3) domestic politics; and (4) the individual factor.

The desire to punish ...

I start with the assumption that, in general, sanctions will always be a most attractive policy option to decision-makers of states of all sizes and ranks, from great powers to microstates. The reason, baldly put, is that sanctions satisfy so well a desire to punish wrong-doing by hurting the wrong-doer – but do not carry the risks of war that are involved in the use of force to inflict serious harm on a wrong-doer.

Such a view springs from a basic assumption that political leaders, when confronted with what they regard as wrong-doing by another government, are moved by a genuine desire to harm the wrong-doer – responding, as Grotius would have it, to evil with evil. It is true that some dismiss such a desire as emotionalism, vengeance, sadism, or irrationality.[20] However, it can hardly be denied that the desire to inflict pain on wrong-doers appears to be a widespread and well-entrenched response to moral wrong-doing within society. Such a desire seems no less evident in international society: when confronted with acts they regard as morally wrongful, given the norms of the contemporary international system, the tendency of leaders of states has indeed been to respond with an act of punishment – that is, an act hurtful to the wrong-doer. (It should be added immediately, however, that, as noted in the introductory section above, context in such matters is all. Australian and Canadian governments, for example, may express outrage and embrace sanctions in response to one act of invasion-and-overthrow; another entirely comparable act will be 'explained away' by officials in Canberra and Ottawa as entirely justifiable and appropriate under the circumstances. Which reaction is forthcoming will, of course, largely depend on who is doing the invading and the overthrowing, and who is being invaded and overthrown.)

If sanctions are attractive in general, one could, however, hypothesize that non-great powers have a particular interest in punishing some kinds of wrong-doing more than others. Unlike great powers, which have the capacity to deter or repel threats to their well-being, non-great powers, by their very nature, are relatively weak, and must always seek to increase their security against the predations of larger powers in whatever ways they can given their more limited resources. And one relatively inexpensive way for small states to increase their security is to try to ensure that those norms and ideas that foster the 'rightness' of small-state existence (for example, by making invasion-and-overthrow a 'wrongful' act) are entrenched in the international system. Violations of that norm thus become doubly 'bad' for small states: not only may the violation of a small state's sovereignty and territorial integrity be 'wrongful' in itself; but to the extent that the violation weakens the norm if it remains unpunished, it weakens the security of all smaller powers. Non-great powers thus have an even greater interest than great powers in inflicting hurts on violators of those norms that weaken their vital interests – such as the moral claim to territorial integrity and sovereignty.

While non-great powers may have a greater interest in punishment than great powers, they will also, paradoxically, be more inclined than great powers to embrace non-violent sanctions as the best means of punishing wrong-doers. Such a predisposition to non-violent statecraft stems not from any greater virtuousness of non-great powers, but from their position in the structure of the international system. It is axiomatic that smaller powers have less capacity to use force as a tool of statecraft than great powers, and thus there is less willingness to perceive force as a sometimes necessary, even if regrettable, tool in the repertoire. Sanctions, because they avoid force while still imposing punitive harms, are thus a most attractive option to smaller powers.

In looking at cases of middle-power sanctions, therefore, we should expect that the target state's wrong-doing may cause the middle power's political leadership to be genuinely and personally disturbed or angered. While calculations of non–great power raison d'état may most frequently underlie this anger, with the concomitant desire to punish, it should be noted that at times the response of the leadership will simply be the result of visceral reactions. For example, Brian Mulroney's well-documented anger at apartheid was quite evident when he lost his temper during a 1985 television interview at the interviewer's expressed sympathy for South African whites; likewise, Malcolm Fraser was disposed to curtly close down backbenchers' criticisms of his sanctionist South African policy; Bob Hawke's tears during the Canberra memorial service in the aftermath of the Tiananmen massacre in 1989 reflected his emotional reaction to that event. In either case, however, we should expect that these leaders will seek to embrace sanctions as an attractive policy response, not with any expectation that the measures will by themselves or even in concert with others move the wrong-doer to 'right' behaviour, but rather simply to give vent to the desire to hurt the wrong-doer.

... but not too much

The hurtful nature of sanctions makes them an attractive policy option; but there are few sanctions that, when implemented, do not inflict some harm on the sender as well as the target. Thus, the very feature that makes them attractive – their capacity to hurt – may also act as a considerable repellent, inclining would-be sanctioners to moderate the harms they seek to inflict on others. In the Australian and Canadian cases, there are both general and specific reasons why neither government has an interest in embracing strong – and therefore self-hurtful – economic sanctions against other states.

Generally, the structural economic condition of middle powers like Australia or Canada impels them away from sanctions. Both countries have open, highly trade-dependent economies, with a traditional reliance on primary-resource exports.[21] Because of this, both governments have usually expressed a generalized interest in minimizing interruptions to international trade, particularly for what are invariably termed 'political' reasons usually associated with international sanctions.

There is, however, a more specific reason why economic sanctions are frequently an unappealing policy response. While the bulk of Canadian and Australian trade is with the industrialized world – the United States, Japan, and the European Community – both Canberra and Ottawa have been reluctant to disrupt economic intercourse with such states as the Soviet Union, China, Iran, and Iraq because of the particular patterns of trade that exist with these states. Both Australia and Canada tend to enjoy highly favourable terms of trade with these states. It is true that, in aggregate terms, the costs of disrupting this trade would not be high; however, both these middle powers tend to be sensitive to marginal declines in the current account balance that disruptions in profitable trade can cause. More important, much of this trade tends to be in products that affect politically important constituencies within both countries – farmers – and that therefore always constitute a more sensitive target for sanctions. Thus, for example, both Australia and Canada proved more than happy to sign lucrative grain contracts with the People's Republic of China during the 1960s, in the process undercutting broader American efforts to hurt China economically.[22]

Finally, bedevilling the middle-power sanctioner's calculus of costs and benefits is uncertainty about returns. Because of their more limited capacity, non-great powers can never be sure that their sanctions package will actually make a difference – that harms caused by Australian or Canadian sanctions will produce an instant (or even quick) instrumental effect in bringing an end to the 'wrongful behaviour' that prompted their imposition. Moreover, their limited capacity means that they do not have the power to stop 'sanctions leakage' – the attempts by other states to find ways around embargoes and boycotts. This can make careful and assiduous attachment to a sanctions package little more than a mug's game. Therefore, there will be an in-built reluctance to embrace a policy that is sure to be harmful to one's own interests, but that may – or may not – have any effect on the target.

Given these considerations, we should not be surprised to discover that while both governments may have found sanctions an attractive

means of punishing other states for their transgressions, neither government has tended to favour measures that seriously disrupted existing
trade relations – unless other compelling circumstances intervened.
Thus, for example, in the cases of sanctions against Vietnam after the
invasion of Cambodia, or sanctions against Iraq after its invasion of
Kuwait, there were no attempts made to limit the self-hurting element
of sanctions. The 'compelling circumstance' in the Iraq case, despite the
high financial costs, was the considerable degree of support in both
countries for a strong policy of sanctions within the context of the
multinational coalition. Even if the Hawke or Mulroney governments
had been inclined to abandon their strong support for a leak-proof
sanctionist approach, the costs, both domestic and international, would
have been too high. The case of Vietnam also demonstrates these costs
at work. The Hawke government was inclined to soften or terminate
Australian sanctions against Vietnam,[23] prompting friends and allies of
Australia to bring pressure to bear to maintain the punishments. And
that international pressure, in turn, generated considerable domestic
political opposition to the move.

But such widespread support for punitive sanctions is relatively rare.
More common is the pattern we saw in the cases of sanctions against
the Soviet Union for its invasion of Afghanistan in 1979, against South
Africa after the outbreak of unrest in the mid-1980s, or against China in
the aftermath of Tiananmen in 1989: in each case, the measures adopted
by both Australia and Canada were designed to limit the degree of
harm rebounding onto the sanctioner. In the words of the then Australian minister for finance, Senator Peter Walsh, these were merely 'Clayton's sanctions' – after Clayton's, the Australian non-alcoholic beverage
that advertised itself as the drink you have when you're not having a
drink.[24]

The push and pull of coalition politics

One of the most obvious gaps in the generic theory of sanctions is the
effect on a state's sanctions policy of its membership in interstate groups
or coalitions – alliances such as the Australia–New Zealand–United
States security agreement (ANZUS) or the North Atlantic Treaty Organization (NATO), or interstate groupings such as the post-ministerial meetings of the Association of Southeast Asian Nations (ASEAN),[25] the G-7
summit, Asia Pacific Economic Cooperation (APEC), or the ad hoc coalition of thirty-six states arrayed against Iraq during the Gulf conflict in

1990–1. Membership in such groups inevitably creates a 'utility' for junior members in being 'onside' with the leading members of the group. Australia and Canada are both formally allied to the United States and belong to numerous other groupings of states; membership in these groups will be an important factor in the making of sanctions policy. However, membership in a group will not simply have a one-way impact (where the smaller state seeks to ensure that its policy is in line with the policy of the group's leaders). Instead, group membership will create a dynamic that will make sanctions either attractive or unattractive, again depending heavily on context.

The coalition dynamic has two aspects. On the one hand, group membership brings with it a considerable emphasis on solidarity; a premium is normally placed on being onside with the group's leadership on a particular issue. This premium, it should be noted, is most of the time self-generated, particularly by smaller members of the group, but there are times when the leader will insist on coalition solidarity. Because of this dynamic, the leader's preferences are crucial: if it decides to impose sanctions (or decides to eschew such measures), the stakes for a junior partner in taking a contrary position are raised considerably. The sanctions imposed against Vietnam are the most obvious example of this dynamic at work: while neither the Hawke government nor successive Canadian governments demonstrated much enthusiasm for these sanctions, it was believed that the costs of defecting from the sanctioning coalition were too high for either government to countenance a contrary position.

The other side of the coalition dynamic is a counter-dynamic that inclines junior partners in a coalition towards defection on sanctions. First, just as middle powers may find sanctions attractive because they match the group leader's approach, so too may they be unattractive for that very reason – when the leader structures the situation so that the smaller power has little choice but to match the leader's policies. However much they may welcome membership in the group, or the protection of alliance, smaller powers are always to some degree resentful of their subordinate position. Ironically, this natural resentment tends to be exacerbated in groupings of Western states, for deeply embedded in the institutional mythology of Western-based groupings is the assertion of equality in decision-making, and the concomitant expectation that all powers, even the smallest, will be duly consulted before decisions affecting the entire group are taken.[26]

The resentment at not being consulted will be heightened even further if the leader sets policy unilaterally and then uses adherence to the line as a measure of the smaller ally's loyalty – as happened in the case of the Afghanistan sanctions, when the Carter administration invoked a range of sanctions against the Soviet Union without having consulted the allies. When the group's leader engages in such unilateralism, members will tend to look for opportunities to defect. For example, American unilateralism on the Afghanistan sanctions had a considerable impact on the Western sanctions imposed on Poland and the Soviet Union in 1982: when the Reagan administration demonstrated comparable unilateralist tendencies, the European allies refused to go along with Washington's sanctions policies.[27]

How this dynamic works itself out in practice is highly dependent on context. For example, the case studies presented below will show that the dynamics of coalition politics impelled Canadians *away from* sanctions in the case of Indonesia, but *towards* sanctions in the case of Vietnam. In the case of Canada's South African policy, the dynamics of coalition membership had both effects, but serially: in the 1960s and 1970s, the coalition dynamic impelled Canadians away from sanctions and in the mid-1980s it impelled the government towards sanctions.[28]

Indeed, the case of the multilateral embargo on sales of strategically important goods and technology to Communist countries during the Cold War era demonstrates how coalition politics can incline countries towards and away from sanctions, but at the same time. The key mechanism for implementing these sanctions against Communist countries was the Coordinating Committee for Multilateral Strategic Export Control (COCOM). COCOM was established in 1949; its membership eventually grew to include all members of NATO except Iceland and Spain, together with Australia and Japan. It sought to establish a multilateral regime for the control of the flow of strategic goods and technology to all Communist countries by establishing and maintaining lists of proscribed goods. The purpose of the COCOM sanctions was thus essentially pre-emptive: to ensure that Communist countries did not benefit by the sale of Western technology.[29] With the outbreak of the Korean War in June 1950, a separate China Committee (CHICOM) was established. CHICOM operated in substantially the same manner as COCOM.[30] Both Australia and Canada participated in COCOM and CHICOM throughout the Cold War era, in part because both governments basically shared the concerns of the main catalyst behind these pre-emptive efforts, the United States, and in part because the costs of defecting from the broad-based coalition would have been exceedingly high, particularly given the obvious attachment of the coalition leader to these sanctions. But at the same time, both the Australian and Canadian governments were keen to do business with the targets of COCOM and CHICOM, and actively sought to develop trade relations with the Soviet Union, China, and others.

On some occasions, however, middle powers will simply not be moved by the costs of defecting from the sanctions being embraced by the coalition leader. The case of American attempts to sanction Cuba and Nicaragua demonstrate how there will be occasions when middle powers will, for a complex of reasons, refuse to embrace the coalition leader's policies, and will be quite willing to suffer American anger as a consequence.

The Progressive Conservative government of John G. Diefenbaker greeted the imposition of American sanctions against Cuba on 18 October 1959 with a certain detachment. If Diefenbaker had little sympathy for the regime of Fidel Castro, he firmly believed that the American policy of sanctioning Cuba was mistaken, according to Basil Robinson, who was External Affairs' liaison officer in the Prime Minister's Office at the time. When Diefenbaker first heard the news of the embargo, he was 'clear in his own mind' that Canada would not participate.[31] However, he conceded that while Canada was not going to stop any trade in non-strategic goods, Ottawa would not allow strategic materials to be sold to Cuba.[32] That policy was to persist throughout the 1960s and 1970s.

In his memoirs, Diefenbaker presents an extensive explanation for his refusal to cooperate with Washington: among the reasons cited were his refusal to accept the idea that governments of different ideological stripes could not co-exist in the western hemisphere; the Canadian government's desire to maintain a dialogue with Cuba as a means of easing tensions; the legal barriers to imposing sanctions; and the overwhelming support of the press and public to his government's stand on Cuba.[33]

However, Diefenbaker might have mentioned that there was also considerable domestic value in taking a line that was independent of the United States, for independence in Cuban policy was an easy way to deflect criticism in Canada that the government was 'too close' to Washington. Indeed, as time went on and members of the administration of John F. Kennedy became increasingly annoyed at the Canadian policy on Cuba, Diefenbaker became increasingly attached to this independent policy. For example, after Kenneth Keating, a United States senator, criticized the Canadian government on the CBC, Diefenbaker openly criticized Keating. Robinson noted in his diary: 'I tried unsuccessfully to persuade the PM not to go after Keating ... but PM obviously thinks anti-American statements are good and timely, and relished another opportunity.'[34]

A similar calculus obtained in the case of the Reagan administration's sanctions towards Nicaragua a quarter-century later. When Reagan announced an American embargo against Nicaragua on 1 May 1985, both the Australian and Canadian governments remained adamantly opposed to the sanctions against the Sandinista regime, despite the obvious desire of the United States to have its allies join in the sanctions.

For its part, the Canadian government was quick to distance itself from the American measures. 'It's their policy, not ours,' was the dismissive comment of Joe Clark, Canada's secretary of state for external affairs.[35] Moreover, Clark complained directly to George Shultz, the United States secretary of state, that the Canadian government had not been consulted about these measures. As a result, the Mulroney government offered no objections when the Nicaraguan government asked that it be allowed to relocate its trade office from Miami to Toronto; likewise, Ottawa made no efforts to disrupt trade; on the contrary, it threatened to prosecute any American firm in Canada that obeyed the United States sanctions; and Monique Vézina, Canada's minister of state for external relations, visited Nicaragua in the summer of 1985 to discuss development assistance projects. Moreover, the Canadian government was not hesitant to criticize openly a policy they thought was entirely mistaken: 'As we consider that the Central American crisis stems largely from socio-economic disparities and problems, Canada believes that these issues should be addressed not by embargoes but by encouraging economic development.'[36]

The reaction in Canberra to the American sanctions against Nicaragua was similar. The minister for foreign affairs, Bill Hayden, had two years beforehand outlined Australian policy in terms that were almost identical to the Canadian position: 'Australia looks to the United States to balance its legitimate right to be concerned about security in [Central America] with a real concern for the promotion of these objectives [improvement of living standards]. Australia considers that military action will not solve the problems of Central America.'[37] When the United States imposed sanctions, Hayden 'regretted' the Reagan administration's decision, claiming that the action was 'severe' and unlikely to change the Sandinistas. Hayden was also quick to point out that Australia had not been consulted in advance: 'Had it been consulted it would have advised against the boycott.'[38] Like Canada, Australia symbolically set itself apart from Washington: Hayden invited the Nicaraguan foreign minister to visit Australia; he criticized American policy; and the Australian government extended aid to Nicaragua.[39] As in Canada, the Nicaraguan sanctions provided the Hawke government with an opportunity to pursue a policy that was independent of the United States.

The push and pull of domestic politics

It has long been recognized that one of the important purposes of external sanctions is to satisfy domestic expectations that the government is 'doing something' in response to some international wrong.[40] What does not seem to be as frequently recognized is the degree to which governments face competing and conflicting demands in their domestic environments that push and pull them in markedly different directions on the issue of sanctioning other states. There are four dimensions of domestic politics to be examined: the domestic context of alliance/coalition relationships; the issue of who is to pay for the sanctions; the impact of ethnic groups; and the electoral connection.

First, being a member of an international grouping of states in general, and of an alliance in particular, has a domestic political context that will push and pull governments in general as well as specifically on the issue of sanctions. It is axiomatic that the relationship with the United States has been the most important external relationship for both these middle powers – for Australians at least since Pearl Harbor and the fall of Singapore, and for Canadians well before Confederation in 1867.[41] It is hardly surprising that the issue of how the relationship with the United States is conducted has come to be a deeply embedded and politically prominent feature of the political culture in both countries. In particular, there appears to be a persistent tension between the requisites of being (and being seen to be) a good ally of the United States on the one hand, and on the other being able to conduct a sufficiently 'independent' foreign policy to avoid being branded by domestic critics as an American 'lackey' or 'lap dog.' There is little doubt that in both countries, good alliance relations make good politics: political leaders in both Canberra and Ottawa must always be attentive to the likelihood that the more their policies begin to drift away from support of the United States, the more severely they will be attacked by domestic critics for 'anti-Americanism' or for imperilling the relationship with the

United States. By the same token, however, they run a comparable risk at the other end of the pendulum's swing: when their policy behaviour begins to mirror too closely the alliance leader's, they will assuredly be accused of lap-dog politics, as, for example, was the case in the Gulf conflict of 1990–1. As we will see in chapter 9 below, charges that Hawke and Mulroney were merely George Bush's lap dogs were a prominent part of Australian and Canadian political discourse during that conflict.

But on the whole, governments in Canberra and Ottawa have tried hard to steer away from sanctions policies that would on the one hand have ensnared them in charges of lap-dog politics, or would have entangled them in domestic charges of endangering the relationship with the United States on the other. Thus, as was noted above, for example, neither government chose to join the Reagan administration in sanctioning Nicaragua; but both governments maintained their sanctions against Vietnam despite their profound misgivings about a policy that isolated Hanoi.

A second aspect of domestic politics is the issue of who will bear the costs of sanctions. While sanctions are always imposed by, and in the name of, the state, in fact it falls to particular individuals, firms, groups, classes, localities, and regions within the state to actually engage in the sanctioning. Who within the political community is to pay for the imposition of hurts against another state, and how these tensions and contradictions get worked out in practice, remain important aspects of the sanctioning process. Equally important is the formal compensation process put into place by the government to offset the costs of sanctions.[42]

The regional dimension of Australian and Canadian politics that springs from both the realities of geography and the federal form of government will have an important impact on the degree to which sanctions will fall on regional interests. Again, this will be heavily dependent on context. As we will see in the case of Afghanistan, for example, much of the visible Soviet activity in both Australia and Canada, and thus an obvious and ripe target for sanctioning, happened to be in the coastal peripheries – in Tasmania and Newfoundland. However, what was attractive to Malcolm Fraser, a Liberal prime minister with an Australian Labor Party (ALP) government in Hobart was anathema to Joe Clark, a Conservative prime minister who not only had a Conservative premier in St John's, but who was in the middle of a federal election to boot. Given these factors, it should not be surprising that when sanctions were announced, measures affecting Tasmania figured prominently in Canberra's list, while Ottawa tried hard to avoid sanctions that affected Newfoundland.

The concerns of those whose concrete interests are directly affected by sanctions – in Australia and Canada, sanctions in the 1980s fell most heavily on primary producers and athletes – will also prove important to the political mix. As we will see, the Olympic boycott in 1980 tended to pit athletes against farmers in both countries, though the debate was sharper in Australia than Canada. Likewise, firms and organizations with direct interests in maintaining links with a target state will be active in pressing their interests by suggesting that a different mix of sanctions – meaning, of course, sanctions that do not adversely affect their parochial interests – be chosen.

But involvement in the sanctions debate tends not to be limited to those who have a financial stake in the outcome; those whose interest in sanctions is purely symbolic will also figure in the domestic political dynamic. For example, in both countries there exist well-organized interest groups that can be counted on to add their voices, pro and con, to the different sanctions debates that may be running concurrently. For example, in both Australia and Canada, anti-apartheid groups were a persistent source of pressure for a sanctionist approach against South Africa. In Canada, well-organized groups that focused on Central America plumped for Canadian sanctions against El Salvador and Guatemala in the mid-1980s – but these groups would have been strenuously opposed had Ottawa joined the Reagan administration's sanctions against Nicaragua. In both Australia and Canada, non-governmental organizations involved in development assistance were at the forefront pressing for lifting sanctions (particularly aid sanctions) against Vietnam, Cambodia, and Laos.

So too will unorganized groups, also with largely symbolic interests, add their voices to the debate. For example, proposals for sporting boycotts tend to generate considerable controversy among sports fans. But the dynamic will differ depending on context: proposals for sporting boycotts against South Africa tended to play well in Canada – where cricket and rugby, the main sports affected, do not rank among popular spectator sports; in Australia, by contrast, proposals to interfere with these sports resonated more sharply. By contrast, Australians tended to be indifferent to ice-hockey boycotts against the Soviet Union; but governments in Ottawa had to tread more carefully to ensure that whatever the disruptions demanded by the course of great-power rivalry, they had better not include the popular Canada-Soviet hockey rivalry.

The impact of ethnic groups on sanctions policy deserves separate mention. Immigrant groups in particular have an impact on sanctions. It is axiomatic that one of the consequences of the patterns of migration into both Australia and Canada in the postwar period is that there are within both countries ethnic groups that tend to be well organized and highly vocal on issues concerning relations with their original home-land.[43] This is particularly true with regard to countries perceived to be on 'the other side' at some point or other in the forty-five years after the Second World War – the Soviet Union, China, and Vietnam. Because many members of ethnic groups from such countries fled to Australia and Canada, they have tended to demonstrate a certain ambiguity towards their homelands. On the one hand, they retain an affinity for their *patria*, particularly when their relatives continue to live there. On the other hand, these immigrants generally seem to bear little goodwill towards the government whose attitudes or policies caused them to emigrate in the first place.[44] As the activities of Ukrainians, Balts, Viet-namese, and Chinese in both countries suggest, these groups tended to strongly resist attempts by Canberra or Ottawa to improve relations with those governments over the course of the Cold War. Indeed, these groups often pushed policy in the other direction: governments seeking electoral support from these voters were frequently inclined towards sanctions as a means of concretely demonstrating antipathy towards the target regime. But in some cases, the politics of ethnicity may incline governments away from sanctions: the debate over Canadian policy towards the Arab boycott of Israel is one manifestation of this response.[45] Finally, ethnic groups can have an impact on how effective the sanctions net around a state will be. For example, Serbs overseas, including many in Australia and Canada, reportedly transferred over US$1 billion in funds to Serbia in 1992, offsetting to a considerable degree the impact of Western sanctions imposed on Serbia in response to its aggression in Bosnia.[46]

Finally, the evolution of sanctions policy may be intertwined with the dynamics of electoral politics. To be sure, it is rare that a sanctions epi-sode will occur at precisely the same time as an election. But the juxtapo-sition of electoral considerations and the imposition of sanctions is likely to muddy the policy process. The case of Canadian sanctions against the Soviet Union following the invasion of Afghanistan provides an instruc-tive example of how the search for electoral advantage can affect sanc-tions policy. We noted above how the Clark government sought to avoid sanctions that would target Soviet economic activity in Newfoundland

and limit the negative effects of grain sanctions on farmers. It would not be unreasonable to assume that the particular sanctions package adopted by the government in January 1980 was designed to minimize regional retribution when the elections were held on 18 February. But the sanctions package was also designed to maximize electoral support, particularly in the electorally important 'Golden Horseshoe' around Toronto.[47] Clark and his ministers made a concerted (and entirely obvious) effort to use a harsh anti-Soviet line to attract support from voters of East European descent (who historically tended to vote Liberal); Bayer has opined that the Conservatives almost succeeded.

In Australia, the invasion of Afghanistan got intertwined with electoral politics, for 1980 was an election year, and it was commonly asserted that Malcom Fraser was using the invasion for electoral purposes. The ALP, for example, charged that Fraser's Afghanistan policy was little more than an attempt to have a 'khaki election' or a 'green and gold election'[48] – using the menace of the Soviet threat in order to scare the electorate.[49]

Vietnam provides another case where electoral politics affected the course of sanctions policy. The ALP's desire to distance its Vietnam policy from Fraser's harsh anti-Soviet line led the party to embrace in its 1983 election platform a promise to end Australian sanctions against Vietnam. When Bob Hawke's minister for foreign affairs, Bill Hayden, tried to make good on the ALP promise, he was met with strident international criticism from Australia's friends and allies around the Pacific rim, and strong opposition domestically. The tortuous demise of the Hayden initiative at the hands of both international pressure and domestic opposition demonstrates the contextual and contingent nature of the sanctions process. The fate that befell the Hawke initiatives on Vietnam, it might be noted, also provided an object lesson for Canadian policymakers. It was not only the harsh pressures of friends and allies against the Hawke initiatives in 1983 that deepened the Canadian commitment to a policy of sanctions against Vietnam throughout the 1980s. It was also the prospect of comparable domestic violence, and possible electoral retribution, from the concentrations of Vietnamese in the electorally important cities of Montreal, Toronto, and Vancouver.

The individual variable

What James N. Rosenau termed the individual (or idiosyncratic) variable in foreign policy – a political leader's particular *Weltanschauung* that manifests itself in the policy process – can push or pull governments on sanctions as a favoured policy instrument.[50] In the case of Australian sanctions against the Soviet Union in 1980, for example, it can be argued that the individual variable – Malcolm Fraser's attitudes about world politics, and how the Soviet invasion of Afghanistan fitted into those views – explains much of Canberra's crusading spirit, the grave rhetoric of the prime minister, and the sanctions eventually chosen. Most analyses of Fraser remark on how his approach to foreign policy was fundamentally shaped by his understanding of world politics, and in particular his view of the threat posed to Australia (and the West) by 'the Other' – for many years China and then, after the mid-1970s, the Soviet Union. Fraser, it has been argued, was 'marked indelibly' by his father's service in both world wars, and by the 'lessons from the 1930s' he learned while at Oxford University in the late 1940s about the fundamental insecurity of the international system, the consequences of appeasement, and the need to respond to aggression forcefully.[51] He seems to have been particularly seized with the 'lessons of the 1930s': in his public statements, he would frequently draw parallels between the response to Soviet aggression in Afghanistan and the failure of the Western democracies to respond to the expansion of German power in the mid-1930s. The analogy may well have been flawed; but viewed from this perspective, Fraser's responses to the Soviet invasion over the first half of 1980 and his eager embrace of sanctions as the key policy instrument become more understandable.

The same variable is also important in understanding both Australia's policy towards South Africa in the late 1970s and early 1980s and Canadian policy towards South Africa in the mid- and late 1980s. At first blush, it might be expected that conservative leaders like Fraser and Brian Mulroney, who came to power in September 1984, would have had views about sanctions against South Africa comparable to those of conservative governments in London or Washington. But both prime ministers evinced visceral personal reactions to apartheid, and both took a strong pro-sanctionist line, to the evident dismay of many in their respective parties.

By contrast, just as their beliefs inclined Fraser and Mulroney *towards* sanctions as a favoured instrument of statecraft in some cases, Pierre Trudeau in Canada was inclined *away* from sanctions because of his own world-outlook. Not only was he sceptical about the appropriateness of sanctions against South Africa, he also believed that it was counterproductive to use sanctions against the Soviet Union. J.L. Granatstein and Robert Bothwell conclude that Trudeau had an unusual view of the Soviet Union, and that this view served to moderate considerably the Canadian government's reactions to the invasion of Afghanistan, the declaration of martial law in Poland, and the shooting down of Korean Air Lines flight 007 on 1 September 1983.[52]

CONCLUSION

To this point, I have argued that the orthodox theory of international sanctions is dominated by a concern with the instrumental purposes of this tool of statecraft. While the generic theory might be useful for explaining the sanctions policies of the international system's major powers – which have the capacity to have instrumental effects – I have tried in this introductory chapter to suggest that orthodox theories of sanctions do not provide a full account of the sanctions process as it actually works itself out in non-great powers like Australia and Canada. Although the instrumental purposes of sanctions may provide an attractive way for the policy-makers of the great powers to frame responses to what they regard as wrong-doing in international politics, the orthodox theory does not provide such a clear guide for the governors – or the governed – of non-great powers, much less offer an illuminating explanation of the essentially symbolic purposes of the sanctions policies of middle powers.

I have outlined here a different set of utilities of sanctions, only one of which – the punitive purpose – bears much resemblance to the utilities of generic theory. It should be noted that while these alternative utilities may also be useful in analysing the sanctions policies of the system's great powers, they are particularly applicable to middle powers.

The alternative utilities, I would suggest, are more non-instrumental, closely resembling what an American commentator once called the 'rain dance' quality of international sanctions: because it appears that something is being done, all the participants feel better – but nothing of substance is actually accomplished.[53]

These alternative purposes, I have argued, have both attractive and repellent qualities that push and pull policy-makers on the issue of sanctions. In keeping with the essentially heuristic purpose of this book, I have sought to identify the contending factors that exert what I characterize as a magnetic quality on the leaders of smaller states, inclining them towards or away from sanctions. Much of the pull and push, I have suggested, will be heavily contingent, and highly dependent on context, making predictive generalizations about how this magnetic dynamic works difficult. However, I would none the less argue that examining the utilities outlined in this chapter, rather than the generic variety, offers a clearer, more nuanced, and more realistic way to account for the sanctions policies of middle powers like Australia and Canada.

PART ONE: CANADIAN CASES

2

Avoiding Sanctions:
Policies towards Indonesia, 1972–91

We begin our investigation of middle-power sanctions by examining the case of the Canadian measures that were invoked against Indonesia in response to a massacre by Indonesian troops of civilians attending a funeral in Dili, the capital of the former Portuguese colony of Timor, in November 1991. What is interesting about these sanctions is that they took so long to be invoked: for nearly twenty years, the Canadian government had actively avoided imposing sanctions against Indonesia, despite the poor human rights record of the government of President Suharto. In the mid-1970s, Indonesia did not enjoy a reputation for human rights observance. It was reported to have the highest population of political prisoners of all states in the international system.[1] Djakarta's policy of 'transmigrating' political prisoners to a series of forced-labour camps, such as those on Buru Island, was widely criticized, most notably by a Committee of Experts of the International Labour Organization in 1976.[2]

Most important, the Indonesian decision to intervene militarily in East Timor drew widespread criticism. The Timorese issue arose after the 1974 coup in Portugal, which brought to power a democratic regime that promised all Portuguese colonies or overseas provinces, including Portuguese Timor, the right of self-determination. In anticipation of this event, numerous groups emerged among Portuguese Timor's 650,000 people, some advocating outright independence as East Timor, some advocating maintenance of the link with Portugal, and some advocating incorporation into Indonesia. In August 1975, a civil war broke out among several competing factions. When the most powerful of these groups, the Revolutionary Front for an Independent East Timor (Fretilin), declared independence in December 1975, the Indonesian government intervened militarily, dispatching troops to East Timor, defeating Fretilin, and subsequently annexing the territory as Indonesia's twenty-seventh province in July 1976. The intervention was widely condemned in the international community as an act, in the words of the *New York Times*, of 'naked aggression';[3] even the United Nations General Assembly, dominated by Third World countries not unsympathetic to anti-colonial struggles, condemned the invasion and subsequent absorption of Timor. Moreover, after its intervention in East Timor, Indonesia faced persistent charges that its troops occupying the territory were engaged in a policy of genocide against the Timorese population.

Thus, it might be expected that the policies that were being pursued by the Suharto government in the mid- and late 1970s would attract Canadian sanctions. However, throughout the 1970s and 1980s, the Canadian government sought to give priority to its relations with Djakarta, maintaining an active aid program and encouraging trade and other links with the government of President Suharto.

The Indonesian case thus begs a number of questions about Canada's sanctions policies. First, although governments in Ottawa have occasionally mooted the idea of using aid sanctions to punish recipients of Canadian development assistance that violate human rights,[4] why did the Canadian government not impose sanctions against Indonesia for its human rights violations in the 1970s and its military intervention in and occupation of East Timor in 1975? What factors prompted the governments of both Pierre Elliott Trudeau and Brian Mulroney to give priority to relations with Indonesia? Second, why were sanctions finally imposed in December 1991 after such an extended time?

This chapter thus addresses two questions. First, it explores the reasons why the Trudeau Liberal government in the 1970s and the Progressive Conservative government of Brian Mulroney in the 1980s chose to ignore both the internal and external aspects of Indonesian policy that had earned the Suharto government such considerable international opprobrium. It begins with an exploration of the reasons why the Trudeau government chose to focus on building up Canada's relations with Indonesia. Ottawa selected Indonesia as a 'country of concentration' in its development assistance program, and devoted considerable economic and diplomatic attention to Djakarta throughout the 1970s, even though at the beginning of the decade the Trudeau government had promised, in its 1970 foreign policy papers, to link development assistance to a specifically Canadian standard of political behaviour:

'Development assistance will tend to be concentrated in countries whose governments pursue external and internal policies that are broadly consistent with Canadian values and attitudes.'[5]

I will argue that a mix of strategic and economic concerns prompted the government in Ottawa to ignore its earlier promises to link aid and human rights performance and to refuse to criticize publicly the more overt human rights violations of the Indonesian government. Instead, these strategic and economic considerations would prompt the government in Ottawa to make Indonesia the centre of its Southeast Asian policy in the 1970s. For Canadian economic interests in Indonesia – the result of policies pursued by the Trudeau government – had developed to the point where sanctions that might have been considered appropriate in the face of these violations would have involved considerable costs for Canadian interests. Moreover, there were broader strategic and diplomatic reasons for a small state like Canada to mute whatever uneasiness officials in Ottawa may have had about close relations with the Suharto regime. Because other members of the Western alliance, particularly the United States, strongly supported the government in Djakarta, public criticism of Indonesia's human rights record by the Canadian government would have resulted in diplomatic isolation. It can be argued that these same strategic and economic concerns also explain the willingness of the Mulroney government not to re-examine seriously the relationship with Indonesia throughout the 1980s.

Second, the chapter explores the implications of the links between Canada and Indonesia for the usefulness of sanctions to coerce 'rightful' behaviour by other states. The case of Canadian-Indonesian relations during the 1970s and 1980s suggests that the closer the relationship between two states, the deeper the interests that exist between them, and the less likely that these sanctions will be used in diplomacy between them. For it is axiomatic that strategic and commercial interests, once created, become inertial imperatives that are not easily ignored, and pose significant impediments to the use of sanctions as a means of securing foreign policy objectives.

Finally, this case also demonstrates the importance of coalition politics on the sanctions policies of middle powers like Canada. In the wake of the American withdrawal from Indochina in the mid-1970s, and the concomitant increase of Soviet interest in the Southeast Asian region, maintaining good relations with the Indonesian government became a priority for an emerging anti-Soviet (and anti-Vietnamese) regional coalition. Included in this coalition were the Western great powers with interests in the region – the United States, Japan, and Britain. Also included was China, for the government in Beijing was intent on opposing what it widely condemned as Soviet hegemonism in the Asia Pacific area. Likewise, the coalition took in many of the smaller states in the region, notably the members of the Association of Southeast Asian Nations (ASEAN), of which Indonesia was a member. These states, despite their many diversities, had a broad common interest in keeping Indonesia firmly within the Western coalition – regardless of the behaviour of the government in Djakarta. As I will argue, the Canadian government, for its part, had little interest in challenging this coalition, particularly when it included the United States and Commonwealth partners such as Britain, Malaysia, and Singapore.

Perhaps the most telling indication of the importance of the coalition dynamic for the Canadian approach to sanctions is to examine what happened to Canada's Indonesian policy once the importance of the anti-Soviet coalition diminished after the end of the Cold War in 1989. We will demonstrate below that once the government in Ottawa was no longer constrained to maintain coalition solidarity, it chose to adopt a harsh sanctionist approach to Indonesia.

PROLOGUE: THE RELATIONSHIP BEFORE 1972

Canada's relations with Indonesia evolved through four distinct phases. Before the foreign policy review of 1968–70, contacts and interests were few. The period 1970–72 marked a substantial shift in Ottawa's interest in fostering an expansion of the relationship. The years after 1972 saw a very rapid increase in Canadian support for the government in Djakarta. And, finally the relationship entered a new phase in late 1991 in the wake of the Dili massacre.

David Van Praagh has characterized the Canadian approach to Southeast Asia in the years before the 1970s as 'innocent.'[6] The government's involvement with the countries of the Pacific rim was largely limited to its truce-supervisory activities in Indochina and its development assistance commitments to members of the Commonwealth on the Indian subcontinent. Whether such a limitation was born of innocence, or, as observers like John W. Holmes have argued, was predicated on a hardheaded calculation of Canadian interests in this region,[7] there is little doubt that Ottawa's interest did not extend to Indonesia.

Contacts were few. A Canadian embassy was opened in 1953 Djakarta after Indonesia joined the Colombo Plan, but there seemed to be little interest in extending the relationship beyond this minimal level. Trade was so slight during the 1950s that as an economy measure the commercial section of the embassy was closed in 1960 because of inactivity. Development assistance was limited. Ottawa's preoccupation was with the Commonwealth members of the Colombo Plan. As a result, Canadian development assistance to Indonesia before 1972 was primarily in the form of food aid.[8] Generally, interest was low. Indonesia was seen by policy-makers in Ottawa during the 1950s and 1960s to be unimportant, both strategically and diplomatically. Only when fellow Commonwealth members were actively threatened by President Sukarno's aggressive foreign policy did the question of Canada's relations with Indonesia assume any prominence in Ottawa. In the wake of Indonesia's 'Crush Malaysia' campaign, the government of Lester B. Pearson responded by reducing Canadian contributions to Indonesia under the Colombo Plan by 82 per cent.[9]

The prevailing attitude in official Ottawa that Indonesia's position in Southeast Asia warranted no special attention changed after Prime Minister Trudeau initiated the review of foreign policy in 1968. Although the results of the review were not published until 1970, the attention accorded to Indonesia in the 1970 foreign policy papers suggests that, in the intervening two years, official thinking had undergone a considerable transformation.

The key factor in the government's Pacific policy during this period was the shifting balance of power in Asia. The British government was withdrawing its military commitments east of Suez. The administration of Richard Nixon had begun the process of extracting the United States from Indochina. The People's Republic of China was still in the throes of the aftermath of the Great Proletarian Cultural Revolution, and the attitude of the government in Beijing towards the Asia Pacific region remained unclear. The significance of great-power shifts in Asia was not ignored by the strategic thinkers in Ottawa who helped formulate Canada's Pacific policies. Officials in the Department of External Affairs felt that it was unlikely that changes in the balance of power would promote strategic stability in Southeast Asia. They believed that it was, therefore, equally unlikely that the Canadian government could achieve its priorities in the Pacific – economic growth, social justice, and quality of life[10] – if there was no military stability in the area. Officials in the Department of External Affairs were at pains to stress the importance of achieving military stability in Southeast Asia so that Canada's other objectives, particularly its economic and commercial ones, could be realized.

The foreign policy paper openly mentioned those states in the Pacific rim that could help provide this necessary strategic tranquillity. Both Japan and Australia were suggested as significant contributors to regional stability. But Indonesia appeared to have attained a new-found importance in the eyes of the Canadian government as one means of enhancing regional security: 'Indonesia must also be regarded as a nascent power among the non-Communist nations because of its position and population, and the development potential of its natural resources.'[11]

The emphasis that the 1970 foreign policy paper placed on defining Canada's foreign policy interests in terms of economic growth is well-known,[12] but nowhere was this emphasis more evident than in the Trudeau government's plans for Canadian relations with the nations of Southeast Asia. The government sanguinely envisaged a rapid increase in commercial relations with the Pacific countries in the 1970s, an optimism no doubt based on the spiralling increases in Canadian trade with the Pacific region as a whole during the 1960s. During that decade, Canadian exports rose over 400 per cent, and imports increased by over 300 per cent.[13] Indonesia was to play an important part in this attempt by the government in Ottawa to transform the Far East into Canada's 'Near West,' as William Saywell put it.[14] The 1970 foreign policy papers saw large-scale Canadian investments in mineral exploitation in that country as a catalyst for increased trade. A corollary was an increase in the amount of official development assistance that was to be channelled to Indonesia.[15]

Ottawa's choice of Indonesia as a Pacific partner of enhanced importance was by no means arbitrary. First, policy-makers in Ottawa were moved by macro-strategic calculations about great-power shifts in the Asia-Pacific region. In particular, some officials were of the view that the reversals suffered by the United States in Vietnam, particularly after the *Têt* offensive of February 1968, would inexorably lead to an eventual substantive withdrawal of the United States from the region. There was, at the same time, little indication that the government in Beijing, emerging from the upheavals of the cultural revolution, would relax its strong support for its Vietnamese ally, or for the Communist insurgents in Laos and Cambodia. In addition, Soviet interest in the Indochinese peninsula had not lessened, despite the continued chill in relations between Moscow and Beijing. While there appears to have been little fear among External Affairs officials in Ottawa that the dominoes would be pushed, one by one, by either of the Communist great powers, there was the fear of continued military instability in the region that could have wider implications. The tenor of the 1970 foreign policy paper, the subsequent actions of the government in the 1970s, and ex post facto assessments by officials in the Department of External Affairs all suggest that these kinds of strategic concerns were not absent from the government's thinking in the late 1960s. The dramatic shift in the Canadian view of Indonesia's importance can be seen as a natural consequence of the shifts in the power balance in Asia, the perceived effects of these shifts on regional stability and security, and their effects, in turn, on economic and commercial possibilities.

Second, Indonesia appears to have been chosen by the government in Ottawa for increased attention because of its development needs. Before the rapid increases in the price of oil that created a boom that was to boost dramatically Indonesia's gross national product per capita to $300 by 1977, Indonesia was ranked as one of the poorest countries in Asia, with a 1968 GNP per capita of only $85. Ottawa's announced intention to focus 80 per cent of its bilateral allocations to 'countries of concentration' – which included the low-income states – meant that Indonesia would be a likely candidate given its poverty. A related factor was Ottawa's belief that Indonesia was well equipped to use development assistance sent by Canada. The domestic political stability achieved by Suharto after the ouster of Sukarno in 1966, together with a pronounced tilt in foreign policy towards the West,[16] made Indonesia an attractive target in the eyes of policy-makers concerned with ensuring that aid was effectively used by recipient countries.

Third, the Canadian government's announcement in 1970 that henceforth it would be concentrating its development assistance in areas in which Canada had a particular expertise had implications for the choice of Indonesia as a country of concentration. Huge natural resources, ready for exploitation, provided a complementarity for Canadian expertise in resource extraction and exploitation. Pulp and paper, hydrocarbon, and mineral resources all attracted the attention not only of the Canadian government, but also of the corporate community in Canada. As a result, for example, the International Nickel Company (Inco) and several Canadian-based oil companies expanded considerably their investments in Indonesia. Similarly, the development of transportation and communications between Indonesia's numerous far-flung islands also became a Canadian development priority, an outgrowth of Canadian expertise in civil aviation.

Finally, Indonesia was selected because the trade and investment possibilities were seen to be considerable over the medium and longer term. Indonesia has the largest population of any state in the Southeast Asian region, and this large population was often cited as a prime market to be tapped by Canadian business. The Suharto government was a relatively compliant host, regulating but none the less facilitating private foreign investment. The investment climate, while not entirely open, was none the less favourable enough to attract considerable Western capital. Of all the states in the region, therefore, Indonesia presented itself as the likeliest opportunity for increased economic activity.

Having laid out Canadian priorities, and the objectives it would seek in the region, the Trudeau government set out to expand and improve the Canadian-Indonesian relationship. Three indicators can be used to measure the government's interest in Indonesia between 1968 and 1972: the flows of development assistance and trade, and interest in the relationship with Indonesia shown by Canadian cabinet ministers.

Aid flows

During the 1960s, Indonesia, as a member of the Colombo Plan, received small amounts of bilateral official development assistance (ODA) from Canada each year, averaging $500,000 annually. Beginning in 1968, however, bilateral disbursements of ODA began to show a marked increase. These disbursements climbed to $0.97 million in 1968–9, $2.33 million in 1969–70, $3.57 million in 1970–1, and $6.95 million in 1971–2. Although this was a sizeable increase, it did not represent a radical change in Canadian development assistance priorities in Asia. Aid to Indonesia amounted to 0.9 per cent of bilateral ODA to all Asia in 1968; by 1972, that figure was only 3 per cent. Development assistance to India, Pakistan, and Sri Lanka continued to claim the lion's share of Canada's ODA budget for Asia. Ottawa was increasing its support for Indonesia through increased development assistance spending, but not at the expense of its traditional aid recipients in the region.

Trade flows

In August 1969, the commercial division of the Canadian embassy in Djakarta was reactivated after a nine-year hiatus. In addition, the Department of Trade and Commerce decided to double its allocation of funds for trade promotion in the Pacific area at the same time. These renewed efforts of Trade and Commerce bore fruit fairly quickly. Exports to Indonesia, which had averaged $1.7 million per year from

1960 to 1969, to a high of $2.9 in 1969, rose sharply to $16.5 million in 1970. Importantly, however, the same was not true on the import side: imports from Indonesia, which had averaged $0.72 million throughout the 1960s, increased only marginally, widening even further the positive trade balance Canada has always enjoyed with Indonesia.

Ministerial interest

One useful indicator of the nature of the relationship between states is the degree to which political leaders engage in exchanges designed to express symbolic support. In the case of Canadian-Indonesian relations in this period, Pierre Trudeau himself sought to provide a concrete and practical manifestation of his government's stated intentions by including Indonesia in a tour of other Asian Commonwealth states – Malaysia, India, Pakistan, and Sri Lanka – following the Commonwealth prime ministers' conference (as it was then known) in Singapore in January 1971. Trudeau spent three days in Indonesia, meeting with Suharto, Foreign Minister Adam Malik, and other senior officials. Trudeau claimed that he would 'view with sympathy' Indonesian requests for development assistance, and indeed announced in Djakarta a $4 million interest-free loan for commodity purchases.[17]

Although in the four years after 1968 the relationship flourished, in many respects the links between Canada and Indonesia in the period 1970–2 were developing in the absence of specific policy objectives. The 1970 policy paper had enumerated general interests and goals, and the concerns about regional instability were cast at a high level of generalization. After 1972, however, Canadian concerns about Indochina and the role of the government in Hanoi in the post-hostilities period crystallized Canadian policy objectives towards Indonesia. Specific strategic ends were laid down, and specific means to achieve those ends were employed. The objective, very basically, was to prevent the government of Vietnam from destabilizing the region by posing a military threat to its neighbours; the policy employed to achieve that objective was strong support for ASEAN, and equally strong support for the most powerful member of that group, Indonesia.

THE RELATIONSHIP AFTER 1972

Of central importance to an understanding of the pronounced shift in

Canadian policy towards Indonesia after 1972 was the deterioration of the situation in Indochina in general, and in Vietnam in particular. The Canadian government did not have the luxury of being able to watch these events from the comfort of the diplomatic sidelines. The Nixon administration, eager to lend legitimacy to the Paris peace accords, pressed Ottawa hard to participate in a revitalized international truce-supervisory commission – consisting of Canada, Hungary, Indonesia, and Poland – to oversee the provisions of the Peace of Paris.

Canada participated on the International Commission of Control and Supervision (ICCS) for only six months before withdrawing in mid-1973.[18] But Ottawa's service on the ICCS put into sharp focus for many Canadian policy-makers, particularly those in the Department of External Affairs, the potential military threat to stability in Southeast Asia posed by the Vietnamese. For the Vietnamese government in Hanoi demonstrated little intention of allowing the opportunity afforded by the withdrawal of the United States to pass. While the North Vietnamese leadership had been constrained to accept the terms of the Paris accords because of the large-scale bombings authorized by President Nixon in December 1972, it seemed unwilling to accept the spirit of that agreement. The North Vietnamese waited until the withdrawal of the remaining United States troops, and the return of the last prisoners of war at the end of March 1973, before resuming the struggle against South Vietnam. The resumption of hostilities was watched over by the ICCS, itself becoming more fractured as a split developed between the East Europeans on the one side and the Canadians on the other. And the government in Ottawa was becoming increasingly frustrated with its role on the Commission. 'Canada,' declared the secretary of state for external affairs, Mitchell Sharp, in a white paper published in May 1973, 'would not take part in a charade.'[19] The government in Ottawa eventually withdrew Canada from the ICCS, arguing that no useful purpose was being served as long as the most important parties to the peace had little intention of reconciliation.[20]

Once Canada had withdrawn from the truce-supervisory role in Indochina, direct attempts to secure military stability in the region by participating in the international machinery put in place by the Paris peace accords were replaced by more indirect methods. The primary focus of this indirect approach was strong Canadian support for the Association of Southeast Asian Nations, whose membership included Thailand and Indonesia, both seen as the primary bulwarks against expansionism by North Vietnam. From bilateral aid flows alone, it could be inferred that ASEAN had assumed a new importance in Canadian eyes. Bilateral disbursements to ASEAN countries doubled between 1971–2 and 1972–3, increasing from 6 per cent of bilateral aid to all Asia to a high of 15 per cent by 1975–6. Most of this increase took the form of expanded assistance to Indonesia. Whereas in 1971–2, 46 per cent of bilateral aid to ASEAN members was directed to Indonesia, by 1972–3, Indonesia was receiving 80 per cent of Canadian disbursements; by 1975–6, that figure would increase to 95 per cent.

Increased development-assistance disbursements to Indonesia after the Canadian withdrawal from Indochina was mirrored by a dramatic increase in trade flows.[21] Exports to Indonesia quadrupled in two years – climbing from $14.4 million in 1972 to $53.6 million in 1974 (and climbing even further by 1976 to $76.9 million). Imports, as before, also rose, but less dramatically, so that by 1976, Canada had a $58.8 million surplus in merchandise trade.

One impulse for much of this economic activity was the increasing uncertainty in Indochina. While increases in investment and trade tended to be the result of private-sector decisions, clearly the increase in official development assistance allocations was the result of the severe deterioration of the military situation in Indochina. By 1975, the rapid demise of the three governments in Laos, South Vietnam, and Cambodia prompted Canadian officials to wonder aloud about the future of the region, and especially about North Vietnamese intentions. For while Ottawa did not hesitate to recognize all the new Communist governments that came to power in 1975, it was slow in reacting favourably to what was openly admitted to be an unknown quantity. As R.L. Rogers, then the director-general of the Bureau of Asian and Pacific Affairs in the Department of External Affairs, asked in a speech to the Canadian Committee of the Pacific Basin Economic Council in April 1977: 'The attitude of the Government of Vietnam is ambiguous at this time. Will Hanoi concentrate on reconstruction or will it attempt to export its revolution to its neighbours?'[22]

Nor was the government in Ottawa hesitant to show the flag in support of ASEAN in general – or Indonesia in particular. In ministerial and bureaucratic statements of policy regarding Southeast Asia, the importance of ASEAN to Canada's policy towards the region was consistently underscored. Two ministerial visits in 1976 – merely months after the invasion of Timor – helped to highlight this Canadian interest. In January 1976, the president of the Canadian International Development Agency, Paul Gérin-Lajoie, led a mission to Indonesia to examine Canada's development assistance programs there, claiming afterwards that there were 'new possibilities' in the country. In March, Don Jamieson, the minister of industry, trade, and commerce, toured ASEAN countries, accompanied by a fifty-member trade mission. While in Djakarta, the minister signed an agreement with the Indonesian government extending a $200 million line of credit, claiming that one of the ways Canada would show its commitment to ASEAN would be to improve trade relations.[23] On his return to Canada, Jamieson was more blunt: he told the *Financial Post* that he could see 'a way to make a hell of a lot of money in Asia now if you're in business and you're hungry.'[24]

The trade mission was followed by a visit from the secretary of state for external affairs, Allan MacEachen, in August and September. Indonesia was the first stop on a four-nation tour that was notable because it marked the first official visit by a Canadian foreign minister to Indonesia, Malaysia, and (interestingly, given historic Commonwealth links) New Zealand and Australia. In Djakarta, MacEachen signed agreements with Indonesia for grants and loans totalling $20.8 million. He also publicly reconfirmed Canada's commitment to both Indonesia and ASEAN, claiming that 'it was natural – indeed inevitable – that Indonesia would be regarded with special interest' by Canada.[25]

The issue of human rights violations in Indonesia was included on MacEachen's agenda. He met with the Indonesian foreign minister, Adam Malik, to discuss the question of political prisoners, and reportedly pressed the Indonesian government to continue its policy of releasing these prisoners. However, such criticisms as Ottawa might have had were communicated privately to the Indonesians;[26] in public, MacEachen said nothing about human rights. Instead, his public concerns remained fixed on peace in the region. In Australia, he claimed that Vietnam was the key to peace in the Pacific region; the onus was on Hanoi to show concrete evidence of its desire to live in peace with its neighbours.[27]

The Canadian government's reaction to the Indonesian invasion of East Timor in December 1975 was perhaps the best indication of the desire to do nothing, in public at least, to disrupt in any way the domestic stability or international standing of the Suharto regime. From the outset of the invasion, Canadian policy had been firmly to avoid public criticism of the invasion. On 12 December 1975, the UN General Assembly approved a resolution deploring the invasion, and called on Indonesia to remove its troops from the disputed territory. Far from condemning Indonesia for the invasion, Canada joined thirty-three other nations in abstaining on Resolution 3485. No consideration was given to suspending development assistance in retaliation or to disrupting the increasingly large trade between the two countries. Moreover, this seeming public indifference would be maintained for over fifteen years.

AVOIDING SANCTIONS, 1975–91

There can be little doubt that in the case of Indonesia, there was what Margaret Doxey has called a 'rhetoric gap' between the professions of concern by Canadian government officials for 'rightful' behaviour in the international system and the actual behaviour of the Canadian government when it is confronted with wrong-doing by other states.[28] Likewise, Indonesia provides a clear example of what T.A. Keenleyside and Patricia Taylor have called the 'dubious selectivity' of the government in Ottawa when it comes to imposing sanctions on acknowledged human rights violators.[29]

How might we explain the Canadian government's reluctance to sanction Indonesian behaviour in the mid-1970s and, as resolutely, to oppose sanctioning Djakarta throughout the 1980s? What factors prompted the government into silence when confronted with not only violations of human rights on a broad scale but also an open violation of a cardinal rule in contemporary international politics – the injunction against violating the sovereignty and territorial integrity of other states?

One common response to those instances where governments choose to eschew sanctions when confronted by wrong-doing by other states is simply to invoke a charge of hypocrisy. The argument is basically that despite all the high-sounding rhetoric of policy-makers, both elected and bureaucratic, about wrongful behaviour by other states in the international system, governments are not really interested in 'rightful' behaviour at all. Rather, they merely use rhetoric to cover their 'real' interests, which are usually claimed to be economic.

However, as I have argued elsewhere,[30] hypocrisy tends to be of limited utility as an explanation for foreign policy behaviour. More compelling are analyses that recognize that the responses of governments to international wrong-doing tend to be inconsistent, and that policy-makers, when choosing responses to wrong-doing, engage in highly selective behaviour, as Keenleyside and Taylor assert. For example, why do some invasions go unremarked while others generate passionate objections? Why do some cases of human rights violations attract sanctions, while others are completely ignored? Explanations that locate the causality for such inconsistency in the putatively ignoble motives of officials are easy to conjure up, but are hardly satisfactory. Rather, we should examine how a commitment by officials to conceptions of internationally 'rightful' behaviour – for example, the sanctity or inviolability of borders, or the humane treatment of citizens by their governments – can be eroded by their attachment to other, often contending, goals. Other national interests, such as economic, diplomatic, or strategic considerations, tend to intervene, prompting governments to turn a blind eye to wrong-doing by other states.

One part of the explanation in the Indonesian case lies in Canadian domestic politics. Unlike other cases of gross human rights violations, or other cases of invasion-and-overthrow, the Indonesian wrong-doing provoked virtually no political response in Canada in the 1970s. The large-scale human rights violations passed largely unremarked. Likewise, media coverage of the invasion of East Timor was minimal; there was no great interest in either issue in Parliament. As a consequence, neither fuss nor comment was raised over the fate of either the huge number of political prisoners or the Timorese.

On the contrary, in the mid- and late 1970s, there were only a few domestic critics of Canadian links with Indonesia. T.A. Keenleyside, a former External Affairs official who moved to the University of Windsor to teach political science, offered a fictional critique of Canada's development assistance policies in *The Common Touch*, a novel published in 1977. Keenleyside's fictional state of 'Bukhara' is undisguisedly Indonesia, and he was not hesitant to criticize what he felt were the misguided priorities of the Canadian government in the concrete support it was giving to the Suharto regime. Likewise, Douglas Roche (PC, Edmonton-Strathcona), the Progressive Conservative critic for relations with developing countries during the 30th Parliament (1974–9), maintained a strong attack on the government's policies towards Indonesia throughout 1977 and 1978. During a nation-wide speaking tour sponsored by the Canadian Institute of International Affairs in January 1977, Roche called Canadian development assistance to Indonesia merely a 'tool' to get Canada's foot in the door for more trade. He called on the Trudeau government to 'press Indonesia to move towards policies of social justice and then ensure that Canadian aid gets through to the village level.' He argued that 'when repression and corruption are added to authoritarianism as hallmarks of a government, it is wrong for Canada to remain mute in the face of these evils and maintain an aid program that Canadians think is intended to help the Indonesian people.'[31]

In short, there was little domestic criticism of Canada's Indonesia policy throughout this period, and little pressure on the government to adopt a more sanctionist approach. It is true that the government in Ottawa was confronted with periodic protests on the issue of human rights violations in Indonesia, as the criticism that greeted Prime Minister Trudeau's January 1983 visit to Southeast Asia demonstrated, for example. Even so, Canadian interest in the East Timor issue remained sporadic at best – usually marked by an annual op-ed piece in the *Globe and Mail* run in early December to mark the anniversary of the invasion.

Certainly the Trudeau government never had to face the kind of outraged public opinion demanding censure and punishment of Indonesia that confronted the Australian government of Malcolm Fraser. Like the Canadian government, the Australian government was not at all eager to sanction Indonesia for its intervention in Timor, although the reasons for this reluctance were more complex than Canada's, since good relations with Indonesia were (and are) so much more important to Australian foreign policy-makers.[32] But the government in Canberra had to face a broad spectrum of critical domestic opinion that included a number of émigré groups linked to Fretilin; a coalition of some forty unions; the Conference of Roman Catholic Bishops; and the peak association of non-governmental organizations involved in Australian development assistance, the Australian Council for Overseas Aid.[33] Moreover, Australian public opinion on Timor was inflamed by the persistently strident criticism of Indonesia in the Australian press, the result of the killing of five young Australian journalists at Balibo during the civil war in October 1975.[34]

If the Canadian public was not pressuring the government in Ottawa to sanction Indonesia, what of those Canadian firms that had commercial interests in Indonesia? It can be argued that one of the reasons for the public silence of the Canadian government on the issue of Timor was economic. This explanation tends to be favoured by those, such as Carty and Smith,[35] who explain all government behaviour in economic determinist terms. However, even those who embrace a more mixed-motives explanation for foreign policy behaviour have been disinclined to ignore the impact of economic links. Keenleyside, for example, has argued that Ottawa's desire to encourage commercial links between Canadian investors and Indonesia was one of the 'transparent' reasons for avoiding criticism or sanctions that surely would have soured the relationship – to the undoubted detriment of future economic ties.[36]

Yet another reason for official reluctance was the role Indonesia played in Canada's development assistance policies during this period. There is little doubt that policy-makers in Ottawa regarded Indonesia as a 'success story' in the Canadian aid program. Officials claimed to be impressed by the degree to which Indonesia under the Suharto regime was able to absorb Canadian development assistance relatively efficiently. At a time when the Canadian International Development Agency was being widely criticized in the Canadian press for wasteful practices and manifestly inefficient and unsuccessful aid projects,[37] the Indonesian experience did stand out. To be sure, one of the reasons for this success was that Canadian aid was part of a wider Western aid effort that was carefully coordinated by a consortium of Western aid donors, organized into the Intergovernmental Group on Indonesia (IGGI), chaired by the foreign minister of the Netherlands.

But it was not only the success of development assistance spending that encouraged Ottawa. Perhaps more attractive was the willingness of the Suharto government to embrace large capital-intensive projects in areas in which Canadian firms had a ready expertise – mining or civil aviation, for example. In short, the success of Indonesia as a development assistance recipient proved to be a not inconsiderable disincentive to disrupting the program.

Finally, a fourth factor that inhibited the adoption of a sanctionist approach to Indonesia was the calculation about Indonesia's strategic importance noted above. Canadian officials were not insensitive to the shifts that were occurring in the regional power balance, and indeed were already in the late 1960s calculating that with the withdrawal of the American commitment to the region, other regional players would have to play a larger role. In such a calculation, the strategic benefits derived from the balancing role of such regional powers would outweigh the costs of developing closer relations with a regime that had a less than pristine record on human rights observance.

Moreover, there were genuine concerns among officials in Ottawa, mirroring fears being expressed in other Western capitals, that if the East Timorese were successful in securing independence, it would seriously destabilize Indonesia by prompting other groups within the far-flung multi-ethnic country to seek self-determination. Adding to such concerns about the stability of Indonesia were the fears about Fretilin being voiced by the Indonesians: that it was a revolutionary group with ties to the Soviet Union. The Soviet-backed regime in Vietnam had only eight months beforehand secured victory, giving the Soviet Union a strategic entree to Indochina that had hitherto been denied them; there was little desire in the West to countenance the possibility that Moscow might be able to add another friendly regime in Dili. In short, there were a range of strategic reasons for acquiescing in the Indonesian action.

It can be argued that these factors – the lack of domestic pressure, the attraction of commercial benefits, the success of Indonesia as an aid recipient, and the broader strategic considerations – all played a part in inclining the government in Ottawa away from a sanctionist position on Indonesia in the late 1970s and throughout the 1980s. But the factor that appears to have weighed most heavily in the determination of the Canadian government's position on sanctions against Indonesia was the position being taken by other states in the region.

There can be little doubt that there would have been a notable lack of multilateral support for a sanctionist policy against Indonesia; indeed, it is likely that Canada would have faced strong multilateral ostracism at the diplomatic level had it moved to impose sanctions against the Suharto regime for the invasion of East Timor and its other human rights violations. Since the United States, Britain, Japan, and the other ASEAN countries were all committed to maintaining Suharto in power, deviation by a smaller player – and one located at the fringe of the region at that – would not have been appreciated.

Had Canada imposed sanctions against Indonesia unilaterally, or attempted to rally multilateral support for a sanctionist response to Indonesia's policies on Timor, the larger powers in particular would surely have moved against Canada, if only to create strong disincentives for other states to defect. Indeed, the experience of Australia must have been instructive in this regard. As Australian-Indonesian relations continued to suffer tensions throughout 1976 over Australia's refusal to accept the incorporation of Timor into Indonesia, the United States finally took the initiative to indicate directly to the Australian prime minister, Malcolm Fraser, that Canberra should not allow the Timor issue to cause a further deterioration in relations with the Suharto regime. American officials argued that Indonesian control of Timor was important for American strategic interests because it would extend Djakarta's control over neighbouring straits, and would, because of Washington's close 'working relationship' with Indonesia, facilitate the passage of American nuclear submarines through these waters, while at the same time denying comparable access to Soviet submarines.[38]

Likewise, it is likely that the smaller countries of the region would have subjected Canada to comparable ostracism. The combined anger of these groups would, quite simply, have frozen Canadian diplomats out of regional diplomatic activity on which Ottawa puts high value: invitations to Ottawa to attend ASEAN's '6+6' post-ministerial meetings as a 'dialogue partner,' for example, might have stopped.[39] Likewise, Canada's membership in IGGI might have been jeopardized. In short, given the importance that Canada's major alliance partners in the area were attaching to the notion of Indonesia as a regional stabilizer and bulwark against Soviet expansionism, the gains from a sanctionist policy would have had to outweigh heavily the costs of deviating from the coalition that supported Indonesia, regardless of its policies on human rights or East Timor.

EPILOGUE: THE RELATIONSHIP AFTER NOVEMBER 1991

One measure of the impact of the coalition dynamic at work in this case can be seen in the evolution of Canada's policy towards Indonesia after the end of the Cold War – in other words, in the period when the threat of Soviet expansionism had receded, and when strategic considerations were no longer at the forefront of Ottawa's foreign policy concerns in the region. In effect, we can see a significant change of attitude when the Canadian government of Brian Mulroney was confronted with fresh evidence of Indonesian human rights violations in East Timor.

On 12 November 1991, Indonesian troops in Dili, the capital of Timor, attacked a group of approximately 2500 mourners at a funeral service for a young Timorese pro-independence activist who had been killed two weeks earlier by Indonesian soldiers. By all accounts, the only provocation that the mourners were offering was to carry the flag of Fretilin, the outlawed Timorese independence movement, and pictures of its guerrilla leader, Xanana Gusmao. At the cemetery, Indonesian soldiers opened fire on the group, and subsequently moved in on the mourners, allegedly bayonetting many of them. In the immediate aftermath of the massacre, it was claimed that numerous Timorese were 'disappeared' by Indonesian authorities. Numerous foreign journalists witnessed the massacre itself; and it was recorded on video by Yorkshire Television.

Barbara McDougall, Canada's secretary of state for external affairs, was at the third Asia Pacific Economic Cooperation (APEC) conference being held in Seoul when the massacre occurred. The day after news of the shootings reached Seoul, she held a meeting with the Indonesian foreign minister, Ali Alatas, during which she expressed Canadian 'outrage' over the behaviour of the Indonesian troops. She revisited this theme at a news conference at the end of the APEC meeting on 14 November, expressing 'anger' at the shootings. The same day, the Indonesian ambassador to Ottawa was called in to External Affairs to hear further criticism. And in Djakarta, Canada's ambassador, Ingrid Hall, called on a number of Indonesian ministers to convey comparable sentiments. At the United Nations, Canada's permanent representative condemned Indonesian actions in Dili before the Third Committee.[40]

Apart from this diplomatic activity, however, no concrete actions affecting Canada's links with Indonesia were taken. Ottawa was disinclined to invoke aid sanctions at this early juncture, even though McDougall ordered an immediate review of the $46 million in Canadian aid projects in Indonesia. In response to criticism in the House of Commons on 18 November, for example, McDougall argued that she was not inclined to invoke aid sanctions, since the vast majority of Canada's aid was 'grassroots' assistance that did not benefit the government or the security forces.[41]

Despite the reluctance regarding aid sanctions expressed by McDougall in the weeks following the shootings, the Canadian government did eventually invoke sanctions involving development assistance. On 9 December 1991, the minister announced that Canada was suspending approval of all new development assistance projects that might 'directly benefit' the Indonesian government. The value of the projects affected was approximately $30 million.[42]

How can one explain Canada's about-face on sanctions against Indonesia? After all, for sixteen years both Liberal and Conservative governments had acquiesced in the Indonesian occupation of Timor; Canada's consistent refusal to vote for resolutions at the United Nations condemning the occupation was but one indication of this. After a decade of assiduously avoiding sanctions against Indonesia, why did the Canadian government change its mind in December 1991?

One reason was that the Dili massacre was caught on video. These images, widely broadcast, proved important, for they galvanized public criticism in many Western states, including Canada. This dynamic is not unusual: other cases reported in this book demonstrate the importance of visual images to a sanctionist response. We will see in the case of Vietnam that even the artificially recreated images of Khmer Rouge slaughter in the film *The Killing Fields* made the Canadian government's attachment to the coalition government of which the Khmer Rouge was a part that much more uncomfortable. In the case of South Africa, one of the catalysts for public demands for sanctions in 1985 was the widely publicized videos of white police officers thrashing black demonstrators and setting dogs on them (a causal relationship quickly appreciated by the South African authorities, who moved to censor all reportage). Finally, the video images in the case of the Tiananmen massacre were important in galvanizing public opinion, and indeed helpful in explaining why the shooting of demonstrators in the Tibetan capital of Lhasa earlier in 1989 by People's Liberation Army soldiers – not widely seen – had not aroused a comparable negative response in Canada.

In the case of the Dili massacre, the impact of the video images propelled the Timor issue onto the national political agenda in a sustained way for the first time in sixteen years. The opposition parties pressed the minister on the issue in Question Period; a subcommittee of the Standing Committee on External Affairs and International Trade, chaired by a Progressive Conservative MP, gave over a day of often exceedingly critical testimony to an examination of the Timor issue.[43]

A second reason why the Mulroney government abandoned its attachment to an antisanctionist approach was that by the time Indonesian soldiers opened fire on the Dili demonstrators, the government in Ottawa had firmly locked itself into linking human rights performance and Canadian development assistance. Over the fall of 1991, Canadian policy on the linkage between development assistance and human rights performance underwent a major shift.[44] In September and October, both Mulroney and McDougall gave a number of speeches insisting that Canadian aid would be linked to human rights performance by development assistance recipients. And the prime minister had carried his human rights/development assistance message personally to both the Commonwealth Heads of Government Meeting in Harare in October and the summit of *la francophonie* in Paris in November.[45] But by making the linkage between aid and human rights performance so explicit, the Mulroney government could not easily ignore blatant human rights abuses by recipients of Canadian development assistance; or the reminders from the Opposition of the government's commitment to use aid sanctions in response to human-rights abuses. On the issue of the Dili massacre, both the Liberal and New Democratic Party human rights critics pushed McDougall on making good the government's promises to link aid and human rights.[46]

But of all the reasons for the reversal of the Canadian attitude towards sanctions against Indonesia, arguably the most important was the change of attitude of other governments that came with the end of the Cold War era.[47] No longer were the various other governments in the region so committed to supporting Indonesia as an anti-Soviet and anti-Vietnamese bulwark that they were willing to overlook Djakarta's human rights abuses (much, it would appear, to the surprise of the Indonesian government). As a result, one by one, Western countries announced that they were invoking sanctions in reaction to the shootings. The chair of the Intergovernmental Group on Indonesia, the Netherlands, suspended aid; Denmark and the European Community also announced aid sanctions. The EC called on the United Nations to impose bans on weapons sales to Indonesia.[48] Perhaps more important, Indonesia's neighbours in the region were clearly upset by the Dili massacre. In other words, it can be argued that Canada was still being influenced by its regional partners, just as it had been in the past; Canada was still following suit, even if its policies were now reversed.

CONCLUSION

The growth of Canadian strategic and economic interests in another country or region inevitably creates powerful inertial forces that often serve as a barrier to major changes in policy priorities. To shift from the predominance of economic, strategic, and diplomatic objectives to a policy shaped by a concern for the maintenance of international law or the observance of human rights through sanctions involves a major change in policy direction. In most instances, such a change becomes too large for governments to contemplate.

The case of Canadian policies towards Indonesia from the 1970s to the 1990s demonstrates how and why sanctionist policies are frequently avoided by smaller states when they involve such a large-scale shift. In this case, sanctions might have allowed policy-makers in Ottawa (and the few domestic critics) the satisfaction of engaging in consistent policy behaviour – punishing violators of international law or human rights by refusing to engage in 'business as usual' with those violators.

But that would have been one of the few positive effects of a sanctionist policy. For Canadian sanctions, no matter how comprehensive, would have had no appreciable impact on the target's behaviour: Djakarta was so committed to the incorporation of Timor that the Indonesian government would not have announced its withdrawal from East Timor or brought its human rights violations to an end had it been the target of Western sanctions in 1975 (much less unilateral Canadian sanctions). Nor, given the degree of international support for Suharto, particularly from the United States, would the Canadian government have been able to create a bandwagon effect, encouraging (or embarrassing) other states into joining a Canadian effort to coerce Djakarta into changing its behaviour.

On the other side of the ledger, however, the costs to Canada of a sanctionist policy during the 1970s and 1980s would have been significant. First, the direct economic costs would have been small but none the less quite harmful to Canadian interests, particularly when the trade balance was running so heavily in Canada's favour. Moreover, the extent of aid, trade, and investment activities by Canadians would surely have generated pressures within Canada to avoid a sanctionist policy that would disrupt this profitable intercourse.[49]

Most important, I have argued that Canadian sanctions against Indonesia during the Cold War period would have drawn the ire of Canada's major power allies, such as the United States, Britain, and Japan. It would also have alienated the region's smaller players, notably Indonesia's partners in ASEAN, all of whom had a greater interest in strategic considerations than in human rights concerns. In short, sanctions, by putting Canada so at odds with its regional partners, would have caused more harm to the sender than the target – a powerful disincentive to embrace this tool of statecraft.

By contrast, after the Dili massacre of November 1991, the Canadian government had little reason to avoid sanctions so assiduously. The strategic calculations of the Cold War period were no longer operative; the attitudes of all of Canada's IGGI partners had undergone a substantial shift. By December 1991, sanctioning Indonesian behaviour was finding considerable favour among precisely those states that had resisted sanctions against Indonesia so strenuously in the years before 1991. And just as Canada had been inclined to follow the coalition in the years before 1991, so too did it take its cue from its IGGI partners in the aftermath of the Dili massacre.

3

Coalition Politics and the 'Punishment' of Vietnam

The Canadian government imposed sanctions against Vietnam in 1979 and did not lift them until 1990, when Ottawa moved to normalize relations and re-establish a diplomatic presence in Hanoi. These sanctions were introduced quietly by the government of Pierre Elliott Trudeau in February 1979 – there was no public announcement from the government that punitive measures had been adopted by Canada – and were maintained for eleven years. They were finally lifted, as we will see in the next chapter, as a consequence of changes both domestic and international.

Canada's sanctions against Vietnam can best be understood if one goes beyond the usual 'utilities' offered by the generic theory of sanctions, which, as we noted in chapter 1 above, tends to focus on the instrumental purposes of these measures.

One of the central themes of this book is that among the various aspects of sanctions that are not well explored in the scholarly literature is the degree to which the sanctions policies of middle powers are affected by coalition politics: the dynamic by which the preferences of other states in the coalition to which a middle power belongs shape that middle power's own policy preferences. In the last chapter, we saw the degree to which the Canadian government was inclined *away* from a sanctionist policy in the case of Indonesia because of coalition politics. In this chapter, we explore how coalition politics inclined the Canadian government *towards* a sanctionist policy.

CANADIAN POLICY TOWARDS VIETNAM

After the end of the Vietnam War in 1975, caution dominated the Canadian government's approach to its relations with Vietnam. The Trudeau government proved reluctant to expand the flow of Canadian development assistance to Vietnam, slowly imposing restrictions on the flow of aid to Indochina as a whole.[1] The eventual collapse of peace in Indochina in the late 1970s caused a further deterioration in Canada's relations with Hanoi. The Vietnamese invasion of Cambodia (or Kampuchea, as it was then called[2]) in late 1978, the ouster of the Pol Pot government in January 1979, the Sino-Vietnamese war of February 1979, and in particular the refugee crisis in 1978 and 1979, provoked by genocide in Cambodia and Vietnam's mass expulsion of its Hoa citizens, all prompted Ottawa to revise Canada's relationship with Vietnam.

When the hostility between Cambodia and Vietnam escalated into a full-scale assault on Cambodian soil by Vietnamese troops in December 1978, the Trudeau government remained publicly indifferent to the swift removal of the Pol Pot regime and its replacement by a government backed by Vietnam. It is true that when Australia, Japan, and Denmark immediately cancelled or froze their aid programs in Vietnam,[3] Canada followed suit and quietly terminated its aid program in February 1979.[4] However, there was no public statement or comment by either the prime minister or the secretary of state for external affairs, Don Jamieson, to the press or to Parliament on these sanctions. Indeed, there was no immediate public comment on the invasion or the overthrow of the Pol Pot regime from Ottawa, even though numerous other states had issued condemnations.

It was not until after China launched an attack on Vietnam in February 1979 that Ottawa's public activity quickened, mainly at the United Nations. On 23 February, Canada joined Australia and New Zealand in publicly urging the Security Council to consider the situation in Southeast Asia. Canada's representative to the United Nations, William Barton, joined in the Security Council debate. On 24 February, he called for the removal of 'all foreign forces' from both Vietnam and Cambodia, claiming that Canadians were 'shocked' by the refugee crisis.[5]

However, the invasion went completely unremarked in the House of Commons among the opposition parties. In the immediate aftermath of the invasion, no question was put to the government; no motion was put under Standing Order 43; no adjournment debate was held on the issue. In fact, the issue was not raised in the House until 27 February, and in the waning months of the 30th Parliament, the Indochina question emerged precisely once after that. On neither occasion was the focus on the Vietnamese invasion of Cambodia. On 27 February Douglas Roche

(PC, Edmonton-Strathcona) asked Jamieson to outline Canada's response to the Chinese invasion of Vietnam. The second question, put by Peter Stollery (L, Spadina) on 14 March, focused on 'the truly scandalous way Vietnam is ridding itself of its citizens of Chinese descent.'[6] This public indifference was no doubt affected by the impending elections, but, I will argue below, the initial silence is important to an understanding of the evolution of Canada's policies towards Vietnam.

The official reticence ended in June 1979 when the newly elected Progressive Conservative government of Joe Clark embarked on what can best be described as a policy of punishing Vietnam. The punishment consisted of both political and economic measures. Politically, the Clark government initiated sustained public criticism of Vietnam in international fora that lasted throughout 1979. The Conservative government also continued diplomatic sanctions initiated by the Liberals: refusing to recognize the Vietnamese-backed Cambodian government of Heng Samrin, and blocking the efforts of the Soviet Union and Vietnam to have that government occupy Cambodia's seat at the United Nations. On the economic front, Clark publicly acknowledged and continued the comprehensive aid sanctions imposed by the Trudeau government. It is unclear whether emergency humanitarian aid was also sanctioned: while Canada had extended some limited emergency aid to Vietnam in the aftermath of typhoons in 1978, it was not until 1985 that a similar commitment was made.[7] It should be noted that these punitive policies were continued by the Trudeau government when it returned to office in February 1980, and by the Progressive Conservatives under Brian Mulroney after the September 1984 elections. Indeed, they were extended in the mid-1980s, when both the Trudeau and Mulroney governments provided limited humanitarian assistance to the coalition seeking to overthrow the government in Phnom Penh by force. In this section, the nature of the Canadian responses to the Vietnamese invasion will be examined; an attempt will then be made to assess the objectives of the sanctions employed against Vietnam.

Public criticism

When Clark came to power in June 1979, Canada's rhetorical pronouncements on Vietnam radically altered. Throughout the remainder of the year, the government, and particularly the secretary of state for external affairs, Flora MacDonald, used every opportunity to condemn Vietnam in terms that left in little doubt the government's anger at both

Vietnam's invasion of Cambodia and its expulsion of the Hoa people. For example, at the United Nations Conference on Refugees held at Geneva on 20–21 July, MacDonald chose to ignore an appeal by the secretary-general to minimize 'political' rhetoric. Instead, she called for 'an end to this flagrant, this continuing, this outrageous violation of human rights.' Referring to Vietnam, Cambodia, and Laos by name, she claimed that the international community would hold them 'responsible for the fate of their citizens,' and that the international community 'rejects as an unconscionable violation of human rights the attempt to expel or otherwise eliminate any ethnic community or any socio-economic group.' She also urged all states to cut off aid to Vietnam. Her open criticisms of Vietnam at the conference were said to be the harshest of any Western delegate.[8]

At the United Nations Pledging Conference for Emergency Assistance to Kampuchea in November, MacDonald continued the attack. In the lead-up to the conference, the Department of External Affairs issued a communiqué accusing Vietnam of exposing the 'entire population' of Cambodia to famine because of Hanoi's continued occupation, and that Vietnamese policies were the 'roots of the problem.'[9] At the conference itself, MacDonald claimed that, in making its pledge, the Canadian government was responding to 'a deep sense of outrage' among Canadians at the situation in Indochina. She called on the Vietnamese and the Heng Samrin and Pol Pot factions in Cambodia to stop playing politics with the lives of millions of people and to restore independence and territorial integrity to Cambodia.[10] A week later, during the General Assembly debate on the situation in Cambodia, Douglas Roche, MacDonald's parliamentary secretary, claimed that, when confronted with the evidence of 'appalling circumstances' in Indochina, 'Canadians feel outrage at the enormity of this obscenity ... The deep concern in Canadians ... is slowly changing its expression from anger to determination' to address the root of the problem. He rejected Vietnam's justification for its invasion, claiming that Hanoi only wanted to establish a 'docile and subservient' regime in Cambodia; MacDonald, in her address to the General Assembly, referred to 'the dismaying number of examples of human rights violations' in Indochina.[11] Finally, on 4 December 1979, in a statement concerning Canadian policies on human rights to the Third Committee, Vietnam was again criticized by name by the Canadian representative, who claimed that the link between human rights violations by Vietnam and Cambodia and the refugee crisis was clearly established.[12]

The reduction in expulsions by Vietnam and in the number of Indochinese refugees generally, the diversion of attention caused by the Soviet invasion of Afghanistan, and the defeat of the Conservative government in the House of Commons and again at the polls all served to bring this phase of public criticism of Vietnam to a close. However, throughout the 1980s, every Canadian government engaged in an annual (and eventually almost ritualistic) public criticism of Vietnam's occupation of Cambodia in two fora. The first was the annual '6+6' post-ministerial conference of the foreign ministers of the Association of Southeast Asian Nations (ASEAN) and of ASEAN's 'dialogue partners' – Australia, Canada, the European Community, Japan, New Zealand, and the United States. The second forum was the United Nations General Assembly, where discussion of the situation in Cambodia was on the agenda annually throughout the 1980s.[13]

Diplomatic responses

After the victory of the Communists in 1975, the Canadian government formally recognized the new Indochinese regimes. Canada had formally recognized the Democratic Republic of Vietnam (North Vietnam) in 1973; Canadian recognition was extended when North and South Vietnam were unified as the Socialist Republic of Vietnam in 1976. Although the Vietnamese had opened an embassy in Ottawa, the Canadian government had decided against having a diplomatic mission in Hanoi. The main reason seems to have been budgetary restraint, although it is clear that External Affairs had little desire to open a mission in Hanoi while the political situation in Indochina remained unsettled and the United States government was urging upon its allies a policy of diplomatic isolation for Vietnam: as a result, until the early 1980s, the Canadian ambassador to China was accredited to the Socialist Republic of Vietnam. With the advent of open conflict between the PRC and Vietnam, these responsibilities were transferred to Canada's ambassador to Thailand.[14] After the invasion of Cambodia and the removal of Pol Pot, no diplomatic sanctions were applied directly against Vietnam by Canada. Although the Canadian government expelled Vietnam's second secretary in Ottawa in March 1979 over alleged extortions of Vietnamese in Canada, this was not a sanction directly linked to events in Indochina.[15] In the words of one External Affairs official, the diplomatic relationship remained 'correct though not overly cordial.'[16]

However, Canada did join other states in imposing diplomatic sanctions against the new Vietnamese-backed government in Phnom Penh, and hence, indirectly, against Vietnam itself. Not only did Canada refuse to recognize the Heng Samrin government; it consistently supported resolutions aimed at keeping the government from taking Cambodia's seat at the United Nations. For example, in the credentials fight over Democratic Kampuchea at the 34th session of the General Assembly in September 1979, Canada joined seventy other states in support of Resolution 34/2A (21 September 1979) upholding the right of Pol Pot's regime to occupy the Democratic Kampuchean seat. At the 35th session, the credentials resolution denying the Heng Samrin regime the Cambodian seat was accepted without a vote.

In the immediate aftermath of Pol Pot's downfall, these sanctions proved to be an acute embarrassment for all Western governments, for in order to deny legitimacy to the government installed by Vietnamese troops, they had to accord recognition to the Khmer Rouge – at the very time that the international community was learning the full extent of the genocide visited on Cambodia by Pol Pot and his regime. The usual practice was to claim that recognizing the Khmer Rouge as the legitimate government did 'not imply Canadian government approval for the Democratic Kampuchean regime of Pol Pot or Canadian acquiescence in the abhorrent human rights abuses perpetrated by that regime.' This is how Roy MacLaren, parliamentary secretary to the minister of energy, mines, and resources, speaking for the government in an adjournment debate in the House of Commons on 16 July 1981 put it to a critical Liberal backbencher.[17]

Such semantic attempts to wriggle out of what in essence was de facto support for Pol Pot and the Khmer Rouge proved too much for at least one Western country: the Australian government withdrew its recognition of the Khmer Rouge in February 1981.[18]

The Western embarrassment was reduced somewhat by efforts of Beijing and ASEAN to make the Cambodian rebels more palatable to the West. In 1982, a tripartite opposition coalition, including the Khmer Rouge and two non-Communist groups led by Prince Sihanouk and former premier Son Sann, was created. Although Australia and the European Community refused to recognize the coalition because of the continued association of Pol Pot and the Khmer Rouge, Canada joined with the ASEAN states in endorsing the formation of the Coalition Government of Democratic Kampuchea (CGDK) as the legitimate government of Cambodia.[19]

The issue of concrete assistance to the anti-Heng forces arose in 1983.

During his Asian trip in January 1983, Trudeau politely refused to consider Thai requests for 'something more than moral support' for the CGDK. Indeed, he was reported to have said that 'Canada does not intend to be, nor can it be, a major player in that game [the stabilization of Cambodia]. We will continue to support the ASEAN initiative which we think is the right one, including the strengthening of the non-Communist forces in the coalition, and we are saying so, but not by supplying arms or anything like that.'[20] However, in 1984, the then secretary of state for external affairs, Jean Chrétien, announced that the government in Ottawa would, like a number of other Western states,[21] be sending limited humanitarian aid to the non-Communist segments of the CGDK located in camps in northeastern Thailand, a pledge that was reiterated by Clark in 1985.[22] In 1984, a minuscule sum – $20,000 – was offered as a 'symbolic contribution' to the non-Communist factions; by contrast, Canadian humanitarian assistance of all kinds to Cambodian refugees in Thailand amounted to $750,000 in 1982–3, $175,000 in 1983–4, $900,000 in 1984–5, and $700,000 in 1985–6.[23]

Aid

While the Trudeau government had first slowed down Canada's development-assistance program to Vietnam, it moved in February 1979 to terminate it completely. Included in the sanctions were all technical assistance, food aid, direct government-to-government disbursements, disbursements to multilateral agencies, and indirect contributions of matching grants to non-governmental organizations such as the Canadian Friends Service Committee. The last shipment of food aid – a $4.75 million shipment of flour authorized in 1978 – left Vancouver in July 1979.[24] As noted above, this decision had remained unannounced until the Clark government made it public in June 1979.

As table 1 indicates, Canada's development assistance program to Vietnam in the late 1970s provided Ottawa with very limited economic leverage against Vietnam. Although at one juncture the Canadian government had envisaged a postwar reconstruction program for Indochina,[25] the political situation in the late 1970s had considerably dampened that earlier enthusiasm. The radical regimes in Cambodia and Laos terminated Western aid projects; the Khmer Rouge did not even bother to respond to a Canadian offer of aid in 1975. Vietnam, however, was interested in Canadian development assistance: Pham Van Dong apparently wished to diversify Vietnam's sources of development

TABLE 1

Canadian development assistance to the states of Indochina, 1975–81

	Government-to-government disbursements[a] (C$ millions)						
	1974/5	1975/6	1976/7	1977/8	1978/9	1979/80	1980/1
Vietnam	2.07	1.49	(0.05)[b]	6.07	0.24	–	–
Cambodia	0.55	0.03	0.01	–	–	–	–
Laos	0.20	0.18	0.09	–	–	–	–
Indochina[c]	–	2.24	1.92	0.69	–	–	–
ASEAN[d]	21.9	38.56	25.71	19.32	17.95	20.66	31.5
Total Asia	244.3	257.8	233.4	253.4	227.1	234.6	223.3

[a] Includes food aid.

[b] Indicates net return to Canada.

[c] Disbursements made under the Emergency Relief Programme to the States of Indochina. A lump sum of $12.71 million was voted by Parliament for 1975/6 for relief aid to Indochina as a whole; portions of this sum were also disbursed to international and non-governmental organizations.

[d] ASEAN comprises Indonesia, Malaysia, the Philippines, Singapore, and Thailand, and (after 1983) Brunei.

SOURCE: Data compiled from Canada, Canadian International Development Agency, *Annual Report* (Ottawa 1974–86)

assistance in the postwar period, hoping that the Western states, including the United States, would provide half of its needs.[26] But the policies being pursued by Hanoi caused sufficient concern in Ottawa about Vietnam's regional intentions that by the late 1970s the Trudeau government was keeping the aid program minimal. It consisted almost completely of food aid: in 1977/8, only $200,000 was provided in technical assistance; in 1978/9, that figure dropped to $100,000.

When Trudeau was returned to power in the elections of February 1980, his government continued these aid sanctions. Likewise, when Clark was appointed Mulroney's external affairs minister in 1984, the sanctions remained in force. Although the issue was periodically reviewed by both the Canadian International Development Agency and the Department of External Affairs, there was, for reasons we will explore below, little sentiment in External Affairs to lift the sanctions. For example, when a Canadian interchurch delegation visited Vietnam in 1986 and returned recommending that a parliamentary delegation visit Vietnam and that Ottawa resume matching grants for NGOs, it reported that External Affairs showed 'no signs of deviating from the policy of the isolation of Vietnam.'[27]

Trade

In contrast to Canadian sanctions on development assistance, the government in Ottawa did not impose formal barriers to trade with Vietnam or Cambodia. There was neither an embargo nor a boycott imposed on goods to the states of Indochina. Likewise, Canadian firms wishing to expand their trade with Indochina remained eligible for assistance under the Program for Export Market Development, although demand for these services were, not surprisingly given the circumstances, minimal.

Full trade sanctions, comparable to the total ban on all economic intercourse maintained by the United States throughout this period,[28] were never enacted for two reasons. First, as table 2 indicates, trade with Vietnam was minuscule. Even at their pre-invasion peak in 1977, Canadian imports from Vietnam amounted to a total of $117,000, a tiny fraction of total imports from Asia alone. Most of the goods exported to Vietnam in the late 1970s consisted not of commercial exports, but of food and medical aid donated by NGOs. Likewise, Canadian trade linkages with Cambodia were non-existent.

Once development assistance had been terminated in 1979, there were virtually no other economic links left to disrupt. And while it is true that economic sanctions intended to disrupt what is not there are occasionally invoked,[29] the Canadian government did not think that a symbolic embargo or a boycott against Indochina was appropriate in the circumstances.

Second, trade restrictions against the states of Indochina were not seen as an important measure because a more subtle impediment to trade existed: the Export Development Corporation refused to extend guarantees to private business transactions with Vietnam and Cambodia.[30] However, the unavailability of EDC financing should not be regarded as a purposive economic sanction imposed by the Canadian government against the states of Indochina, for the policy of not extending guarantees to these states does not appear to have been introduced with the deterioration of the diplomatic relationship in the late 1970s. It existed prior to other sanctions introduced in 1979, and had been based primarily on economic grounds. The disruptions in Indochina during the period meant that, regardless of the tenor of political rela-

TABLE 2
Canadian trade with the states of Indochina, 1976–86

	Imports to Canada					
	1976	1978	1980	1982	1984	1986
Indochina ($ thousands)						
Vietnam[a]	27	50	62	161	2220	6671
Cambodia/Laos[b]	1	6	4	–	–	35
Other Asia ($ billions)						
ASEAN[c]	0.19	0.26	0.39	0.40	0.68	0.73
Total Asia	2.78	3.82	5.03	7.10	10.33	13.85
	Exports from Canada					
	1976	1978	1980	1982	1984	1986
Indochina ($ thousands)						
Vietnam	171	22,744	358	250	1898	2845
Cambodia/Laos[b]	1	66	15	8	14	28
Other Asia ($ billions)						
ASEAN[c]	0.23	0.32	0.75	0.72	0.79	0.65
Total Asia	3.29	4.81	7.45	8.08	9.74	10.10

[a] The figures for Vietnamese imports to Canada are for direct imports only; throughout
this period there existed a substantial *entrepôt* trade through Hong Kong and Singapore.
[b] Statistics Canada reports trade with Laos and Cambodia (Kampuchea/Khmer Republic)
in a single category.
[c] Indonesia, Malaysia, the Philippines, Singapore and Thailand, and (after 1983) Brunei

SOURCE: Data compiled from Canada, Statistics Canada, *Summary of External Trade*
(Ottawa: December 1976–86)

tions between Canada and Indochina, the EDC would not normally
regard either Vietnam or Cambodia a sufficiently sound risk to extend
assistance under its various programs for export financing, export-
credits insurance, or foreign investment guarantees. None the less, it
might be noted that, to the extent that the lack of EDC financing was a
disincentive to Canadian trade, it produced largely the same result as
a formal disruption of trade.

One can see clearly the effects of the aid sanctions on the movement
of goods between Canada and the states of Indochina. Between 1977
and 1979, over $56.2 million in goods were exported to Vietnam, pri-
marily wheat and hard spring wheat flour, drilling equipment, and
medical equipment and supplies.[31] In 1980, the value of those exports

abruptly tumbled: the 1979 level of $22.4 million fell to merely $358,000 – the bulk of that in medical supplies. However, one can also see the medium-term effects of the absence of formal trade sanctions. After 1980, a small trade between Canada and Indochina began to develop slowly. By 1986, Vietnamese direct exports to Canada, primarily clothing and fish products, had grown considerably in value; in addition, there was an increase in indirect Vietnamese exports to Canada through Hong Kong and Singapore.[32] In turn, by the mid-1980s Canadian commercial exports to Vietnam had also increased.

CANADA'S PUNISHMENT OF VIETNAM: CATALYSTS AND PURPOSES

There are two parts to an inquiry into what Vietnam was punished for: first, an examination of the 'wrong' committed by Vietnam that warranted a punitive response from Canada; and, second, an examination of the ends Ottawa hoped to achieve by its punishment of this wrongdoing.

Catalysts

Canadian rhetoric suggests that punitive economic sanctions were imposed because the Vietnamese invasion of Cambodia represented a violation of the sovereignty and territorial integrity of another state, and for that reason alone had to be punished. The argument that the invasion itself was sufficient explanation for punishment is, however, not compelling. Despite its obvious attachment to the principle of territorial integrity, Canada has never reacted to violations of that principle in an absolute or entirely consistent fashion. Such violations simply do not automatically trigger Canadian condemnation and punitive sanctions. Instead, Ottawa's response to armed invasions that result in the ouster of a legitimately established government has always been heavily dependent on the political context: Ottawa's responses have ranged from the use of force to implicit approval.

At one end of the spectrum, as we will see in chapter 9 below, the Canadian government eventually used force against Iraq following its invasion of Kuwait. As chapter 7 will show, Ottawa responded to the Soviet invasion of Afghanistan in December 1979 with sanctions; it likewise imposed sanctions on Argentina for its invasion of the Falkland Islands in April 1982. But, as we saw in the last chapter, when the

Suharto government in Indonesia took East Timor by force in 1975, the Canadian government did not publicly condemn Djakarta or impose sanctions against Indonesia. Likewise, when French forces invaded the Central African Empire in 1979 and relieved Emperor Bokassa I of his throne, or when the United States invaded Grenada in October 1983 or Panama in December 1989, there was no Canadian response that invoked the sanctity of territorial integrity. Indeed, at least one invasion-and-overthrow was greeted with implicit approval: when Tanzanian forces ousted Idi Amin in April 1979, Ottawa immediately recognized the new government installed in Kampala and participated in a Commonwealth scheme for economic rehabilitation.[33]

One indicator of the lack of importance of the invasion issue to the Canadian government's subsequent punitive measures against Vietnam is to be found in the immediate reactions in Canada to the invasion. The public indifference to the overthrow of Pol Pot in January 1979 strongly suggests that the moral consciences of Canadians were neither shocked nor outraged by Vietnam's military actions. (The subsequent disquiet in some quarters over Canada's continued recognition of the Khmer Rouge[34] suggests that there may have been some muted feeling of utilitarian satisfaction that the overthrow of a genocidal regime was a just end, even if achieved by unjust means.) Immediate reactions to an event provide a not unimportant indicator of the degree of 'wrongness' attached to an action: the strong, swift, and vociferous condemnations by Canadians of the Soviet invasion of Afghanistan, the Argentinean invasion of the Falkland Islands, the imposition of martial law in Poland, the Soviet downing of Korean Air Lines flight 007, or the June 1989 massacre in Beijing all stand in marked contrast to the silence after the downfall of Pol Pot.

Rather, I would argue that the action that prompted the Canadian punishment of Vietnam in 1979 was Hanoi's expulsion of the Hoa. This is suggested by the fact that the increase in Canadian verbal attacks on Vietnam coincided with the massive increase in the number of refugees leaving Indochina. If Canadians, and their representatives in Parliament, appeared unmoved by Vietnam's forcible removal of Pol Pot, they were disinclined to greet the 'boat people' crisis with such indifference. Such a reaction to the plight of the thousands of people expelled from their country was not only humanitarian in origin. It was also strongly grounded in self-interest, for the expulsions created a potent demand, not only for resettlement in other states, but also for additional aid for the refugees themselves and for the neighbouring states of first refuge – Indonesia, Malaysia, and Thailand.

Purposes

While the expulsion of ethnic Chinese citizens was the proximate cause of Canadian anger, and of Ottawa's concomitant desire to punish Vietnam, the multi-faceted punishments imposed on Hanoi were designed to achieve specific policy objectives. To what extent does conventional theorizing about the purposes of economic sanctions contribute to our understanding of the purposes of Canadian sanctions against Vietnam? On the one hand, it could be argued that three of the five conventional categories – domestic symbolism, international symbolism, and compliance – could be used to explain the sanctions in this case. However, it will be argued that a focus on these conventional categories, and their putative 'targets,' provides an incomplete view of Canada's punishment of Vietnam.

Domestic symbolism

Numerous students of economic sanctions have noted that often the 'real' target of these measures is the sender's own public. One can see in Canada's punishment of Vietnam domestic political purposes – in 1979 in particular. The 'boat people' issue assumed considerable political visibility in Canada during the Clark government's tenure in office;[35] a policy of criticizing – and economically hurting – the state deemed responsible for the plight of the refugees was a natural complement to the government's overall attempts to rally domestic support for additional aid funds and increased immigration levels. Certainly it would have been politically difficult (if not psychologically uncomfortable) to have to grapple with the massive human distress caused by Vietnamese behaviour while at the same time approving development assistance disbursements to the government in Hanoi. However, after that crisis abated, it is difficult to see the domestic purposes of a continued policy of punishment, although, as we will see in the next chapter, the Canadian government had to be concerned with how Canadians of Vietnamese origin, many of whom were among the 'boat people,' would have responded to an abandonment of that policy.

International symbolism

The 'target' of this objective, which involves expressing outrage at behaviour seen as objectionable, is assumed to be the international community. The vigorous rhetorical attacks by the Canadian government do suggest that by mid-1979 international symbolism was one of Ottawa's objectives. As Flora MacDonald explained to the House of Commons in November 1979, 'We took [the suspension of aid] further because we believe that the activities in Vietnam, the present expulsion of thousands of Indochinese, the invasion of a neighbouring country, Cambodia-Kampuchea, with all of the disaster and tragedy that has brought forward, does [sic] not in any way elicit our support.'[36] Certainly she and the Clark government took every opportunity in 1979 to criticize Vietnam in front of the international community: the attacks were pressed twice in the General Assembly, in one of the Assembly's committees, and at two international conferences on Indochinese refugees. Likewise, the undiplomatic language favoured by MacDonald in her speeches in international fora and her propensity to attack Vietnam by name also suggest a strong expressive objective. Again, however, it should be noted that much of that rhetoric was directed against Vietnam primarily for its expulsion of the Hoa, and not for the invasion of Cambodia.

Compellence

Sanctions that seek compellence are directed at the target. It might be argued that, in sanctioning Vietnam, the Canadian government was engaging in a classical calculation about economic sanctions. In other words, Ottawa was hopeful that its punitive policy of open criticism and diplomatic and economic sanctions would, when joined with comparable deprivation from other states, impose sufficient hurts on Vietnam to prompt the government in Hanoi to alter its objectionable behaviour, specifically the expulsion of the Hoa and its occupation of Cambodia. There was optimism that a policy of punishment would lead to a halt in the expulsions, the issue that had the most direct and immediate consequences for the Canadian government. A calculation that the leadership in Hanoi would be sensitive to international criticism of its expulsion policy drove the sustained Canadian verbal attacks on Vietnam in international fora throughout the year. It was, as MacDonald herself recognized, a largely successful effort. In November 1979, she told the House of Commons that 'there is no question that in speaking out about what Vietnam has been doing' Canada had an impact. 'The effect of that has been ... to cut down on the number of expulsions.'[37]

After the expulsions slowed and then ceased, the government in Ottawa none the less continued to explain the maintenance of sanctions in terms of compellence, as indeed did some commentators.[38] As the Vietnamese demonstrated little willingness simply to withdraw its military forces from Cambodia, Canadian rhetoric on aid sanctions shifted to linking the restoration of aid with Vietnamese compliance with one demand: their military withdrawal from Cambodia. As the following quotations from three secretaries of state for external affairs indicate, the formal rhetoric embraced classical arguments about economic sanctions: economic deprivation would impose sufficient costs on Vietnam that it would abandon its wrongful behaviour.

So long as Hanoi refuses to end its occupation of Cambodia, Canada for its part will not help subsidize its military activities by extending development aid to Vietnam.

Mark MacGuigan, June 1982

I can assure you that Canada will continue to support ASEAN in opposing Vietnamese challenges to the credentials of the Coalition Government of Democratic Kampuchea in the United Nations. At the same time, Canada will not support in either its bilateral programmes or through multilateral institutions the provision of economic assistance to Vietnam which would have the effect of subsidising or rewarding Hanoi's continued military occupation of Cambodia.

Allan MacEachen, June 1983

Canada fully supports the consistent efforts of ASEAN to achieve a Vietnamese withdrawal, and, until that happens, Canada will continue to deny Vietnam development aid.

Joe Clark, July 1985[39]

However, it is difficult to believe that these punishments of Vietnam remained in place for so long primarily to secure compliance with Canada's publicly stated objective of a military withdrawal from Cambodia. Vietnam's security interests were always linked to preventing a return to the *status quo ante bellum*: Vietnam's leaders, one observer has remarked, concluded that 'the economic deprivation and diplomatic isolation they are experiencing are outbalanced by retaining the dominant position in Indochina for which they fought so long and sacrificed so much to achieve.'[40] In short, the stakes were so high for Vietnam that it is hard to believe that the Canadian government was maintaining its punitive sanctions in the expectation that these measures would actually compel Hanoi to abandon its occupation of Cambodia.

THE PUNISHMENT OF VIETNAM RECONSIDERED: COALITION SOLIDARITY

If the discussion is taken no further than the conventional categories, we are left with an incomplete view of the purposes of Canadian policy towards Vietnam. At worst, Canadian policy appears almost sadistic – as it did to one Liberal MP who in 1981 criticized as 'obscene' a 'Vietnam-bashing' policy that would 'inevitably fail.'[41] At best, Canadian policy, which remained unchanged for a decade, appeared to be motivated by a quixotic and idealistic belief in the eventual ability to compel the leadership in Hanoi to change their calculation of Vietnam's vital interests and withdraw from Cambodia.

Such conclusions are perhaps inevitable only if the usual range of categories of objectives – and their assumed 'targets' – are used to analyse a sanctions episode. However, it is argued here that this case suggests the need for expanding the category of 'international symbolism' in order to understand why the Canadian government imposed sanctions on Vietnam in 1979, and why they remained so firmly in place. For the states that comprise the 'international audience' should not be treated as an undifferentiated whole. Margaret Doxey explictly recognized this fact when discussing the different 'targets' of sanctions: 'there is a wider audience in the world at large – which may include allies of the sanctioning government. Here too, there will be a drive to display and confirm ability to defend national interests and deter future challenges. For super-powers however, there will also be a leadership role ... [T]hey will expect their allies to back them up.'[42]

One corollary of this is that the friends and allies of the sanctioning state will have an interest in demonstrating their solidarity, even if the issue that prompted the sanctions might not directly affect them, and even if they might have no particular quarrel with the target of the sanctions. Paradoxically, in this view, sanctions – an instrument of interstate hostility – are employed primarily to demonstrate friendship for another state.

Canada's persistence in maintaining its eleven-year punishment of Vietnam becomes more understandable if it is assumed that the sanctions against Vietnam were designed primarily to demonstrate both symbolically and concretely Canadian solidarity with a coalition of other states. The coalition in this case was a loose one ranged against the Soviet Union. It included the members of ASEAN (Indonesia, Malaysia, the Philippines, Singapore, Thailand, and, after 1983, Brunei) and ASEAN's 'dialogue partners' (Australia, Canada, the European Community, Japan, New Zealand, and the United States).[43] And to the extent that Chinese interests in Indochina coincided with those of the United States and ASEAN, Beijing was associated – albeit more loosely – with the coalition.

The ASEAN states developed, not without some difficulty, a common diplomatic front on what they perceived as a threat to their security posed not only by Vietnam's regional expansionism, but also the introduction by Vietnam of great-power politics – notably the Sino-Soviet rivalry – into the region.[44] The key features of this common ASEAN approach, which has been called a 'strategy of attrition,'[45] involved (1) denying international legitimacy to the Vietnamese-backed government in Phnom Penh; (2) maintaining formal recognition of the government of Democratic Kampuchea; and (3) maintaining international pressure on Vietnam to withdraw from Cambodia. By implication, ASEAN's strategy of attrition also involved minimizing economic assistance to Vietnam.

The ASEAN coalition tended to be perceived by decision-makers in Ottawa as being of cardinal importance to the Pacific thrust of Canadian foreign policy, both economically, as tables 1 and 2 indicate, but also strategically. Canada's standing as an ASEAN 'dialogue partner' provided the government in Ottawa with an institutional entrée, and therefore a voice, in Southeast Asian affairs. Canada, which since 1970 had sought to be a player in Southeast Asia, consistently put a premium on good relations with ASEAN; maintaining that standing required that Canadian policy on Vietnam conform to the minima of the 'strategy of attrition.'

Certainly the Canadian government had little interest in creating the kind of conflict that emerged between the ASEAN states and Australia after the election of Bob Hawke in 1983. Before the 1983 elections, the Australian Labor Party pledged that, if elected, it would open a dialogue with Vietnam, and examine the possibilities of restoring a development assistance program. In 1983, Australia voted for, but did not co-sponsor, ASEAN's annual resolution at the United Nations, a symbolic departure that prompted considerable ASEAN criticism. Likewise, the ASEAN governments have taken the position that the Australian plan to resume aid to Vietnam was 'premature and likely to sabotage ASEAN strategy.'[46]

Thus, Canada refused to recognize Heng Samrin; it maintained diplomatic recognition of, first, the Khmer Rouge, and later the CGDK; it supplied moral and some limited concrete support to the coalition government favoured by ASEAN; the external affairs minister made an annual speech at the post-ministerial conference that was in varying degrees critical of Vietnam. For example, Mark MacGuigan's speech to ASEAN in Bangkok in June 1980 was notable for its severe anti-Soviet and anti-Vietnamese tone. He accused the Soviet Union of threatening world stability and financing the Vietnamese occupation of Cambodia, and even claimed that a recent Vietnamese incursion into Thailand 'was an indirect result of the Soviet Union.' Using the terms favoured by polemicists in Beijing, he claimed that 'the Soviet Union is the big hegemonist and Vietnam the little hegemonist.'[47] And, finally, Canada refused to consider a resumption of aid to Vietnam or to engage in any activity that might be interpreted as providing Hanoi with legitimacy or support. In short, Ottawa never deviated from the ASEAN line and, by doing so, maintained its *bona fides* in ASEAN eyes.

It is not incidental that both China and the United States found themselves on basically the same side on the Indochina issue in the 1980s. Again, Canada had little interest in directly opposing the United States position on Vietnam, which was one of keeping Vietnam isolated diplomatically and economically. The Reagan administration, for its part, always made it clear that the United States would 'seriously question' aid from 'any source to Vietnam' as long as Cambodia was occupied.[48] Moreover, Washington believed it could use economic statecraft to coerce the Vietnamese to negotiate on those American soldiers listed as missing in action and still unaccounted for.[49]

Likewise, Canada had little interest in confronting Chinese policy on Indochina. Beijing provided large-scale military assistance to the Khmer Rouge and maintained military pressure on Vietnam's northern border – both of which increased the costs to Vietnam and thus served as a useful complement to ASEAN's non-military strategy. Again, the Canadian government had little to gain in pursuing a policy on Vietnam that might have jeopardized the Sino-Canadian relationship, which, before Tiananmen Square, at least, was friendly and profitable.

In short, it can be argued that Ottawa's definition of Canadian strategic objectives in Indochina did not differ radically from those of the loose coalition organized around ASEAN; Canada was regarded as a small player in what was a classical case of great- power geopolitical rivalry. As a result, Canada chose to be guided in its policy towards Vietnam by the preferences of other states more directly affected. While the positions of both China and the United States were not unimportant to the definition of Canadian interests in the region, the government in Ottawa was most sensitive to the policy preferences of the members of ASEAN. Indeed, this was explicitly put by Allan MacEachen at the 1983 meetings: 'We do not make any important decisions about this region without taking full account of the views and interests of ASEAN.'[50] It thus can be argued that the requisites of maintaining solidarity with this coalition go further in explaining Canadian policy towards Vietnam than the conventional explanations of economic sanctions.

This objective, it might be noted, does not explain why the sanctions were introduced in the first place, but rather why they were maintained. For, in 1979, the different coalitions to which Canada belonged took six months to achieve some commonality of response, and so at different times that year the Canadian government found itself out of step with some coalition members. At the beginning of January, for example, all the Western industrialized states were out of step with the United States, which alone maintained a total ban on economic intercourse with Vietnam; by the middle of the month, Australia, Denmark, and Japan were well ahead of other Western states in imposing aid sanctions on Vietnam; in June, Canada found itself out of step with Britain, Germany, and the European Community, all of which waited until July to impose their own bans on development assistance programs. At the United Nations, by contrast, the various coalitions had little difficulty in establishing a common response for the two resolutions on the Vietnamese invasion and the Cambodian credentials question.

CONCLUSION

This chapter has attempted to evaluate the common assumptions about the utilities of economic sanctions by examining the case of Canada's policies towards Vietnam in the aftermath of the invasion of Cambodia in 1979. It has suggested that the government in Ottawa adopted a multi-faceted approach of open criticism and diplomatic and economic sanctions that can best be characterized as a policy of punishment of Vietnam. However, it has also argued that the conventional 'utilities' of economic sanctions usually identified in the literature have limited value in explaining the case of Canada's persistent attachment to its sanctions policy. Rather, the conclusion posited here is that small states, with a limited capacity or willingness to define their strategic interests independently, may still impose economic sanctions on other states, but for reasons very different than those usually identified. Of particular importance is the role of coalitions in shaping sanctions policy. Indeed, there is no better example of this dynamic at work than the problems the Canadian government encountered in bringing Canadian sanctions against Vietnam to an end, which is the subject of the next chapter.

4

Necessary and Sufficient Conditions: Ending the Indochina Sanctions

I argued in the previous chapter that when the Canadian government quietly imposed a range of economic and diplomatic sanctions against Vietnam and Cambodia in the spring of 1979, its major motive in doing so was to demonstrate in a concrete way its objection to the Vietnamese invasion of Cambodia in December 1978 and the overthrow of the Khmer Rouge government of Pol Pot in January 1979. From the outset, Ottawa's formal position was clear: the invasion of Cambodia and the overthrow of a legitimate foreign government, however barbaric and genocidal that regime might have been, represented a serious and unacceptable violation of international law and norms.

But it was also noted that the Canadian government had a number of additional reasons for imposing sanctions against Vietnam in 1979. First, the government in Ottawa wanted to demonstrate solidarity with its friends. For numerous aspects of Vietnamese foreign and domestic policy – its alliance with the Soviet Union; its clashes with the People's Republic of China (PRC); its domination of Laos; its expulsion of its indigenous Chinese population, the Hoa; its maintenance of a large standing army – were of considerable concern to other key govern-ments, both those in the Southeast Asian region and extra-regional powers like the United States. By the beginning of 1979, numerous states were ranged against Vietnam, comprising what amounted to a grand anti-Hanoi coalition. As we noted in the last chapter, the coalition's core included the People's Republic of China and the United States, together with the six members of the Association of Southeast Asian Nations (ASEAN), particularly the 'front-line' state of Thailand. But it also included Japan and a number of smaller Western states, such as Denmark and Australia. All these states were friends or allies of Canada.

Likewise, as the crisis generated by the expulsion of the 'boat people' by Hanoi deepened, the government in Ottawa had every reason to demonstrate to the Canadian public that it was doing something about a Vietnamese policy that was resulting in a massive influx of Vietnamese refugees into Canada. Thus, while the Liberal government of Pierre Elliott Trudeau had not felt the need even to publicize its punitive measures in February 1979, the government of Joe Clark was moved to embrace a loud condemnatory and sanctionist policy against Hanoi as the number of boat people increased.

But if one can see numerous motives for the Canadian government's sanctions, Ottawa's justificatory rhetoric for these measures tended to hinge on one factor alone: the presence of Vietnamese troops in Cambodia. The logic of Canada's position dictated an inertial sanctions policy that admitted no possibility of change until Vietnam ended its military occupation: Hanoi was being punished for invading Cambodia and maintaining its troops there in support of the new government in Phnom Penh; as long as those troops remained, Canada would provide no assistance to Vietnam and would not improve relations with Hanoi beyond a minimal level of cordiality; the necessary condition of lifting these punishments, therefore, was the removal of the Vietnamese troops. From this position the Canadian government would not shift over the course of the 1980s.

WESTERN SANCTIONS AND THE VIETNAMESE WITHDRAWAL FROM CAMBODIA

It should be noted that this was not an uncommon position among the various governments ranged against Vietnam in the early part of the decade. By 1988, differing measures were being employed by the United States, China, ASEAN, and other Western states to punish Vietnam. The Chinese engaged Vietnam in military harassment along the Sino-Vietnamese border, and initiated forays in the disputed Spratly and Paracel Islands that saw Vietnamese ships allegedly sunk by Chinese fire. The Thai army occasionally engaged the forces of Vietnam's other Indochinese ally, Laos. Moreover, military assistance was provided to the various Cambodian rebel groups, including the Khmer Rouge, that were fighting the Vietnamese occupation forces in Cambodia. In addition, diplomatic sanctions were imposed by numerous Western states against both Hanoi and the Heng Samrin and Hun Sen governments in Phnom Penh. Economic sanctions of all kinds were used, from the harsh prohibitions on any form of economic intercourse dictated by the United States Trading with the Enemy Act of 1917 to some more unorthodox economic harms meted out by China. China's campaign of economic harassment and subversion across the border, the Vietnamese government claimed in 1988, included offering Vietnamese peasants huge cash prices for water-buffalo horn (thus inducing peasants on the Vietnamese side to kill their water buffalo) and flooding the border area with cheap consumer products (thus destabilizing Hanoi's attempts to dampen the demand for these products further south that had spawned an active black market).

These measures both contributed to, and compounded, the considerable economic difficulties that Vietnam was suffering domestically by the late 1980s. These economic problems included chronic unemployment or underemployment owing to a lack of capital expansion capable of accommodating a rapidly expanding but predominantly young population; a succession of poor harvests due to bad weather, a scarcity of high-grade fertilizers, and highly inefficient agricultural management; an unstable currency and low supply of consumer goods, both of which encouraged a pervasive and active black market; and the continuing inability of central planners in Hanoi to achieve a truly national integration of the often divergent northern and southern economies.[1]

To be sure, both the Soviet Union and the states of Eastern Europe continued to trade with Vietnam throughout the 1980s; they provided Hanoi with assistance, particularly military aid and capital-intensive projects; and large numbers of Vietnamese continued to be flown to the countries of Eastern Europe and the Soviet Union as low-wage 'guestworkers.' In addition, states like India and Sweden continued to maintain development assistance projects. And a limited regional trade persisted despite the sanctions. However, such limited economic activity could not mitigate or offset the deeper problems.

To what extent were Vietnam's economic difficulties the direct consequence of the coalition's measures? Certainly for Western diplomats, whose governments' policies were, after all, purposely designed to cause Vietnam as much hurt as possible, it was tempting to attribute these economic problems directly to the maintenance of the coalition's sanctions. But because the question involves the elusive 'what if?' of the counterfactual condition – How would the Vietnamese economy have performed had the sanctions not been in place? – a definitive answer to this question is virtually impossible to obtain. Nevertheless, there can be little doubt that the sanctions either deterred, or in some instances stopped outright, Western capital-investment possibilities in the 1980s. Likewise, it can be assumed that had Vietnam pursued different foreign and domestic policies after the fall of the Saigon regime in 1975, aid projects would likely have been more forthcoming from Western development assistance agencies. In short, while we cannot with any certitude make a direct connection between the sanctions and Vietnam's economic condition, we can note a variety of potential opportunities foregone.

If an unequivocal answer to this question is impossible, it is clear that the more reform-minded Vietnamese leadership that emerged in the late 1980s did indeed made a linkage between the coalition's sanctions and the economic problems of their country. For, in addition to embracing domestic economic and political reforms in an effort to reduce inefficiencies and increase productivity, the government in Hanoi also embraced a foreign policy that sought to solve domestic economic difficulties by reintegrating Vietnam into the Southeast Asian regional economy and lessening Vietnam's economic dependence on the Soviet Union. Broadly speaking, this policy involved the encouragement of foreign investment, foreign trade, and Western development assistance. In particular, Japanese investment was avidly sought, for Japanese business was by all accounts eager to establish enterprises in Vietnam to take full advantage of an exceptionally well-educated population, high pent-up demand for consumer goods, and a considerable potential overall for economic growth. But expanded trade – with the ASEAN area, the European Community, the United States, and smaller peripheral capitalist countries like Canada and Australia – was also seen as a means of encouraging economic growth. Finally, development assistance was seen as a limited means of putting in place some infrastructural foundations.

In the Vietnamese view, the major impediment to such expanded economic linkages with ASEAN and the West was the Vietnamese policy on Cambodia, notably the presence of Vietnamese troops there. Hanoi's view appeared to be that if that impediment were removed, Western sanctions would be removed, allowing for the development of normal economic intercourse that would, by fostering economic growth, solve a number of Vietnam's problems. Hence, by 1988 the leadership in Hanoi adopted a policy that was quite unbending: by 1990, all Vietnamese troops would be out of Cambodia. Indeed, Vietnam advanced this timetable: by the summer of 1988, it had withdrawn its officer corps from Cambodia; by September 1989, all of its troops were withdrawn.[2]

To be sure, Hanoi was being pushed strongly in this direction by the Soviet government of Mikhail S. Gorbachev, which was actively seeking to reduce its support for its allies around the world, for states like Vietnam were costing the Soviet treasury billions of rubles a year in aid and trade subsidies. But Gorbachev was also seeking to defuse regional conflicts on a global scale, in order to reduce friction with Moscow's superpower rival, the United States. Finally, Gorbachev also wanted to normalize Moscow's strained relations with Beijing.

For all these reasons, therefore, the leadership in Vietnam was eager to withdraw from Cambodia, with many policy-makers in Hanoi believing that a withdrawal from Cambodia would prove to be a watershed in Vietnam's economic fortunes.

The degree to which the government in Hanoi pinned its hopes on what would follow a withdrawal can be seen in the explicit trade-off that seems to have been made in terms of Vietnamese security. It can be argued that the invasion of 1978–9 – which catalysed so much of the opposition from the United States, China, and ASEAN – was an attempt by Vietnam, with the explicit support of the Soviet Union, to achieve three interrelated objectives. The ouster of Pol Pot was designed, first, to maximize Vietnam's regional security sphere by extending Hanoi's dominance over all of Indochina; second, it sought to eliminate the source of the 'negative externalities' being inflicted on Vietnam as a result of the genocidal policies of the Khmer Rouge, especially border skirmishing and the influx of refugees down the Mekong River; and, third, the invasion was intended to increase Hanoi's own security and independence, particularly vis-à-vis China, which in part through its strong support of Pol Pot was seeking to blunt the Soviet presence on China's southern borders.

In the short run, the invasion did indeed remove the pro-Chinese regime and did eliminate the worst aspects of the genocide. But over the longer term, the invasion did not manage to eliminate armed opposition to the new Vietnamese-backed regime in Phnom Penh entirely. In place of Pol Pot, Vietnam faced instead a loose coalition of armed opponents. The Coalition Government of Democratic Kampuchea (CGDK), formed in 1983, comprised three groups that had, at different times in the postwar period, governed Cambodia: the National United Front for an Independent Neutral Peaceful and Cooperative Cambodia (FUNCINPEC) under Prince Norodom Sihanouk; the Khmer People's National Liberation Front (KPNLF) under the leadership of Son Sann, a former prime minister in the Lon Nol regime that had been backed by the United States; and the Khmer Rouge, which included the former Pol Pot faction. Moreover, throughout the 1980s, the various parts of this coalition were sustained by military aid from their client great powers, with the active cooperation of Thailand: China supplied military aid to the Khmer Rouge; and FUNCINPEC and the KPNLF were sustained by aid from the West (including, it might be noted, non-lethal assistance from Canada). On the other hand, without Vietnamese military assistance, the government in Phnom Penh was at that time widely regarded as having limited capacity to sustain itself against a concerted post-withdrawal offensive by the rebels, particularly the Khmer Rouge, which allegedly had access to large arms caches hidden throughout the Cambodian countryside.

However, despite these initial aims, and despite the considerable resources that Hanoi devoted to the occupation of Cambodia over the course of the 1980s, the Vietnamese position shifted considerably on the desirability of maintaining the Heng Samrin regime in power by their continued military presence. By 1988, officials in Hanoi were freely admitting the possibility that their withdrawal might bring a breakdown of peace and order in Cambodia, and the possibility of what was widely called the 'Lebanonization' of the country. Thus, the Vietnamese leadership eventually abandoned linking a military withdrawal to the provision of firm assurances that the power of the present government in Phnom Penh be maintained. Instead, it commonly claimed that the possibility of a change in regime – such as a coalition of the government in Phnom Penh and the various opposition forces – would not alter their proposed timetable for withdrawal. To be sure, the leadership in Hanoi did not view the prospect of a return to power of the Khmer Rouge with equanimity. The scenario of a government in Phnom Penh that was dominated by the Pol Pot faction of the Khmer Rouge – and that excluded other groups – was seen as the only major impediment to an orderly Vietnamese withdrawal. Such a scenario on occasion prompted speculation about an occupied buffer zone in eastern Cambodia that would serve to provide a *cordon sanitaire* against what officials were more than ready to suggest would be another round of massive killings if the Khmer Rouge were to return to power unrestrained.

Thus, as their own self-imposed deadline of 1990 approached, the government in Hanoi appeared sanguine that an end to the occupation would eliminate what Western states like Canada claimed was the barrier to better aid and trade relations. In other words, the leadership in Hanoi believed what governments like Canada had claimed throughout the 1980s: the reason for the sanctions was the presence of Vietnamese troops in Cambodia. The implication was that the withdrawal of those troops would bring an end to the sanctions. In other words, they believed that withdrawal, a *necessary* condition, was also a *sufficient* condition for the removal of Canadian sanctions.

EXPLAINING THE END OF CANADIAN SANCTIONS

As the Vietnamese troop presence in Cambodia progressively diminished during 1989, the government of Canada began the process of reconsidering its sanctions against Vietnam. Finally, on 25 January 1990, Joe Clark, the secretary of state for external affairs, rose in the House of Commons to announce that Canada had reviewed its Indochina policy and was preparing to re-establish development assistance programs for Cambodia, Laos, and Vietnam. To be sure, the projects envisaged were to be 'small scale and focused on humanitarian needs'; none the less, Clark's announcement marked a significant reversal in Canadian policy.[3]

At first blush, it would appear that the reason for the ending of Canada's sanctions was straightforward: Vietnam had in essence bowed to the demands of other countries, including Canada, that it withdraw from Cambodia; the sanctions, which had been predicated on the Vietnamese invasion and occupation of Cambodia, had 'worked,' and were thus no longer necessary.

The political dynamic that brought these sanctions to an end on 25 January was, however, somewhat more complicated. For there were powerful inertial factors, both domestic and external, that had constrained the Canadian government from altering its relations with Vietnam in the 1980s. It was only changes in these factors that altered the correlation of forces affecting Canada's Vietnam policies. It can be argued that the Vietnamese military withdrawal from Cambodia was not, in itself, enough to bring a speedy end to Canada's sanctions: withdrawal, in short, was a necessary but not a sufficient condition.

Changes in bureaucratic attitudes

One of the impediments to altering Canada's sanctionist policy towards Vietnam was the attitude of many members of the Department of External Affairs. Canada's nineteen years of service on the two international commissions in Vietnam had longer-term effects that extended well beyond 1973, when the Canadian government withdrew from the second commission – the International Commission of Supervision and Control (ICCS) – that had been established by the Paris peace accords. From 1954, when Canada joined the first commission – the International Commission of Control and Supervision (ICSC) – the Department of External Affairs tended to rotate newly recruited foreign service officers through the commission as part of their apprenticeship. Thus, meant that by the early 1970s, well over one-third of DEA officials had experience in Indochina. And, in general, it would appear that this experience was not one that generated a great deal of sympathy for the government in Hanoi among Canadian officials. Indeed, many Canadian foreign service officers would emerge from their time in Vietnam with a strong antipathy towards the regime in the north.[4]

In other circumstances, such attitudes would not have had such long-term effects. The negative perceptions of North Vietnam gained on the ground by Canadian foreign service officers would have been leavened by the passage of time and the retirement of successive cohorts of diplomats. The institutional memory of Vietnamese 'badness' would by slow degrees have diminished. But in this case, such was not to happen: North Vietnamese policies after 1973 were to delay the process of decay. Instead, Vietnamese behaviour in the 1970s merely served to perpetuate the negative perceptions gained in the 1954–73 period.

For example, the leadership in Hanoi did not tolerate the southern regime that had emerged victorious in 1975 for long. In 1976, the government in the north eliminated the independent southern regime through reunification, and then, for good measure, purged many of the southern fraternal compatriots who had served in the Provisional Revolutionary Government (PRG) during the war against the Americans. A number were forced into re-education camps; others managed to make it to exile. To be sure, the fate of the southern PRG élite did not concern Canadian officials directly; but their harsh treatment at the hands of the Hanoi regime did confirm the perceptions of those Canadian policy-makers who saw North Vietnam as essentially Leninist in nature, unable to tolerate other centres of political power and authority.

Furthermore, some of Hanoi's domestic policies affected Canada directly. The leadership's attempt to solve the economic difficulties of reunification by 'exporting' what they saw as the root cause of these problems – the Hoa – was not only regarded as abhorrent by Canadian officials; it also had profound effects on Canada as Ottawa felt obliged to admit some of the 'boat people' as refugees. Moreover, in the 1980s, many Canadian officials would come face to face with Vietnamese officials in trying to implement the family-reunification program. Hanoi's attitude to this program was characterized by some Canadian officials as both unpredictable and frequently intransigent, and by all accounts officials did not relish the trips to Ho Chi Minh City, where most of the family-reunification negotiations were held. Finally, the activities of the Vietnamese intelligence service in Canada – particularly extortion and subversion operations among the Vietnamese immigrant community in Toronto – did not endear Hanoi to Canadian policy-makers.

Vietnamese foreign policy was also cause for concern among DEA officials. For the government in Hanoi had, since 1975, sought to expand its influence over Indochina as a whole. It consolidated its hold over Laos by political means, and then, by invasion, over Cambodia. It tied itself more closely to the Soviet Union, both economically and militarily, and engaged in fighting with China, Cambodia, and Thailand. Hanoi's policies thus would not only reinforce the institutional memory about Vietnam within External Affairs, but would also serve to strengthen, not diminish, the idea that in fact the older generation had been right about the nature of the leadership in the North.

Likewise, there was also opposition to improved relations from those in External Affairs who were responsible for Canada's relations with the United States. The argument was that any improvement in Canadian-Vietnamese relations should be linked to the state of Vietnamese-American relations. If improvement in Canadian relations with Vietnam was likely to cause annoyance in Washington, it should be opposed, because of the damage it would cause to Canadian-American relations.

In short, in the decade after 1975, Vietnamese behaviour, both domestically and externally, did little to foster any sympathy within the Canadian government. Rather, such attitudes lingered on in External Affairs: some officials remained viscerally and vociferously opposed to any proposal advanced in the late 1980s to increase cordial relations with Vietnam.

By 1989, however, their strength had diminished somewhat. The transformation in the international system was having an impact on attitudes within the department. Moreover, changes in bureaucratic leadership within the DEA itself were altering the traditional antipathy towards Vietnam by bringing to the fore a cohort that openly doubted the wisdom of the sanctionist policy that Canada had pursued over the course of the 1980s.

The collapse of the coalition

A key external change involved the attitude towards Vietnam of the broad anti-Soviet coalition lead by the United States, ASEAN, and China. To be sure, the coalition was never a monolith, acting in unison, for the interests in the Indochina issue of the eight states at the coalition's core were never entirely coincidental. Some interests were at best complementary: both the United States and China, for example, wanted to see an end to Soviet access to the naval facilities at Cam Ranh Bay and the airfield at Da Nang. Some interests, however, were discrete: the United States government, for example, had a variety of concerns about Vietnamese policy, including the question of prisoners of war (POW) and those missing in action (MIA) from the period of United States involvement in the Vietnam War. But the MIA/POW issue was not one that concerned other members of the coalition. Other interests, moreover, were not at all harmonious: for example, the PRC periodically needled Vietnam by asserting its claims to the disputed islands in the South China Sea,[5] tactics that brought Beijing into conflict with some of the ASEAN members who also claim sovereignty over the islands. And China's continued support for the Khmer Rouge found little favour among Western political leaders, who not only personally abhorred the Khmer Rouge for their brutal attempts to alter Cambodian society, but who also had to face domestic publics who had been politicized on this issue by the success of the film *The Killing Fields*. Likewise, the ASEAN states themselves were never completely united over what would constitute an acceptable resolution of the Cambodian question, since they remained uneasy over the consequences of the return of a Chinese-backed Khmer Rouge government to Phnom Penh. But for all these differences, the coalition remained relatively united in one common desire throughout the 1980s: to damage Vietnam as much as possible economically, to isolate it as far as possible, and thus to demonstrate to the leadership in Hanoi the short-sightedness of its alignment with the Soviet Union.

We saw in the previous chapter that the anti-Vietnam coalition had a powerful effect on smaller states like Australia and Canada. And it can be surmised that had the coalition held together after 1989, where – and when – the members of the coalition moved on the issue of sanctions against Vietnam following a military withdrawal from Cambodia would have had a profound effect on smaller states like Canada, which never had direct or concrete interests at stake in Indochina. As long as the coalition held, the Canadian government, or so it would appear, had little interest in stepping outside the bounds of what the coalition as a whole considered appropriate and seemly.

Such reticence was entirely understandable: Ottawa was only too mindful of what had happened to the Australian government when Canberra stepped outside the boundaries of policy acceptable to the coalition. In 1983 the new government of Bob Hawke sought to implement the plank in the Australian Labor Party platform that determined to improve Australia's relations with Vietnam. Canberra's initiatives provoked harsh criticism from both ASEAN and the United States. (Indeed, the Australian initiative must stand as one of the few occasions on which a United States secretary of state has publicly characterized the policies of an American ally as 'stupid.'[6])

Moreover, the Canadian government was not insensitive to the impact of geographic location on how diplomatic outriders are perceived by others. Australia, because of its geographic position, could at least claim to have a legitimate stake in the Indochina situation. By contrast, Canada could make no such claim, and thus a Canadian defection would have been perceived all the more harshly by its friends in the region. As Hervouet has so succinctly noted, in the late 1980s, Canada had no interest in souring its expanding relations with China or the ASEAN members, and no interest in a conflict with the United States over Vietnam.[7] Each of these states had, in effect, a determining influence on the evolution of Canadian policies towards Vietnam: any of them singly could deter whatever proclivities the Canadian government may have had to improve Canadian-Vietnamese relations; together, they could maintain a policy of hostility regardless of what the Vietnamese did on the issue of Cambodia.

It is thus crucial for an understanding of Canadian policies towards Vietnam in 1990 to note that the coalition did not in fact hold. It began to break apart by slow degrees over the course of 1989. The most serious fragmentation occurred between China and the other Western states over the massacre in and around Tiananmen Square on 4 June. The immediate souring of relations between China and the West had the effect of prompting Western countries, including Canada, to reassess the value that had been placed on maintaining the relationship with China. But Tiananmen was important because it occurred at precisely the same time that profound transformations were occurring in the relations of the great powers elsewhere in the international system. The breaching of the Berlin Wall in the fall of 1989; the sudden and successive political transformations in Eastern Europe; and the decision by the Soviet government of Mikhail Gorbachev not to respond to these changes with force – all these contributed to a profoundly altered strategic calculus in Southeast Asia.

These transformations in Europe also had an impact on the ASEAN states, which began to recalculate the nature of the military threat from Vietnam given the Soviet withdrawal from the region and the growing weakness of the Vietnamese economy. No longer was such a premium being placed on isolating, weakening, and containing Vietnam. Rather, ASEAN leaders themselves began a process of limited rapprochement with Hanoi, even toying with the idea of admitting the Indochinese states to ASEAN.

In short, by the end of 1989, the coalition that had been so important for sanctioning Vietnam was fractured; the main security threat in the region was in full retreat.

The attitude of the United States

One of the difficulties for those in the Canadian government who doubted the wisdom of the sanctionist approach against Vietnam was that throughout the 1980s, Hanoi and Washington were both unwilling and unable to alter their fundamentally hostile relationship.

For its part, the Vietnamese government, no doubt both emboldened by its ability to prevail militarily against the United States during the period of direct American military intervention in Vietnam from 1965 to 1973, and embittered by the shattering effects of that war, demonstrated no concern at all over whether or not the vanquished was losing face in the making of peace. As a consequence, the leadership in Hanoi insisted on pressing a set of strident demands on the United States in the post-1975 period. The United States, Vietnam argued, had an 'obligation' to pay huge sums in war reparations for postwar reconstruction. The United States, Hanoi insisted, had an obligation to 'repatriate' all the 'Amerasians' in Vietnam – the young men and women born of Vietnamese mothers and American GI fathers.

For its part, the United States steadfastly refused to undertake any improvement in relations with Vietnam. In part this was because Hanoi's attitudes towards such matters as reparations and Amerasians were guaranteed to aggravate American policy-makers; indeed, Vietnamese officials seemed quite unaware of – or, if they were aware, they seemed altogether indifferent to – the degree to which making demands on a polity with a degree of nationalistic pride rivalling that of Vietnam itself would only yield intransigence and hostility. Moreover, Vietnamese demands blithely and simplistically ignored the realities of domestic politics in the United States. Even if they had been inclined to take a conciliatory attitude towards Vietnam, American policy-makers would have had to contend with domestic political opinion, which remained vigorously opposed to any improvement of relations with Vietnam.[8] Paradoxically, Hanoi's demands served to strengthen, not lessen, American resolve to contribute as much as possible to the deepening of Vietnam's economic woes.

But in part the American refusal to normalize relations with Vietnam was a logical consequence of the issue of American GIs listed as missing in action or taken prisoner of war. Early in his presidency, Ronald Reagan discovered that the MIA/POW issue had dramatic domestic political appeal in the United States. His administration chose not to disabuse Americans of the largely mythological claims that American GIs officially listed as MIA were in fact alive but being held in secret jungle camps in Indochina, allowing, for example, photographs of GIs supposedly held in Indochina – but which were known to be doctored – to circulate as 'evidence' of the MIA claim. Indeed, Reagan actively encouraged what eventually became a deeply rooted belief in American political culture: that Vietnam was still holding American 'boys' as POWs.[9]

For their part, the Vietnamese did not help matters by initially responding to the MIA claims with complete dismissiveness. The initial Vietnamese position, baldly put, was that in any war there will always be casualties whose bodies will never be found, and that it was utterly unreasonable of the United States to insist that the remains of each and every MIA be accounted for in order to demonstrate unequivocally that they were not being held in some Laotian prison camp fifteen years after the end of hostilities. But the Vietnamese position, however reasonable, did not take sufficient account of the symbolic importance in American political culture of where those killed in foreign wars are buried. Other countries bury those who die in overseas wars where they fall; the United States, by contrast, is the only country in the world that brings the remains of each of its soldiers killed abroad in war home for burial. Given this tradition, any proposal simply to leave the remains of a pilot whose fighter was downed in inaccessible jungle would deeply violate American sensibilities: ideally the remains should be located and repatriated. More important, however, the dismissive Vietnamese response was hardly likely to assuage American public opinion.

The MIA issue thus continued to bedevil American-Vietnamese relations throughout the 1980s, and indeed made it difficult to improve relations. For one of the key consequences of elevating the MIA claims to national prominence in American politics was to make any improvement in relations with Vietnam virtually impossible, since those who would propose improving relations would have to contend with considerable domestic anger about the fate of American GIs.

Such a continuation of the quarrel between the United States and Vietnam had inexorable consequences for Canadian diplomacy. Simply put, smooth relations with the United States were always more important to Canadian policy-makers than smooth relations with Vietnam. Thus, to the extent that Canada was called on to take sides in the ongoing dispute between Washington and Hanoi, there was never any doubt where Canadian policy-makers would stand: Ottawa would refuse to upset the relationship with the United States over the issue of Vietnamese-American relations.

By 1989, however, several aspects of American policy had changed. First, Reagan was no longer in the White House, and with his departure had come a noticeable shift in American policy. Second, given the shifts in Soviet policy, such anti-Vietnam attitudes as still remained in Washington could no longer be underpinned on strategic grounds. One could no longer argue that regional security depended on keeping Vietnam weak and isolated, for manifestly Vietnam, shorn of its great-power lifeline, could not pose a security threat to any of its neighbours. With the diminution of the Soviet-backed threat, opposition in Washington to a reintegration of Vietnam into the regional economy could be too easily written off as merely a visceral dislike of an ex-enemy whose 'victory' over the United States continued to affect the American polity. Moreover, by 1989, the Vietnamese had realized that on the MIA/POW issue it was smarter to reveal the mythological status of the American claims by demonstration rather than by denial: Hanoi began to cooperate actively with American searches, digging through inaccessible jungle to twenty-five-year old crash sites and repatriating the remains of downed American pilots to the United States.

Because of these factors, 'defections' on the part of smaller states were no longer regarded with such antipathy by American policy-makers as they had been at the middle of the decade: certainly Joe Clark was not excoriated as 'stupid' by his counterpart in Washington for the Canadian announcement of 25 January 1990.

Changes in domestic politics

Throughout the 1980s, no secretary of state for external affairs made improved economic relations with Hanoi a priority. A brief examination of the domestic political context in Canada reveals why, on the contrary, the government had every interest in avoiding the Vietnam question altogether. First, there was little mileage for politicians in embracing what was at best a non-issue for most Canadians throughout this period, but one that had every possibility of arousing the essentially negative view of Vietnam so pervasive in 1979 and 1980, when large numbers of ordinary Canadians were engaged in accepting more than 100,000 of the 'boat people.' And even those who at one time sympathized with Vietnam would likely be disinclined to see the improvement of relations in positive terms. Whatever popular image there might have been in Canada during the Vietnam War of the valiant Vietnamese struggling for their right of self-determination against the might of United States imperialism seemed to have been washed away, in large part by Vietnam's own not-so-valiant behaviour after the imperialists had been beaten. Indeed, it is indicative that Victor Levant, no great admirer of the capitalist West, would feel obliged to denounce the Vietnamese government for the sins it committed after 1975 – even though his polemical history of Canadian involvement in Vietnam extended only to 1973.[10]

Second, and more important from a domestic political point of view, changes in policy towards Vietnam would have had to confront the views and interests of those in Canada of Indochinese origin who, by the mid-1980s, were both citizens and well established within the community.[11] It is no small irony that by expelling so many people in such a brutal fashion, Vietnam created the structural seeds of staunch opposition to it within many other states. While a warming trend in relations between Ottawa and Hanoi was welcomed by some Canadians of Indochinese extraction as a means of advancing family reunification, it also held out the prospect of arousing significant and possibly violent opposition.

The experience of Australia in this regard was not reassuring. Over the course of the 1980s, Australians of Vietnamese extraction engaged in sporadic violence in opposition to the regime in Hanoi that had expelled them.[12] For example, Vietnamese embassy officials in Canberra were beaten up and a shot was fired into the embassy.[13] In April 1985, on the tenth anniversary of the fall of Saigon, there were violent riots in the suburbs of Sydney involving members of the Australian Communist party celebrating the 'liberation' of Saigon and anti-Hanoi Vietnamese youths protesting the event; one man was stabbed and another bashed with a brick.[14] Emotions ran so high that an academic conference on Indochina, scheduled for July 1985, was cancelled on the advice of the police after threats of violence and the call of a Vietnamese-language newspaper in Sydney for a massive demonstration.[15] And, as late as December 1987, Melbourne shopkeepers who refused to join a boycott of goods from Vietnam organized by the local Vietnamese community received death threats and had their shop windows smashed.[16]

Given the experience in Australia, it would have been difficult to convince a Canadian politician that he or she should seek to brave ethnic opposition that just happened to be concentrated in the electorally important cities of Vancouver, Toronto, and Montreal for the relatively minor economic or diplomatic benefits of a better relationship.

By the end of 1989, however, the domestic political environment was shifting as it became clearer that the Vietnamese government was engaged in a full retreat from Cambodia, along with serious economic and political reform domestically. To be sure of the sentiments of ethnic groups in Canada, the government in Ottawa decided to send up a trial balloon before announcing a shift in policy. In December 1989, the Department of External Affairs hosted a one-day Ministerial Round Table, to which were invited representatives of non-governmental organizations involved in the delivery of development assistance to the states of Indochina; members of Indochinese ethnic groups from Montreal and Toronto; and academics and journalists with an interest in Vietnam. It was clear at this meeting that there was division between the representatives of the Indochinese ethnic groups and the other participants over the appropriateness of shifting Canada's policies on Indochina. On the other hand, it was also clear that the opposition of the ethnic groups to such a course of action had lessened considerably.

CONCLUSION

When one examines the domestic and external context in which decisions about economic relations with Vietnam were taken in the mid- and late 1980s, it is clear that the withdrawal of troops by Vietnam was not the key factor that brought Canadian sanctions to an end. Rather, the changes in the broader political contexts of Canadian foreign policy provided policy-makers in Ottawa who were coming to doubt the wisdom of Canada's sanctionist approach with an opportunity to alter the relationship. The government was able to do so in January 1990 with so few costs because virtually all the factors that had constrained the Canadian government throughout the 1980s had changed. No longer were punitive sanctions made necessary by the inertial forces of bureaucratic attitudes, coalition demands, or the concerns of ethnic groups.

5

The Impact of the Individual: Explaining Mulroney's South African Sanctions, 1985–6

Much of the orthodox theorizing about international sanctions does not accord great weight to the role of the individual policy-maker in embracing these measures. Rather, explanations for a state's sanctions policy tend to fix on the other variables commonly used to explain foreign policy, such as systemic, role, societal, or governmental determinants.[1] Examining the individual, or idiosyncratic, variable[2] is generally deemed to be least useful in explanations of sanctions policy.

In general, such a focus on variables other than the individual is perfectly sensible in the Canadian context. The highly bureaucratized and institutionalized nature of the Canadian state; the weakness, dependence, and vulnerability of Canada as an actor in international politics; and the capacity of societal actors to influence policy outcomes – these factors all serve to mitigate the impact of the individual decision-maker on Canada's external behaviour. However, it can be argued that in some cases such a focus can be misleading, for it diverts our attention from the effects that individual decision-makers can have on policy change and innovation.

The case of the Canadian policy towards South Africa after the fall of 1984 stands as an instructive example of the impact of personality on sanctions policy. From early 1985, the new Progressive Conservative government of Brian Mulroney increasingly shifted Canada's traditional approach to South Africa. In a relatively brief period, the government abandoned an essentially reactive policy that mixed rhetorical denunciation of apartheid with a 'business as usual' approach (to use T.A. Keenleyside's apt characterization[3]). Such a policy had steered well clear of either imposing concrete harm on South Africa, or intervening directly in South African affairs. Instead, from the autumn of 1984 on, the

Canadian government adopted what might be argued was an increasingly activist and hard-line policy against South Africa. This included the imposition of economic and other sanctions against South Africa, active interference in South Africa's domestic affairs, and vigorous diplomatic efforts on a number of different international fronts that produced a sharp conflict with both Britain and the United States.

The purpose of this chapter is to explore how we can understand this change of policy. First, it will review the extent to which policy changed between 1984 and 1986 by contrasting the broad outlines of the approach taken by the Liberal government of Pierre Elliott Trudeau in the 1970s and the early 1980s, on the one hand, with the approach adopted by the Progressive Conservatives, on the other. It will then analyse the views of Mulroney and his non-bureaucratic advisers towards sanctions, and assess the degree to which these views were reflected in policy outcomes. An examination of contending explanations for this change strongly suggests that the individual variable exercised a powerful influence on the change in Canada's external behaviour on sanctions against South Africa.

THE TRUDEAU GOVERNMENT'S APPROACH TO SOUTH AFRICA, 1968–84

The Trudeau government's rhetoric and its concrete actions on the issue of apartheid demonstrated a remarkable consistency. On the one hand, at the rhetorical level, Canada was consistent in both its denunciation of apartheid and its expressed hope that South Africans would move to abandon institutionalized racism.[4] On the other hand, for sixteen years the Trudeau government consistently proved unwilling to take the kind of concrete actions that would effectively match its rhetorical denunciation of apartheid. Rather than using disruptions in economic relations as a tool of statecraft for the promotion of human rights in South Africa, the government appeared to eschew any form of sanction, but particularly economic sanctions, that had not been legitimized by the United Nations. Thus, Ottawa did embrace the arms embargo agreed to in 1963 by the UN Security Council, but not until 1970, and on terms that attracted considerable criticism from anti-apartheid groups worried about both the 'leakiness' of the sanctions and the narrowness of the government's definition of what constituted 'arms.'[5] Indeed, as Clarence Redekop has noted,[6] from the publication of the foreign policy papers in 1970 to the policy review of late 1977, Ottawa expressly justified its decision to maintain economic links with South Africa on the grounds that trading in peaceful goods 'with all countries and territories regardless of political considerations' was a fundamental tenet of Canadian foreign policy.[7] In 1977, a policy review was undertaken, prompted by the juxtaposition of the killings in Soweto; the death of the student leader Steve Biko while in the custody of the South African security forces; the new emphasis placed on human rights by the new American administration of President Jimmy Carter; and the election of Canada to the United Nations Security Council.[8] As a result of this review, Ottawa acknowledged in December 1977 that the systematic denial of rights on the basis of skin colour was a *cas unique* in the international system,[9] and thus 'business as usual' could not be justified on the grounds that South Africa was just another state with which Canada disagreed.[10]

The government imposed limited economic sanctions against South Africa in December 1977. These included the withdrawal of Canada's commercial counsellors from the missions in Johannesburg and Cape Town; the closure of commercial offices; the withdrawal of some Export Development Corporation financing; a promise that a 'code of conduct' for Canadian corporations with subsidiaries in South Africa would be introduced; and the imposition of visa requirements for South Africans wishing to visit Canada. However, these limited measures had little effect on the steady growth of economic links between the two countries, as most students of Canada's South African policies have clearly demonstrated.[11]

In short, it can be argued that by the time Trudeau resigned as prime minister in 1984, Canada's approach to South Africa had not shifted markedly since 1968. Redekop has argued that what changes were introduced in December 1977 have 'tended to camouflage the essential continuity in post-war Canadian policy.'[12] He suggests that there were four interrelated strands to this policy. First, there was a emphasis on maintaining normal bilateral and multilateral relations with South Africa. Second, a succession of Canadian governments between 1948 and 1984 put a premium on the use of 'quiet' diplomacy in dealing with South Africa. Third, Canadian governments were adamant in their opposition to force or violence as a means to achieve political change in South Africa. Finally, before 1984, every government in Ottawa evinced a strong preference for the maintenance of economic relations with South Africa, and, as a corollary, had an equally strong aversion to the use of disruptive economic measures.

It could be argued that these four strands comprised a set of beliefs and assumptions that dominated the Canadian approach to South Africa before 1984. During this period there was little propensity among decision-makers to think of South Africa as an 'outlaw' state within the international community; rather, it was seen more as a wayward member of the family of nations that needed to be treated with patience and understanding. Thus in 1961, for example, the Canadian delegate to the United Nations stated that 'we are dealing here with an evil philosophy which can ... only be overcome by moral suasion.' Such a goal could not be achieved by 'measures which would only further isolate South Africa from the world community.'[13] To be sure, this theme was more pronounced in the 1950s than in the 1970s, though some of the same language and assumptions lingered well into the 1960s, particularly about the 'effectiveness' of punitive measures.[14] It followed naturally that there would be little desire to put South Africa beyond the pale by disrupting the pattern of normal bilateral and multilateral diplomatic relations. Indeed, only when the Commonwealth was threatened by the continuation of South African membership did the Canadian government deviate from this general pattern. Thus, what has passed into Canadian mythology as the 'expulsion' of South Africa from the Commonwealth in 1960 stands as a key exception to this general desire to keep South Africa actively engaged in the international community.

These kinds of views inevitably had an impact on the kind of statecraft favoured by the government. Although over this period the stridency of the criticism levelled at South Africa by Canadian officials increased considerably, particularly at the United Nations, there persisted in Ottawa a belief in the diplomatic process as the most appropriate method of dealing with South Africa. Certainly no Canadian government appeared comfortable with any stratagem, such as support for armed struggle, that might disrupt the 'peace' and 'stability' that the white minority was able to impose on the polity. For all the abhorrence expressed by Canadian officials, the government in Pretoria was seen as the legitimate sovereign government of South Africa.[15]

Given this desire for normal relations, it should not be surprising that economic sanctions were seen as an inappropriate tool of statecraft vis-à-vis South Africa.[16] Such an aversion to disruptive economic measures both flowed from, and fitted well with, this mind-set. On the one hand, the imposition of sanctions is essentially an act of hostility, one invoked when the peaceful means of diplomacy have faltered; and such hostile measures were seen as an inappropriate act against what was seen as a legitimate, if misguided, member of the international community.

On the other hand, there was also a widespread belief that the encouragement of economic activity would be a more effective means of bringing about peaceful change in South Africa than cutting economic ties. It is true that this line of thinking enjoyed less and less support in official Ottawa over the course of the postwar period. Indeed, after their discussions with External Affairs officials and Mitchell Sharp, the secretary of state for external affairs, in 1970, the authors of the 'Black Paper' on Canadian relations with South Africa concluded: 'Although these views are still expressed by Canadian officials, they are not offered with much sign of conviction that they are valid.'[17] However, economic intercourse was still a strategy to be embraced because of what the government, particularly in the late 1960s and early 1970s, saw as 'better-than-normal opportunities for trade and investment in the growing economy of South Africa.'[18] It was only after the events of 1976 and 1977 that Ottawa moved to embrace economic sanctions – and even then, only in a way that was both tentative and half-hearted.

There is, however, a fifth strand that could be added to Redekop's list: throughout the postwar period, Canadian officials evinced an abiding attachment to the notion of national sovereignty as an organizing principle for international relationships in general, and for Canada's relations with South Africa in particular. As I have argued elsewhere,[19] Canada's approach to human rights violations in general in the three decades after the Second World War tended to be predicated on a belief that it is both improper and inappropriate to weaken the principle of national sovereignty by interfering in the internal affairs of other countries. This attachment to sovereignty had a clear effect on policy towards South Africa. In the 1950s, the numerous Canadian objections to United Nations action on the South African question were prompted by a concern to uphold the importance of the principle of the hard shell of a state's sovereign rights.[20] It is true that the support of policy-makers for this strand (like the other strands) grew progressively weaker over the forty years after 1945, particularly as the international discussion of human rights violations by governments became increasingly legitimized. However, it might be noted that as late as 1977, Don Jamieson, the secretary of state for external affairs, was still claiming that human rights 'are essentially the domestic concerns of other states.'[21]

THE MULRONEY GOVERNMENT'S APPROACH TO SOUTH AFRICA, 1984–6

In 1985 and 1986, four of these strands of relatively consistent Canadian policy would basically be abandoned by the Mulroney government. By

1986, the Canadian government no longer was attached to the importance of maintaining 'normal' diplomatic relations with South Africa; it
no longer placed a premium on quiet diplomacy; it no longer was
averse to the use of economic measures to inflict hurt on South Africa;
and it completely rejected the idea that how South Africans organized
their laws and their polity was a matter over which other sovereign
governments had no legitimate say.

Even on the issue of the use of force the Mulroney government
altered Canadian policy: by 1987 the Canadian government was no
longer so adamantly opposed to the use of force to secure the elimination of apartheid, or to the maintenance of links with the African
National Congress. The change on the use of force came during the
prime minister's trip to Africa in early 1987. While in Harare, Mulroney,
in a sharp break with traditional policy, said that while Canada could
not condone the use of violence by any party to the South African
conflict, 'we understand the ANC's contention [that they cannot merely]
accept more brutality from an apartheid state armed to the teeth.'[22] In
1986, the Canadian government also established well-publicized links
with the ANC, much to the chagrin of the South African government and
the displeasure of at least one member of the Progressive Conservative
caucus: Don Blenkarn (PC, Mississauga South) publicly criticized the
prime minister for meeting with leaders of the African National Congress, on the grounds that the ANC had adopted terrorist tactics and was
aligned with Communist states.[23] Such criticisms were, however, dismissed by the Conservative front bench; indeed, in August 1987, following his trip to South Africa, the secretary of state for external affairs, Joe
Clark, was to go so far as to say that the ANC 'is not the cause of violence [in South Africa].'[24]

Any discussion of these considerable changes in the Mulroney government's policy on apartheid should begin by noting that the issue was
in a sense sprung on the new government by the renewed outbreak of
violence in South Africa in the fall of 1984. Certainly, there is little
evidence to suggest that before this either Mulroney or his party had
any fresh ideas on how to respond to apartheid. If the newly selected
leader of the Opposition had any views about Trudeau's policies
towards South Africa before he assumed the prime ministership in
September 1984, he kept them well concealed; no attention seems to
have been devoted to the on-going issue of South Africa by the Progressive Conservative party. In the public statements made between his
selection as leader and the 1984 election, Mulroney's focus was firmly

fixed on demonstrating what were to become the major foreign policy themes of the 1984 election campaign: anti-Sovietism and pro-Americanism.[25] South Africa was neither mentioned publicly by Mulroney nor made a focus of the Progressive Conservative campaign.[26]

It should also be noted that the appearance of the South African issue on the foreign policy agenda in the fall of 1984 coincided with a general policy review initiated by the secretary of state for external affairs, Joe Clark – a review process that was to take well over two years to complete. While the issue of apartheid could not be ignored by the new government, there appeared to be an unwillingness to take firm decisions on this (and other issues) before the process of review was even under way.

As a result, the immediate and initial response to the renewed outbreak of violence strongly suggested that there was to be a continuation of traditional Canadian policies. For example, speaking to the United Nations General Assembly in November 1984, Canada's newly appointed permanent representative, Stephen Lewis, reiterated a number of familiar themes. He claimed that Canada, while expressing abhorrence for apartheid with 'every fibre of moral strength,' opposed attempts to isolate South Africa diplomatically. Continued membership in the UN would force South Africa to confront 'the pressures of world opinion' and 'international condemnation.' On the issue of economic sanctions, little change was forecast: Canada, Lewis asserted, would be considering 'long and hard' the effectiveness of this tool as a means of helping alter the situation in South Africa.[27] Such a line would be reflected in the government's reaction to calls for economic sanctions throughout the winter of 1984–5. When Bishop Desmond Tutu visited Ottawa in December 1984, for example, there was pressure by opposition members in the House of Commons for the imposition of concrete sanctions. The government's reaction was lukewarm: the prime minister would only say that he appreciated Tutu's suggestions for their 'helpfulness' in the process of the policy review then under way, and that Canada's South African policy would be 'very carefully re-examined.'[28] Likewise, further calls in February 1985 for strengthening the code of conduct for Canadian firms operating in South Africa were met with the standard concern that legislating Canadian corporate behaviour in South Africa would involve the extraterritorial application of Canadian law, and was thus to be avoided. On 26 February 1985, Gerry Weiner, Clark's parliamentary secretary, claimed that the government had 'reservations about the effectiveness of economic sanctions in fostering peaceful change and we are concerned about the effects they would have on the poorest segments of the population.'[29]

Nor did the first product of the foreign policy review – the publication in May 1985 of a green paper that was intended to frame a national debate on foreign policy – give any indication that the government would be embracing substantial change in South African policy. Only one paragraph was devoted to apartheid in the green paper, framing the issue in broad and vague terms.[30] Redekop has suggested that this paragraph was 'so detached as to suggest that the official outrage, such as it was, over institutionalized racism in South Africa had burned itself out.'[31]

In retrospect, however, it can be suggested that the lack of movement in policy over the first nine months of the Mulroney government was indeed because of the 'very thorough review of the appropriate Canadian policy' towards South Africa that was under way, as Clark put it when he rejected a call in April by Liberal MP Warren Allmand for the immediate imposition of sanctions against South Africa.[32] In early February, Clark had asked his officials for a review of Canada–South Africa relations; from the middle of February, a group of officials had been coordinating the reassessment.[33] By June, the results of the review had been presented to cabinet. Its decisions were announced by Clark in the prime minister's own riding of Manicouagan on 6 July 1985. In his Baie Comeau statement, the external affairs minister asserted that 'the time has come for basic change' in Canadian policy, 'for the repudiation of apartheid as a concept and a policy.' Claiming that Canada 'cannot tolerate a course which means continued repression within South Africa, and lawless raids outside,' Clark announced a package of twelve substantive measures, intended to either put pressure on Pretoria or punish the South African government.[34]

Specifically, these measures included strengthening the voluntary 'Code of Conduct Concerning the Employment Practices of Canadian Companies Operating in South Africa' by the appointment of an administrator to receive and publicize information about compliance; tightening the application of the UN Security Council arms embargo by not allowing 'sensitive' equipment to be sold to the South African security apparatus; imposing an embargo on the importation of arms manufactured in South Africa; terminating the double taxation agreement; closing the availability of the Programme for Export Market Development (PEMD) to Canadian exporters seeking to develop markets in South Africa; terminating South Africa's eligibility for insurance under the

Export Development Corporation; strengthening the sports boycott first agreed to at the 1977 Commonwealth meetings; imposing a ban on the toll-processing of Namibian uranium by Eldorado Nuclear; discouraging the sale in Canada of South African Krugerrands; monitoring all contacts between departments and agencies of the Canadian government and their South African counterparts; appointing a labour attaché to the embassy in Pretoria; and increasing 'very substantially' funding made available for non-white education and training.[35]

Over the remainder of the summer of 1985, the situation in South Africa deteriorated further, with a state of emergency being declared by Pretoria on 21 July. While the South African president, P.W. Botha, had been widely expected to announce new reforms in a speech scheduled for 15 August, he had instead roundly denounced foreign intervention and internal agitation. These developments prompted Ottawa to prepare a new round of punitive measures. Both Mulroney and Clark overtly threatened South Africa in August 1985. On the eve of Botha's speech, for example, Clark indicated that Canada would adopt further punitive measures if South Africa failed to take 'concrete action' to abolish apartheid. Following the speech, both the prime minister and Clark indicated that 'serious' measures would be forthcoming.[36]

In the wake of Botha's hard-line speech, the Canadian government made good on its threats: in September, further sanctions were imposed, announced by Clark in the House of Commons on 13 September. He noted that 'Canada's influence is limited but real, and our challenge is to take practical steps which help to end apartheid.'[37] The 'practical steps' included increasing governmental pressure on Canadian companies doing business with South Africa by calling three meetings in September between Clark and representatives of the business community in Canada 'to examine areas of cooperative action against apartheid.' Clark also called for a 'voluntary' ban on loans to South Africa: 'We are asking all Canadian banks to apply such a ban and we have reason to believe that they will do so ... The ban will not affect any outstanding credits nor prevent loans that would clearly be to the benefit of blacks.' Another 'voluntary' ban was placed on oil. All air traffic between the two countries was embargoed. The government also opened a 'register' to allow individuals and institutions, both public and private, to indicate their own limited measures of protest against apartheid. Finally, an additional $1 million was allocated to assist the families of political prisoners and detainees, to be channelled through non-governmental organizations.

In the speech that announced these measures, Clark also indicated that Ottawa had decided on a substantial shift in its approach on other strands of traditional policy. First, no longer would a premium be placed on maintaining normal relations with South Africa: 'It is also our duty,' Clark declared, 'to make clear to South Africa that Canada is prepared to invoke total sanctions if there is no change.' Although he claimed that, 'As a general principle, we believe that diplomatic and economic relations should exist even though governments might disagree,' Clark left in little doubt that Canada's 'responsibility to provide both moral and practical leadership' would lead the government to invoke 'full sanctions.' Indeed, the threat of total sanctions – 'to end our relations absolutely' – was repeated no less than three times in Clark's address to the House.[38]

Second, the government outlined eight explicit demands for domestic political change in South Africa, thus abandoning an approach that had kept Canadian concerns about apartheid implicit. Clark called for the establishment of common citizenship and the concomitant establishment of equal political rights, including the right to vote; the abolition of racial classification; the abolition of the 'pass laws'; independence for Namibia; the granting of freedom for political prisoners, specifically the imprisoned leaders of the African National Congress and the United Democratic Front; and the establishment of a 'process of consultation and negotiation with the true leaders of those who are referred to as Indians, blacks and coloureds. In other words, such consultations cannot be restricted to the leaders of the homelands.' Finally, the government in Ottawa sought the 'initiation of a process of reform based on consent, not imposition or coercion.'

The Commonwealth Heads of Government meeting in Nassau in October 1985 – and its year-long aftermath – proved to be a galvanizing event for the Mulroney government's policies on South Africa. The Commonwealth was openly split between Britain and all other members on the issue of sanctions. With the British prime minister, Margaret Thatcher, remaining firmly opposed to any movement, a compromise of sorts was fashioned, with Mulroney playing a key role in the negotiations. It was agreed that a 'Group of Eminent Persons' from the Commonwealth would attempt to persuade the South Africans to reform; if no progress were reported, each member the Commonwealth would decide for itself on the implementation of further sanctions.[39]

The publication of a gloomy report by the Eminent Persons Group (EPG) on 11 June 1986 – with its call for effective economic sanctions as 'the last opportunity to avert what could be the worst bloodbath since the Second World War'[40] – occasioned a further round of Canadian measures, some of which had been agreed to at Nassau. The government imposed a voluntary ban on the promotion of South African tourism; a ban on government purchases of South African goods; and a cancellation of the credentials of four South African diplomats accredited to Canada but resident in the United States. It also added $2 million to the Canadian fund used for black education in South Africa.[41]

A mini-summit of seven Commonwealth countries in London in August 1986 ended once again in deadlock, with all states but Britain endorsing a package of eleven sanctions, some of which Canada had already implemented. The government in Ottawa introduced three new measures in the wake of the mini-summit: a ban on a range of imports from South Africa, including agricultural products, coal, iron, and steel; a ban on new investments; and the withdrawal of consular facilities in South Africa.[42]

By October 1986, therefore, a significant transformation in Canadian policy had been effected. A reluctance to embrace sanctions and to engage in overtly hostile relations with Pretoria had been replaced by an abandonment of 'business as usual.'

CONTENDING EXPLANATIONS

The approach that has been characterized here as a transformation in policy towards South Africa in the two years after 1984 was frequently criticized for either being too little too late or not being forceful enough in promoting the abolition of apartheid.[43] On the other hand, even critics of Canada's South African policy acknowledged that the changes introduced by the Mulroney government constituted a significant departure from the previous approach of all postwar Canadian governments.[44] However, what concerns us here is not an evaluation of this policy, but an assessment of its well-springs. It could be suggested that three possible factors accounted for this change.

The first explanation focuses on external, or systemic, factors. In other words, it can be argued that the Mulroney government was prompted to shift its approach to South Africa substantially not only by events in that country, but also by the reactions of other states to the renewal of violence there and the expectations of others that Canada would respond positively.

At least one author, Richard J. Payne, has suggested that the unrest in South Africa itself is the explanation for the change in policy. As Payne put it, 'Growing violence there following the state of emergency in 1985 and its extension in 1986 significantly contributed to Canada's decision to impose stronger sanctions.'[45]

Of course, there can be no denying that events in South Africa – and more specifically their extensive reportage in Canada – propelled the issue onto the agenda in 1984 and 1985. But it might be noted that this is how the issue of apartheid has tended to be treated in Canadian politics: it has always been a persistent, but sporadic, issue, emerging suddenly and periodically with the sudden and periodic surges in the overt violence to which a system like apartheid must inevitably give rise, and in the state repression that is inexorably needed for the maintenance of that system. The surges in violence in South Africa have also always prompted promises of a 'tougher' response from Canada. In the year after the Sharpeville shootings in March 1960, for example, it was frequently asserted that Canadian policy would 'harden' substantially; yet, however active Prime Minister John Diefenbaker might have been in Commonwealth diplomacy on this issue, in fact his government did not change policy significantly.[46] Likewise, the Trudeau government's review of Canadian policy towards South Africa, prompted by the violence in 1976 and 1977, culminated in December 1977 with the promise of a harder line; we have already noted that economic links between the two countries actually increased after these 'tougher' initiatives.

Thus, it would have been unusual had the renewed unrest in 1984 not produced a comparable reaction from both Canadians and the government in Ottawa, particularly since the disturbances of 1984–5, unlike previous instances of violence, were widely filmed on video and as widely broadcast. However, it is not at all clear why the Progressive Conservative government's response to the violence in 1984–5 differed so markedly from that of its predecessors. The violence alone, or the numbers killed, or even the fact that the disturbances were widely captured on video do not provide a compelling explanation for the sharp break with traditional Canadian policy introduced by the Mulroney government.

In a similar vein, it could be argued that the international response to the renewal of violence triggered a greater activism in Canadian policy. Thus, Godfrey argues that the effective failure of the policy of 'constructive engagement,' championed by U.S. President Ronald Reagan, led to the 'disintegration of US dominance of international diplomacy in southern Africa,' creating a 'vacuum' filled by the European Community, the Nordic states, and the Commonwealth.[47] Likewise, Bernard Wood raises the possibility that international pressures would have forced Ottawa's hand: any Canadian government after 1984 would have moved to embrace comparably anti-apartheid policies 'by dint of the pressures and expectations inherent in Canada's middle-power roles.'[48] Again, there is little doubt that the sanctionist policies of other states, many of which sought to coordinate their responses to the crisis in southern Africa, would have impelled some Canadian action. Indeed, the traditional response from Ottawa had been to move more or less in step on this issue with other key Western states, notably the United States.[49] Unilateral action, particularly when it would have put Canada out of step with the Western coalition, had traditionally been rejected by Ottawa as ineffective and therefore inappropriate.

But, again, it might be noted that in 1985 and 1986, Mulroney, whose campaign promises in 1984 had stressed to a cloying degree the intention of a Progressive Conservative government to remain in step with Canada's 'great allies,' moved well beyond both Britain and the United States, producing sharp – and in the case of Thatcher, personally bitter – breaks with both London and Washington. To be sure, the policy that emerged after 1984 was not unilateral – in the sense that several other states, notably the Scandinavians and members of the Commonwealth, were moving in ways similar to Canada. Moreover, the divergence with the United States was greatly mitigated by the fact that Canadian policies mirrored almost exactly the approach being adopted by the United States Congress.

However, the question is why the Mulroney government chose to break with the 'Summit Seven' coalition on the South African question when a majority of the heads of government of the states attending the annual G-7 economic summit (notably the United States, Britain, Germany, and Japan) remained consistently and personally opposed to strong economic sanctions as a means of prompting political change in South Africa.

Domestic political factors provide a second possible explanation for the change in the Mulroney government's policy on South Africa. It may have been that the government wanted to be seen to be responding in a positive fashion to domestic political demands for action on apartheid. That there was a dramatic increase in domestic political demands cannot be denied: in 1984 and 1985, anti-apartheid activity intensified as individuals, interest associations, and organizations, both public and private, were galvanized by the vivid images of repression and violence

that were suddenly appearing on television and in newspapers. Divestment campaigns, particularly on university campuses, became more
vigorous; consumer boycotts escalated; public demonstrations were
more strident. Was it that the government in Ottawa, spotting a trend,
decided to try to capitalize on the public support that a more activist,
sanctionist, Canadian policy would possibly bring? Certainly in other
spheres of policy, the Mulroney government had shown its preference
to follow the dictates of public opinion in order to maximize its support
and minimize domestic criticism; why not on South African policy?
Although Redekop does not try to provide an analysis of what he
describes as Mulroney's policy of 'constructive disengagement,' he
clearly hints at the importance of such a factor when he notes that some
of the sanctions imposed by Ottawa during this period had clear 'public
relations value.'[50]

While one would not wish to dismiss this factor entirely, there are
some considerable problems with a perspective that suggests that the
government was following rather than leading mass opinion on this
issue. All the increased domestic political activity notwithstanding, the
results of opinion surveys, at least, suggest that if the government were
in fact looking to the polls as a guide for policy, there would be little
impetus for change. It is noteworthy that by July 1985 – a full nine
months after the well-reported renewed outbreak of unrest and an
equally well-reported flurry of international activity – a surprising 52
per cent of respondents in a Gallup poll claimed not to have heard
anything about the South African government's racial policies. Moreover, of the 48 per cent who had heard, only a small minority (19 per
cent) appeared to favour strong punitive action by the Canadian government as a means of dealing with the problem of apartheid.[51] Moreover, when the results of polls conducted *after* the Mulroney government's initiatives of 1985 are examined, one might conclude that public
opinion was in fact following the government's lead and not the other
way around. Indeed, a poll conducted in October 1987 by the North-
South Institute suggested that the majority of Canadians – 75 per cent
– were either satisfied with the direction of policy, or thought the government should be doing more; only 9.7 per cent thought that Ottawa
was doing 'too much to help end the racial policies in South Africa.'[52]
Because public opinion, broadly conceived, changed only *after* the
adoption of a new approach, one cannot with any certainty point to this
as a critical influence on the shifts in policy.[53]

Another possibility is that élite opinion had an impact on the Mulroney government. It is true that there was a striking coincidence between the program of sanctions embraced by Mulroney in 1985 and 1986 and the recommendations of the leading Canadian public-interest association on the South African issue, the Taskforce on the Churches and Corporate Responsibility.[54] Could it have been that Mulroney was merely responding positively to pressure from the Taskforce? There can be little doubt that the Mulroney government drew on the Taskforce's recommendations in shaping policy in 1985, but the sequence here is important. Rather than being influenced directly by the Taskforce, it would appear that the Mulroney government appropriated the recommendations *after* it had already decided on a stronger sanctionist line, and needed a coherent package of sanctions to embrace.

In short, when we look at each of these explanations for the shift in Canadian policy towards South Africa after 1984, we are left with a sense that each of them begs further questions about the well-springs of the changes introduced by the Mulroney government.

THE INDIVIDUAL VARIABLE

There is a further possibility, however: that the one variable that *had* changed after September 1984 made a critical difference to the Canadian approach to South Africa. After the election, there were substantial changes in what might be termed the foreign policy 'leadership' in Canada. In the context of the South African issue, a number of key new actors in the policy process at the 'political' (or, more correctly, non-bureaucratic) level emerged: Mulroney himself, of course; Clark as the secretary of state for external affairs; Stephen Lewis, the former Ontario New Democratic Party leader, whom Mulroney appointed as Canada's permanent representative to the United Nations; Bernard Wood, executive director of the North-South Institute, who was appointed by Mulroney as his personal envoy to southern Africa; Roy McMurtry, Canada's high commissioner in London, who was to chair a key Commonwealth committee on sanctions; and Tom Hockin (PC, London West), the co-chairman of the Special Joint Committee of the Senate and of the House of Commons on Canada's International Relations.

As a group, these individuals manifested three interesting similarities. First, in their public statements on South Africa after 1984, none of them gave any indication that they were prepared to accept the numerous arguments for 'business as usual' with South Africa that had been used to justify Canada's previous aversion to concrete punitive measures;

indeed, most were overt supporters of a sanctionist approach to the issue of apartheid.

Mulroney's reaction to the emergence of the South African issue was unexpected, given his corporate background and his obvious admiration for both Ronald Reagan and Margaret Thatcher. As Redekop put it, 'Logically, it might have been expected that the new Canadian policy [on South Africa] would be even less sympathetic to the disruption of normal business relationships than had been the policy of the previous government.'[55] But Mulroney instead demonstrated a visceral and intensely personal anger at the institutionalized racism of apartheid, an anger frequently evident in public statements and interviews. For example, during a wide-ranging television interview with Peter Trueman and Peter Desbarats at the end of his first year in office, broadcast on Global Television on 2 September 1985, the prime minister clearly displayed both anger and impatience when discussing the South African issue; as notable in this interview was his obvious and frank lack of sympathy for the concerns of white South Africans about their future, claiming brusquely that they had had over twenty-five years to deal with the consequences of their racism. Likewise, in his address to the UN General Assembly in New York in October 1985, Mulroney openly embraced a maximalist approach to economic and other sanctions, threatening not only to impose further sanctions, but to sever relations 'absolutely' if no progress was made on dismantling apartheid.[56]

Clark was the least enthusiastic sanctionist of the group, in the sense that he evinced a strong preference for a step-by-step approach to punitive economic measures.[57] In particular, he remained a vocal opponent of the 'absolute' termination of Canada–South African ties, arguing that the maintenance of diplomatic relations serves a useful and positive political role. Reportedly, Clark was instrumental in persuading the prime minister to delay the implementation of his October 1985 promise to sever all relations if there was no progress in dismantling apartheid.[58]

Still, for all his caution Clark was no supporter of a 'business as usual' approach. As Munton and Shaw have noted, Clark and Mulroney 'both apparently have strong personal feelings about apartheid, induced in part by experiences at the [1979] Lusaka and [1985] Nassau summits.'[59] While he opposed legislating compliance with the corporate code of conduct on the grounds that such legislation would have serious implications for Canada's traditional rejection of extraterritoriality, there is little evidence that Clark viewed Canadian investment in South Africa as a positive force or that he had a particularly soft spot for the interests of capital operating there. For example, in June 1986, he urged 'the whole country' to start writing letters of protest to Canadian companies that failed to comply with the code of conduct, threatening that if private pressure did not change corporate behaviour, the government would resort to 'forced action.'[60] Likewise, he publicly applauded the anti-apartheid initiatives of private individuals and associations, many of which focused on the importance of sanctionist activity.

Of the key actors, Stephen Lewis had the most unambiguous record of where he stood on the most appropriate approach to South Africa. As a backbench member – and then the leader – of the New Democratic Party in the Ontario legislature in the 1970s, Lewis had been consistent in his criticism of the contacts that the provincial government under the Progressive Conservative premier, William Davis, maintained with South Africa. Lewis was also a confirmed sanctionist: until the Ontario Liberal government of David Peterson pre-empted the issue in the summer of 1985 (discussed in the next chapter), the provincial NDP had consistently pressed for the imposition of provincial sanctions against apartheid.

The views of other members of this group may be briefly noted. Like Lewis, Bernard Wood had a well-established record of pressing for a more activist Canadian role in southern Africa. As the executive director of the North-South Institute since its founding in 1976, Wood had been critical of an approach that condoned, if not encouraged, the continuation of strong economic links between Canada and South Africa. His appointment as Mulroney's personal emissary provided the prime minister with not only a perspective that was critical of established policy, but also an important conduit to other African Commonwealth leaders outside normal diplomatic channels. Roy McMurtry, whom Mulroney appointed as high commissioner to London in 1985, was active in the implementation stage of policy following the Nassau meetings. Although we have no indication of his views on sanctions against South Africa during his time as a minister in the Davis government in the 1970s, he was to play an important role not only as chair of a Commonwealth coordinating committee after 1985, but also in managing the deteriorating relationship between the British and Canadian prime ministers on the sanctions issue.[61] Tom Hockin, the House of Commons co-chair of the special parliamentary committee appointed to assist in the process of foreign policy review, was not one of the key decision-makers. But it might be noted that he also was a sanctionist. The report of the special committee, issued in June 1986, recommended that since the Eminent Persons Group had reported that there had been no progress in dismantling apartheid, 'Canada should move immediately to impose full economic sanctions.'[62] While the committee's deliberations – and its final report – did not directly contribute to the change in policy that had largely already taken place, it could be suggested that the sanctionist bent of the chairman contributed to the general approach that had been taken by Mulroney.

A second similarity of the members of this group was that, with the exception of Clark, who had been prime minister in 1979, none had had prior close ties to the Department of External Affairs. This aspect would be critical, for there is evidence that the bureaucracy preferred a continuation of the traditional approach that would have seen Canadian policy remain in step with other Western states and would have involved as few disruptive measures as possible. Indeed, the departmental review of the Canadian approach to South Africa was prompted by the 'active encouragement' (as Clark euphemistically put it to the Commons[63]) of a prime minister distinctly uncomfortable with existing policy. Likewise, it is clear that following his appointment as Canada's permanent representative at the United Nations, Lewis was not content with External's existing policy and pressed hard for a reconsideration of the Canadian approach[64] – apparently with considerable success, as can be seen in the tone of his addresses to the UN General Assembly on the issue of apartheid in 1984 and 1985. As noted above, the 1984 speech, delivered shortly after his appointment, touched on several familiar themes, and it can be assumed that it bore the heavy imprint of External Affairs. By 1985, by contrast, the rhetoric was more emotional and, it might be surmised, less influenced by the bureaucracy: 'We have to maintain the faith with the black leadership that never gives up: faith with those who suffer the policy in the townships, with those who languish in detention, with those who face trial, with those who are hanged at dawn, with those whose lives are already forfeit in the desperate struggle for freedom.'[65]

Moreover, some of the mixed signals over sanctions in the summer of 1985 have been attributed to a difference between DEA and the political leadership.[66] Indeed, as late as October 1987, Michael Valpy of the *Globe and Mail* was reporting that, within the department, there was still considerable concern with what one senior official was reported to have termed Mulroney's 'African adventurism'; there was also 'a marked lack of interest and enthusiasm by External's professionals for the southern African issue.'[67] In short, it could be argued that the absence of strong prior links to DEA meant that the political leadership that assumed office in 1984 would not be bringing with them a particular sympathy for the inertial preferences of the bureaucracy.

A final similarity of this group's members was that all belonged to roughly the same age cohort, and it is possible that the sharp generational break that occurred with the shift in personnel in 1984–5 might explain the willingness of this group to embrace a rather different approach for Canadian policy.[68] Most of the Mulroney cohort was born in the late 1930s: Mulroney and Clark were both born in 1939, Hockin in 1938, and Lewis in 1937. Born in 1932, McMurtry was the oldest of the group; Wood, born in 1945, was the youngest. By contrast, those in comparable positions who had been responsible for Canada's South Africa policy in the 1970s and early 1980s had for the most part been born twenty years earlier. Trudeau was born in 1919. His secretaries of state for external affairs during this period were Mitchell Sharp (1911), Allan MacEachen (1921), Don Jamieson (1921), and Mark MacGuigan (1931). Canadian permanent representatives at the United Nations during the last decade of Trudeau's tenure were William Barton (1917) and Gérard Pelletier (1919). Jamieson also served as Canada's high commissioner to Britain from 1982 to 1984. Ivan Head, who had served as Trudeau's special assistant on international relations in the 1970s, was born in 1930.

Those two decades may have been an important factor in how each group looked at the most appropriate response to apartheid. The older group had been in their thirties and forties in the 1950s, when South Africa was still widely seen as a state friendly to Canada;[69] the racial situation there tended to be seen either as a temporary phenomenon or as a purely 'internal' matter; and the architects of apartheid were believed to be amenable to rational persuasion. In the circumstances, the most appropriate policy response was seen to be an approach that combined patience, dialogue, and the maintenance of contacts (particularly economic contacts). Judging by their actions while in power in the 1970s, this group appeared to have been persuaded that this approach continued to be the most appropriate policy response.

By contrast, by the time Mulroney came to power in 1984, the long-term structural consequences of the consolidation of state power by the Afrikaaners in the 1950s were clearly evident; the bankruptcy of the thesis that economic intercourse with the rest of the world would cause South Africa to liberalize had been laid bare by the increasing disaffection of the South African capitalist class and the failure of the growing black middle class to secure any change in their political rights. In short, it seems to have made a difference that the Mulroney group had spent their adult lives listening to a succession of Canadian governments claim that a policy of 'business as usual' would help eliminate apartheid. (It might also be noted, *en passant*, that the scepticism of the Mulroney cohort is not unusual: in their examination of public-opinion polls, Munton and Shaw have noted a correlation between age and support for tougher measures against apartheid.[70])

CONCLUSION

When the changes in Canada's South African policies in the mid-1980s are examined, it is tempting to conclude that there were numerous factors at work pushing and pulling the government of Brian Mulroney into a more sanctionist approach to the persistent problem of apartheid. On the other hand, there is some utility in trying to tease out the most important of these factors, if only to test that widespread assumption in the literature noted at the outset of this chapter: that individual decision-makers do not much matter to policy outcomes.

Thus, it is worthwhile to pose the question explicitly: Did the essential like-mindedness of the political leadership on the issue of sanctions against South Africa have a decisive impact on the evolution of a sanctionist policy in the two years after 1984? The answer, I have argued, must be a tentative yes, if only by a process of elimination. For it can be seen that other explanatory variables put forward to account for the significant changes in Canada's South African policies introduced after 1984 – external or domestic – do not provide a full and convincing explanation for policy change. On the other hand, these policy changes do seem to be more fully explained by the changes in personnel at the political, or non-bureaucratic, level in Ottawa. I have suggested that in this case the emergence of a relatively like-minded generational cohort with a markedly different view about the most appropriate response to institutionalized racism in South Africa was able to dampen considerably the inertial forces within the government – notably from within the Department of External Affairs – that seemed to find little favour with an 'adventurist' departure from the traditional 'business as usual' approach to Canada–South Africa relations. In short, in this particular case, the individual factor provides a more plausible explanation for what in the context of postwar Canadian policy was a radical change in policy direction.

6

Federalism and International Sanctions: Ontario and South Africa

One of the pervasive assumptions of the generic literature on international sanctions is that sanctionist behaviour is essentially centralist: in other words, the only sanctions that really matter are those invoked by a country's central government. On the one hand, such a centralist bent in the literature is understandable given the pervasive centralism of the great powers on which the literature tends to focus. Of the system's great powers of the last two centuries, only one, the United States, has been a functioning federation. And even in that case, it could be argued that the much-celebrated pluralism of the American federation did not extend to the conduct of foreign affairs.

On the other hand, such a centralist focus is clearly inappropriate in those federal systems where the non-central governments have come to play an important role in some elements of foreign policy. The generic theory's fixation on the central government alone leaves an incomplete picture in those cases where non-central governments have, for one reason or another, chosen to insert themselves into a sanctions episode. This chapter focuses on one such case: the role of the Ontario government in sanctioning South Africa in the 1980s. It also underlines the importance of provincial involvement for our understanding of sanctions theory. It examines the sanctions policies of the government of Ontario towards apartheid in South Africa. The policies of the Progressive Conservative governments of Premiers William Davis and Frank Miller in the 1970s and early 1980s will be compared with those of the Liberal government of David Peterson, which after the general election of May 1985 abandoned Ontario's traditional silence and inaction on human rights violations in South Africa and imposed a range of economic sanctions against that regime.

I will show that, in this case, the sanctions policies of the Ontario government, not unlike those of other governments operating in the international system, were impelled by a mixture of 'individual,' 'external,' and 'domestic' imperatives and opportunities.[1] As was the case at the federal level, the personal, or individual, factor – the election of a new premier with little apparent attachment to existing approaches – was a major impetus for change. However, external and domestic conditions also contributed significantly to the adoption by the Ontario government of a new approach to the South African issue. 'External' influences – notably the attitudes on this question of other provincial governments and the federal government in Ottawa – were critical in prompting the Ontario government to embrace economic sanctions against South Africa. 'Domestically' – that is, within the province – there was the palpable desire of a new government with a tenuous minority in the legislature at Queen's Park to be seen as 'doing the right thing' on South Africa in order to maximize support and minimize criticism from interest groups within the province that were becoming increasingly vocal as the situation in South Africa deteriorated in the summer of 1985.

THE CONSTITUTIONAL SETTING

Any discussion of the sanctions of non-central governments must be prefaced by a recognition that the international activities of a non-central government, such as a province, will depend heavily on the constitutional regime that defines the legal and conventional parameters of involvement in international politics. The formal constitutions of the vast majority of federal states are quite explicit in delineating federal and subnational competence in international affairs. The degrees of competence range from the extremely permissive case of the former Soviet Union, where the union republics were explicitly granted the three broad rights of sovereign states in the Westphalian international system, to the tightly restrictive regime under the United States constitution, where intercourse with any 'foreign power' can only be conducted with the explicit consent of Congress. Moreover, much of the attention that has been devoted to the 'foreign policies' of non-central governments in federations has focused on the issues usually classed by students of international politics as 'low' policy – the essentially functional or economic interests of subnational governments derived from their needs to coordinate services with bordering states, promote foreign trade, encourage foreign investment, or protect the local environment.[2] Only rarely has attention been focused on issues of 'high' politics such as sanctions imposed for human rights violations.[3]

The Canadian federation is, as far as the constitutional definition of non–central government involvement in international politics is concerned, sui generis. No other federal constitution is as silent on the issue of the rights and powers of the constituent units in international affairs as the Canadian constitution. To be sure, the silence in the basic document does not mean that there has been either juridical silence or failure to manage Canada's international relations as a whole. First, there have been judicial clarifications over the years as to the competence of both the federal and provincial governments to engage in different aspects of international activity; of particular importance has been the clarification of the rights of the provinces to be protected from jurisdictional intrusions by the federal government through the use of international treaties.[4] Likewise, there has emerged a modus operandi between the provincial and federal levels of government on the day-to-day management and coordination of their international operations. As a result, there have been ongoing attempts at both the central and provincial levels of government to develop norms and expectations of each other's behaviour in the international realm.[5] The eleven governments have managed, with but few exceptions, to keep the areas of dispute between them on international affairs limited.

To be sure, the case of the government of Quebec complicates the picture considerably.[6] Its motivations for involvement in world politics have been the focus of sustained attention from students of both federalism and Canadian foreign policy. However, Quebec's micro-diplomacy in the realm of high politics, it can be argued, stands as an unusual case, primarily because it stems from the nationalist or *indépendantiste* aspirations of successive governments in Quebec City and from the obvious need of aspirants to sovereign statehood to give expression to these aspirations at the international level.

None the less, neither judicial clarification nor convention have proved a sufficient deterrent to dissuade Canada's provincial governments from pursuing distinctly parochial definitions of interest when it has suited them. The absence of the kind of constitutional bar to a wide range of international activities that exists, for example, in the United States or Germany means that the potential for independent provincial action in the international sphere can never be ruled out. Certainly the international activities of the government in Quebec City over the last twenty-five years, designed to give expression to *québécois* perceptions of the province's special status in the federation, have been made easier because of the looseness of Canada's constitutional regime.[7] It might therefore logically be assumed that it was precisely because there was no constitutional impediment to such involvement in an issue normally considered the prerogative of the central government that the Ontario government was able to indulge its policy preferences on the issue of human rights violations by South Africa. However, as I will argue, the constitutional regime was an important, but not determining, factor in this sanctions case.

ONTARIO'S SOUTH AFRICA 'POLICY' UNDER THE PROGRESSIVE CONSERVATIVES, 1971–85

The purpose of this section is to examine the evolution of the Ontario government's attitudes and behaviour towards the Republic of South Africa in the fourteen years before the defeat of the Progressive Conservative party under Premier Frank Miller in the general election of May 1985. It should be noted at the outset, however, that in this case one must use the word 'policy' with some care. For 'policy' usually connotes a set of carefully formulated governmental objectives on a particular issue (or, in the context of interstate politics, towards relations with another jurisdiction or government); normally, these policy ends are publicly articulated in a formal, symbolic and often institutionalized, way; and finally, 'policy' suggests the application of well-defined and often routinized policy instruments, or means, to achieve these objectives.[8]

Such a usual understanding of the term would indeed be accurate in some cases of provincial international activity. For example, one can speak confidently of a 'French policy' and a 'United States policy' pursued by the PQ government of René Lévesque in the three years leading up to the 1980 referendum. During this period, Quebec had a clear articulation and definition of external objectives that it wished to achieve.[9] Foremost among these was a desire to alter the attitudes and behaviour of both France and the United States. Having defined the objectives sought, the Quebec government set about in a calculated fashion to secure for the *indépendantiste* cause support from the government of France and acquiescence from the government in Washington. Likewise, the Ontario government developed a clear set of objectives in its approaches to the free-trade negotiations begun by the federal government with the United States in 1984.

By contrast, the word 'policy' would *not* accurately capture the essence of Ontario's approach to the issue of human rights violations in South Africa. The various decisions (and non-decisions) of Ontario on this issue after 1971 could not realistically be called a 'South African policy' pursued by either the Progressive Conservative governments of Premiers William Davis and Frank Miller or, as I will argue, the Liberal government of David Peterson after 1985. Certainly, one cannot find a clear public articulation of Ontario's objectives vis-à-vis South Africa. Nor can the collection of often unconnected decisions be described as being impelled by a rational calculus of means and ends that had as its direct object the behaviour of the South African government. One is left to conclude that the Ontario government never developed carefully defined objectives towards South Africa that it wished realized. While individual members of the provincial government expressed a personal abhorrence of apartheid, it could be argued that the government as a whole did not care much whether what it did (or did not do) had an impact on the behaviour of the South African government or on the existence of apartheid. The Ontario government dabbled in this issue: its decisions and non-decisions on South Africa were not systematic or sustained, but were a set of ad hoc reactions to the episodic appearance of the South African issue on the provincial political agenda.

Until the 1985 election, a succession of Ontario governments adopted an inertial, and often semi-conscious or thoughtless, policy of business as usual with South Africa. The provincial government countenanced a variety of public and private contacts with South African interests and, with but few exceptions, consistently refused to consider interrupting or otherwise decreasing provincially controlled economic or other interactions with that country. The semi-conscious nature of the Ontario government's responses to the South African issue under the Progressive Conservatives should be stressed. Some have argued that the economic links between the provincial government and South Africa particularly reflect, or indeed are a direct consequence of, the Ontario government's (and the Progressive Conservative party's) active support for apartheid.[10] However, there is little evidence that Ontario's 'policy' towards South Africa stemmed from a set of conscious political decisions taken to engage in active support for the white-minority regime in Pretoria. Rather, a more compelling argument is that Ontario's approach resulted from a series of 'non-decisions' (decisions to take no action or decisions not to consider the issue) and decisions that were semi-conscious, or thoughtless, in the sense that little sustained con-

sideration seems to have been given to the cumulative political consequences of the maintenance of such links. Indeed, it could be suggested
that the Ontario government's position on this issue was not unlike that
in which several university boards of governors in Canada found themselves on the South African issue in the 1980s. Like their counterparts
elsewhere, Canadian universities maintained a variety of links – particularly investment ties – to South African interests. But such links tended
to be maintained out of thoughtlessness about their political import,
rather than from an express intention to support and maintain the
system of apartheid in South Africa. One could with more accuracy
argue that such ties to South Africa – whether maintained by governments, firms, organizations, or individuals[11] – particularly when they are
semi-conscious, constitute 'complicity in oppression,' as Canadians
Concerned about South Africa would have it,[12] rather than intended
support for apartheid.

At the same time, however, these links were not unconscious or
inconsistent. This can be seen from the Davis government's responses
to the rare, but periodic, appearance of the issue on the provincial
political agenda. Although they are of minor importance, these are
'critical' episodes – in the sense that they serve to illustrate the nature
and tenor of the Davis government's approach to the issue. The first
was a trade mission organized by the ministry of trade and tourism for
representatives of Ontario firms in the autumn of 1973. When he discovered that the mission was being organized, Stephen Lewis, then the
leader of the New Democratic Party in the Ontario legislature,[13] criticized the government for its attempts to generate trade between South
Africa and the province, claiming that such efforts meant that the
Ontario government was 'affording economic advantages to a white
racist group in South Africa and assisting the oppression of a very large
majority of the population.' Lewis concluded that 'it ill behooves
Ontario for the few dollars involved to prop up white racism in South
Africa.' Such criticism fell on deaf ears: the minister of trade and tourism, Claude Bennett, responded with an argument that was familiar at
the federal level – that if Canadian trade were predicated on political
considerations, then the number of potential trading partners would
decrease dramatically: 'When you say we should walk out of countries
we don't agree with, you know ... we'd be dealing with ... countries
where we can't sell our products anyway. Look at the difficulties we
have trading with the European Economic Community.'[14]

The second episode occurred in 1981. In 1980, the Institute of Natural

Resources in Pietermaritzburg in Natal had approached the Ontario government proposing an exchange program between officials to explore comparative land-use techniques in their respective jurisdictions. Importantly, the Institute was proposing that officials from the Ontario Ministry of Natural Resources would also conduct studies in KwaZulu, a Bantustan declared independent under the South African government's 'homelands' policy. Unperturbed by the implications of engaging in official relations with a homeland, the Ontario government proceeded, so that by January 1981, the officials were ready to be exchanged. At this juncture, however, the federal Department of External Affairs intervened. In a letter to Ontario, DEA argued that in light of Canadian relations with South Africa, such an exchange would be 'inappropriate.' The exchange proposal was dropped.[15]

Finally, in February 1982, the Toronto Committee for the Liberation of Southern Africa (TCLSAC) learned that Donald Morand, the Ontario ombudsman, was planning to attend a seminar on ombudsmen sponsored by the International Bar Association in Cape Town. When TCLSAC threatened to stage a public protest, Morand cancelled the trip.[16]

However minor their significance, these episodes, together or separately, do indicate that the Ontario government was not completely unaware of the official links between the province and South Africa, limited and sporadic though these ties may have been. The episodes also indicate that in the intervening years between the 1973 trade mission and the protests of the early 1980s, government officials in Toronto had become somewhat more sensitive, if not to the propriety of ties with South Africa, then at least to public opinion on the issue.

The consciousness and consistency of the Ontario government's approach to the issue of South Africa before 1985 can also be seen in its refusal to engage in economic sanctions against South Africa. In particular, the provincial cabinet did nothing to prevent the Liquor Control Board of Ontario (LCBO), the provincial agency that regulates the sale of wine and liquor, from selling wines and spirits imported from South Africa. By 1984, Ontario was importing $783,000 in wines and spirits from South Africa, 0.7 per cent of its total imports of wines and spirits of $109 million.[17] Likewise, no bar was placed on provincial purchases of South African goods. Hence, for example, institutions run or regulated by the province – notably reformatories and hospitals – continued to purchase South African fruit, though an official in the office of the premier admitted that Queen's Park did not know precisely how much of the $27.1 million in fruits imported into Canada from South Africa in 1984 had made its way to provincially controlled institutions.[18] Perhaps most important, no attempt was made to place restrictions on the investments of the various pension plans over which the provincial government had authority to exclude investments in firms with ties to South Africa.

Nor did the policies of other provincial governments have an effect on the attitude of the Davis government at Queen's Park. Throughout the 1970s, in those provinces where the New Democratic Party (NDP) – and, in the case of Quebec, a self-styled social democratic party, the Parti québécois – had come to power, limited or full sanctions on the import and sale of South African wines and spirits had been imposed. By the early 1980s, Manitoba, Saskatchewan, British Columbia, and Quebec had each moved to restrict the importation and sale of alcoholic products from South Africa. It should be noted that these provincial boycotts were often not total, and often self-serving or symbolic. For example, when the PQ invoked sanctions in 1978, the ban included only South African wine; brandy continued to be imported and sold. In Manitoba, the NDP government ordered South African wines and spirits off the shelves in 1982; however, until 1985, Manitoba Liquor Control Commission stores continued to stock the banned products, which were available on request, but kept out of sight in stockrooms in the back of MLCC stores.[19] However, despite considerable and persistent lobbying from anti-apartheid groups in Toronto urging the Ontario government to follow the sanctionist examples being set by other provinces, Queen's Park remained adamantly opposed.

A number of factors account for the approach taken by Ontario during this period. First, of all the major provinces, Ontario under the Progressive Conservatives had always embraced the most conservative interpretation of provincial international activism. There was a fundamental satisfaction with the primacy of the federal government's role in the formulation and execution of Canadian policy, and a disinclination to challenge the federal government on anything but the most critical of foreign policy issues. The views of Denis Massicotte, the director of information in the office of the Ontario minister of intergovernmental affairs, are indicative of this approach: in 1982 he claimed that 'l'Ontario demeure satisfaite de la situation actuelle. Le gouvernement fédéral est le seul représentant du Canada à l'étranger, mais il doit faire un effort soutenu pour obtenir l'impact provincial nécessaire.'[20]

It is true that on occasion Ontario departed from this general line. For example, when the federal government decided to admit representatives of the Palestine Liberation Organization to a United Nations conference on crime scheduled to be held in Toronto in 1975, the Davis government was insistent and vocal that PLO representatives should be denied permission to enter Canada.

But such unusual stridency is rare, and in that instance can best be explained by the provincial general election that was under way and a concomitant fear that unless the Conservatives were clear on the issue, they would end up losing considerable electoral support from a highly exercised Jewish community concentrated in Toronto.[21] More common was Massicotte's approach. And given the federal government's policy on the South African question – a policy that, as we saw above, during this period also persistently refused to embrace punitive measures such as economic sanctions – it remained unlikely that Ontario would move to fracture the single voice for Canada in international politics that it so often stressed.

A second, and related, reason for Ontario's approach was the evident agreement of members of the provincial cabinet with the official position of the federal Liberals on economic sanctions vis-à-vis South Africa. That position, succinctly put, consisted of the following, not entirely related or logically consistent, propositions: (1) economic sanctions as an instrument of policy are fundamentally ineffective and therefore should be avoided; (2) trade is a liberalizing force, and the encouragement of economic intercourse will promote reform in South Africa; (3) economic sanctions would hurt South African blacks more than they would help; (4) if sanctions were adopted, consistency would demand that all violators of human rights should be equitably sanctioned, and clearly that would be damaging to the national interest; and (5) for a trading nation like Canada, it would be damaging to the national interest to politicize trade relations.

Third, and most important, the Davis government calculated that there was not a great deal of voter interest in the question of provincial links with South Africa, despite the persistence of the small but vocal anti-apartheid movement concentrated in Toronto. Nor did there appear to be the intensity of feelings on the issue that might prompt electoral retribution. One small, but telling, measure of this lack of interest was the debate in October 1984 on ways in which the Ontario legislature might respond to human rights violations by other states. Although considerable interest in the question was shown by members of the legislature, the debate quickly became polarized, with the Progressive Conservatives focusing on the human rights violators of choice for the right (the Soviet Union and its allies in Eastern Europe) and the NDP on the favourites of the left (Chile, El Salvador). However, it is indicative that in a one-hour debate on global human rights violations, South Africa was not mentioned even once before the Conservative majority in the assembly voted the resolution down, this despite the considerable and widely televised escalation in the violence in South Africa that fall.[22]

Fourth, the financial implications of liquor sanctions for the provincial treasury may have acted as a minor constraint on an alteration of policy. By 1984, the province was importing $783,000 in South African wine and liquor, which it was then selling through LCBO outlets for a total of $10.8 million.[23] While this represents but a minuscule proportion of provincial revenues, it might be argued that in the absence of widespread demands for a boycott of these products, the opportunity costs of foregoing not only such sizeable profit margins, but also what by then was a secure niche in the market (particularly for South African brandies), represented a disincentive, however marginal, to act.

Finally, it might be suggested that the Progressive Conservative governments of Davis and Miller were hesitant to act on the issue of provincial purchases of South African products because of partisan considerations. To have imposed any limitation on provincial procurements of South African goods would have been to follow the lead of, and in a sense join in common cause with, NDP or PQ governments. Both Davis and Miller had such an overt dislike of the New Democratic Party – for example, both frequently attempted to link the NDP in the minds of voters with the Soviet Union[24] – that it is unlikely that they would have embraced a policy so closely identified with the NDP unless there were other, far more compelling, reasons to do so.

ONTARIO'S SOUTH AFRICA 'POLICY' UNDER THE LIBERALS, 1985

Ontario's approach to the South African issue was to change swiftly after the change in government that followed the May 1985 general election, which resulted in a minority Liberal government supported in the legislature by the New Democratic Party. By August, the government of Premier David Peterson had thrust itself into the debate on relations with South Africa and embraced the economic sanctions so studiously avoided by the Conservatives.

The catalyst for a change in policy was, however, not the change in government per se, but rather the situation in South Africa itself, notably an escalation of racial violence and killings in that country. As we noted in the previous chapter, the federal government in Ottawa, following the lead of the United States Congress, invoked a range of measures against South Africa on 6 July 1985, including a series of economic measures. In Ontario, the NDP immediately pressed the Peterson government to join in the disapproval by imposing sanctions on those areas under provincial jurisdiction.

The campaign in the legislature was spearheaded by D.W. Warner (NDP, Scarborough-Ellesmere). On 8 July, he cited the example of Manitoba's sanctions on South African liquor and asked Monte Kwinter, the minister of consumer and commercial relations, whether Ontario would be imposing sanctions on South African wines and spirits; Warner raised the issue again on the 9th. Kwinter's initial answers indicated that a change in policy was unlikely; he merely repeated the reasons for not invoking sanctions. First, Kwinter claimed that he agreed with the federal position that harsh economic measures were inappropriate 'because they would hurt the very people Canada is trying to help.' Second, he mirrored the reluctance at the federal level for unilateral action: 'I do not think it would be prudent for Ontario to act unilaterally. I do not think it should ban the import of wine without some assurance it would not be a counterproductive move.' Third, reminding the legislature that 'we do not live in a vacuum,' he expressed some fear that such a move would have 'very serious implications' under the General Agreement on Tariffs and Trade (GATT). Finally, he claimed that the LCBO procedures for listing items are apolitical: they 'are really governed by demand as opposed to other considerations.'[25]

By early August, however, the government was being criticized both inside and outside the legislature for inaction on the issue. For example, on 2 August, the Law Union of Ontario staged a demonstration of lawyers, law students, and legal workers, demanding that Kwinter ban the sale of South African wines. An official in Kwinter's ministry announced that 'while he [Kwinter] abhors the situation in South Africa, the fact is that he must follow the lead of the federal government.'[26]

However, there was a sizeable group in Peterson's cabinet, led by the premier himself, who did not believe that the government of Ontario had to follow the lead of the federal Progressive Conservatives on an issue that fell exclusively within Ontario's jurisdiction. At a lengthy and divided meeting shortly afterwards, the Ontario cabinet eventually settled the issue, with those who were plumping for sanctions overcoming those ministers who believed either that this was a matter of federal jurisdiction or that Ontario, by taking such a move, was opening itself to the possibility of economic retaliation.

On 14 August, Peterson announced the ban on future imports and sales of wines and spirits from South Africa. Saying that he saw the issue 'in moral terms,' he called on all Canadians to boycott all products from South Africa, expressing the hope that the Ontario move would prompt other provinces and firms to join the sanctions. He recognized that the move was a 'symbolic gesture,' but noted that 'we can join the chorus of international disapproval for a racist regime.'[27]

Within two months of being sworn in, the Peterson government had not only altered a long-standing policy, but had also changed its own approach outlined in early July by Kwinter. What accounted for this change? First, and most simply, it appears that Peterson, and thus the government, did not share the assessment of sanctions against South Africa embraced by his predecessors, and very simply believed that limiting ties with South Africa was 'the right thing to do.' Second, and more important, he and his government had by the summer of 1985 no incentive to subordinate those personal normative views to other (notably federal) conceptions about economic sanctions. Indeed, the interplay of what at the outset of the chapter was termed the 'domestic' and 'external' environments – in other words, the impact of events and politics outside Ontario on political considerations within the province – strongly suggested that the Ontario government had every incentive to abandon the approach of its predecessor.

There is little doubt that the 'external' environment contributed considerably to the alteration of approach. The escalation of violence and the declaration of the state of emergency in South Africa itself, along with global reaction, made it more difficult to ignore the implications of a 'business as usual' approach. Indeed, it might be argued that it was the crisis of apartheid that emerged in the summer of 1985, rather than apartheid's existence, that triggered the considerable changes in Ontario's 'external' policy environment.

Within Canada, South Africa had become an issue of concern at both the federal-provincial and inter-provincial levels in the summer of 1985. It was clear that sanctions against South Africa would be discussed at the summit of provincial premiers in St John's, Newfoundland, that August, and there was considerable discussion of sanctions in the preparatory talks leading up to that meeting. In such a forum Peterson wished to distance his government not only from his predecessors, but also from other Progressive Conservative governments; aligning Ontario with Manitoba and Quebec on the South African issue was a costless tactic.

It would also appear that the Peterson government's calculations about federal-provincial relations played a role in determining the outcome of this decision. Certainly the federal government was not pleased with the Ontario move, if the public reaction from the Department of External Affairs immediately after the decision is any indication. In a statement, DEA claimed that the moves would necessitate an investigation by the federal government into the implications of the provincial sanctions to determine whether they violated Canada's trading agreements. 'Is Canada's reputation as a trusted trading partner being undermined?' asked one External Affairs official, adding that she feared that such provincial actions could be 'the thin edge of the wedge, having provinces lop off markets.'[28] What could not be said publicly by the federal government was that the unilateral action of a provincial government, or worse, a number of provincial governments, might have the effect of pushing the federal government into adopting harsher policies towards South Africa, which for its own parochial reasons Ottawa did not want to do. (Indeed, René Lévesque was to charge in *La Presse* at the premiers' conference later in August: 'What we didn't know but found out this morning, is that the federal government, apparently in the corridors, is putting pressure [on the provincial premiers] against movement in reaction to the South African situation, while saying in public that it [that is, apartheid] is unacceptable.' Mulroney later denied the charge.[29]) Unlike Ontario, the Canadian government had to worry about reactions from other sovereign governments, particularly its allies – a constant concern for the federal government on this issue, as we saw above. By contrast, for the Peterson government, there was no percentage in deferring to Ottawa on the issue, for it would have been criticized anyway on the grounds that liquor remained under Ontario's jurisdiction. Indeed, in early August Peterson was criticized for 'hiding behind the kilts of the Tories,' as one anti-apartheid activist put it.[30]

Likewise, the increased visibility of the South African issue in the summer of 1985 also prompted an important change in the 'domestic' environment within the province. For there was an increase not only in the level of intensity of interest-group activity, but also in the awareness of a larger public, particularly in Toronto. Moving to ban those South African products under the exclusive jurisdiction of the province would in essence render the government immune to criticism on a position that had proved exceedingly hard for politicians (and others) to defend. Such a calculated desire to minimize criticism in an effort to maximize support must have come naturally to a government in a minority situation. In the event, the Peterson government was indeed well rewarded, for, as the reactions from anti-apartheid activists in Toronto indicated, it was to prove surprisingly easy to turn biting criticism to glowing praise,[31] and to abruptly remove the issue from the provincial political agenda.

What had not changed in August 1985, however, was the ad hoc nature of the Ontario government's response to the South African issue. Peterson's approach was radically different from that of his predecessors, but what emerged in the summer of 1985 can no more be described as 'policy' than the fifteen years of discrete decisions that marked the approach of Progressive Conservative governments before it. There was no statement of purpose or clear articulation of objectives. There was little articulation of any instrumental purposes for these sanctions. Rather, it is likely that these measures were intended to have very limited 'domestic' objectives, being limited simply to eliminating the South African issue from the provincial political agenda by invoking sanctions against South Africa in areas of provincial competence.

CONCLUSION

The case of Ontario's embrace of sanctions as a means of addressing the issue of human rights violations in South Africa suggests that in federal systems one has to look beyond the central government for a full understanding of some sanctions episodes.

First, the constitutional regime that underwrites a federation will, obviously, have an impact on both the legal ability and the willingness of a subnational government to tread in areas usually reserved for the central government, such as the adoption of sanctions against foreign states for human rights violations. In the case of the Canadian federation, the silence of the Constitution Acts, 1867–1982, on this issue provides all of Canada's provinces with considerable latitude to engage in international activities. But, as this case demonstrates, constitutional latitude is not a determining factor, neither a necessary nor a sufficient condition for provincial international activity in 'high politics.' On the one hand, it is clear that subnational governments in federations where the constitutional regime on foreign policy is unambiguous have been as eager to engage in high policy as those whose constitutional situation is permissive. For example, in 1974, all the state governments of Australia, including the Labor governments in Tasmania and South Australia, successfully pressed the federal Labor government in Canberra not to invite representatives of the PLO to visit Australia.[32] A number of states in the United States adopted sanctions against South Africa not dissimilar to Canadian provincial sanctions;[33] likewise, the South African issue also engaged the state and federal governments in Australia.[34] On the other hand, the Progressive Conservative governments of Davis and Miller demonstrate that a loose constitutional regime does not necessarily impel a subnational government into the sphere of high policy. We are left with the rather obvious – and tautologous – axiom that regardless of the permissiveness of the constitutional regime, subnational governments will involve themselves in matters of high policy when it is perceived to be in their interests to do so.

However, the case of Ontario's sanctions against South Africa does alert us to those few occasions when constituent governments will be most likely to define their interests in ways that require involving themselves in foreign policy issues usually dealt with by central governments. For what both the Progressive Conservative and Liberal governments had in common in this case was an extraordinary attentiveness to the issue of electoral support and the requisites of maintaining or increasing that support. For Davis, premier during a period when (with but one brief exception in 1977) apartheid was not an issue of great importance provincially or nationally, there was little to be gained by pursuing a course that would have won plaudits from the few anti-apartheid activists, but would likely have raised the ire of both the federal Liberal government and other provincial Conservative premiers. By contrast, Peterson found himself grappling with the issue under a very different set of circumstances. The situation in South Africa was critical; the visibility of the issue in Canadian politics was considerable; the ranks of the anti-apartheid movement had swelled; and the pressure to act was intense. Moreover, the government's minority position provided an impetus to embrace a posture on South Africa that finessed the traditional pro-sanctionist stand of the New Democratic Party. There was, in short, every reason in the summer of 1985 for Peterson to involve himself personally in foreign policy to remove the issue of South Africa from the provincial agenda in a manner that maximized support for his government.

PART TWO: CANADIAN/AUSTRALIAN COMPARISONS

7

The Symbolic Purposes of Sanctions: The Invasion of Afghanistan

In the first chapter I argued that academic and political debates about international sanctions tend to focus on the instrumental purposes of these measures – their ability to hurt a target state sufficiently to cause it to change its behaviour. By contrast, the symbolic purposes of sanctions are commonly assumed not to be as important. Such assumptions, I have suggested, might be appropriate for states that have the capabilities necessary to achieve these ends – great powers or regional powers targeting very weak neighbours, for example. But are these assumptions useful in explaining the sanctions policies of non-great powers, particularly those that impose sanctions against great powers?

This chapter explores the case of Australian and Canadian sanctions against the former Soviet Union after its invasion of Afghanistan in December 1979. It recounts the measures imposed against the USSR by these countries and explores the dynamics that drove each state's sanctions policies. It demonstrates that the orthodox assumptions that underlie the theory of sanctions – a theory that ironically frames debates over international sanctions in both Australia and Canada – had little connection to practice in the Afghanistan case. Instead, this case suggests that the orthodox theory tends to hide a complex political dynamic that drives the sanctions process in smaller states, a process in which non-instrumental, or symbolic, utilities feature more prominently than the instrumental purposes. I argued in the introduction that these non-instrumental purposes of sanctions are likely to be found in smaller states; by examining the post-Afghanistan sanctions of two middle powers – Canada and Australia – this chapter illustrates the alternative perspective laid out in the introduction.

THE INVASION OF AFGHANISTAN AND ITS AFTERMATH

The Western response to both the overthrow of the Afghan government by Soviet troops and the killing of President Hafizullah Amin on 27 December sharpened considerably over the New Year's holiday. It was at that time that the United States administration of President Jimmy Carter decided that the invasion represented a major threat to world peace. By 4 January, the United States government had publicly proclaimed that the purpose of the Soviet invasion was to expand its military control beyond Afghanistan, perhaps to the Persian Gulf; that this aggression constituted a clear and serious menace to international peace; and that therefore the aggression had to be countered by stiff measures. Such measures included strengthening the United States military position in the region, the refusal to proceed with strategic arms limitation agreements, and the imposition of sanctions – to ensure that the Soviet Union continued to 'pay a heavy price' (as Cyrus Vance put it) for its invasion. The 'price' that was to be exacted by the United States was in the form of six sanctions: a delay in opening new consulates; a deferment on cultural and academic exchanges under negotiation; a stiff ban on the transfer of high-technology items to the USSR; curtailing the privileges of Soviet fishing vessels in United States waters; a partial ban on grains – notably the denial of seventeen million metric tonnes of extra grains requested by the USSR after the failure of the harvest in 1979; and a threat to withdraw from the summer Olympics in Moscow.[1]

The pattern of responses in Australia and Canada almost exactly mirrored the course of the American reactions.[2] The initial responses were muted, followed in the new year by a wave of anti-Soviet rhetoric in the local press that seemed to taking its lead from the political discourse of both the United States president and the American media. While, as we will see below, Carter took all the allies by surprise by presenting them with a fait accompli on sanctions on 4 January, the Australians and Canadians soon followed with sanctions of their own.

Most of the Australian sanctions imposed against the USSR were announced on 9 January 1980, following a bureaucratic review of Australian-Soviet relations and an assessment of those links that could best be disrupted. Speaking to Parliament a month later, Prime Minister Malcolm Fraser enumerated the thirteen different measures taken by his Liberal–National Country Party coalition government to that point:[3]

1 Australian support for the partial grain embargo imposed against the USSR by the Carter administration, notably a promise to Washington that Australian grain growers would not seek to make up the difference in the 17 mmt of grains embargoed by the United States

2 Suspension of new maritime cooperation

3 Suspension of cruise-ship operations after 31 May 1980

4 Suspension of fishing feasibility projects

5 Refusal to proceed with earlier agreements on fisheries and expansion of consular offices

6 Refusal of permission for Soviet scientists and research vessels to visit Australia

7 Indefinite suspension of all bilateral scientific collaboration

8 'Non-acceptance' of Soviet approaches to establish direct air links between the two countries

9 Refusal to allow Aeroflot, the Soviet airline, to station technicians in Sydney

10 Withdrawal of support for bilateral cultural agreements

11 Indefinite suspension of all visits at the ministerial and senior official level

12 Indefinite suspension of high-level 'periodic consultation' between the Australian and Soviet foreign ministries

13 Promotion of a boycott of the Moscow Olympics

Prime Minister Joe Clark, whose Progressive Conservative government had been defeated in the House of Commons on 13 December 1979, and who was thus in the middle of a general-election campaign, closely followed the lead of the United States in reacting to the situation in Afghanistan. As the Carter administration's line on the invasion hardened, so too did Ottawa's policies. While the initial Canadian reaction had been muted, the imposition of sanctions against the new regime in Kabul quickly followed on 4 January, merely hours before the announcement by Carter of a set of sweeping sanctions against the Soviet Union. Like the Australians, the Canadians were surprised by these unilateral sanctions, and quickly moved to subject Canadian-Soviet links to a substantive review. On 11 January, Clark announced the Canadian government's sanctions imposed against the Soviet Union:[4]

1 Future sales of Canadian grain to the USSR would be restricted to

'traditional levels'; there would be a compensation scheme for farmers who lost income as a result of disruptions

2 Exports of strategic and high-technological goods to the Soviet Union would be 'tightened up' following consultation with other members of the Western alliance

3 Postponement of negotiations between the USSR and the Export Development Corporation for the renewal of a long-term credit agreement

4 Elimination of scientific and cultural exchanges with the USSR

5 Banning of high-level visits between the two governments

6 Aeroflot was denied permission for its normal one extra flight per week into Gander during the summer season

7 Canada would urge the International Olympic Committee to move the Games to a city outside the Soviet Union

EXPLAINING THE POST-AFGHANISTAN SANCTIONS

To what extent do we find orthodox sanctions theory resonating in the cases of the Australian and Canadian sanctions imposed against the Soviet Union for its invasion of Afghanistan? On closer examination, we find an interesting irony. On the one hand, there were throughout the Western alliance strong similarities in the terms of the sanctions debate, the political rhetoric employed, and the justifications offered for sanctioning the USSR. Such cross-national similarity is hardly unusual: Richard Leaver has observed that a great deal of the Australian debate over sanctions against South Africa in the mid- and late 1980s was derivative of debates being conducted in the United States and Western Europe;[5] this observation could be applied with equal force to the debate in Australia and Canada over Afghanistan in 1980. Both the debate itself, and the justificatory rhetoric used for (or against) sanctions, tended to mirror the rhetoric heard elsewhere in the international system. Malcolm Fraser and Bill Hayden, leader of the opposition Australian Labor Party (ALP), and Joe Clark and Pierre Elliott Trudeau, leader of the opposition Liberal party in Canada, were all using essentially the same language over the Soviet invasion, echoing not only each other (quite unconsciously, it would appear), but also American and European leaders.

Paradoxically, however, the considerably smaller size of middle powers, and thus their much diminished capacity to inflict harm on others, did not alter the terms of the debate over how to respond to the

Soviet invasion of Afghanistan. Rather, the purposes of middle-power sanctions were conceived, at least in public rhetoric, to be indistinguishable from the purposes of great-power sanctions. In other words, while there was usually a formal recognition of the relative smallness of their state, the public justifications offered by both those who proposed and opposed sanctions in the case of Afghanistan suggest that the purposes of these sanctions were essentially instrumental: they were hurts designed to compel others by invoking the dynamic of pain-avoidance. Thus, sanctions advocated on, or by, the governments of Australia or Canada seemed to be designed by their advocates to deter the Soviet Union from 'marching to the Gulf,' or to compel it to withdraw from Afghanistan. Much of the rhetoric made it appear, or worked on the assumption, that the behaviour of the Australian or Canadian governments mattered – that is, that it could have had an instrumental effect on the international political environment. In short, the rhetoric implied a certain universality of purpose and motive at work, suggesting the appropriateness of orthodox theory.

On the other hand, when one examines the actual sanctions policies of these middle powers in response to the invasion of Afghanistan, one finds little that is as tidy or as rationally instrumental as orthodox sanctions theory would indicate. Instead of the instrumentality suggested by the public rhetoric of Australian and Canadian politicians, the sanctions of these middle powers were driven, I will argue, by largely non-instrumental considerations. Instead of the clean rationality predicted by sanctions theory, where the ends and means are clearly conceived, actual policy behaviour by Canberra and Ottawa was seemingly inconsistent, frequently hypocritical, and invariably confused about ends and means. Instead of the tidiness of pigeon-holing motives in four abstract and theoretical 'utilities' (deterrence, compellence, symbolism, or subversion), the actual policy behaviour of the Australian and Canadian governments revealed a much messier mix of motivations.

THE PUNITIVE CALCULUS

While most students of sanctions prefer to stress the fundamental instrumentality of this tool of statecraft, I have argued elsewhere[6] that what has consistently made sanctions such an attractive instrument of statecraft is the punitive aspect of sanctions – in other words, the desire to hurt a wrong-doer for having done evil. To be sure, as I noted in the introductory chapter, there is nothing automatic in this punitive compulsion, for it is heavily dependent on the context of international 'wrong-doing,' as international reactions to the frequent incidence of interventions and invasions shows. But it can be argued that political leaders will frequently feel a compulsion to do something in response to acts that they regard as wrongful, if only for fear that by doing nothing, one becomes *particeps criminis* – a participant in the wrong-doing. At the same time, however, they discover that because some kinds of punishment can be a most costly policy option, they can also be most unattractive.

There is little doubt that for Australian and Canadian leaders, sanctions were an attractive policy option, particularly after it was clear that Jimmy Carter was going to be using the invasion of Afghanistan as a critical issue in American foreign policy. As we will see below, other leaders may not have shared Washington's analysis of either Soviet motivations or the most effective method of response, but once Carter had indicated that there had to be a response, sanctions presented themselves as the option of choice. For sanctioning the USSR achieved three essential purposes: first, insofar as sanctions hurt the Soviet Union, they served to punish the leadership in Moscow for 'doing wrong'; second, insofar as sanctions gave the impression that the sanctioning government was doing more than merely condemning wrong-doing, the problem of appearing to condone the wrong by inaction was avoided; and, finally, sanctions as a policy response avoided – at least for the moment – the slide towards the harsher and more uncertain tools of statecraft, such as the use of force.

On the other hand, policy-makers in both Canberra and Ottawa were eager to avoid hurting the Soviet Union too much. As I noted in the introductory chapter, the hurtful nature of sanctions makes them an attractive policy option; but there are few sanctions that, when implemented, do not inflict some harm on the sender as well as the target. This feature of sanctions may act as a considerable repellent, inclining would-be sanctioners to moderate the harms they inflict on others. With respect to the Australian and Canadian sanctions against the Soviet Union after Afghanistan, there were both general and specific reasons why neither government had an interest in embracing strong economic sanctions against the USSR unreservedly.

First, as I noted in the introduction, the structural economic condition of middle powers like Australia or Canada impels them away from economic sanctions. Both countries have open, highly trade-dependent economies, both with a traditional reliance on primary-resource exports, even though there are significant differences in the economies of both countries. Because of this, both governments have traditionally expressed a generalized interest in minimizing interruptions to international trade, particularly for what are invariably termed the 'political' reasons usually associated with international sanctions.

There is, however, a more specific reason why in the case of the Soviet Union economic sanctions were an unappealing policy response. While the bulk of Canadian and Australian trade is with the industrialized world – the United States, Japan, and the European Community – both Canberra and Ottawa have been reluctant to disrupt economic intercourse with the Soviet Union because of the particular patterns of trade that have developed since 1960. Both Australia and Canada enjoyed highly favourable terms of trade with the Soviet Union: at the time sanctions were being discussed in January 1980, it was frequently pointed out that Australia was exporting A$264 million and importing merely A$7.5 million; for its part, Canada was exporting C$567 million and importing C$37.3 million.[7] It is true that in aggregate terms, the costs of disrupting this trade were not high; however, both the Australian and Canadian governments have tended to be highly sensitive to marginal declines in the current-account balance that disruptions in this profitable trade can cause. Indeed, some have suggested that for a country in Australia's position, a grain embargo 'should only be considered *in extremis*.'[8] Moreover, the bulk of this trade was in products that affected politically important constituencies within both countries – farmers – and therefore constituted a more sensitive target for sanctions, as we will see below. Finally, there was a considerable problem in gauging costs and benefits in the case of Afghanistan. It was unclear that the harms caused by Australian or Canadian disruptions in trade would have an instant (or even quick) instrumental effect in bringing an end to the 'wrongful behaviour' that prompted their imposition – the Soviet occupation of Afghanistan.

It is not surprising, therefore, that while both governments found sanctions an attractive means of punishing the USSR for the invasion, neither government favoured measures that would have seriously disrupted existing trade relations with the Soviet Union. Both found numerous reasons why bans on the goods traded with the USSR would be ineffective, or counterproductive, or would hurt them more than the intended target. For example, Doug Anthony, the Australian minister for trade and resources, openly plumped in Parliament for embracing an Olympic boycott rather than a ban on goods.[9] Instead, both governments adopted what Senator Peter Walsh, Bob Hawke's minister for finance, was to label 'Clayton's sanctions' – after the Australian non-alcoholic beverage that advertises itself as 'the drink you have when you're not having a drink.'[10]

Walsh's characterization was not inappropriate: the sanctions adopted by the governments in Canberra and Ottawa after Afghanistan were basically measures designed not to hurt Australian or Canadian inter-ests significantly. Indeed, an editorial cartoon in the *Sydney Morning Herald* nicely captured this non-hurtful feature of the Australian sanc-tions: it depicted Fraser handing N.G. Sudarikov, the Soviet ambassa-dor, Australia's sanctions package; Sudarikov is saying, 'Thank you. I don't think they will hurt us.' Fraser is smiling in reply: 'More impor-tant. They won't hurt us either.'[11]

For example, Australia imposed sanctions against some primary products, but in the case of rutile the ban was lifted almost as quickly as it was imposed. Rutile is a mineral used in paints, but it is also the basic material for titanium, used in the skins of aircraft and rockets. Towards the end of January 1980, it was discovered that an Australian firm had contracted to send A$700,000 worth of rutile to the USSR under a multi-year agreement. Without checking whether it was a 'strategic' mineral, Fraser suddenly banned the export of rutile before leaving on his trip to the United States for consultations with Carter; without an explanation, the prime minister lifted the ban on the day of his return, 12 February.[12] In other cases, marketing boards for affected agricultural goods were given long lead times to secure signatures on contracts before the bans took effect. For example, the New South Wales Barley Board signed its contract with Soviet purchasers on 19 January, merely four days before the 23 January deadline; the NSW Yellow Maize Board, by contrast, had completed negotiations for a A$3.4 million sale, but had not secured signatures on the contracts, with the result that A$400,000 in compensation was originally placed in some doubt.[13] Still other products, like wool, exhibited a remarkable immunity to any kind of disruption. For example, on 13 February, the government announced the cancellation of academic exchanges with the USSR; on the same day, the minister for trade and resources announced that a Soviet wool-buying mission would be granted visas to attend local wool auctions.[14] Other sanctions sounded tough but had limited concrete impact: for example, the ban imposed on Soviet cruise ships operating out of Aus-tralian ports was to come into effect on 31 May 1980 – which just hap-pened to coincide with the end of the regular cruise season. Likewise, despite the fisheries bans, and the expulsion of a Soviet research vessel, the *Professor Bogorov*, from Newcastle harbour, there was no mention of disrupting Soviet cargo lines, such as the Far Eastern Shipping Company (FESCO). FESCO, which regularly undercut North Pacific conference freight prices by 15 per cent, continued to carry Australian goods abroad at discount rates throughout this period.[15] In some instances, Australian sanctions disrupted non-existent links: the civil-aviation ban, for example, was meaningless given the absence of aviation links to disrupt.

The Canadian government chose a similar route. It invoked only a symbolic disruption of the civil-aviation links that were worth a great deal to Gander. Its bans on high-technology goods sounded fierce, but in fact there was little trade in such goods, and most of the high-tech items would already have been covered by the Coordinating Committee for Multilateral Strategic Export Control (COCOM). Despite its refusal to allow a Soviet oceanographic research vessel, the *Victor Bugav*, to put into Halifax, Ottawa chose not to sanction the lucrative fisheries. Likewise, export financing was not really 'terminated'; for in fact the government was merely replacing a standing C$500 million line of credit, which had not been fully used anyway, with a new procedure under which projects would henceforth be considered on a case-by-case basis. So too did the ban on cultural events involve a bit of legerdemain. As Bayer has noted, events that involved or appealed to a large number of Canadian voters were not tampered with, while those with minimal attraction were banned.[16] For example, the Canadian government immediately cancelled a hockey series between teams from the Canadian and Soviet embassies in Beijing to protest the invasion; it pressured the Canadian Track and Field Association into banning Soviet athletes from an indoor sporting meet being scheduled for Edmonton. However, the very popular hockey series between the National Hockey League and the Soviet Union, which opened in Canada shortly after the invasion, was allowed to run its course safely before the government began to threaten hockey bans for the future: in mid-January, the secretary of state for external affairs, Flora MacDonald, threatened to ban the Canada Cup hockey series between Canada and the USSR – but this series was not scheduled to begin until September, a safe nine months into the future.[17]

Perhaps the best indication of the unwillingness to engage in self-hurting measures was the Australian and Canadian participation in the partial grain embargo. Neither government was willing to follow the

Carter administration's lead by disrupting the existing grain trade. Instead, both took refuge in their promise not to do anything to undermine the Carter embargo, such as seeking to replace any of the seventeen million metric tonnes of grain embargoed by the United States. This was, however, an easy promise for both Canberra and Ottawa to make, for neither had the capacity to make up such vast quantities of grain in the immediate term. Indeed, in Canada's case, negotiations for 3.8 mmt in wheat sales to the USSR were actually carried out *after* the embargo announcement. Because the crop year in Canada falls later in the calendar year than for other wheat producers, contracts for Canadian grain sales to the USSR for 1980 had not yet been negotiated; a group of Canadians had been scheduled to go to Moscow when the invasion took place. It was agreed at the meeting of grain exporters on 12 January that Canada would negotiate for no more than 'historical levels.'[18] As a result, neither government actually had to cut shipments of grain to the USSR after the invasion.

Indeed, in the years after 1979, Australian and Canadian grain sales to the Soviet Union actually rose dramatically from previous years. Australian grain sales to the USSR rose from A$15.2 million in 1978–9 to $629.4 million in 1979–80 and $483.6 million in 1980–1. Overall, Australian exports to the USSR rose from $264.9 million in 1978–9 to $978.3 million in 1979–80 and $831.8 in 1980–1. Canadian grain sales rose from C$342.0 million in 1978 to $416.9 in 1979, $1288.9 million in 1980, and $1757.9 million in 1981. Overall Canadian exports also demonstrated growth: from $567 million in 1978 to $762 million in 1979, $1.5 billion in 1980, $1.9 billion in 1981, and $2.1 billion in 1982.[19] In short, before the United States grain embargo was dismantled by the incoming administration of Ronald Reagan in 1981, neither Australian nor Canadian interests suffered at all seriously, despite the tough-sounding rhetoric of Australian and Canadian leaders. These were indeed the sanctions you have when you're not having sanctions.

ALLIANCE POLITICS

The fact that Australia and Canada were both members of American alliances proved to be important in making the post-Afghanistan sanctions at once attractive and unattractive. On the one hand, alliance membership brings with it a considerable emphasis on solidarity; a premium is normally placed on being onside with the alliance leader on issues of importance. This premium, it should be noted, is most of the time self-generated, particularly by smaller members of the alliance, but there are times when the alliance leader will insist on solidarity. Because of this, the leader's preferences are crucial: if it decides to impose sanctions (or decides to eschew such measures), the stakes for a junior partner in taking a contrary position are raised considerably. In the case of Afghanistan, the position of the United States was critical. Once the Carter administration had decided by early January that the invasion represented the 'greatest threat to peace since the Second World War,'[20] and once the United States government had publicly announced its sanctions on 4 January, smaller allies had little room for manoeuvring. To analyse the invasion in terms other than those being used by the alliance leader, or to respond in other ways would be to break alliance solidarity, and thus not only jeopardize the strategic benefits of presenting a 'united front' to the rival power, but also risk a backlash from the alliance leader. Indeed, it is instructive to note that a U.S. congressional subcommittee, reflecting on the role of the allies in the Afghanistan sanctions, complained sourly that 'the reactions of the allies have been found wanting.'[21]

In the event, both Canada and Australia were quick to get on side after 4 January: the measures adopted by Canberra and Ottawa during January 1980 matched almost exactly the sanctions imposed by the United States. And one part of that coincidence of policy approach, it can be argued, was due to the constraints imposed by the requisites of alliance solidarity. This, it should be noted, seemed important at both the political and the bureaucratic levels. In Canada, Prime Minister Clark, his minister of national defence, Allan MacKinnon, and his secretary of state for external affairs, Flora MacDonald, all seemed genuinely convinced of the gravity of the threat, the appropriateness of the American response, and as well as the need to demonstrate solidarity the political importance of being onside with the United States. For example, Clark claimed that Carter's State of the Union message 'requires allies of the United States to be very clear in our position of support.'[22] Likewise, in Australia Prime Minister Malcolm Fraser, his deputy prime minister, Doug Anthony, and the minister for home affairs (also the minister responsible for sport), Robert Ellicott, were all committed to such sanctions as the Olympic boycott – not only because they thought it an appropriate response, but also because they too thought it was critical to present a united front: 'solidarity,' Weller concludes, 'was the driving force of the policy.'[23] The only front-bench member who did not share this general enthusiasm for the Olympic boycott was Andrew Peacock, the minister for foreign affairs. However, since Peacock was engaged in a running feud with Fraser (indeed he would eventually resign from the cabinet), his influence was minimal.

At the bureaucratic level, there was more scepticism about both the gravity of the situation and the appropriateness of the American response, but a similar commitment to the importance of being onside. In Australia, differences of view between the prime minister on the one hand and officials in the Office of National Assessment and the Department of Foreign Affairs on the other frequently spilled into the open.[24] But there was little doubt that if officials remained sceptical about the gravity of Soviet motivations, they were convinced that Australian policy could not deviate significantly from Western policies. Likewise, External Affairs officials in Ottawa remained, as Kirton put it, 'massively sceptical' that sanctions would have an impact, but sought to define their response within the context of the alliance.[25] For example, on the issue of the Olympic boycott, one Canadian official later put it this way: 'Once the United States was committed to a boycott, it was tacitly accepted among the DEA officials involved that Canadian participation in the boycott was inevitable. There may have been doubts about the wisdom of such a policy, but the feeling was that Canada had to maintain solidarity with the Western alliance.'[26]

On the other hand, I have argued that there is also an important counter-dynamic at work that inclines junior alliance partners towards defection on sanctions. First, just as middle powers may find sanctions attractive because they match the alliance leader's approach, so too may they be unattractive for that very reason – when the alliance leader structures the situation so that the smaller power has little choice but to match the leader's policies. However much they may welcome the protection that membership in an alliance may bring, the smaller members of an alliance are always to some degree resentful of their subordinate position. Ironically, this natural resentment tends to be exacerbated in the Western alliance, for deeply embedded in its institutional mythology is the assertion of equality in decision-making and the concomitant expectation that all powers, even the smallest, will be duly consulted before decisions affecting the entire alliance are taken.[27] The resentment at not being consulted will be heightened even further if the leader sets policy unilaterally and then uses adherence to the line as a measure of the smaller ally's loyalty.

And this was precisely what happened in the case of the Afghanistan sanctions: on 4 January, the Carter administration invoked a range of sanctions against the USSR without having consulted the allies. Indeed, in Canada's case, officials from the United States Department of Agriculture called Canadian grain officials merely hours before Carter's 4 January announcement to inform them of American actions and to invite them to the 12 January meeting of grain exporters in Washington.[28] The result was considerable disharmony and disunity in the Western alliance: the more powerful allies, such as Japan, France, and Germany, tended to diverge from the United States line. Faced with this kind of disarray, small states like Canada and Australia, which had initially fallen quickly into line, looked for – and took – opportunities to defect, particularly on those issues that affected their material well-being. Thus, for example, by July 1980 Peter Nixon, the minister for primary industry, was assuring farmers in New South Wales that Australia was ready to abandon the partial grain embargo, and was merely waiting for the United States. A comparable breakdown was also occurring in Canada as evidence of leakage in the grain embargo began to surface: for example, Senator Hazen Argue, minister responsible for the Canadian Wheat Board, openly suggested that Canada would be increasing its grain sales to the Soviet Union, claiming that 5 mmt, not 3.8 mmt, was the 'traditional' level for Canada.[29]

DOMESTIC POLITICS

It has long been recognized that one of the important purposes of external sanctions is to satisfy domestic expectations that the government is 'doing something' in response to some international wrong.[30] What does not seem to be as frequently recognized is the degree to which governments often face competing and conflicting demands in their domestic environments that push and pull them in different directions on the issue of sanctioning other states. There are four dimensions of domestic politics to be examined: the domestic context of the alliance relationship; the 'who pays' issue; the electoral connection; and the ethnic factor.

It was suggested in the introduction that being a member of an alliance also has a domestic political manifestation that will push and pull governments in different directions on sanctions. It is axiomatic that the relationship with the United States has been the most important external relationship for both Australia and Canada. It is hardly surprising, therefore, that the alliance relationship with the United States is of considerable political importance in both countries. In particular, I have suggested that there appears to be a persistent tension between the requisites of being (and being seen to be) a good ally of the United States on the one hand, and on the other being able to conduct a sufficiently 'independent' foreign policy to avoid being branded by domestic critics as a lackey of Washington.

In the case of Afghanistan, one can see some evidence of this dynamic at work. In Canada, the sporadic criticism from the Opposition (by turns Liberal and Conservative) was that the government (by turns Conservative and Liberal) was not doing enough to support the United States in what both editorial and popular opinion generally regarded as a righteous struggle against Soviet expansionism. For example, in early January the Liberal opposition was arguing not only that Clark was an unreliable ally of the United States, but even that he was partly responsible for the invasion of Afghanistan! The argument, put by Trudeau, was that Clark's reluctance to demonstrate stronger support for the United States during the Iranian crisis convinced the USSR that it could invade Afghanistan with impunity.[31]

To be sure, when the Conservatives were returned to the opposition benches, they sounded a similar note about the Trudeau government's support for the United States: on several occasions in April, opposition spokesmen castigated the government for refusing to take a decision on the Olympic boycott.[32] Given the popular mood, neither Clark's Conservative government nor Trudeau's Liberal government allowed such criticism to linger for long: both were keen to keep Canadian policy aligned with that of the United States, and so both sought to defuse opposition criticism by adopting a sanctions policy that as closely as possible reflected Washington's position.

In Australia, by contrast, the prime minister tended to be criticized for going too far in the other direction, for his 'prompt and unquestioning support' and 'ostentatious enthusiasm' for the United States, as one critic put it.[33] Hayden, for example, argued in Parliament that the government's policies on Afghanistan merely demonstrated Fraser's 'sycophancy and eagerness to be praised' by the United States.[34] Likewise, when the *National Times* wrote that Fraser's was an 'all the way with the Americans' policy, it was purposely echoing Harold Holt's 1966 catch-cry 'all the way with LBJ' – the phrase that in Australia parsimoniously evokes a posture of the country's subservience to American strategic interests.[35] But even newspapers that generally supported the government's policies on Afghanistan were inclined to urge greater moderation. For example, at the end of January, *The Age* suggested that the prime minister should 'pause' to allow other states to catch up with Australia, and to engage in a 'cool appraisal' of existing policies; likewise, by March, the *Financial Review* was calling the 'fervour and headlong speed' of Australian support for American initiatives 'mistaken.'[36]

A second domestic element was the issue of who within the national community was going to bear the costs of sanctions against the USSR. It will be clear that while international sanctions are always imposed by, and in the name of, the state, in fact it falls to particular individuals, firms, groups, classes, localities, and regions within the state to actually engage in the sanctioning. Who within the political community is to pay for the imposition of hurts against another state, and how these tensions and contradictions get worked out in practice, remain important – and fundamentally political – aspects of the sanctioning process. In the case of the Afghanistan sanctions, we can see this dynamic at work in both regional and occupational contexts.

Once the United States had declared itself on the sanctions question, both the Fraser government in Australia and the Clark government in Canada moved to review their relations with the Soviet Union to determine where they could be disrupted. As it happened, much of the most visible Soviet activity was occurring in the coastal peripheries of both countries, and thus proved a ripe target for disruption. Australia and the USSR had reached a proposed agreement for a joint venture in mackerel fishing that would have involved the use of Hobart, Tasmania, by Soviet trawlers. The ALP premier of Tasmania, Doug Lowe, calculated that this would create 1000 jobs in the state.[37]

The situation was not dissimilar in Newfoundland. A federal-government estimate noted that a sizeable proportion of the revenues of the town of Gander was generated by Aeroflot's use of the airport as a refuelling stop. Soviet vessels fished in Canadian waters under a 1976 bilateral treaty, and made substantial annual purchases from merchants and shipyards in St John's.[38] Newfoundland's Conservative premier, Brian Peckford, argued that a ban on fishing and on Gander refuelling stops would exacerbate his province's already depressed economy.[39]

When Australian and Canadian sanctions were eventually announced, however, the peripheries received rather different treatment. As noted above, the disruption of the fisheries featured prominently in the Australian sanctions announced on 9 January. The fact that other economic activity was not disrupted – notably by a full ban on wheat, wool, and minerals – prompted considerable criticism from state politicians. As Michael Tate (ALP, Tasmania) argued in the Senate, his state had been 'singled out ... selected to bear the brunt of the only significant retaliation.'[40] By contrast, Newfoundland was spared any significant disruption when Clark announced the Canadian measures on 11 January. Soviet fishing, and the lucrative port visits that came with it, were to continue; likewise, Aeroflot flights were to continue to put down in Gander. The only sanction was to deny the USSR permission to add one customary weekly flight during the summer season.

The Olympic boycott also demanded disproportionate sacrifices from a small segment of the community, and so it too proved to be a thorny political issue – though, as we shall see, more in Australia than in Canada. Following Carter's lead, both governments had included disrupting the 1980 Moscow games in their sanctions packages. Initially, it was thought this could be done by having the International Olympic Committee move the games to another site; and when that option was ruled out by the IOC, a boycott of the Moscow games was embraced. In both countries, however, the governments were being pulled in different directions by the debate over whether the Olympic athletes should be the ones to 'pay' for a protest against the USSR, particularly when the interests of others were being protected.

In Australia, the Fraser government was inclined towards an Olympic boycott.[41] First, the prime minister, like Carter, was personally convinced that an Olympic boycott was an ideal punishment for the invasion. Moreover, as we will see below, a boycott of the 1980 games fitted well with Fraser's own view of the historical similarities between the 1930s and the 1980s. Second, opinion polls revealed that boycotting the Moscow games was a popular policy option in the immediate aftermath of the invasion, and thus disrupting the games presented itself as a most attractive alternative to other sanctions available to Australia but difficult to embrace – such as a full ban on primary products. As we noted above, Fraser had little desire to disrupt Australia's profitable trade in primary products. His reasons were not simply economic, however; he also had little desire to alienate his fellow primary producers. Not only were they well represented within the Liberal–National Country Party coalition government – in the 31st Parliament, 45 of the 125 members of the Liberal–National Country Party coalition were primary producers – they were also very vocal. The primary producers lost few opportunities to press through their associations the view that bans on their products would be ineffective or counterproductive or hugely expensive; and that therefore it was in Australia's national interests to keep these products from being sanctioned.[42] (The most imaginative defence of continued wool sales was put forward by former prime minister Sir William McMahon [LP, Lowe, NSW]. Speaking during the parliamentary debate on the invasion, Sir William argued that because the West was weak, it needed time to build its strength; the sale of wool would help the growth of the GNP, which in turn would make Australia – and the West – stronger.[43]) Indeed, the Victorian Farmers and Graziers Association was quick to seize on the idea that since a wheat and wool embargo would not be leak-proof, a far more 'effective' response to the invasion was an Olympic boycott.[44]

As a result, the Australian government tried hard to be in the van on the Olympic boycott issue, actively seeking international support for the original American position. For example, Robert Ellicott, the minister responsible for sport, travelled to Washington, London, and Bonn in March to lobby for a boycott; Australia co-sponsored a pro-boycott meeting with the United States and Britain.[45] Fraser also tried hard to move the Australian Olympic Federation and the athletes themselves, using a variety of tactics, some rather heavy-handed. For example, while Fraser's advisers had recommended that the government 'massage the AOF,' and not do anything that might appear as though the government was 'dictating to them,'[46] on one occasion Fraser asserted that to compete in Moscow would be to support Soviet foreign policy; on another he drew a comparison between the Afghanistan invasion and Hitler's entry into the Rhineland, followed by the refusal of the British and French to take a strong stand against Germany.[47] However, the government's high-profile pro-boycott campaign, conducted at the same time as it was refusing to embrace full sanctions on primary products such as wool or wheat, ended up making the games a contentious political issue in Australia. For the disjuncture between the Fraser government's Olympic policy and its policy on trade in primary products led inexorably to the charge that the government was selling out the interests of the athletes while protecting the interests of farmers and graziers.

For its part, the ALP found the opportunity to use Fraser's sanctions policy to score easy political points too tempting to resist. To be sure, the ALP's own posture on sanctions was both inconsistent and contradictory, and it was not clear from the statements of party spokespersons whether the ALP wanted sanctions or not. On the one hand, Hayden castigated the government for engaging in 'a welter of rhetoric' and refusing to adopt wheat and wool sanctions. In the same speech, however, he criticized the government for engaging in 'empty gestures, or in counterproductive measures that damage Australia ... more than they do the Soviet Union.' On other occasions in the parliamentary debate, ALP MPs claimed they supported sanctions only if they could be proved 'effective.'[48] But the ALP leadership none the less decided early on to make the boycott a political issue. Fraser was frequently charged with hypocrisy: claiming that he was engaged in 'a series of double standards' in his policies towards the USSR, Hayden termed the government's attitude on the Olympic boycott 'futile and pigheaded as well as selfish and hypocritical.'[49] The coalition was also criticized for its willingness to put 'rubles before runners,' as one MP put it.[50] Likewise, the ALP made much of its allegation that several hundred bales of the wool clip from the prime minister's own farm, Nareen, had been sold to Soviet buyers, and was sitting on the docks at Melbourne and Portland, awaiting shipment to the USSR.[51] Fraser eventually confirmed that forty-eight bales from Nareen, worth some A\$20,000, had indeed been sold to Soviet buyers in November 1979, but had not been shipped.[52] The story did, however, give the ALP political ammunition: while ministers in Parliament were exhorting Australian athletes to embrace the boycott 'as an act of protest' (as Ellicott put it in the House[53]), the prime minister himself was selling wool to the Russians. Mick Young (ALP, Port Adelaide, SA), the manager for opposition business, remarked dryly that if Australian athletes could be loaded into a wheat bag or a wool pack, they could go to the Olympics unhindered.[54]

The government's Olympic campaign eventually failed, in part because of the eagerness with which it was pursued. As the weeks passed, support for a boycott of the games slipped, so that by the time the AOF finally decided the matter in late May 1980, the government's position was not as popular as it had been in January and February. The problem for Fraser was that by this time, he and his government had invested a great deal of energy – and face – in the boycott. Despite his own misgivings about using the Olympics in such a fashion, Andrew Peacock, the minister for foreign affairs, had lined up support for the boycott from Southeast Asian governments, which had accepted Peacock's assurance that Australia's team would not be going; Ellicott and Fraser had been at the forefront in the North Atlantic region, cajoling other Western leaders into a posture of solidarity.[55] But by May it looked as though Fraser would be caught in the embarrassing position of being unable to keep his own federation on side. And the more it looked as though the AOF would not side with the government, the harder the government, to save face, pressed; and the harder it pressed, the less sympathetic the anti-boycott forces on the AOF executive became. On 23 May, by a narrow margin of six votes to five, the federation executive voted to compete in the games.[56]

In Canada, the government was also inclined towards the Olympic sanction, though for rather different reasons. To be sure, editorials and opinion polls in Canada, as in Australia, leaned heavily towards refusing to participate in the games in the first months of the year. As in Australia, the athletes themselves were opposed to a boycott. As in Australia, some key members of the national Olympic association publicly refused to bend to the government's advocacy of a boycott. Indeed, the president of the Canadian Olympic Association, Dick Pound, remained the principal anti-boycott voice, calling it an abuse of amateur sport, and going so far as to recommend that anyone boycotting the games be suspended from the IOC. But there the similarities end.

There were three major differences. First, while both Clark and Trudeau embraced the Olympic boycott, they were not particularly enthusiastic supporters; unlike Fraser, they had not been at the forefront of the boycott movement and had less invested, politically and diplomatically, in a successful boycott. Second, both major parties ended up being more or less united on the desirability of disrupting the games, so that the issue did not become a central focus of partisan politics, either during or after the election. The Conservatives, while in power, had urged that the Olympics should not go ahead in Moscow; they did not change that position following their defeat. In opposition, the Liberals under Trudeau opposed a boycott on the grounds that it would be ineffective; however, as they caught the public mood and read their own polls, the party slowly shifted ground – to a somewhat convoluted Catch-22 position in which they asserted they would support a boycott if enough other states also boycotted to ensure its effectiveness.[57] Third, the issue of who was to pay for Canadian sanctions did not become a major political issue, the unhappiness of the athletes themselves notwithstanding. Canadian grain farmers had it both ways: they could argue that they were 'paying their fair share' of the Canadian sanctions, though in reality they were well protected by Clark's compensation scheme and the high definition of 'traditional levels' of grain exports. Certainly they did not have to campaign for an Olympic boycott while arguing that their products be excluded, for problems with the grain embargo did not emerge until *after* the games boycott had been embraced.[58] Moreover, the sanctions selected by the Clark government ensured that Ottawa did not have to face charges that it was making its athletes pay while primary producers (or others) were being protected.

Despite the stridency of the anti-boycott voices in Canada, their impact was feeble: in the end, the weight of pro-boycott opinion prevailed. The Conservative promise to boycott was eventually carried out by the Liberal government on 22 April. While Ottawa did not forbid Canadian athletes from competing, or withdraw their passports, it did announce that athletes choosing to participate in the Moscow games would do so 'without the moral or financial support' of the government. The possibility that athletes would be in a position to compete regardless of the government's decision was eliminated when the Olympic Trust, a private fund sponsored by several major corporations, decided that no funds were to be made available to athletes who chose to go to Moscow. On 26 April, the COA lent the final vestige of legitimacy to the government's decision, overriding its president by a vote of 137 to 35.[59]

I argued in the introduction that a third element in the domestic politics of international sanctions was the electoral connection. In the case of the post-Afghanistan sanctions, the evolution of sanctions policy was inexorably intertwined with the dynamics of electoral politics in both Canada and Australia. For the invasion of Afghanistan occurred in the middle of a Canadian federal election, and at a time when Australia was on the verge of an election. In each country, electoral politics made the policy process murkier.

In Canada, the Clark government tried to use the invasion to best advantage electorally over the seven weeks between the invasion and the election of 18 February. According to Bayer, this strategy involved in the first phase keeping the Afghanistan issue *off* the political agenda. Clark was concerned that this was an issue that was capable of alienating special-interest groups on whose support the Progressive Conservatives were relying. Ottawa's sanctions policy, enunciated in the middle of January, succeeded in virtually eliminating domestic opposition: those who were arguing that Clark was letting the Americans down, or not doing enough to 'stop the Russians,' fell silent; those whose interests were most directly affected, such as grain farmers, were content with the compensation scheme announced by Clark on 11 January.

However, at the end of the month, Clark adopted a much harder line on Afghanistan, and not only sought to put the issue back *on* the electoral agenda, but indeed to make it the major issue of the campaign by embarking on a stridently anti-Soviet foreign policy. Bayer has argued that the decision to reverse course on the Afghanistan issue was a conscious attempt to revitalize Conservative fortunes that were, by the third week of January, sagging dramatically. The turnaround in the political fortunes of Jimmy Carter in January had not gone unnoticed in Ottawa. Private polls were confirming the stridently anti-Soviet mood of the public, the widespread support of Canadians for American policy, and the strong support for an Olympic boycott, particularly in the electorally important 'Golden Horseshoe' region around Toronto. One indication of this was that a majority of the Progressive Conservative candidates in the thirty-two Toronto-area constituencies called on Clark to adopt an Olympic boycott.[60] The possibility that Clark could achieve a comparable swing in public favour prompted the adoption of a more strident anti-Soviet policy. This involved giving a series of stiffly anti-Soviet speeches, beginning in late January; announcing the Canadian intention to boycott the Moscow Games if the USSR had not withdrawn its troops from Afghanistan by 20 February; a series of defence-related policies, such as active Canadian support for the Carter Doctrine and an increase in the number of active personnel in the Canadian Forces; and even a symbolic promise, made after Carter reinstituted registration for the draft, that Canada would not accept future draft dodgers as it had done during the Vietnam war.

The strategy, Bayer argues, almost worked. In the fortnight following the shift in tactics, support for the Liberals and the New Democratic Party softened; both opposition parties were thrown on the defensive by the Clark initiative; Conservative support grew; Clark's foreign policy received widespread plaudits. However, inexplicably, a week before the vote on 18 February, the Conservatives abruptly shifted focus again back to the domestic agenda, losing the momentum of early February.

In Australia, 1980 was an election year, and it was commonly asserted that the Fraser government was merely using the invasion for electoral purposes. The ALP in particular argued that Fraser's Afghanistan policy was little more than an attempt to have a 'khaki' or a 'green and gold' election, using the menace of the Soviet threat in order to 'scaremonger' and 'divert public attention from other issues.'[61] It may be, as Weller asserts, that Fraser had a keen eye for electoral opportunities;[62] it is undoubtedly true that some options, such as a full primary-products boycott, were never seriously entertained as a possibility because of their domestic political impact. However, on balance, it seems unlikely that Fraser's Afghanistan policies were single-mindedly driven by a concern for the government's electoral prospects. Since the elections were not due until later in the year, a poll-driven prime minister would have been much more sensitive to the clear waning of support for a hard line. But, as we have seen, instead of fudging on the Olympic boycott issue as Australian public support for this measure softened, Fraser not only remained firm; he became more strident and intimidating as the prospects for the endorsement of the Australian Olympic Federation diminished. Likewise, a prime minister concerned to maximize electoral support would have taken some care, as Clark did in the case of Newfoundland, to avoid sanctions that had such discriminatory regional impacts, such as the measures that affected Tasmania.

A final domestic element is the impact of ethnic groups. One of the consequences of the patterns of immigration into both Australia and Canada in the post-1945 period is that there are within both countries ethnic groups that tend to be well-organized and highly vocal on issues concerning relations with their original homeland. In the case of Afghanistan, one can see some indication of ethnic-group activity in Australia. For example, representatives of the Baltic states in NSW called on the government to go further than Fraser had gone – seeking a complete ban on Soviet shipping, a down-grading of diplomatic relations, and a complete cancellation of the Olympics.[63] However, there seems to be little evidence that the Fraser government was at all attentive to such groups, let alone inclined to base Australian policy on their preferences.

In Canada, the situation differed. The ethnic groups were initially no more vocal, but the shift in Clark's electoral strategy ensured that they received greater attention. It was not by coincidence that Clark chose to unveil his new anti-Soviet campaign on 26 January to 2500 Canadian-Ukrainians celebrating Ukrainian Independence Day in Toronto.[64] A few days later, Flora MacDonald, Clark's foreign minister, was the featured speaker at a Toronto rally sponsored by the Committee for Captive European Nations. The nature of the event, not surprisingly, encouraged the politicians present to engage in the kind of rhetoric that draws wild cheers from the crowd, the stuff of which lead-off stories on the nightly news are made. 'Our government was not surprised by the Soviet invasion of Afghanistan, but we were nevertheless outraged!' MacDonald was reported to have shouted. 'We said stop right there! Here's where Canadians stand up to be counted!' By contrast, when a local Liberal candidate tried to read a telegram from Trudeau, he was drowned in boos. However, the leader of the Ontario Liberal party, Stuart Smith, drew great cheers when he called the USSR an 'international leper' and asked, 'Why can't we keep their vodka off our shelves in our liquor stores?'[65]

THE INDIVIDUAL VARIABLE

We explored in chapter 5 above the impact of the individual on sanctions against South Africa. In the case of Australian and Canadian reactions to the invasion of Afghanistan, the political leaders differed in not only how they saw the invasion, but what they thought the best response.

In Canada, for example, Pierre Trudeau's reaction to Afghanistan differed fundamentally from that of Clark and MacDonald. The Conservative leadership tended to analyse the invasion in terms that were almost identical to those adopted by the Carter administration: Clark embraced the view that the USSR was using Afghanistan as a stepping-stone to the Gulf; he also believed that the sanctions selected by Washington were the most suitable response. Indeed, judging from his public statements, Clark even appeared to believe that the primary purpose of the sanctions was to secure a Soviet withdrawal. As he said when announcing the Canadian sanctions: 'We are expecting that our actions and, more particularly, the actions of a number of countries acting together may persuade the Soviet Union to withdraw from Afghanistan. That is the point of the exercise.'[66]

Trudeau, by contrast, had a calmer view of Soviet intentions: he was disinclined to regard the West as being in mortal danger. Moreover, he had a decidedly sceptical view of the usefulness of sanctions as an instrumental tool of Canadian statecraft. 'Every Canadian knows,' Trudeau said, 'that our boycott of the Olympics will not by itself move one soldier or one tank out of Afghanistan.'[67]

What is important in the Canadian case, however, is that the individual preferences of the leadership did not seem to have had a determining impact on Ottawa's sanctions policies as they evolved. For all his willingness to see the world through Carter-coloured lenses, Clark always remained sensitive to the imperatives of domestic politics, taking care to fashion sanctions policies that would best suit parochial interests. By the same token, Trudeau might have been sceptical about the Soviet menace and the utility of sanctions, but he was not indifferent to the requisites of alliance politics: however unenthusiastic he might have been, his sanctions policies were fashioned with an eye on Washington and on American expectations about alliance solidarity.

In the Australian case, by contrast, it can be argued that the individual variable explains much of the Australian government's crusading spirit, the grave rhetoric of the prime minister, and the sanctions chosen by Canberra. It is true that one could interpret the Australian response to the invasion as posturing – merely Fraser 'rattling his gum leaves at the Russian bear,' as one opposition MP disparagingly put it.[68] Likewise, one could cite Fraser's critics and dismiss the sanctions invoked after Afghanistan as so much sanctimonious hypocrisy.[69] As hustings rhetoric, this might do; as explanation, it is less than satisfactory, for it tells us little about why Fraser devoted so much energy to this cause.

A more compelling explanation, it might be suggested, would focus on that idiosyncratic aspect of Fraser's political persona: his attitudes about world politics, and how the Soviet invasion of Afghanistan fitted into those views. Most analyses of Fraser as prime minister, sympathetic or not, remark on how his approach to foreign policy was fundamentally shaped by his understanding of world politics, and in particular his view of the threat posed to Australia (and the West) by 'the Other' – for many years China and then, after the mid-1970s, the USSR.[70] It may be, as Renouf and others have argued, that Fraser was 'marked indelibly' by his father's service in both world wars, and by the 'lessons of the 1930s' he learned while at Oxford University in the late 1940s about the fundamental insecurity of the international system, the consequences of appeasement, and the need to respond forcefully to aggression.

Whatever its origins, what is striking about his reaction to the invasion of Afghanistan is the degree to which Fraser, more so than any other Western leader, seems to have been seized with the 'lessons of the 1930s.' It is true that he may have been taking his cues from Jimmy Carter, whose earliest responses to the invasion made implicit reference to the 'Munich syndrome.' In his televised address on 4 January, Carter said: 'History teaches perhaps very few lessons. But surely one such lesson learned by the world at great cost is that aggression unopposed is a contagious disease.'[71] Fraser repeatedly returned to this theme in his public statements, frequently drawing explicit parallels between Afghanistan and the expansion of Germany in the mid-1930s, along with the failure of the Western democracies to respond to the expansion of German power. His view seemed to be that with the expansion of the Soviet Union in the late 1970s, the Western democracies (together with the anti-hegemonial Chinese) needed to avoid the mistakes of the 1930s. Fraser clearly feared that if the West did not respond the right way to the invasion of Afghanistan, it was a prelude to a major war, for the appeased merely hunger for more.

The analogy may well have been deeply flawed, as Renouf, for one, has argued. But viewed from this perspective, Fraser's responses to the invasion over the first half of 1980, and his eager embrace of sanctions as the key policy instrument in dealing with it, become more understandable. Moreover, one can see more clearly why he adopted the sanctions he did with such zealousness. To begin with, it is not surprising that the Olympic boycott proved to be a primary cornerstone of his policy, for the 1936 Berlin games seemed to hang heavily in Fraser's imagery. His reaction to the AOF decision is indicative: 'I pray that those Olympians who do go to Moscow will not pay the price that many of those who went to the Berlin Olympics paid once the War started in 1939.'[72] Likewise, given his view of the importance of alliance solidarity, it is not surprising that Fraser should have become increasingly concerned about the fractures in the Western alliance as 1980 wore on. Concern over solidarity also explains why he should care so little about sanctioning Australia's primary products, even though bans on a full range of primary products would have hurt the USSR. For it can be suggested that the instrumental effect of the Australian sanctions was not important; rather, what mattered was the degree of unity of purpose demonstrated by the broad coalition ranged against the USSR and its putative expansionism.

CONCLUSION

The orthodox theory of sanctions, with its assumptions of value-maximization and pain-avoidance, suggests that this tool of statecraft is primarily useful because of its instrumentality – its ability to deter, compel, or subvert target states that have done wrong. However, the case of Australian and Canadian sanctions against Afghanistan suggests that, while such an emphasis on instrumentality may be useful to explain the sanctions policies of states that have the capacities to achieve instrumental results, the usual focus of sanctions theory does not illuminate well the sanctions process as it actually works itself out in non-great powers like Australia and Canada.

Rather, the case of Australian and Canadian responses to the Soviet invasion of Afghanistan demonstrates that sanctions were driven by symbolic rather than instrumental concerns. True, sanctions were being talked about by policy-makers in Canberra and Ottawa in the same instrumental terms being used by great-power leaders like Carter. But when the policy process is examined in greater detail, it is clear that a concern with instrumentality did not underlie the sanctions policy of either government. On the contrary: the magnetic dynamic to which I referred in chapter 1 pushed and pulled Australia and Canada in often divergent ways. Thus, both governments were much more concerned about the symbolic effects of their sanctions than the instrumental effects – about what impact their sanctions policies would have on their domestic political environments and on their relations with the alliance leader, rather than the impact these measures would have on Soviet policy. This is, of course, a rather different conclusion than the one suggested by the justificatory rhetoric of policy-makers themselves, or the predictions of the scholarly literature, suggesting that in some sanctions episodes, particularly when non-great powers seek to sanction great powers, we look to the primacy of the symbolic utilities of sanctions.

8

The Tiananmen Massacre:
The Impact of Domestic Politics

According to the orthodox theory of international sanctions, one of the reasons why this tool of statecraft remains so persistently attractive for foreign policy makers is their 'domestic symbolic' value.[1] This view has been put most parsimoniously by Lindsay: sanctions provide not so much an effective means of altering the behaviour of the state against which these measures are imposed (the 'target'), but rather a most effective way to 'increase domestic support' and to 'blunt criticism' within the sanctioning state itself (the 'sender').[2] In this view, sanctions are directed primarily at domestic opinion: they are a useful 'in-between' and supposedly peaceful way of responding to an international crisis provoked by another state's 'wrong-doing' – avoiding the option of 'doing nothing' on the one hand and all the risks of using force on the other.

In this view, the purpose of international sanctions is symbolic rather than instrumental. One does not embrace sanctions to actually affect the behaviour of the target state (to coerce it into ceasing its wrong-doing, or to deter it from engaging in further wrong-doing). Rather, one embraces sanctions for the purely symbolic reason of trying to assuage domestic demands for some kind of action against the wrong-doer. In other words, the 'target' of such measures becomes the sender's domestic public, not the 'target state.' In this view, it thus does not matter what impact the sanctions actually have on the target state; whether the target state changes its behaviour is immaterial.[3]

Lindsay argues that the evidence for the domestic symbolic utility is mixed. On the one hand, he claims, sanctions did not appear to have increased domestic support in two cases (the American embargo against Cuba in 1960 and the sanctions against the USSR and Poland in 1981–2);

on the other hand, Lindsay suggests, sanctions increased domestic support in four other cases. And he notes that sanctions have generally been useful in deflecting domestic criticism.[4]

The purpose of this chapter is to test Lindsay's conclusions about the domestic symbolic purpose of sanctions by examining the sanctions imposed by Australia and Canada against the People's Republic of China following the Tiananmen massacre of 4 June 1989. This case of middle-power sanctions is particularly suggestive, for in both countries there was not only a great deal of anger expressed at the events in and around Tiananmen Square, but there were also insistent demands from a wide range of domestic groups that their governments punish the authorities in Beijing by imposing a wide range of concrete sanctions against China.

Moreover, the Sino-Australian and Sino-Canadian relationships were sufficiently well developed that economic sanctions were an obvious measure to be pressed on both governments.[5] China was Australia's ninth-largest customer, importing A$1.3 billion in 1987–8 and A$1.2 billion in 1988–9 (2.8 per cent of Australia's exports).[6] Moreover, trade ran favourably to Australia's advantage: Australia imported A$851 million in 1987–8 and A$1.03 billion in 1988–9 (2.2 per cent of total imports). Canadian trade was likewise lucrative: exports had risen from C$1.4 billion in 1987 to C$2.6 billion in 1988 (2 per cent of total exports); imports had risen from C$812 million to C$955 million in the same period (0.07 per cent of imports).[7] There was also substantial two-way investment: besides Australian and Canadian companies operating joint ventures in China, Chinese state enterprises also had investments in both Australia and Canada. For example, China had a $250 million investment in CRA Mount Channar, a joint-venture iron-ore facility in Western Australia, and was a substantial investor in the Celgar pulp mill in Castelgar, BC.[8]

It should be noted that in Australia's case, the commercial relationship also extended to the telecommunications field: by 1989, AUSSAT, the agency responsible for the management of Australia's satellite communications, had selected a bid by Beijing to launch Australia's second-generation satellites using Chinese Long March rockets. Australia's first generation of communications satellites was launched in the 1980s using the American Space Shuttle and the European Arianne rocket. For the second generation of satellites procured by AUSSAT from Hughes Aerospace in the late 1980s, a range of launch options was considered, including the American Titan III and the European Arianne IV. However, the Chinese also bid to launch the Australian satellites using Long

March 2E rockets and, in an effort to break into the aerospace market, the Chinese government was offering the launch at a substantial discount. Using a Chinese rocket would have saved AUSSAT more than A$100 million – approximately 25 per cent of the procurement package. AUSSAT therefore decided to use the Long March, and by early 1989 had secured approval from both the United States government and the Coordinating Committee for Multilateral Strategic Export Control (COCOM) for shipping the American-made satellites to China for launch.[9]

The development assistance relationships were modest but not inconsiderable: the figures being used in the press at the time of Tiananmen put the Australian aid package at A$40 million, including $21 million in project aid and technical assistance, $9 million in import financing, $2.6 million in co-financing, and $6.8 in educational aid. Canadian development assistance totalled C$30 million in project aid and another C$60 million channelled through multilateral agencies.[10]

By comparing the reactions to Tiananmen of domestic groups in Australia and Canada on the one hand, and those of the two governments on the other, this chapter explores the degree to which the sanctions policies of these two countries were driven by domestic symbolism. I will show that a considerable gap existed between the sanctions being urged on both governments by their publics and the sanctions packages these governments eventually adopted. Other reasons, I conclude, underlay the post-Tiananmen sanctions of the Australian and Canadian governments.

BACKGROUND TO TIANANMEN: 'BEIJING SPRING,' 1989

The origins of the crisis in Chinese politics in the northern spring of 1989 need only brief outline here.[11] The large-scale demonstrations of students and workers had their origins in the conjuncture of two broad, albeit deeply interrelated, forces – a radical transformation in the domestic Chinese economy and a struggle for power within the leadership of the Chinese Communist Party (CCP) over appropriate policies for the People's Republic of China.

In brief, it can be argued that Tiananmen marked the culmination of a struggle between two competing visions of China's future. On one side were those who were concerned to increase the pace of China's economic modernization and development. The economic reformers argued that one key to the success of such a push for modernization was to reduce the role of the state in the economy; another was to spur an increase in trade with the West, which also required economic reform and a departure from the tenets of central planning.

On the other side were those who had profound misgivings about abandoning central planning and state direction in favour of more market-oriented economic policies. A reduction in the role of state planning would also mean a sharp reduction in the role and importance of the Party. Moreover, such economic reforms also had considerable implications for the power and privileges of Party cadres and their kin. A more market-oriented economy promised to bring with it an end to the widespread official corruption that had flourished in the mid-1980s as parts of the Chinese economy liberalized. In the Chinese economy that emerged in this period, elements of state-directed central planning were mixed with some elements of a market economy, with the result that some officials were able to get exceedingly rich by selling goods allocated to them at low prices by central-planning agencies for much higher prices on the domestic black market (or the even more lucrative international market), pocketing the 'profit' for themselves.

Such sharply divergent visions of the future of the Chinese economy – and the Chinese polity – were, not surprisingly, reflected in those who made up the leadership of the CCP in the mid- and late 1980s, and the struggle between the economic reformers and the conservatives was carried on in the leadership group. Indeed, the proximate origins of the 1989 crisis are usually located in the student protests of 1986 over economic reform, after which Hu Yaobang, a reformer, was forced to resign as general secretary of the CCP in January 1987 for the sin of 'bourgeois liberalization.' He was replaced by Zhao Ziyang, who was premier at the time, and also was an economic reformer. However, the more conservative members of the leadership sought to balance Zhao's reformist tendencies by appointing Li Peng, a conservative protegé of the paramount leader Deng Xiaoping, as premier.

In 1988 and early 1989, the struggle between these forces was played out in the area of economic policy. By 1988, the Chinese economy had experienced eight quarters of high economic growth. Inflation surged from 7.3 per cent in 1987 to 18.5 per cent, and even higher in the cities. The current-account deficit plunged from US$200 million in 1987 to over $4.3 billion in 1988. Moreover, these trends were even more distorted by the widespread cheating and corruption that affected the supply of raw materials and energy.

In response to these trends, Zhao continued to press for economic reform, proposing in the spring of 1988 to introduce widespread price reforms by lifting centrally imposed prices. The main result of these initiatives was merely to fuel the economy's overheating, as consumers, flush with incomes that had risen rapidly with China's economic expansion in the mid-1980s, embarked on a massive buying spree, seeking to make purchases before expected price hikes.

The panic buying and the spectre of hyper-inflation prompted the conservatives in the Politburo to respond by backing away from Zhao's plan. In September 1988, following an acrimonious meeting of the leadership in Beidahe at the end of July, the Third Plenum of the Thirteenth Party Congress agreed to the introduction of a broad range of measures to address the economic crisis. In an attempt to control inflation, an austerity plan was introduced; administrative controls were reimposed; and measures designed to 'rectify' some of the irregularities that had grown up in the wake of economic reform were adopted. However, these kinds of measures usually require some time to have an effect. Therefore, it was not surprising that the policies embraced by the Chinese leadership in 1988 had little immediate impact on the inflation rate, which continued to spiral upwards over the remainder of 1988.

Moreover, at the same time, the economic crisis was spawning a political crisis, as increasing calls were heard for greater political reform that would, inter alia, bring an end to the corruption spawned by the process of liberalization. The political crisis escalated dramatically in February 1989, when Fang Lizhi began to circulate a petition calling for the release of political prisoners. Fang, a scientist, was also a prominent dissident who had been expelled from the Chinese Communist Party in January 1987 – the day after Hu. Like Hu, Fang had been charged with advocating 'bourgeois liberalization.' Fang's decision to press for political reforms in early 1989 added to the other pressures on the leadership.

It was in this highly charged environment that Hu Yaobang, the former general secretary of the Party who had been the students' favourite in 1986, suddenly died on 15 April 1989. Rumours quickly swept through Beijing that Hu had died of a heart attack after having been criticized by Premier Li Peng at a Politburo meeting. His death catalysed Beijing's university students into open action: they used his memorial service as a means of protesting the slow pace of economic and political reform. In the days following, more and more students in Beijing joined the protests, calling class strikes on 24 April and issuing demands for greater democratization and respect for human rights. On 26 April, while Zhao Ziyang was safely out of the country visiting North Korea, Li Peng ordered *Renmin Ribao* (*People's Daily*), the official publication of the Chinese Communist Party, to issue an editorial denouncing the protests. The *Renmin Ribao* editorial argued that the pro-democracy demonstrations were the work of a small band of counter-revolutionaries bent on overthrowing the leadership of the Communist Party and subverting socialism. The following day, over 50,000 students marched on Tiananmen Square, calling on the leadership to withdraw allegations that they were unpatriotic. The emphasis on patriotism happened to coincide with the seventieth anniversary of the May Fourth Movement, a nation-wide protest that had begun on 4 May 1919 when it was learned that the Chinese delegation to the Versailles Peace Conference had signed a treaty ceding German possessions in China to Japan, betraying the hopes of Chinese nationalists that foreign concessions in China would revert to Chinese sovereignty after the First World War. The historic symbolism of the May Fourth Movement galvanized protestors, prompting them to push the political leadership hard: on 2 May, student leaders demanded to meet with the leadership, threatening further rallies if their demands were not met. It was not only the increasing boldness of the student protestors that confronted the leadership; the protests also posed a practical problem. For the frequent presence of protestors in the centre of Beijing promised to disrupt the historical visit by Gorbachev, scheduled for 15 May. Indeed, on 13 May, the students announced that they would occupy Tiananmen Square until their demands were met, and a thousand of them began a hunger strike. So concerned was Zhao Ziyang that the hard-line conservatives on the Politburo might take action in advance of the Gorbachev visit that on 13 May he visited the students, imploring them to end the occupation because of the impending summit – but to no avail. However, despite Zhao's fears, the Politburo did not order the use of force to clear protestors from the centre of the city.

As a result, the Gorbachev summit proved to be a huge loss of face for the Chinese leadership. What should have been a happy moment for the government in Beijing – the welcoming of the Soviet leader for an historic visit that re-established Sino-Soviet friendship after years of bitter hostility – was instead an ongoing, and very public, testament to the inability of China's leaders to control the centre of its capital. For example, the formal welcoming ceremony, originally scheduled to be held in the magnificence of Tiananmen Square, had to be moved to the drearier ambience of Beijing's airport; as the formal reconciliation between China and the Soviet Union proceeded in the Great Hall of the People, 250,000 protestors gathered noisily in Tiananmen Square outside; even Gorbachev's visit to the Forbidden City had to be cancelled as over one million people packed Tiananmen on 17 May.

It was only after the Gorbachev visit that the hard-liners finally took action. Zhao Ziyang disappeared from public view after a visit to the protestors on 19 May and there was widespread speculation that he had been purged. Troops were moved into the centre of Beijing on 19 May; the next day, martial law was declared. Massive protests greeted this decision, including demonstrations by over a million people in Hong Kong. These demonstrations continued for the remainder of the month. On 30 May, a ten-metre-high styrofoam statue, modelled after the Statue of Liberty in New York City, made its appearance in Tiananmen Square. Quickly dubbed the 'Goddess of Democracy,' the statue became an instantly recognizable symbol of the protests. We do not know if it was the statue's appearance that served as the catalyst for the decision to bring the protests to an end, or whether it was the appearance of office workers and peasants in the ranks of the protestors on 31 May, or whether it was because Zhao had by this time been removed from the Politburo.

The denouement began on Friday, 2 June, when unarmed troops were ordered to march on Tiananmen in the early morning hours to disperse the demonstrators. The attempt was unsuccessful: the troops were turned back by the protestors, who erected barricades and set fire to several vehicles. Although there was relatively little violence, the government denounced the actions of the protestors as a 'counter-revolutionary rebellion.' The following day, troops, this time from different units, were again ordered to march against the protestors. And this time, the confrontation was more violent, with dozens of protestors being beaten before the troops were finally withdrawn. Later, on Saturday evening, the troops regrouped and tried again: units of the 27th Army of the People's Liberation Army, accompanied by police, tanks, and armoured personnel carriers, converged on Tiananmen Square from different parts of the city. Some units moved down Changan Boulevard, one of Beijing's main thoroughfares leading to Tiananmen, firing on people, foreign embassies, and foreign businesses located along this street as they went. In the early hours of Sunday morning, the troops forced their way across the barricades, and entered the square.

THE PUBLIC'S REACTIONS: AUSTRALIA AND CANADA

In both Australia and Canada, as in most other Western countries, there was a ubiquitous and emotional reaction to the visual images of the killings in Beijing that were transmitted via television and the newspapers – the same kind of emotionalism noted above in the cases of the Dili massacre in 1991 (chapter 2) and the South African 'emergency' in 1985 (chapter 5). Moreover, the reaction was made more palpable by the concern for the safety of the numerous Australian and Canadian nationals in Beijing.

In both countries, this emotional response was given vent in a variety of ways. Calls for consumer boycotts of Chinese products, condemnatory or exhortatory statements, and press releases from numerous organizations were common. Petitions, letters to the editor, and letters to the government were also a popular form of protest. Indeed, in Canada, the Department of External Affairs received more correspondence from the public on the Tiananmen issue than it had received on any previous issue. Among the more imaginative protests was the campaign mounted by Chinese students in Montreal to jam 'hot line' phone numbers in Beijing that had been set up by the authorities there to encourage people to inform on protestors. Shifts of students dialled these numbers twenty-four hours a day and kept the lines occupied. The sizeable long-distance phone charges for this operation were paid for by a Chinese-Canadian businessperson in Montreal.[12]

Certainly the large-scale protests that occurred in all major cities with a sizeable Chinese ethnic (or university student) population helped to galvanize and focus opinion in the immediate aftermath of Tiananmen. There had been sporadic, albeit well-attended, public demonstrations in several Australian and Canadian cities, designed to express solidarity with the demonstrators in Beijing before 4 June. After Tiananmen, however, the number of both demonstrations and demonstrators increased dramatically. In Adelaide, Brisbane, Melbourne, Perth, Sydney, Toronto, Vancouver, and the two national capitals, thousands of people gathered to hear speeches and to march on the nearest Chinese diplomatic office to register a protest; in smaller centres, the protests were more sparsely attended, but they were held none the less. In Toronto, more than thirty thousand people came to hear speeches at a rally in Grange Park near City Hall, and then marched to the Chinese consulate two kilometres away. In Sydney, two thousand people gathered in Chinatown for a previously scheduled concert, 'Sing for Democracy,' whose original purpose had been to demonstrate support for the Beijing protests, but that became a focal point for a spontaneous protest against Tiananmen.

In Australia, a nation-wide memorial ceremony was quickly organized for the afternoon of Friday, 9 June, with simultaneous services held in all eight capital cities. This service was organized by Bill Jenner, a professor at Australian National University, and Stephen FitzGerald, Australia's first ambassador to the People's Republic of China. Attendance at these services was indicative of the popular mood: for example, six thousand people attended the service at Town Hall in Melbourne and two thousand the service in Canberra, which was held in the Great Hall of Parliament House. In Toronto, a candlelight service was held a week after Tiananmen, attended by 7500 people.

Not surprisingly, ethnic politics played an important role in the responses to Tiananmen.[13] To be sure, what is usually referred to as the 'Chinese community' in the singular in Australia and Canada actually includes several 'communities,' not always sharing the same outlook, interests, or even language. These communities would include the most deeply rooted descendants of those who came primarily from the south of China to work the Australian gold fields and the Canadian railways in the nineteenth century; the postwar waves of Cantonese-speaking immigrants from Hong Kong, Singapore, and Malaysia; the ethnic Chinese expelled from Vietnam in the late 1970s; and, finally, the short-stay students, predominantly Mandarin speakers from northern China and Shanghaiese from the central coast, who in the 1980s came to Western countries like Australia and Canada in large numbers as part of China's Four Modernizations program. But in both countries ethnic Chinese from all groups tended to be vocal in their protests against the massacre.

In Canada, in 1989, there were between 360,000 and 400,000 Canadians of Chinese origin, and about 6800 students from China studying at Canadian institutions. Early estimates put the Chinese student population at 4500; the actually figure was closer to 7000.[14] In Australia, there were 15,400 nationals of the People's Republic of China, of which about 10,600 were students, the vast majority enrolled in English-language schools. The exact number of Australians of Chinese descent remains unknown, with estimates ranging widely from 50,000 to 250,000. Exact figures are unavailable because Australian Bureau of Statistics census data no longer distinguish on the basis of race or ethnicity, only on place of birth and country of origin for overseas arrivals. Estimates thus have to be culled from these two data groups (a method that of course misses second- and third-generation Australians of Chinese descent). The 1986 census data reveal that 536,000 Australians were born in 'Asia' (a generally unhelpful category that includes all countries from Lebanon eastward): the largest 'birthplace groups' were Vietnam (83,040), Lebanon (53,340), India (47,820), and Malaysia (47,800).[15]

In both countries, the pattern of ethnic involvement was similar. Besides the well-established ethnic and community groups – such as the Federation of Chinese Canadians, the Chinese Canadian National Council, or, in Australia, the Ethnic Communities Council of NSW and the Australian Chinese Forum – numerous ad hoc groups appeared to organize protests, coordinate events, and distribute news received from sources in China. Some of these ad hoc groups were formed by students from China. For example, Chinese students at universities in southern Ontario (Guelph, McMaster, Queen's, Waterloo, Western Ontario, and York), issued a joint statement condemning the 'anti-people, anti-democracy crime' on 3 June.[16] In Australia, pro-democracy students gravitated towards such groups as Democratic China, an all-Australia umbrella students group. After an initial flurry of activity, however, the student organizations tended to fade from view as the government in Beijing began its post-Tiananmen crack-down. In both Australia and Canada, reports began circulating that security agents operating out of the Chinese embassies in Canberra and Ottawa and the consulates in major cities in both countries were monitoring student protests;[17] moreover, reports that people in China who had appeared on international television news programs had been arrested made students fearful that reports of their protests carried on local television stations would be videotaped and analysed by Chinese consulate and embassy officials. Australian and Canadian government officials expressed concern and urged caution. In Canberra, although the Department of Foreign Affairs and Trade claimed not to be aware of Chinese security agents operating in Australia, it none the less formally advised students who were being harassed or followed to contact Australian police. In Ottawa, Secretary for External Affairs Joe Clark thought it prudent to call the Chinese ambassador, Zhang Wenpu, in to warn him about harassing students. Canada's ambassador to China, Earl Drake, also made a point of warning Chinese students in Canada to keep a 'low profile.'[18]

As a result, the primary source of pressure-group activity tended to be the well-established members of the community of Chinese descent. Both ad hoc and institutionalized groups were involved. Numerous ad hoc groups quickly appeared on the scene. For example, in Canada, the Chinese Action Committee was formed in Halifax, and in Vancouver the Canadian Chinese Committee for Democratic Movement in China in Vancouver; in Australia, the Chinese Alliance for Democracy was formed in Melbourne, along with the South Australian Chinese Democracy Support Group in Adelaide and the Canberra Support Committee for Chinese People.

Some of these groups had a wider base of community support than others. In Toronto, for example, the Toronto Committee of Concerned Citizens Supporting the Movement for Democracy in China was organized on an initiative by Joseph Wong, a local physician. Its many supporters included Toronto City Council; John Polanyi, a Nobel laureate at the University of Toronto; many members of the New Democratic Party élite in Toronto; numerous unions, including the Ontario Federation of Labour; two university-student umbrella organizations, the Canadian Federation of Students and its Ontario counterpart; several Toronto-area peace groups; Oxfam Canada; and numerous individual members of Toronto's Chinese-Canadian cultural and business communities.[19] The Toronto committee was primarily involved in organizing letter-writing campaigns, coordinating such events as a candlelight memorial service held at Toronto City Hall on 10 June, mounting a weekly protest vigil throughout the summer, and monitoring the Canadian government's policies on China. But the committee's activities were also closely coordinated with those of the more institutionalized Chinese-Canadian ethnic groups. All these groups pressed the government in Ottawa, both publicly and privately, to take a hard punitive line. They recommended, for example, imposing economic sanctions, withdrawing the ambassador from Beijing, and raising the issue of Tiananmen on the UN Security Council (where Canada was serving a two-year term).

Likewise, in Australia, much of the protest and pressure-group activity was coordinated by either established Chinese community groups or groups with broad community support. In Canberra, for example, supporters of the Canberra Support Committee for Chinese People included former prime minister Gough Whitlam, three former Australian ambassadors to China, a former head of the Department of Foreign Affairs and Trade, numerous professors and students at the Australian National University, the ANU student association, several local Chinese business establishments, and the Canberra branch of the Australia-China Friendship Society.[20]

In Sydney, by contrast, established community groups took the lead. On 6 June, approximately one hundred representatives from dozens of community organizations, including the Ethnic Communities Council of

NSW and the Australian Chinese Forum, met at Sydney Trades Hall to discuss the Chinese community's reaction to Tiananmen. A series of motions was put forward by Chinese students at the University of New South Wales and, as a group, they voted to call on the Australian government to condemn the violence; impose economic sanctions; withdraw the Australian ambassador from Beijing; ban all services to China's embassy and consulates in Australia; direct the embassy in Beijing to grant asylum to anyone who asked for it; raise Australian concerns internationally; and urge China to lift the media ban.[21]

In both countries, it was to the established groups that the governments turned for policy input. On 16 June, the Australian prime minister, Bob Hawke, met a delegation of twenty representatives from Chinese communities throughout Australia, headed by Henry Tsang, the vice-chair of the Ethnic Communities Council of NSW.[22]

In Canada, cabinet ministers were sent out to meet Chinese community groups, particularly in Vancouver and Toronto, where most of Canada's Chinese population is centred. Indeed, Toronto's Chinese population had grown so large – 250,000 – that by the late 1980s it had four distinct 'Chinatowns,' including forty thousand Chinese Canadians in the suburb of Scarborough. As a result, fully three cabinet ministers were sent to meet local groups. Monique Landry, the minister for external relations and international development, met in Toronto on 9 June with representatives of industry and non-governmental organizations to discuss Canada's aid program in China. Gerry Weiner held a dinner with Lan Sum, president of the Federation of Chinese Canadians, and other community representatives in Scarborough on 21 June. And Barbara McDougall, at that time the minister of immigration, met with representatives of the Chinese community in Toronto on 23 June.

Moreover, the secretary of state for external affairs, Joe Clark, met with representatives of the Chinese community on several occasions. Community representatives, including Lewis Chan, president of the Canadian Ethnocultural Council, and Jacky Pang, executive director of the Chinese Canadian National Council, were also invited to attend a round table of fifty China experts convened by Clark in Ottawa on 22 June.[23]

The labour movement in Canada played only a peripheral part in the Canadian response to the events of 4 June, helping, for example, to pay for newspaper advertising and lending its symbolic support to groups like the Toronto Committee. By contrast, union activism – and union politics – formed an important part of the Australian reaction. The secretary of the Labour Council of New South Wales, Michael Easson, sought to coordinate a union effort to 'ignite international trade union activity focussed on China.' To this end, he secured an immediate industrial ban on the Chinese consulate in Sydney, closing down garbage pickup, mail delivery, and 'reliable' supplies of electricity.[24] He wrote to the secretary of the Australian Council of Trade Unions (ACTU), urging that the ACTU do more than deplore the killings, such as seeking the expulsion of the Chinese ambassador. In Canberra, the Australian Capital Territory (ACT) Trades and Labour Council endorsed bans on the Chinese embassy, and building union workers decided to forgo a day's wages 'as a strong protest' and stopped work on a new Chinese embassy being constructed in the Canberra suburb of Yarralumla.[25] But such support was not universal in the union movement: for example, the Victorian Trades Hall Council voted to condemn the massacre, but stopped short of imposing bans on the Chinese consulate in Melbourne.[26] Easson's initiative for a trade-union campaign eventually collapsed completely in the face of opposition from union leaders on the far left, such as the Sydney branch secretary of the Waterside Workers Federation, Jim Donovan, who was reported to have expressed open support for the use of force in Beijing, claiming that had the government not 'dispersed' the 'counter-revolutionaries,' there would have been anarchy.[27]

Editorial opinion in both countries harshly condemned the Chinese government for authorizing the use of force, but there was comparatively little editorial discussion of how the governments in Canberra or Ottawa should respond. None the less, one can find some evidence of editorial support for a hard sanctionist line, though it was by no means universal.

In Australia, for example, the *Courier-Mail* in Brisbane remained persistently opposed to sanctions, but even it recognized that 'Western trade, economic and political relations with China cannot continue simply as if nothing has happened.'[28] The *Northern Territory News* (7 June 1989) was likewise of the view that 'emotional calls' for sanctions were 'wisely rejected' by the government, for they would only drive China into isolationism. *The Age* in Melbourne was the most persistent supporter of sanctions, editorializing on 8 June that, 'however lucrative our trade ... it would be incumbent on the Federal Government to institute trade sanctions against Beijing in much the same way as Canberra blocks economic links with South Africa. It may even be necessary to break all diplomatic ties as an extreme signal of disapproval' – a theme repeated on 20 and 23 June. Both *The Australian* (10–11 June) and *The Advertiser* in Adelaide (10 June) bruited the idea of improving relations with Taiwan as a way to punish the government in Beijing.

In Canada, the *Ottawa Citizen* was the most ardent proponent of a sanctionist approach. On 6 June 1989, it called for Canada to impose a full range of sanctions: withdraw the ambassador, embargo technology transfer and all flights, and link Canadian aid to human rights performance; on 14 June, it urged that Canada's aid program be cut, a call repeated on 23 June. The *Financial Post* (6 June) also called for a range of sanctions, including withdrawing the ambassador, reviewing the Export Development Corporation line of credit to China, and postponing consideration of China's re-entry to the General Agreement on Tariffs and Trade. The *Toronto Star* (15 June) urged that Canada fashion its response so as to continue 'people' contact with China. The *Globe and Mail* did not express a view on sanctions until 22 July – well after the G-7 Summit in July – when it offered a qualified endorsement of the summit sanctions. Its few editorials on Canada's China policy in June made no mention of sanctions.

Amid the widespread calls for sanctions within the community, there were few voices besides those of government officials – or former officials[29] – publicly echoing Henry Kissinger's view that the West 'cannot afford emotional outbursts' on China.[30] This was particularly true of the academic community. In Australia, academic responses to Tiananmen tended to come in the form of visceral denunciations of the crack-down and exhortations for harsh action by the government in Canberra.[31] In Canada, by contrast, there was no comparable public reaction: the strident tone that marked Australian academic commentary was simply absent.[32]

Even those whose interests might in other circumstances have led them to oppose sanctions – Australian and Canadian firms with operations in China – tended to remain quiet. Many of them quickly decided to impose their own form of sanction by temporarily closing down their operations and evacuating their non-Chinese personnel. For example, by 7 June, the three Australian banks with operations in China – ANZ, National Australia, and Westpac – had closed their doors and followed American transnational corporations such as IBM, Xerox, Dow Chemical, and Chrysler out of China. Australia's largest firm, BHP, announced that it would withdraw by 10 June.[33] One of the Canadian corporate casualties was Canadian Airlines International: it immediately suspended its flights to Shanghai and Beijing and closed its offices there. It should be noted that for many firms the shut-down proved to be merely a temporary interruption; many Western businesses were back in operation by the end of the year. But for some, the evacuation provoked by the Tiananmen massacre proved to be a catalyst for abandoning the China market altogether. For example, Canadian Airlines International chose not to re-establish its flights to Shanghai and Beijing, instead opening a new route to Taiwan.

If most Australian or Canadian firms with operations in China proved hesitant to press their view on sanctions, not all business people were so reticent. For example, John Garrety, executive director of the Australia-China Business Cooperation Committee, claimed the day after Tiananmen that he saw 'no reason whatsoever' why there should be any change in the relationship. Likewise, Peter Just, head of Just Australia China Holdings, was due to sign a joint-venture agreement with a Chinese delegation three days after Tiananmen. Asked by the press if he thought it appropriate to sign an agreement given the bloodshed in Beijing, Just responded that he found the question 'a little offensive.' Calling the initial response from Canberra 'very measured' and 'very good,' he urged Australia not to join Britain and take the 'very backward step' of introducing sanctions.[34]

The only other source of hesitation on the issue of sanctions came from non-central governments. In both countries, state, provincial, and city governments expressed their abhorrence, and in a few instances they imposed their own sanctions. Mostly the sanctions involved freezing relations and cancelling trips (mirroring, as we will see below, the sanctions imposed by the central governments). For example, claiming that it was 'the only thing we can do to express our shock and dismay,' Art Eggleton, the mayor of Toronto, announced that the city was freezing all its dealings with China, including relations with its twinned sister city, Chongqing.[35] John Bannon, premier of South Australia, banned all South Australian official visits and trade delegations to China, but did not sever relations with South Australia's sister province of Shandong. The Queensland government immediately cancelled two ministerial trips. In New South Wales, both the premier, Nick Greiner, who was due to visit China in July or August as part of sister-city celebrations between Sydney and Guangzhou, and Wal Murray, the deputy premier, who was to have visited China in July as part of a trade delegation for NSW companies operating in China, cancelled their trips. But both the Victorian government of John Cain and the Northern Territory government in Darwin announced that relations would remain unaffected.[36] In Ontario, the Liberal premier, David Peterson, issued a statement expressing his 'outrage,' and members of his cabinet, particularly the minister of energy, Bob Wong, took an active part in the condemnations after Tiananmen. Peterson did, however, reject opposition calls to close the Ontario-Jiangsu Science and Technology Centre in Nanjing.[37]

In sum, the domestic environment in both countries was both palpably disturbed by the events in Tiananmen and generally united in pressing on both governments demands for strong punitive action against China, as this brief survey demonstrates. How the two federal governments reacted to Tiananmen – and to domestic pressures for strong sanctions – is the question to which we now turn.

THE GOVERNMENTAL RESPONSE

On the surface, the official public reactions of the Australian and Canadian governments to the events in Beijing up to 4 June appeared generally muted. Indeed, in the initial period of protest after Hu Yaobang's death, there had been considerable optimism in both Canberra and Ottawa that the protests would not affect the generally warm and close relationship with the West. In the Australian case, much of the optimism appeared to stem from the repeated assurances gives to Australian officials by senior Chinese leaders during this period about its policies towards the student movement. For example, Hu Qili, a senior Politburo member, assured the Australian treasurer, Paul Keating, who was in Beijing in early May for a meeting of the Asian Development Bank, that the Chinese leadership regarded the student movement as a 'healthy positive force.'[38] (As it turned out, Hu was a less than reliable source: as noted above, he was one of the reformers, and a close ally of Zhao Ziyang. He was one of those purged from the leadership following the Tiananmen massacre. On 24 June, Hu Qili was dismissed from the Politburo along with Zhao Ziyang.)

Only after martial law was declared on 20 May did the Australian and Canadian governments, like other Western governments, openly press the leadership in Beijing to maintain a non-violent course. On 20 May, the Mulroney government immediately issued a statement urging the Chinese government to exercise restraint and avoid using force.[39] Two days later, Australia's minister for foreign affairs, Senator Gareth Evans, issued a statement on the 'current crisis,' expressing his government's 'strong hope that it can be resolved without violence and with respect for fundamental human rights.' Evans pointedly made reference to the Australian relationship with China in the previous decade, expressing the hope that the situation could be resolved without jeopardizing either the policies of openness and reform or the growing Sino-Australian relationship that had been built on it.[40]

In private, however, both governments had taken the lead among Western states in pressing the Chinese leadership to settle the growing dispute with the students peacefully. When it became clear that the protests would interfere with the state visit of Mikhail S. Gorbachev, the president of the Soviet Union, to Beijing on 15 May, and seriously embarrass the Chinese leadership, both governments were out in front of other Western countries in delivering explicit warnings to the Chinese leadership of the consequences of violent repression. Like many other Western governments, both Australia and Canada were growing increasingly concerned about the possibility of violence. As a result, officials consulted other Western governments and continued to make their hopes for a peaceful resolution of the dispute known to the Chinese, through both their ambassadors in Beijing and the Chinese ambassadors in Canberra and Ottawa. Moreover, the Australian and Canadian ambassadors were in close touch with each other and with several other diplomats in Beijing, including the American, British, German, Indian, and Sri Lankan ambassadors. In addition, embassy evacuation plans were drawn up in the event that the protests resulted in violence.[41]

Despite these private moves, both governments sought to maintain an optimistic front publicly: as late as 29 May, Evans was still assuring the Senate that despite the events in Beijing, the Australian government was committed to ensuring that trade and investment between Australia and China would continue to grow as it had in the past.[42] Likewise, the Canadian and Chinese governments had officially designated May as a mutual 'Friendship Month' – an opportunity to hold a number of promotional activities. The theme adopted by the Canadian embassy in Beijing for the promotion was 'Sharing Our Future.'[43] Prime Minister Brian Mulroney suggested that the burgeoning demonstrations represented a positive development: two days after the symbolic seventieth anniversary of the 1919 patriotic movement, Mulroney was publicly suggesting that the peaceful transformation under way in China was 'astonishing,' and indicative of a new era in international relations.[44]

The official reticence came to an end as news of the killings in and around Tiananmen Square reached Australia in the early hours of Sunday, 4 June, and Canada (because of the international date line) mid-day on Saturday, 3 June. Like many other governments,[45] Australia and Canada sought to respond to these events with a mixture of rhetorical criticism and punitive measures.

Canadian reactions[46]

The lead for the Canadian government was taken by the secretary of state for external affairs, Joe Clark; it was not until Monday, two days afterwards, that Prime Minister Brian Mulroney commented publicly on the massacre, claiming that he was 'outraged' and 'appalled' by the use of force.[47] Until the G-7 summit in July, Mulroney maintained a low public profile on Tiananmen, even though he was involved on a daily basis in the decision-making on China policy. The rhetoric embraced by Clark reflected a mounting anger as the extent of the violence in Beijing became known.

On Saturday, Clark's rhetoric mirrored the tentative reactions of the United States. President George Bush, from his summer home in Kennebunkport, Maine, initially greeted news of the massacre with a statement that he 'deeply deplored' the use of force and urged 'a return to non-violent means' to resolve the conflict. Secretary of State James Baker, interviewed on CNN, refused to say if the United States would impose sanctions, claiming that he did not want to 'interfere in China's internal affairs.' This tentative reaction produced what the *New York Times* called a 'galloping Congressional movement for immediate action,' with such key members of Congress as Senator Alan Cranston, chair of the Senate subcommittee on Asia Pacific Affairs; Jesse Helms, ranking Republican on the Senate Foreign Affairs Committee; Representative Stephen J. Solarz, chair of the House subcommittee on Asia Pacific Affairs; and Representative Mickey Edwards, chair of the Republican Policy Committee in the House, all pressing for a stronger response.[48]

Clark's initial statements were similar: he indicated the Canadian government's abhorrence and 'great regret' at the use of force. By Sunday, however, Clark was claiming that the attacks were 'inexcusable' and demanding that the government in Beijing stop the 'senseless killing.' Indeed, so harsh was Clark's statement on Sunday that the Liberal external-affairs critic, André Ouellet, approvingly called it one of the toughest statements he had ever heard from a Canadian government.[49] By Monday, Clark was declaring in Parliament that the events in Beijing had filled him with a 'deeply-felt sense of horror and outrage.' Calling the 'indiscriminate and brutal' shooting of citizens a 'tragedy of global proportions,' he urged that the House 'unequivocally condemn this brutal use of force against the peaceful populace of Beijing.'[50]

The government also moved to back up its rhetorical condemnation with several concrete responses. On Sunday, Clark had summoned the Chinese ambassador in Ottawa, Zhang Wenpu, to the Department of External Affairs, where the acting under-secretary of state for external affairs, Raymond Chrétien, lodged Canada's protest and condemnation of the use of force. On Monday, the government indicated that it was advising the six hundred Canadian residents in Beijing, together with the seventy-five Canadian students and an undetermined number of tourists and business people, to leave the Chinese capital. It also set up a toll-free 800 telephone 'hot line' number to External Affairs so that Canadians with relatives in China could get information, and began negotiations to evacuate Canadian nationals, seeking permission to fly a Canadian Forces Boeing 707 into Harbin and several other Chinese cities to evacuate Canadian students. While the Chinese foreign ministry agreed to allow an evacuation, the Chinese military denied permission for the Canadian Forces plane to land. In the end, the Australian and Canadian governments agreed to help each other with the evacuation of their nationals: Canadian Airlines International, which at that time was servicing the Canada-China route, laid on three extra flights free of charge to help in the evacuation.[51]

The government also announced measures affecting the 6800 Chinese students in Canada, claiming that Ottawa would be 'sympathetic' to any requests to extend their stay 'until calm returns to their homeland' and that all deportations to China under the Immigration Act would be suspended for two months.[52]

In the House of Commons, Clark tabled a resolution condemning 'the use of excessive and indiscriminate armed force on a scale and scope which appals all Canadians' and calling on 'the authorities of China to cease this senseless killing and immediately adopt a course of dialogue with the people of China.' He also set up External Affairs briefings for Members of Parliament. This approach generated strong bipartisan support: the government's motion was seconded by both the leader of the Opposition, John Turner, and the leader of the New Democratic Party, Ed Broadbent. Clark's speech was given a standing ovation by members on both sides of the House.[53]

In addition, Ottawa imposed a series of punitive sanctions on China. These included the following:

1 All official events planned for the near future would be deferred or cancelled.

2 Memorandums of understanding on five development assistance projects, worth about C$60 million, which had been scheduled to be signed that week, would remain unsigned.

3 Nuclear cooperation consultations, due to begin after China joined the International Atomic Energy Agency, would be suspended.

4 All other consultations would also be suspended.

5 All provincial governments and non-governmental organizations would be advised to impose similar suspensions on dealings with their Chinese counterparts.

6 Although no high-level visits were expected or planned, the government announced that all potential visits would be put off 'until a more appropriate time.'

7 The Canadian permanent representative at the United Nations would be instructed to begin multilateral consultations on ways of bringing the moral suasion of the UN to bear on the Chinese leadership.

8 Although Canada had no bilateral military cooperation agreement with China, and although there were no arms sales to the Chinese military, Clark none the less affirmed that Canada would not engage in such sales; moreover, the modest program of defence relations between the People's Liberation Army and the Canadian Forces – basically consisting of a visit by the Canadian Chief of Defence Staff to China in 1988 – would be suspended indefinitely.[54]

This initial response was followed a week later by further punitive measures. The first was a decision to delay the showing of a film produced by the National Film Board of Canada, *The First Emperor*, at the gala opening of the newly constructed National Museum of Civilization in Ottawa. The reason for this measure was simple: the film was a C$7 million project co-produced by Chinese film-makers. This sanction was quickly hailed as a 'silly decision' that was, in the words of the *Ottawa Citizen*, 'pathetic, parochial, so quintessentially Canada.'[55]

A more serious measure was the decision to recall Earl Drake, Canada's ambassador to China, as an 'indication of disapproval' (as Clark put it[56]) of the Chinese government's actions. This diplomatic sanction had been urged on the government from the outset by a number of voices in Canada: the organizers of a protest in Toronto on 4 June; an *Ottawa Citizen* editorial on 6 June; and Howard McCurdy, the New Democratic Party MP who led off the emergency debate in the House of Commons on 5 June. In his speech, McCurdy suggested that the government should consider withdrawing the ambassador if the situation in Beijing did not improve.[57] Drake himself acknowledged that External Affairs had considered withdrawing him on the weekend of the massacre, but that he had requested that he be left in place until the airlift of Canadians had been completed.[58] There was an additional concern, expressed to Drake by several envoys in Beijing: it was feared that a recall of the Canadian envoy would precipitate a band-wagon effect and would prompt other states to withdraw their ambassadors. There was, however, another and more pragmatic reason for the withdrawal: the government had decided to undertake a full review of the relationship with China, and Drake's participation in that process was deemed essential.[59] As part of the review, the government convened a ministerial round table to which members of the Chinese-Canadian community, academics, and other people with an interest or an expertise in China were invited.

The results of that review were announced on 30 June: in a broad-ranging statement, Joe Clark outlined the refinement of Canadian policies towards China generally and of Ottawa's post-Tiananmen sanctions in particular.[60] He sought to be explicit about the assumptions the Canadian government was using to guide policy on China. First, Clark asserted that future policy would be based on the assumption that Tiananmen Square had changed the nature of the Sino-Canadian relationship, and that it would not therefore be 'business as usual' with China. However, the government valued the 'friendship' between the two peoples: Clark stressed that Canada would not become 'anti-China.' Moreover, the government in Ottawa would 'try to avoid measures that would push China towards isolation.' Finally, an attempt would be made to 'maximize the impact' of sanctions by coordinating these measures with like-minded countries.

Given these assumptions, Clark argued, Canadian policy initiatives would be assessed according to three broad criteria. First, because Sino-Canadian linkages were valued, existing links were to be preserved 'to the extent possible.' However, any new initiatives in the relationship should focus on people-to-people exchanges. And finally, 'programs which benefit or lend prestige to the current hardline policies of the Chinese government, most particularly the military or state propaganda apparatus' would be 'avoided.'

Further sanctions were announced in the 30 June statement. Ottawa decided to withdraw from three development assistance projects that it claimed failed to meet the new criteria: a lubrication-oil centre in the city of Lanzhou in the western province of Gansu; a training program for state auditors; and a training program for urban traffic management. The traffic-management program was apparently terminated because authorities in Beijing had used traffic-monitoring cameras installed under a British-sponsored traffic-management project to spy on demonstrators.[61] Four of the five development assistance agreements whose signing had been postponed on 5 June would be kept on hold; only a C$7.5 million project linking community colleges would be signed. All Canadian activity associated with the massive (and environmentally contentious) Three Gorges hydroelectric project – a C$13 million pre-feasibility study, paid for by the Canadian International Development Agency – would be suspended indefinitely. It should be noted, however, that the project was in a state of suspension even before the Canadian announcement: in April 1989, the Chinese government had announced that it would not be taking a decision on the project for five years.[62] Funding for a television transmission tower (a facility 'clearly supportive of China's state propaganda apparatus'), which was to have been paid for out of an existing $2.3 billion Export Development Corporation line of credit to China, would be cancelled. Consideration would be given to halting the liberalization of the COCOM (Coordinating Committee on Multilateral Export Controls) sanctions against China.[63] Funding for trade shows would be halted for the balance of 1989, and trade representation in Beijing would be downgraded. The Canadian Broadcasting Corporation would be asked to suspend its joint-production cooperation with Chinese state radio and television.

The announcement of these sanctions was, however, accompanied by an encouragement to Canadian provinces, municipalities, and non-governmental organizations to maintain their ties with China (reversing the government's earlier position). Clark claimed that the maintenance of 'people-to-people links' was particularly important: 'The more contacts people from all walks of life in China can have with their Canadian and other friends, the less likely the success of the onslaught of the hardline propaganda machine.' Moreover, additional measures for the Chinese students in Canada were put in place, notably the provision for extensions of student visas for a year.

Australian reactions[64]

The responses of the government of Bob Hawke were not dissimilar to those of the Mulroney government in Canada. Indeed, they were even structured like the Canadian sanctions: an immediate set of responses that eventually included setting in train a full-scale review of the relationship with China, which in turn was followed some weeks later by a refinement of policy.

The news first broke in Australia early on Sunday morning. (It is useful, when comparing the first Australian and Canadian reactions to Tiananmen, to keep the international dateline in mind. North Americans, roughly half a day ahead of Beijing, first learned of the massacre during the day on Saturday; in Australia, the news came in on Sunday morning. Thus, when reactions are reported in local time, it can at first appear that Canadians were quicker off the mark than others. Indeed, it was a source of considerable pride to officials in Ottawa that Clark had been the first foreign minister to issue a condemnatory statement and that Canada had been one of the first governments to call in the Chinese ambassador in Ottawa, Zhang Wenpu, to hear the Canadian protest – at noon on Sunday. By contrast, the ambassador in Canberra, Zhang Zai, was not called in by the Australian government until Monday morning. However, when the reactions are measured in hours after receipt of the news, there was little difference in the speed of the two responses.)

Hawke's first response was to 'deeply regret and deplore' the attack. Like Bush, who also 'deeply deplored' the use of force in Tiananmen Square, Hawke avoided using the stronger diplomatic word 'condemn' to characterize Australia's official reaction. He also expressed the hope that the massacre was a 'temporary aberration.' He indicated that he had instructed the Australian ambassador in Beijing, David Sadleir, to inform the Chinese government that Australia 'could not accept' the deaths of the students. But when asked about trade with China, or sanctions, Hawke responded that it was 'too early' to talk about trade sanctions. However, the prime minister did cancel a goodwill visit to Shanghai by an Australian naval vessel, HMAS *Parramatta*, which was to have occurred later in the week.[65] The Department of Foreign Affairs and Trade (DFAT) immediately issued a travel advisory to Australians, urging them to postpone all travel to China. In Beijing, the Australian embassy began sending cars for students from Australia, New Zealand, and Papua New Guinea, and one student from Fiji; they were sheltered in the embassy before the evacuation that was being arranged with other Western states.[66]

As noted above, on Monday morning, Zhang Zai, the Chinese ambassador in Canberra, was summoned to Parliament House to hear the minister himself convey Australia's critical reaction. Gareth Evans told Zhang that Canberra was 'deeply distressed' at the abandonment of restraint and 'profoundly deplored' the 'brutally excessive use of force against peaceful demonstrators.'[67] Like both the Canadian and United States government, Australia also moved to offer some protection to the 15,000 Chinese nationals in Australia. On 6 June, Canberra had moved to extend the visas of all Chinese to 31 July 1989; on 16 June, with the news of student arrests and trials in China, temporary visas were automatically extended to 31 July 1990, and those on these visas were allowed to work twenty hours per week.[68] And like the United States embassy, the Australian embassy in Beijing gave refuge to a Chinese dissident, Hou Dejian.[69] This action, together with the decision in mid-June to grant a Chinese diplomat from the Sydney consulate, Dong Qi, political asylum, prompted strenuous Chinese protests; there were even rumours that China was thinking of severing diplomatic relations with Australia.[70]

It was several days before parliament registered a formal opinion, however. The House of Representatives was not sitting and MHRs were not due to return to Canberra until 15 June. Although the Senate was sitting, and though Evans did brief the upper chamber on the situation in China on 5 and 6 June before he left for a trip to India and Europe, it was not until Thursday, 8 June, that the government introduced a motion condemning 'the massive and indiscriminate slaughter' and calling on the authorities in Beijing to 'commence a process of open and democratic consultation with the Chinese people.' A similar motion was introduced by the prime minister when the House returned on 15 June.[71]

While Parliament may have been slow in issuing a formal condemnation, there were several opportunities for other expressions of official Australian opinion. For example, at the end of that week, the prime minister attended the nation-wide memorial ceremony, which in Canberra was held in the Great Hall of Parliament House. Hawke's performance left in little doubt his own emotionalism on the issue. Calling his appearance at the memorial service 'the saddest and the most compelling duty I have had to perform as prime minister,' he bitterly condemned the Chinese government for 'crush[ing] the spirit and body of youth.' He read excerpts from a diplomatic despatch from the Australian embassy in Beijing that recounted in exceedingly graphic detail an eyewitness account of the slaughter in the square that evening.[72] During his speech Hawke wept openly, and at the conclusion he stood for several minutes in a tearful embrace with a representative of Chinese students in Australia.

The Australian government also adopted several concrete measures to protest the massacre. The initial sanctions imposed by the government in Canberra almost exclusively fell into the category of cancellations or suspensions of upcoming events:[73]

1 An official visit by Hawke to China, which had been planned for October, was cancelled.
2 The visit of HMAS *Parramatta* to Shanghai was cancelled.
3 The visit to Australia of a nineteen-member joint delegation from the Chinese Ministry of Foreign Economic Relations and Trade and the Foreign Finance Administration, due to begin on 10–11 June, was cancelled.
4 All further ministerial visits between the two countries were cancelled until further notice.[74]

Other sanctions, while they were being pressed on the government, were rejected at this juncture. In particular, the government persistently refused demands from opposition parties and others to recall David Sadleir, the Australian ambassador to Beijing, as 'a minimum diplomatic protest,' as a Liberal party critic for foreign affairs in the House, Ian Macphee, put it. Evans and other ministers argued that such a move would be 'inappropriate,' since Australian interests would be better served by a diplomatic presence in Beijing.[75] As noted above, Hawke himself rejected trade sanctions from the outset, claiming that cutting trade links would drive China into isolation, and thus would be counterproductive.

Likewise, Australia's A$36 million development assistance program to China was not affected, despite the widespread calls for the use of aid sanctions. Calls for freezing aid came from Andrew Peacock, leader of the Opposition;[76] Robert Hill, the opposition foreign-affairs critic, and John Spender, his predecessor.[77] In addition, the Australian Council for Overseas Aid, the peak organization that oversees Australia's NGO activities in international development assistance, also called for aid sanctions.[78] Two former Australian ambassadors to China, Stephen FitzGerald, ambassador between 1973 and 1976, and Garry Woodard, a former ambassador to both China and Burma, called for using aid freezes.[79] Even the government's own caucus was plumping for an aid suspension: the ALP Caucus Foreign Affairs, Trade and Defence Committee was pressing the front bench to reassess the Australian aid program with a view to suspending it.[80]

Despite this pressure, the Hawke government was unmoved. One project was suspended at the end of June for logistical reasons: two weeks after Tiananmen, the Australian International Development Assistance Bureau (AIDAB) announced that its forestry education program on the Sino-Vietnamese border would be 'suspended' for as long as the Department of Foreign Affairs and Trade travel advisory remained in place.[81]

Calls for stronger action mounted after the Chinese authorities began putting demonstrators on trial on 16 June and sentencing them to death. The execution of three of protestors in Shanghai on 21 June, over the objections of many governments, prompted the Bush administration in Washington to impose an additional range of sanctions. By this time, however, Hawke was out of the country on a long-planned visit to Bonn, London, Paris, and Washington. The overseas trip came at a useful time in the evolution of Australian policies towards China, since it afforded Hawke the opportunity to exchange views with other Western leaders.[82] The trip also provided the impetus for the harmonization of Canberra's China policies with those of other Western countries. Because of the prime minister's absence, the government decided to delay further action on China. Instead, DFAT was ordered to prepare a report on Australian policy towards China to be presented to cabinet on Hawke's return.[83]

On 13 July, Gareth Evans revealed the results of the review. Twelve decisions were announced:

1 The government would continue to make 'vigorous' representations to China on human rights issues.
2 It would 'maintain 'an appreciably downgraded relationship' by suspending ministerial visits for the balance of 1989.
3 Official contacts at the senior level would be 'severely' constrained until the end of 1989, 'except those of a narrowly economic or commercial nature.'
4 All party and parliamentary visits would be suspended for the remainder of 1989.
5 All high-level defence visits (including ship visits) would be suspended indefinitely.
6 All visits by public-security and police officials would be suspended indefinitely, 'except visits considered operationally essential by Australian law-enforcement authorities.'

7 State premiers would be encouraged to adopt comparable policies on visits.

8 Consideration of new technical cooperation and agricultural-research proposals by China would be postponed until further review.

9 The Market Advisory Program for 1989–90 would be suspended.

10 New aid proposals under the Concessional Finance Facility/ Develpment Import Finance Facility would not be accepted until further review.

11 Australia would support initiatives of international financial institutions to defer consideration of new loans to China.

12 Further liberalization of COCOM regulations would be opposed.[84]

Like Clark, Evans sought to lay out the underlying assumptions of these refinements of Australian policy. First, he acknowledged that it was imperative that Australia 'signals its abhorrence' and 'strongly condemns' the human rights violations: 'An easy or early return to "business as usual" is, in the aftermath of the Beijing massacre, simply not an option.'

At the same time, Evans asserted that Australian policy was driven by a commitment to 'a long-term cooperative relationship with China,' and thus the government actively sought to avoid 'action which would harm the Chinese people, further turn the country in upon itself and stifle the pressures of reform.' The Australian government would 'try to keep open as many channels of access and communication as possible, with as many segments of Chinese society as possible.' For these reasons, Evans argued, there would no cuts to the existing aid program or limits on cultural, economic, and student exchanges. Finally, Evans noted that the government's approach was also shaped by its recognition of Australia's 'limited' capacity to influence events in China unilaterally. Thus, Canberra had taken 'closely into account the reactions of like-minded countries' in drawing up its broad policy approach.

EXPLAINING THE POST-TIANANMEN SANCTIONS

The sanctions embraced by the Australian and Canadian governments in the immediate aftermath of Tiananmen bore all the hallmarks of symbolic, rather than instrumental, purposes. In other words, neither Canberra nor Ottawa embraced sanctions in order to try to change the future behaviour of the Chinese leadership by deterrence or compellence, but rather for purely symbolic reasons.

It is difficult to argue that Australian and Canadian sanctions were designed to have a deterrent effect on the Chinese government – in other words, to deter the leadership in Beijing from using force to suppress demonstrations again.[85] For the wrongful behaviour had already occurred, and was unlikely to recur. The regime's very willingness to order tanks and troops to fire on students made it unlikely that such tactics would have to be used again, for they utterly crushed the demonstrators and reasserted the power of the leadership.

Australian or Canadian sanctions might have been designed to compel China – in other words, to prompt the leadership to abandon its hard line, welcome the demonstrators and their symbolic figurine back to Tiananmen Square, and generally 'embrace democracy' – but, again, it is highly unlikely. It is true that in most sanctions episodes, the sender wittingly or unwittingly embraces the compellent purpose by linking sanctions to the future behaviour of the target – usually by insisting that sanctions will only be lifted when the wrong behaviour that provoked the imposition of sanctions in the first place ceases. But, judging by the governments' own rhetoric, compellent purposes were not part of the Australian or Canadian sanctions imposed on China after Tiananmen. Indeed, most of the Australian sanctions were even limited in time, designed to allow the frozen relations to resume automatically (and inconspicuously) at the end of 1989, thus avoiding the 'termination trap' into which international sanctioners so frequently fall (which is discussed at greater length below in chapter 10).

A further indication of the symbolic rather than instrumental purpose of these sanctions was the nature of the measures themselves. Aspects of the relationships were 'suspended' or 'frozen,' not terminated or broken. Visits were cancelled. But key segments of both relationships, such as trade and investment, were not seriously touched. Moreover, 'people-to-people' contacts were maintained, and indeed encouraged. In the opinion of one commentator, these measures did 'not amount to very much';[86] certainly they were not designed to impose sufficient hurts on China to prompt the government in Beijing to change its behaviour.

What, then, were the purposes of these sanctions if not deterrence or compellence? Domestic symbolism inexorably suggests itself: these sanctions, it might at first be supposed, were designed to soothe the anger of domestic groups and meet their insistent demands for punitive action – but in a way that essentially preserved the relationship. It might be argued that these sanctions reflected an attempt by both the Hawke government in Canberra and the Mulroney government in Ottawa to balance conflicting objectives. On the one hand, the palpable anger of the domestic environment in both Australia and Canada was so great that a soft response would have been difficult politically. On the other hand, both governments were trying to avoid seriously disrupting the relationship with China that had been so carefully nurtured over the previous two decades. For both governments had compelling economic and strategic reasons for wanting to take the longer view of the relationship with China. Both foreign ministers sought to outline as explicitly as possible these reasons in their various statements during June 1989.[87] Thus, the measures both governments adopted were designed, quite explicitly, to do as little damage to the respective relationships as possible.

But these sanctions were more than simply the result of the two governments managing demands being expressed by domestic groups in each country: as I have sought to show above, the gap between the sanctions domestic groups were urging on their governments, and those the governments were embracing was simply too large. This gap suggests that both governments had not only their own separate preferences on China that differed from those of most domestic groups, but also a willingness to impose their own preferences without regard for the supposed twin domestic symbolic purposes that seek to 'increase political support' and 'avoid criticism.' Rather, I would argue that both governments adopted the particular sanctions mix they did for reasons that had little to do with the pressures of domestic groups.

First, we should not forget that Australian and Canadian policy-makers were disposed to punish the Chinese leadership in some way for Tiananmen, a desire that existed independently of the pressures of the domestic environment. As I have argued elsewhere,[88] we should not underestimate the personal and visceral reaction of political leaders and their bureaucratic advisers when confronted with wrong-doing by other governments. Policy-makers may be constrained by their political roles, and by the responsibilities of the offices they occupy, to eschew emotionalism, embrace *Realpolitik*, and take a pragmatic 'longer view' of the international relationships they are charged with managing. But such propensities will surely not diminish their own emotional responses to acts they regard as outrageous, horrifying, or wrongful. They will experience not only anger at the wrong, but also that most universal of human urges, the desire to do harm to wrong-doers. And sanctions, to the extent that they harm the target, more than adequately fulfil the symbolic purpose of punishment.

Moreover, it can be argued that in this case the anger of Australian and Canadian political leaders was a special kind of anger – the intense anger that comes with betrayal by a friend. There can be little doubt that by 1989 there was a widespread perception in both Australia and Canada that China was a 'friend' in international politics, a country – and a government – that could be counted on to behave in a friendly way. Evidence that this 'friendly' government in Beijing was capable of ordering – and then openly justifying – such behaviour as was evidenced on the night of 3–4 June made the reaction all the more bitter.[89]

The theme of betrayal was particularly evident in parliamentary debates. Many of the MPs participating in the debates in both Canberra and Ottawa voiced a similar line: how they had visited China, and how warm were the ties of friendship – until 4 June, that is, when the 'real' face of the Chinese leadership revealed itself to have betrayed that trust and friendship. Nor did the leaders of either government make much effort to hide comparable emotions, though it was more in evidence in Australia than in Canada. Such emotions were clearly evident in Bob Hawke's tearful address at the Parliament House memorial service, or his plea to the leadership in Beijing to save the life of the purged general secretary of the Chinese Communist Party, Zhao Ziyang (whom Hawke had come to regard as a personal friend).[90] It has been suggested that Hawke's warm relationship with China – backed up by such concrete measures as setting aside for China half of Canberra's A$400 million concessional development loan allocation, or taking a hard line on Taiwan – was the 'foreign policy initiative he holds most dearly,' and thus Tiananmen was an even more 'shattering' betrayal to him.[91] For his part, Joe Clark was less emotionally committed to China than many of the Australians, but he none the less bitterly denounced China on 4 June and in his speech to the Commons the next day.

Such anger, which was directed at the Chinese leadership personally, goes some distance to explaining the apparent inconsistency of the main thrust of the Australian and Canadian sanctions: cancelling visits, high-level contacts, and suspending some aspects of the government-to-government relationship while encouraging other relations to continue, including 'people-to-people' contacts and economic relations. To be sure, this approach was in part designed to ensure that visits and contacts could not be misrepresented by anyone as endorsements of the regime.[92] But it went beyond this: such a bifurcated approach reflected the hunt for what might be thought of as 'surgical sanctions' – sanctions that were sufficiently precise that they would 'hurt' the leaders who authorized the army to suppress the protestors so violently, but not the 'people' of China. Finally, it should be noted that in part this approach was designed to ensure that political leaders could urge that important elements of the relationship (that is, the actual 'people-to-people' linkages) be maintained, while they themselves could avoid having to deal officially with those responsible for Tiananmen – shake their hands, make after-dinner toasts at dinners in their honour, and generally engage in the pleasantries of diplomacy.

Second, trying to explain Australian and Canadian sanctions policies by reference to internal pressures misses the degree to which these policies were also shaped in coordination with other governments. For the Australian and Canadian reactions as they evolved in June and July 1989 must be placed within a wider, multilateral, and essentially Western context, one in which there was a constant exchange of cues between and among Western states as they sought to coordinate their behaviour.

Some of the initial cues, for example, came from the first reactions of the Bush administration as it scrambled to keep up with congressional criticism. The American bans on high-level contacts and military sales then rippled through the sanctions policies of other countries. Other cues came from the Europeans, who favoured limited investment bans. Sometimes, however, the lead was taken by countries like Canada, which adopted such additional sanctions as the suspension of development assistance projects or the recall of the ambassador in protest well ahead of the United States or the Europeans.

But, in general, all Western states placed a premium on common action, and went to some lengths to coordinate their behaviour. Thus, for example, reluctant sanctioners like Japan allowed themselves to be dragged into the symbolic fold, as occurred at the G-7 summit meeting in Paris in mid-July. For smaller states like Canada and Australia, this process of 'coordinating' the Western response had a considerable impact on the nature of their sanctions.

For example, although Ottawa was one of the more active sanctionists, it none the less also sanctioned aspects of the Sino-Canadian relationship that were not even there to disrupt. In early June, there were no high-level visits planned or in prospect, nor were there sales of military equipment; Clark none the less included these in Canada's sanctions package. Likewise, such measures as opposition to COCOM liberalization, the suspension of concessional financing, and the downgrading of marketing programs had not been pressed on the government by domestic groups, but appeared in Ottawa's sanctions on 30 June – shortly after the announcement of similar measures by the European Community (EC).

In the Australian case, there were high-level visits in the offing, and these were cancelled immediately. But the Australian government also placed a premium on like-mindedness, and that meant bringing Canberra's sanctions policies into line with those of other Western states – despite its own scarcely concealed reservations about the utility of any punitive measure that went beyond cancelling high-level visits. For example, a DFAT working paper, produced on 16 June as part of the review of Australian policy, argued that the government should take a 'soft' approach to China – that relations should be maintained in order to maintain Australian influence and to retain Australia's 'good trade prospects.'[93] This reluctance was underscored by Hawke himself at the end of June. Following meetings with Bush shortly after the United States intensified its sanctions following the Shanghai executions, Hawke expressed optimism that there would be no need for further sanctions.[94] The process of 'coordination' inexorably pulled the Hawke government into embracing a tougher sanctionist line. The measures announced by Canberra on 13 July – merely three days before the G-7 summit leaders in Paris embraced similar sanctions – mirrored sanctions imposed over the previous month by the United States, Britain, the EC, and Canada.

CONCLUSION

I have argued that the post-Tiananmen sanctions embraced by Australia and Canada in 1989 can be better explained by examining factors other than the domestic pressures that were so palpably urging the governments in Canberra and Ottawa to adopt a hard sanctionist line against China. We have seen that although the Canadian and Australian approaches to post-Tiananmen sanctions differed somewhat – Canada being one of the most sanctions-prone of the Western countries and Australia being one of the more reluctant – neither government adopted anything close to a harsh and stiff sanctionist line against China. This is not to suggest that there was not a desire to punish the leadership in Beijing for having authorized the use of force. On the contrary, I have suggested that policy-makers in both Canberra and Ottawa were indeed moved by the desire to punish. But the measures that were invoked tended to be surgical sanctions – aimed at as narrowly defined a target as possible. These sanctions were designed to keep as much of the relationship intact as possible; they were also designed to be lifted smoothly – and soon.

Such an approach hardly mirrored the demands that were being articulated by numerous groups and individuals in both Australia and Canada. To the insistent calls for harsh measures – full trade or aid sanctions, for example – both governments remained as insistently deaf. This imperviousness has implications for the general argument about the symbolic purposes of sanctions, however. We noted at the outset that at first blush the case of the post-Tiananmen sanctions appears as an archetypal example of the domestic symbolic purpose at work: palpably disturbed domestic environments, with reluctant governments moving to embrace sanctions – not to have any effect on the target, but simply to 'deflect criticism' and 'maximize political support,' as Lindsay would have it.

I have argued that, on the contrary, the evidence suggests that the sanctions approach of the governments in Canberra and Ottawa was shaped by several factors and often conflicting desires: to punish the leadership in Beijing; to save as much of the relationship with China as possible; to avoid the discomfort of dealing with the Chinese leadership; and to produce as much 'like-mindedness' as possible among the Western states.

9

'Give Them a Chance':
Sanctions in the Gulf Conflict, 1990–1

In many of the other cases of Australian and Canadian sanctions explored in this book, I have demonstrated the degree to which coalition membership has been a determining factor in shaping the evolution of the policies of these two countries. The sanctions that were imposed against Iraq after its invasion, occupation, and annexation of Kuwait after 2 August 1990 provide yet another example of this dynamic at work: both Australian and Canadian policies towards the invasion of Kuwait were heavily determined by the membership of these countries in the broad international coalition consisting of thirty-six states from six continents and all four points of the compass that the United States administration of President George Bush decided to organize in response to the invasion.

However, the Gulf conflict of 1990–1 provides us with an interesting twist. In this case, both countries became involved in the sanctions against Iraq convinced that their involvement would go no further than international sanctions. Given the wide participation of the international community in the sanctions effort, and given Iraq's high degree of dependence on international intercourse, the governments in both Canberra and Ottawa had every reason to believe that this would be one of those rare cases where sanctions would actually have instrumental effects. In other words, there was a widespread belief that sanctions, applied hard and effectively by the vast majority of states in the international system, would soon coerce Iraq into withdrawing from Kuwait; alternatively, following the assumptions of the 'naive theory,' it was believed that these measures would prompt domestic opponents to overthrow Saddam Hussein.

Indeed, the sanctions invoked against Iraq quickly became central to the debates about the Gulf conflict in both Australia and Canada. In particular, those opposing the use of force to bring the Iraqi occupation of Kuwait to an end argued strenuously that the multinational coalition should give the sanctions more time to work before resorting to force.

However, I will argue in this chapter that right from the beginning sanctions were in fact peripheral to the efforts of the multinational coalition's attempts to coerce or subvert Iraq into a withdrawal. Opponents of the war option in both Australia and Canada might argue that sanctions should be given time, and it is quite true, as Richard Leaver has argued, that there were opportunity costs in moving to a more forceful option.[1] But there can be little doubt that the multinational coalition to which both Australia and Canada belonged had already been led, right from the very beginning, in another direction.

As we have seen in other sanctions cases, being a member of a coalition creates a dynamic for the coalition members that binds them tightly to the preferences of the coalition's leader once they have joined. Once the leader has gathered a coalition around itself, it can radically alter the preferences of the coalition as a whole, relying on its superordinate power to keep the smaller members with it, regardless of their preferences. Like a rider on a roller coaster, the junior coalition partner, once aboard, has few options: there is no stopping the ride; getting off may be possible theoretically but involves such massive costs as to make it totally impractical; and, most important, it makes no difference whether or not the rider actually enjoys the ride as it unfolds, perhaps in ways not anticipated at the outset.

The case of Australian and Canadian participation in the Gulf coalition demonstrates this dynamic at work. When one sets an examination of the process of decision about sanctions within the context of United States policy, it can be argued that these middle powers joined the coalition believing that they were joining a multilateral coalition that was going to advance conceptions of world order by using international sanctions to impose a non-offensive and non-violent blockade against the violating state. We will see, however, that the purposes of the coalition shifted over the course of the conflict, pulling the coalition into a situation that had only been dimly anticipated by both governments in August 1990.

THE INVASION AND THE AMERICAN RESPONSE

The Bush administration decided on its approach towards the invasion of Kuwait in the first hours of the crisis.[2] The National Security Council convened early on the morning of 2 August, and decided not to accept the invasion. By all accounts, Bush's hard line on the invasion was prompted by two factors. The first was a visit from the British prime minister, Margaret Thatcher, who apparently pressed the president to respond vigorously to the Iraqi action. The second was that Bush appears to have been caught by the ratcheting-up effect of his own rhetoric. During a press conference on 5 August, the president became visibly more heated as questions were put to him, leading to his angry, and apparently unrehearsed, declaration: 'I view very seriously our determination to reverse out [sic] this aggression ... This will not stand. This will not stand, this aggression against Kuwait.'[3]

Bush's goals thus coalesced early in the crisis, and the strategy pursued by the United States government followed these goals. The American strategy to secure an Iraqi withdrawal proceeded along several tracks. First, Washington sought to move Iraq by economic strangulation: freezing assets and imposing economic sanctions. Another track was diplomatic: to widen international condemnation of the Iraqi move and secure international support for the sanctions net. A third track was to order the Central Intelligence Agency to begin a campaign of subversion against Hussein.

The fourth, and most important, was the military track. Early in the crisis, Bush decided to seek to deploy American ground, air, and naval forces to the Gulf region. The role of the American forces, even in the planning phase, was always ambiguous. Once they were in position, these forces could be used for numerous purposes: to deter a possible Iraqi attack on Saudi Arabia; to aid in imposing a blockade on Iraq to make sanctions as leak-proof as possible; to stage a demonstration of American power designed to coerce Baghdad into withdrawing; and, of course, actually to secure an Iraqi withdrawal from Kuwait by force.

The success of the diplomatic, economic, and military tracks depended heavily on coalition-building. In the first instance, other governments had to be convinced to refuse to accept the take-over of Kuwait as a fait accompli that could not be reversed. Likewise, a policy of economic strangulation depended on casting the sanctions net as widely, and as tightly, as possible. Finally, and most important, Washington's plan to deploy military forces in the Gulf depended on multilateral support. While technically the United States could have deployed its forces with the cooperation of but one state – Saudi Arabia, where the forces would be based – the Bush administration recognized that a military deployment would be most effective if it had a broad base, ideally including other Arab states.

The administration thus embarked on a concerted effort to secure support for economic sanctions and contributions to the military deployment. Bush conducted much of this diplomacy himself, mostly by telephone. Other senior officials, including the secretary of state, James Baker, the secretary of defense, Dick Cheney, and the permanent representative at the UN, Thomas Pickering, also were active in rallying international support.

By the end of the first week, there were two distinct coalitions of states ranged against Iraq. One had taken only five days to emerge – that large group of states (including all members of the Security Council but Yemen and Cuba) participating in sanctions against Iraq. Some of these states had moved to impose sanctions bilaterally immediately after 2 August; other measures were imposed under the auspices of the UN Security Council Resolution 661, passed on 6 August.

The other coalition was in a more nascent form by the end of the first week. It consisted of those states contributing military units to an emergent coalition being built around the initial deployment of American and British naval units to the Gulf. Both Britain and France had indicated their willingness to use naval forces to blockade Iraq, and indeed, on 6 August, Thatcher committed British naval forces for that purpose. By 8 August, Saudi Arabia had issued its 'request' for American military assistance.[4] The night Saudi approval was secured, Bush announced his decision to send air and ground forces to Saudi Arabia. This action served to catalyse the growth of this second coalition: it triggered numerous commitments of forces from other states, including the commitment of ground troops by members of the Arab League and naval forces by members of the North Atlantic Treaty Organization (NATO). The size of this coalition would grow over the course of the crisis, so that as of 17 January 1991, thirty-six states were contributing units to the coalition: Argentina, Australia, Bahrain, Bangladesh, Belgium, Canada, Czechoslovakia, Denmark, Egypt, France, Greece, Hungary, Italy, Kuwait, Morocco, the Netherlands, New Zealand, Niger, Norway, Oman, Pakistan, Philippines, Poland, Qatar, Romania, Saudi Arabia, Senegal, Spain, Sierra Leone, Singapore, South Korea, Sweden, Syria, the United Arab Emirates, the United Kingdom, and the United States. To these governmental contributions can be added the several hundred Afghani *mujahideen* who joined the coalition in a private capacity.

It should be noted, however, that at this stage the publicly stated purpose of the military coalition was to deter an Iraqi attack on Saudi Arabia. In his announcement, Bush was at pains to deny that these troops were designed to attack Iraq; rather, the president stressed that 'the mission of our troops is wholly defensive.' Indeed, in his address and the news conference that followed it, Bush reiterated the defensive nature of the deployment no less than nine times.[5] Likewise, the publicly stated purpose of the naval forces was to aid in enforcing the UN sanctions.

AUSTRALIAN AND CANADIAN RESPONSES

The Australian and Canadian policy responses in the first ten days after the invasion reflected the rapid evolution of international reactions. Both governments began cautiously with a rhetorical condemnation, which escalated three days later to unilateral and limited sanctions, and two days after that to multilateral and comprehensive sanctions. And within eight days of the invasion, both middle powers had committed themselves to the military coalition.

Given that there was no clear indication of how other states would react to the invasion, it is hardly surprising that the initial response from both Canberra and Ottawa was limited to condemnation. Both foreign ministers happened to be travelling abroad at the time, but both condemned the invasion in comparable terms on 2 August. Returning to Canada from a visit to the Asia-Pacific region, the secretary of state for external affairs, Joe Clark, termed the aggression against Kuwait 'totally unacceptable'; from India, the Australian minister for foreign affairs, Gareth Evans, called the invasion 'just indefensible.' In both capitals, the Iraqi ambassadors were summoned to the foreign ministries to receive formal protests.[6]

Neither Australia nor Canada rushed to embrace sanctions, however, even though the United States had immediately indicated its intention to impose economic sanctions against Iraq. Indeed, Bush signed the executive orders freezing all Kuwaiti and Iraqi assets in the United States merely nine hours after Iraqi troops began crossing the Kuwaiti border. While Canada took measures to achieve similar results, the process took somewhat longer, for Canadian law does not grant the kind of sweeping powers over foreign assets granted to the president under American law. The only way to control assets in the immediate term was to ask Canada's chartered banks to ensure that the estimated C$3 billion in Kuwaiti investment would not be moved out of the country without the authorization of Kuwait's government-in-exile. By 3 August, Clark indicated that the government had 'made an arrangement' with the Canadian Bankers Association to effectively protect Kuwaiti assets.[7] Although it was no less concerned about protecting the estimated A$1 billion in Kuwaiti assets in Australia, Canberra adopted a different approach: what to do with these assets was tied to the broader question of trade sanctions, and so it was not until other sanctions were imposed that Kuwait's assets in Australia were frozen.[8]

Although the United States had also placed an immediate trade embargo on Iraq, both the Australian and Canadian governments moved more slowly on the trade front. Government officials in both Canberra and Ottawa did make a point of indicating that their countries would abide by any decision on trade sanctions taken by the Security Council (on which Canada was sitting as a non-permanent member), particularly if it employed 'Chapter VII language' – in other words, if it were justified under articles 39-51 (chapter VII) of the United Nations Charter, which outline what steps may be taken by the UN 'with respect to threats to the peace, breaches of the peace, and acts of aggression.'[9]

It is clear, however, that the initial preference of these governments was not to adopt trade sanctions ahead of a wider international decision. This was in large part because of the nature of the trade of these middle powers with Iraq, which not only ran heavily in their favour, but also was dominated by sales of primary products. In 1989, Australian trade with Iraq amounted to A$340 million, a full $327 million of which was in wheat sales. Total imports from Iraq were valued at a minuscule A$199,000, none of which was for petroleum. For Australia imported no oil from Iraq; and its oil purchases from Kuwait accounted for no more than 2 per cent of Australian consumption. Likewise, the live-sheep trade with Kuwait was worth A$81.6 million in 1989.[10]

The Canadian trade picture was similar. In 1989, farmers sold C$245 million in wheat and barley to Iraq, which accounted for 95 per cent of Canada's exports to Iraq. By contrast, Canadian imports from Iraq in 1989 totalled C$61.8 million, mostly in petroleum-related products.[11] But the grain trade in 1990 had been exceptionally profitable: in the first eight months, Iraq had bought approximately 10 per cent of Canada's exports of wheat and barley, the country's main crops.[12]

By the time the United States began its diplomatic push for stricter measures against Iraq, both the Australian and Canadian governments had moved somewhat closer to embracing economic sanctions. On Saturday, 4 August, Mulroney had a long telephone conversation with

Bush 'to review efforts to bring collective international pressure on Iraq to end its occupation of Kuwait.'[13] By Sunday, Canada had imposed the following sanctions on Iraq: oil imports were banned; controls on exports were strengthened; most-favoured-nation status and Export Development Corporation coverage of new business ventures were terminated; trade, academic, cultural, and trade-promotion activities were suspended. However, notably absent from the list was any disruption of Canada's lucrative grain trade with Iraq.

Australian officials also met through the weekend to consider what sanctions might be adopted in response to the United States request; indeed, Evans indicated to reporters in Islamabad on Saturday that he fully expected a decision by the end of the weekend. However, according to one account,[14] officials were unable to agree on a course of action to recommend to cabinet. Instead, when ministers met on Sunday, 5 August, they were presented with little more than lists of options on sanctions. Moreover, there was a split within the cabinet. Favouring sanctions were those ministers with responsibility for foreign affairs – Hawke; the attorney-general, Robert Duffy, who was acting minister for foreign affairs in Evans's absence; Robert Ray, the minister for defence; and, participating from Asia by fax machine and telephone, Evans himself. On the other side were those ministers with economic portfolios – John Kerin, the minister for primary industries and energy; Paul Keating, the treasurer; and John Button, the minister for industry, technology, and commerce.[15] Given the lack of agreement at the official level and lack of enthusiasm from some ministers, cabinet eventually decided to postpone a decision until it was clearer what others were planning to do. As one Australian official said, 'It's pretty pointless to go through with work to invoke sanctions if there is no international support. We have to measure our own policy by what others do.'[16]

As it became clearer in the twenty-four hours after the Sunday postponement that the UN was likely to move on the sanctions question, the Hawke government, like the Mulroney government in Ottawa, did not wait for the UN before making its own move on sanctions. Meeting in the early evening of Monday, 6 August (which was before dawn on the same day in New York), the cabinet took but twenty-five minutes to decide to impose a series of sanctions against Iraq. Included in these sanctions was a freeze on all Kuwaiti assets in Australia; the imposition of an embargo on oil imports from Kuwait and Iraq; the imposition of an embargo on sales of defence-related equipment to Iraq; and, for good measure, the rejection of an Iraqi Airways request to open an office in

Sydney.[17] Like Canada, Australia did not include a ban on grain in these sanctions. Speaking to reporters later, Kerin was blunt about the reasons for Canberra's reluctance: Iraq owed Australian vendors a total of A$600 million from previous wheat sales, including US$380 million in credits insured by the government and A$123 million owed directly to the Australian Wheat Board, and there was a fear that a wheat ban would not only jeopardize future sales, but might prompt Iraq to default on this $600 million.[18]

Whatever reluctance both governments might have been displaying in their sanctions policies disappeared completely when firm international action was taken by the UN on Monday, 6 August. By a vote of 13–0, with Cuba and Yemen abstaining, the Security Council adopted Resolution 661, which invoked the enforcement provisions of chapter VII of the Charter, and established a comprehensive ban on all but humanitarian economic intercourse with Iraq and occupied Kuwait. The Canadian and Australian governments, having previously asserted that they would be bound by UN decisions, moved to embrace a stiff sanctions policy: the day after the UN vote, formal announcements were issued extending sanctions to bring them into line with Resolution 661.[19]

In particular, both governments adopted a restrictive interpretation on the issue of food exports to Iraq. The language of Resolution 661 was somewhat ambiguous on the issue of food. Paragraph 3(c) asserted that all states should halt the sale or supply of all goods, 'but not including supplies intended strictly for medical purposes and, in humanitarian circumstances, foodstuffs.' However, both Canberra and Ottawa decided not to invoke 3(c) in order to continue shipping grains to Iraq.

Needless to say, the wheat boards in both countries were not pleased. In Canada, the wheat board strenuously opposed adding food to Canada's list of embargoed items. Charles Thompson, a spokesperson for the board, noted publicly that the board had a consistent policy of opposing food sanctions. 'Food is above politics,' Thompson claimed, since food is a necessity of life. In the end, however, the argument from External Affairs in favour of the strongest possible response prevailed: 'The wheat board wasn't happy about the embargo,' Canada's director-general of the federal government's grain-marketing bureau, Maurice Hladik, noted later, 'but they have no alternative but to honor it.'[20] The same was true of the Australian Wheat Board. It had sent an official from its Melbourne headquarters to Canberra to argue against including food in the Australian sanctions; like their Canadian counterparts, Australia's wheat board officials were clearly upset with the cabinet's decision.[21]

However, no sooner had Australia and Canada joined the sanctions coalition than the focus of American coalition-building had already shifted, fixing instead on the deployment of military force to the region. By Friday, 10 August, both Australia and Canada had also shifted their Gulf policies again: both governments announced that they were each despatching two warships and a supply ship to the Gulf.

In Australia, the first public indication that the government was considering moving beyond a passive sanctions policy came on Wednesday, 8 August. Amid reports that Washington was planning a multinational naval force to enforce a blockade against Iraq, the minister for defence, Robert Ray, who was in Townsville, Queensland, on a tour of defence facilities, was asked by a reporter whether Australian forces were also preparing for action. Ray responded that the government was 'looking at all contingencies,' and suggested that he could not imagine cabinet saying no to a request for a military contribution, particularly if it were organized as a 'United Nations action.' The minister's comments prompted officials in Canberra to issue a hasty 'clarification': the United States had not asked for a contribution, and no units of the Australian Defence Force were preparing for action. However, the government would 'seriously consider' a request from the United States to participate in a multinational force.[22] In Canberra, it was 7:15 on Friday morning, 10 August, when Bush called Hawke at the prime minister's official residence, The Lodge; they spoke to each other for twenty minutes. Three hours later, at 10:30 Canberra time, Hawke announced at a news conference that Australia would be joining other countries in sending forces to blockade Iraq. He said that Australia was joining 'with the rest of the world in saying that we will not tolerate, will not stand idly by while any member of the international community purports to break the rules of civilised conduct.' He announced that he had authorized the despatch of two guided-missile frigates, HMAS *Adelaide* and HMAS *Darwin*, and a supply ship, HMAS *Success*, to the Gulf region to join the multinational force. In his comments to reporters, Hawke clearly intimated that the decision to participate in the coalition came as a result of an American request: 'The matter was raised with us initially in the United States, and we therefore responded. We had discussions with them and it was out of those preliminary discussions that were initiated from the United States that the president rang me today and that out of those discussions we agreed that this Australian naval asset would be provided.'[23]

This was, as one columnist put it a month later, 'a somewhat generous approximation of the facts.'[24] According to later reconstructions of the decision,[25] the sequence of events suggested that the process by which Australia joined the coalition was no less complex than that by which the Saudi 'request' had been secured. When it appeared likely that the international response would go beyond passive sanctions, and that both the United States and Britain were preparing for a naval role, Australian officials in Defence, DFAT, and the Department of the Prime Minister and Cabinet had all been quick to conclude that Australia should seek to be a member; Ray himself favoured sending two warships and a supply ship; indeed, Grigson suggests that, after 7 August, 'no real consideration was being given to other options.'

Officials at the embassy in Washington had raised the possibility of a contribution with American officials. In addition, Hawke had talked to Mel Sembler, the American ambassador in Canberra, about a military contribution on 8 August.[26] Because of the dateline, it was Thursday morning, 9 August, when Bush made his announcement about the deployment of forces. Immediately after that speech, Hawke moved to firm up the Australian commitment. Although it is clear that the naval contribution was very much 'Mr Hawke's decision' (as a critical *Canberra Times* editorial put it on 15 August), he consulted other key members of the cabinet. He phoned Evans, who was in Dacca, Bangladesh; Ray, who was by this time in Cairns; and John Button, the government leader in the Senate, who was in Melbourne, to get their views on an Australian naval contribution. He then met over lunch in his office with the treasurer, Paul Keating, and the acting minister for foreign affairs and trade, Robert Duffy, together with several officials. At this meeting, Hawke reported that Evans, Ray, and Button had indicated that they favoured a naval contribution; Keating and Duffy were also in favour. Indeed, according to one account of this meeting, Keating was described as being exceedingly 'gung ho' about a naval commitment against Hussein, whom he apparently described as 'that turd.'[27]

The deployment decision was finalized: Michael Cook, the Australian ambassador in Washington, was ordered to ask American officials in Washington if they would arrange a phone call from George Bush. (This explains why American officials characterized the phone call from Bush as a thank-you call for a contribution already made, while Hawke was portraying this call as an urgent American request that needed a positive response.)

It is clear that Hawke wanted Australia to be part of the sanctioning coalition. He therefore did not want to do anything that would slow the bandwagoning that was seen as important to the coalition-building process. Thus, he readily agreed to Bush's suggestion that the announcement be made immediately in order to create a 'bow wave' effect – in other words, creating a momentum that would push others into joining. Indeed, so keen were the Americans that they put the story about Australian involvement out to the wire services immediately after the phone call – a full three hours before Hawke make his announcement. And so hurried was Hawke that, although he had intended to consult John Hewson, the leader of the Opposition, before making the announcement, he never managed to get around to it.[28] Nor did he consult the full cabinet or the ALP caucus.

What did the Australian government think it was contributing to when it committed the warships to the international coalition? All indications are that the decision was taken on the assumption that the purpose of the multinational force was not offensive, but defensive. It was meant to enforce an economic blockade against Iraq, in order to deter Saddam Hussein from launching an attack on Saudi Arabia and to coerce the Iraqi government into withdrawing from Kuwait. According to Oakes, Hawke had had persistent concerns that Australia might become involved in something more than a blockade, but such concerns had apparently been 'set to rest' the day before Bush's phone call by the president's public promise not to use the forces gathering in the Gulf to retake Kuwait.[29]

The clearest indication that Hawke (and the other members of the cabinet whom he consulted on this decision) believed that the purpose of the coalition would essentially be peaceful is that the prime minister committed the Australian ships to the coalition without recalling Parliament, which was not due to begin its spring session until 21 August, in order to consult with his own back-bench members. Hawke was well aware of the sensitivities within the Australian Labor Party to the commitment of troops abroad. Historically, the ALP had opposed overseas deployments, most recently in the case of the Vietnam War. Indeed, so entrenched was the party's opposition to the commitment of forces abroad that Clause 15 of its standing policy on international relations mandated that an ALP government would 'not commit Australian forces for combat overseas unless there is a clear and imminent threat to Australian security and lives.'[30] Moreover, the more radical tendencies of some of the ALP factions had in the past caused Hawke considerable personal embarrassment (as, for example, when he had been forced in February 1985 to reverse his decision to support American tests of the

MX missile[31]). Given this background, it is likely that Hawke would have moved to reassure his own caucus – and, more important, secure factional agreement – had he had an intimation that the Australian ships would become involved in combat operations. Instead, he left the caucus and the full cabinet out of the decision loop, no doubt on the assumption that the commitment of ships for an economic blockade was a 'safe' political decision that would be supported by the parliamentary wing of the ALP when it returned for the spring session of Parliament.

As it turned out, Hawke was mistaken. Before Parliament resumed, negotiations between the three factions – Left, Centre Left, and Right – were necessary to deal with the obvious unhappiness of many in the Left faction with the deployment. The Left was planning to ask the full ALP caucus at its meeting scheduled for 20 August to approve a motion calling for putting the Australian ships under UN command. Moreover, the Left argued that the ALP caucus had to be given authority over further Australian involvement. When Hawke and the cabinet strongly objected to this suggestion, arguing that national decisions had to be made by cabinet, the meeting of the caucus had to be delayed for a day while a compromise was negotiated. Not until the afternoon of 21 August, shortly before Hawke's ministerial statement and motion to the House, was a compromise reached: the Left would withdraw its planned motion; for his part, Hawke would acknowledge to caucus that greater consultation was needed; and the government would also agree to insert a call for placing the blockade under UN auspices into the government's motion.[32]

A final indication that the Australian government viewed the purpose of the naval deployment as primarily blockade-related was the degree to which Canberra saw its commitment as a crucial concomitant to the decision to stop its lucrative grain sales to Iraq. Without a blockade, grain sanctions were unenforceable; shipments slipped onto the high seas could make their way to Iraq with relative impunity. Oakes quotes one Australian official as saying that the blockade was a useful means of making sure that 'no other bastard takes over the trade.' The 'other bastard' Australian officials clearly had in mind was Canada, which, like Australia, had been reluctant to embrace full wheat sanctions. Unlike Australia, however, Canada had approximately 200,000 tonnes of grain in transit at the time of the invasion. For in the four months prior to 2 August, Iraq had purchased large quantities of wheat from Canada, pushing grain sales well above traditional levels. Canadian wheat shipments to Iraq had averaged 400,000 tonnes annually in the late 1980s. However, between April and July 1990 alone, Iraq had purchased fully 500,000 tonnes. Moreover, much of this grain was already on the move when the Kuwait crisis broke: 25,000 tonnes of Ontario wheat were already on the high seas and another 100,000 tonnes of Ontario wheat were being shipped through the St Lawrence Seaway; 60,000 tonnes of western Canadian wheat and barley were in Vancouver being loaded for shipment.[33]

Some Australian officials, according to Grigson's account, were concerned that this grain would be allowed to slip out of port before the sanctions took effect. Australian officials in Ottawa called Canberra on 8 August to alert DFAT about the possibility that the grain still in Canada would be slipped onto the high seas – and thus beyond the reach of any sanctions package put into place.[34] However, the Canadian government had already moved that day to stop the shipments still in Canadian waters.[35]

Whether it was out of concern over Canada's fidelity to the UN sanctions – as the story put out by the Office of Prime Minister and Cabinet to the Australian media suggests – or simply to compare notes, Hawke called Mulroney on 9 August to tell him of the Australian decision to deploy two frigates and a supply ship for the blockade. According to Grigson's account, Hawke urged Mulroney to make a similar commitment. In his own reference to this phone call – on ABC's '7.30 Report' on 10 August – Hawke indicated that Mulroney told him that a Canadian decision was expected soon.[36]

By the time that Hawke and Mulroney talked, however, the Canadian cabinet had already made a similar decision to commit ships to the Gulf blockade, and was merely waiting for an appropriate moment to announce it publicly. Although at the outset of the crisis Canadian participation in a military operation had seemed unthinkable to officials – on 3 August, for example, Clark had ruled out any possibility of the use of force by Canada[37] – by 6 August it was more plausible. That evening, Mulroney flew to Washington to have dinner with George Bush; consideration of a Canadian military commitment began the next day. The official line afterwards was that Bush had asked for no commitment from Canada and Mulroney had offered none: at separate news conferences on 8 August, both Mulroney and Clark asserted that no forces had been requested or volunteered.[38] However, journalistic reconstructions of this decision, based on interviews with officials, suggest that Mulroney unilaterally gave Bush a commitment for a Canadian naval contribution that evening, without discussing it with his cabinet.[39]

It does seem improbable that the two leaders did not at least discuss the issue of a multinational naval blockade, particularly since that very afternoon Thatcher had dropped by the White House on her way back to London from Aspen, and had been in the Oval Office when Bush received the call from Cheney indicating that King Fahd ibn Abdul Aziz of Saudi Arabia had approved an American deployment; following this meeting, Thatcher had announced the despatch of two more British frigates to the Gulf and had declared that Britain was considering imposing a blockade on Iraq.

On his return to Ottawa, Mulroney himself started the process of developing military options at the bureaucratic level, since William McKnight, the minister of national defence, was abroad and Clark was in his riding in Alberta. Cabinet met on Wednesday, 8 August, by which time both Clark and McKnight were back in Ottawa. Discussion focused on possible responses to the emergence of a multinational blockade headed by the United States. As in Australia, there was general agreement at both the bureaucratic and ministerial levels that the most appropriate contribution would be the kind of limited naval deployment that Britain had announced and that France, Australia, and other European allies were considering. But because Bush had yet to make an announcement regarding American plans, it was decided to take no decision on a naval deployment in advance of other states. Rather, cabinet decided to wait until after a meeting of NATO foreign ministers scheduled for Friday, 10 August, in Brussels.

As in Australia, Parliament was not recalled to discuss the commitment of forces to the Gulf. In part this was because the government expected to be called on at the NATO meeting to announce its contribution, and there was little desire to have to respond to the NATO allies that the issue was still being debated. But there was another disincentive: the cabinet had just sent Canadian Forces units to Oka, Quebec, to deal with an armed confrontation between native people and the provincial police force, the Sûreté du Québec. On 11 July, Mohawks in Oka opposed to the expansion of a golf course on lands regarded as sacred had erected a barricade on the main road into town. The SQ was sent to dismantle it; a gunfight broke out, in which a police officer was killed. On the same day, Mohawks in the neighbouring community of Kahnawake set up a sympathy blockade of the Mercier Bridge, one of the main commuter bridges across the St Lawrence River into Montreal. Since then, 1500 members of the SQ – fully one third of the force – had been maintained at the two blockades. The government in Ottawa did not particularly want to recall Parliament over the Gulf, then have to face queries and criticisms of its handling of the Oka crisis.

At the NATO meeting in Brussels on 10 August, Baker issued his public appeal to the allies to contribute forces to defend the Gulf states, asking that each ally contribute 'in its own way.' At the conclusion of the meeting, numerous NATO countries announced their participation: Belgium, Canada, and the Netherlands committed naval vessels; Germany, which was constitutionally bound to keep its armed forces within the NATO perimeter, pledged four minesweepers and a supply vessel for the Mediterranean to take the place of American vessels sent to the Gulf; Spain, Portugal, and Italy promised to allow American forces to use air bases on their soil.[40]

The Canadian decision to participate in the multinational coalition was announced by the prime minister at a press conference in Ottawa following the meeting of NATO foreign ministers.[41] The justifications offered by Mulroney indicated that he, like Hawke, saw the purposes of the multinational coalition as defensive: to deter a further Iraqi advance. Noting the reports of atrocities coming out of Kuwait, Mulroney called Hussein 'a criminal of historic proportions' and invoked 'the lessons of history' about responding to aggression: 'Turning a blind eye to aggression only encourages further aggression ... If a clear warning is not sent to Iraq now, it will only be emboldened to find new victims.' But Mulroney stressed that Canada's contribution was intended to convey disapproval of the invasion – but, he added, 'not in an aggressive manner.'

Like both Hawke and Bush, Mulroney allowed his public rhetoric on the Gulf commitment to become exaggerated. For example, Mulroney argued that Canada had to participate in the multinational coalition in order to fulfil Canadian obligations to NATO and the UN, even though the Persian Gulf patently lay outside the NATO area and the impetus for the multinational coalition was coming from the United States, not the UN. Likewise, he argued that Ottawa had a responsibility to respond to attacks and threats 'on friends and allies of Canada,' but none of the states under threat was an ally and it was stretching a point to term any of the states in the Gulf region 'friends' of Canada.[42]

The Canadian contribution consisted of what was fast becoming a standard commitment from smaller states – two warships accompanied by a supply ship: the destroyer HMCS *Athabaskan*, the destroyer escort HMCS *Terra Nova*, and the supply ship HMCS *Protecteur*, all based in Halifax. These ships ranged in age from eighteen to thirty-one years old;

none of the new frigates being acquired by the Canadian Forces was ready for deployment. The ships were configured for anti-submarine duty, and thus they had to be modernized and refitted. By the time they left Halifax, additional forces were despatched with them: a squadron of Sea King helicopters and units of the Royal Canadian Artillery to work the close-in weapons systems installed in the refit.

The Canadian flotilla left Halifax for the Gulf on 24 August. However, because the government did not want to recall Parliament before it was due back on 24 September, it had to structure its Gulf decisions to fit the requirements of the National Defence Act, which requires that if Canadian Forces units are put on 'active service,' or combat status, Parliament must be recalled within ten days. The government thus announced that the task force would not be put on active service until it arrived in the Gulf region. Indeed, when it appeared that the ships would arrive too early, they were slowed down by arranging a special port call in Sicily for degaussing. Finally, on 15 September, these units were put on active service;[43] in what a DND official, his tongue firmly in his cheek, termed 'a happy coincidence,' the flotilla arrived in the Red Sea the following day.[44]

FROM SANCTIONS TO FORCE

The multinational coalition that Australia and Canada joined on 10 August 1990 changed dramatically over the six and a half months that Iraqi forces occupied Kuwait. Usually resulting from policy decisions taken in Washington, these changes altered the purposes of the coalition as a whole, and thus of the individual members.

Indeed, the United States was changing the nature and purposes of the coalition even as it was being formed. While ministers in Australia and Canada were considering what contributions they might make to what they thought was going to be a multinational naval coalition to enforce sanctions, the United States had completed negotiations with Saudi Arabia for the deployment of ground and air forces. As smaller governments were announcing their naval flotillas at the end of the week, American units were being flown into Saudi Arabia, altering the dynamics of the conflict – and therefore the nature of the coalition.

In the next three months, the focus of the international community was fixed on the United Nations, and on UN efforts to resolve the dispute. In a series of resolutions, the Security Council moved to tighten existing coercive measures and to respond to new developments in the Gulf. With virtual unanimity among the permanent members, the Security Council declared itself on such issues as the formal Iraqi annexation of Kuwait (Resolution 662, 9 August 1990); foreign nationals being forcibly held in Kuwait and Iraq (Resolution 664, 18 August 1990; Resolution 674, 29 October 1990); violation of diplomatic missions (Resolution 667, 16 September 1990); and the destruction of Kuwait's population records by Iraqi forces (Resolution 677, 28 November 1990). It also moved to tighten the embargo by allowing states to interdict shipping to and from Iraq and Kuwait (Resolution 665, 25 August 1990); more rigorously defining humanitarian exemptions (Resolution 666, 13 September 1990); and extending the embargo to aircraft (Resolution 670, 25 September 1990).

However, over this period, the focus of the Bush administration remained fixed on the military option, even though it remained an active participant in UN diplomacy. American troop levels continued to rise until, by early October, they had reached the pre-arranged level of approximately 200,000, the figure originally agreed to by Bush in August.[45]

Such large numbers of troops might have been enough to repulse an Iraqi attack on Saudi Arabia. Thus, these troops may have served as a successful deterrent against such an attack. On the other hand, the force was not large enough to be used to forcibly remove the 400,000 Iraqi troops believed to be in Kuwait. As a result, on 31 October, Bush gave his approval for another change in American policy: he redoubled the number of United States forces in Saudi Arabia (a decision not announced until after the 6 November mid-term elections). Importantly, Bush's announcement on 8 November also shifted the posture of American forces from a defensive deterrent against an Iraqi attack on Saudi Arabia to an offensive compellent designed to threaten Iraq into withdrawing from Kuwait.

This significant change was made quite unilaterally by the Bush administration. The decision was taken without the prior knowledge of the Saudi government; only after the decision was made was Baker sent to speak to key allies in Europe and the Middle East. But it was not just the allies who had been kept out of the loop: the decision was apparently taken without the participation of Colin Powell, chairman of the Joint Chiefs of Staff. Moreover, Sam Nunn, chairman of the Senate Armed Services Committee, was also reported to be unhappy about being informed rather than consulted.[46] For all its unilateralism, this decision had inexorable multilateral implications: it meant that, as of 8 November, all states in the United States–led coalition were also committed to the offensive option.

To be sure, this decision was subsequently ratified by Security Council Resolution 678, which authorized the use of 'all necessary means' to 'uphold Resolution 660 ... and to restore international peace and security in the area.' This resolution, passed on 29 November 1990 by a vote of 12 to 2, with China abstaining, provided for a 'pause of goodwill' until 15 January 1991 before action would be taken. But Resolution 678 also represented the end of UN input into the process: arming the United States with the authority of the Security Council put the final decision in Washington's hands. From that point on, all the final stages of the conflict were driven by American decisions. Even the smallest decision, such as deciding exactly when the UN deadline expired, was made by Washington: Resolution 678 had indicated a deadline for withdrawal – 'on or before 15 January' – but was silent as to the time zone in which the resolution became effective. The determination that the resolution meant midnight Eastern Standard Time (rather than midnight Kuwait time, eight hours earlier) was made by American, not UN, officials.[47] Needless to say, the most important decisions – such as deciding to launch the air attacks on 17 January 1991, to open the ground war on 23 February, and to declare a ceasefire four days later – were made unilaterally by the United States.

CHANGES IN AUSTRALIAN AND CANADIAN POLICY

The governments in both Canberra and Ottawa faithfully changed their policies in order to mirror these changes being imposed on the coalition by Washington. In the months between 10 August 1990, when they joined the coalition, and the 27 February 1991 ceasefire, both governments moved more or less in step with the coalition and particularly the United States.

The Australian government both expanded the role its ships played in the Gulf, and augmented the units it was deploying. Once the UN Security Council approved Resolution 665 on 26 August, giving states authority to impose a blockade, Canberra agreed to expand the rules of engagement for its ships; the changes were announced on 11 September, following a naval conference in Bahrain of all the countries engaged in the blockade. The new rules allowed the use of 'minimum force short of sinking,' and specified a graduated series of steps that could be used in interdictions, from shots across the bow to shots into the steering gear.[48] Likewise, the Australian response to the public appeal by the United States to its NATO allies for more contributions to the coalition expanded its contribution: on 16 September Robert Ray announced the decision to send a twenty-member naval medical team, which would eventually be deployed on the United States hospital ship *Comfort*.[49] After the passage of Resolution 678, the government announced that the task force would be available to participate in whatever action arose out of the interpretation of that resolution.[50] By war's end, the Australian commitment included a doubling of the medical contingent to forty, and the despatch of twenty-three Navy divers for mine disposal. An almost unnoticed Australian contribution to the coalition's war efforts were the joint facilities at Pine Gap and Nurrungar, which played a critical role in providing the United States with early warning of Iraqi missile attacks.[51]

The Canadians also augmented the original commitment of three ships. Ottawa responded positively to Baker's appeal by announcing on 14 September that Canada would commit a squadron of eighteen CF-18 fighters from Germany to fly air cover for the Canadian ships.[52] In addition to the 450 pilots and ground crew, units of the Royal Canadian Regiment and the 22nd Canadian Regiment (the 'Van Doos') were deployed to protect 'Canada Dry,' the air base that was established in Qatar and shared with an American squadron of F-16s. A Canadian headquarters to coordinate the naval and air operations was established in Bahrain in mid-October, necessitating the deployment of a signals squadron. In the new year, it was decided by the coalition to give Canada responsibility for arranging logistics for all the naval contingents in the Gulf. As the UN deadline approached, an additional six CF-18s were flown in to Qatar to bring the squadron up to normal strength; a Boeing 707 refueller was also deployed.[53] In response to a British request, a 100-bed field hospital was set up in Jubayl in Saudi Arabia after the war had broken out. A team from the Royal Canadian Engineers was also sent to the Gulf to assist in mine clearance and bomb disposal. The role of the fighters also underwent a transformation: when they were first deployed in October, they were assigned a defensive role, providing air cover for coalition shipping; after 17 January, they were ordered to fly 'sweep and escort' missions, accompanying allied planes on attack missions. On 20 February, the role of the CF-18s was altered again, this time to allow pilots to engage in combat attacks on Iraqi targets.[54]

EXPLAINING AUSTRALIAN AND CANADIAN POLICY

To this point, I have explored the decisions that Australia and Canada took in response to the Gulf crisis, and the premises that underlay them. In particular, I have tried to show that when they joined the multi-national coalition in August 1990, the governments in both Canberra and Ottawa believed that they were contributing military forces to a coalition that had two primary purposes. The first was to enforce a tight sanctions net around Iraq in order to squeeze the Iraqi economy and precipitate the dynamics of the 'naive' theory of sanctions (the favourite 'naive' scenario was that economic deprivations would cause the support of the Iraqi armed forces for Saddam Hussein to weaken, prompting a coup by those in the lower ranks and a negotiated withdrawal from Kuwait by the new regime). The second was to demonstrate sufficient force to Iraq that Saddam Hussein would be deterred from attacking Saudi Arabia (if indeed he had had any intention to launch such an attack).

It is clear from the sequence of events that, in this case, both countries responded positively to the idea of participating in a coalition – when it appeared that a coalition was possible. In other words, both states participated in a classical bandwagoning dynamic: left to their own devices, and in the absence of negative reaction from other states, Australia and Canada might have been concerned about the violation of the principle of territorial integrity, but neither would have moved unilaterally to disrupt their profitable relations with Iraq by imposing sanctions against Baghdad. However, as it became apparent that numerous other states were prepared to join a sanctioning coalition, Australia and Canada quickly moved to join, regardless of the considerable damage it would do to their economic interests. Likewise, as it became apparent that numerous other states would join a multinational blockading force, Australia and Canada again moved to join. And it should be stressed here that the account above makes clear that both states were not simply agreeing to join at the behest of the United States – both Canberra and Ottawa *actively* sought to join.

Second, the account here suggests that both Australia and Canada sought to join the sanctioning coalition for a complex admixture of reasons. The most important was a concern over the violation of territorial integrity by Iraq, more because of its implications for world order than because of any abiding concern for the fate of the al-Sabah emirate. Both countries shared a generalized desire that the international community as a whole respond to this violation of one of the key norms of the contemporary international system as a means of entrenching it. It is true that many critics in Australia and Canada argued that because their governments had not condemned other cases of invasion (most notably Indonesia for invading East Timor or the United States for invading Grenada and Panama), their expressions of concern for Kuwait's territorial integrity had to be disingenuous. However, it can be argued that smaller countries will always experience private concern at violations of territorial integrity, even if political considerations lead them to remain silent on some occasions.

To be sure, this concern resonated in different ways in both countries. In Australia, concern over territorial integrity was more instrumental than in Canada. The Australian experience in the Second World War, which left a widespread belief that conquest by Japan had only been staved off by American intervention, continued to linger in the collective memory.[55] A frequently sounded theme was that support for the coalition was necessary for Australia's own security. It was likely, the argument ran, that the United States would soon be withdrawing its protection from the South Pacific, and that Australia would have to rely on the upholding of international norms to defend itself from threats to its territorial integrity; if the international community acted in concert to uphold the sanctity of borders, would-be violators of the territorial integrity of others would be deterred, and Australia would be the safer for it.[56] For Canadians, by contrast, concerns for the sanctity of territorial integrity were entirely symbolic. Since they have not worried about being invaded for over a century, it is not surprising that the instrumental deterrent argument was never made in the Canadian Gulf debate.

A related world-order desire was to capture the moment presented by the unprecedented Soviet-American cooperation that emerged immediately after the invasion to build up the UN as an effective means of channelling interstate conflicts and imposing a particular order on the state system. Moreover, both governments were genuinely impressed by the multilateral impulses the Bush administration displayed from the outset of the crisis, a happy departure from the more unilateral tendencies of the Reagan administration. It was clear that Bush and Baker were devoting considerable energy to consulting friends and allies and working within a multilateral framework. There was thus a desire in both Canberra and Ottawa to encourage this behaviour. In previous conflicts, Canadian governments regarded multilateral linkages as useful for restraining the more unilateral impulses of American administrations.[57] In the Gulf conflict, there was some evidence of this restraint at work, particularly at the outset of the crisis, when several members of the Security Council, including Canada's permanent representative, Yves Fortier, successfully pressed the United States to seek UN authorization for its proposed interdiction of ships in the Gulf.[58]

Likewise, both Australia and Canada were concerned about the effects of future Iraqi behaviour on the international economic order. Given the interest of Western industrialized states in keeping control over oil supplies as divided as possible, there was a fear that Iraqi expansionism, particularly an attack on Saudi Arabia and the smaller Gulf states, would have profoundly negative consequences for the supply and price of oil, which in turn would have a negative effect on the international economy and, by extension, on Australia and Canada.

Finally, the account here suggests that the deployments cannot be attributed to the personal relationship between the American president and the prime minister. This was an explanation that was commonly put forward as an explanation for both the Australian and the Canadian commitments, with numerous variants on essentially the same theme. Mulroney and Hawke were portrayed as eager to please their good friend George Bush. It was commonly asserted that Hawke or Mulroney were just fawning or toadying to the Americans; the analogy of choice on both sides of the Pacific was the servile canine, with both prime ministers referred to as lap dogs, puppy dogs, and presidential poodles.[59]

In fact, Bush's 'telephone diplomacy' played no part in Australia's Gulf decision: Hawke had no contact with Bush until after the Australian decision was made. By contrast, Bush and Mulroney had two long conversations before the Canadian decision, one by phone and another in person over dinner. But it can be argued that the president's personal relationship with Mulroney had no impact on *whether* Canada would contribute to the coalition, only on *when* Canada would make the commitment to deploy. In other words, had there been no personal contact between Bush and Mulroney, a commitment might not have been given on 6 August, but it would eventually have been made by Friday, 10 August.

There were other factors that also moved both governments to join in the sanctioning coalition: the desire, mentioned above, to widen and tighten the sanctions net to ensure that no other state profited from their own self-abnegation; and the complex dynamic of international 'friendship' that tends to produce in Australian and Canadian governments a desire to be alongside the United States and Britain – especially when the cause is deemed right. Finally, both governments were angry at Iraqi behaviour, particularly at the emerging Iraqi strategy of holding foreign nationals as hostages, and about initial reports of Iraqi atrocities in Kuwait.[60]

DOMESTIC OPPOSITION: 'GIVE SANCTIONS TIME'

As we have seen, both the Australian and Canadian governments maintained consistent rhetorical support for the international coalition over the six months of the crisis,[61] even though both governments were facing increasingly strident domestic opposition as the coalition's purposes shifted over the course of the conflict. Likewise, participation in the coalition continued to enjoy broad support in both countries. For example, editorial opinion in Canada and Australia generally approved not only the initial naval deployment but also the subsequent decisions. And public-opinion polls showed that 60 per cent or more of Australian and Canadian respondents approved of the Gulf policies of their respective governments.[62]

In both countries, however, the prolongation of the crisis, and the moves towards a more forceful option heralded in the passage of Resolution 678, prompted considerable opposition. Opposition came from similar sources: a newly revitalized peace movement, some church leaders, and some members of the Arab-Australian and Arab-Canadian communities. The pattern of opposition in both countries was also similar, with the emphasis placed on street demonstrations (frequently in front of the closest United States diplomatic mission) and public meetings, and reaching a crescendo in the days before the war broke out. Even the language of protest – most of it, ironically, imported from the United States – was the same: Australian and Canadian protestors alike chanted the catch-cry 'no blood for oil' and sang the refrain from John Lennon's 'Give peace a chance.'

Only in the parliamentary sphere did the pattern of opposition differ. In Australia, both the Liberal and National parties supported the government's Gulf policy throughout the crisis; some members of the Left faction of the ALP were unhappy with Hawke's Gulf policy, but most either acquiesced or stayed away. This resulted in virtual unanimity in the lower house: Ted Mack, the independent member for North Sydney, was the lone voice of protest. (Because under Australian parliamentary rules a formal division requires the call of two members, motions on the Gulf never came to a vote in the House; Mack had to invoke a special provision in the standing orders to have his opposition registered in *Hansard*.) In the Senate, the Australian Democrats (who were not represented in the House of Representatives) and an independent member – Jo Vallentine of Western Australia – strongly opposed the Hawke government's Gulf policy throughout the conflict.

In Canada, by contrast, the House of Commons was more divided. The official Opposition, the Liberal party, opposed the government's Gulf policy throughout the conflict, altering their position only after war had broken out. Indeed, as late as the emergency debate on 15 and 16 January 1991, the Liberals were still arguing that if force were used, the government should withdraw Canada's forces from the Gulf immediately. Once war broke out, however, the Liberals abruptly changed direction, and supported the government.[63] The New Democratic Party consistently opposed the Mulroney government's approach, even after the outbreak of war.[64] The Bloc québécois, newly formed from the ranks of Quebec Progressive Conservative MPs who quit the party after the failure of the Meech Lake accord in June 1990, did not take a formal position in the Gulf debate: while several of its members supported the government on Gulf votes, most BQ members, including its leader, Lucien Bouchard, did not vote.

Much of the opposition to government policy in both Australia and Canada focused on the sanctions issue, in particular on the idea that sanctions should be given time to 'work' before the harsher tools of statecraft were invoked against Iraq. Governments, it was suggested, should 'give peace a chance' by 'giving sanctions a chance.' The essence of the argument usually advanced was that Iraq, hugely dependent on oil sales for its foreign exchange, was the perfect target for an effective sanctions strategy. It would not, in this view, take too much time before sanctions began to 'bite,' and when they did, Saddam Hussein would recognize that it would be to Iraq's benefit to withdraw from Kuwait. In some versions of this argument, it was claimed that as Iraq began to suffer economic deprivation, factions within the army opposed to Hussein would move to topple him in a coup.

This line of argument featured prominently in the Canadian parliamentary debates that were held on the issue in November and January. Numerous speakers from both the Liberals and the New Democratic Party expressed their opposition to Resolution 678 and to the Mulroney government's support for the possible use of force against Iraq while the sanctions option was still available to the international community.[65] In Australia, similar concerns about giving sanctions more time to work were expressed in parliamentary debates. Some Australian Labor Party members in both houses, including two former cabinet ministers and Bruce Childs, convenor of the Left faction, were distinctly unhappy with the abandonment of the sanctions option and criticized the government for not giving sanctions a chance to work; likewise, the Australian Democrats in the Senate were consistent in their view that sanctions should have been given more time before force was used.[66]

A SANCTIONING COALITION?

The basic assumption of those arguing for giving sanctions a chance was that the multinational coalition had begun its life as a sanctioning coalition, devoted to the purpose of blockading Iraq and imposing sufficient economic deprivations on Iraqis that Saddam Hussein (or a successor regime) would 'come to their senses' and withdraw from Kuwait. Opponents of the transformation of the coalition from a sanctioning coalition to one intent on using force to remove Iraqi forces from Kuwait believed that it was both possible and appropriate to maintain the original purpose of the coalition.

It can be argued, however, that in the Iraqi case, sanctions as a tool of statecraft became virtually irrelevant, almost from the beginning, and that sanctions were never intended to be the main tool in the attempt to secure an Iraqi withdrawal from Kuwait. Rather, what might have begun as a sanctioning coalition in the first hours of the crisis was transformed almost immediately into a military coalition.

It is true that had the United States been content to limit its actions to a naval blockade of Iraq and Kuwait, there would not have been a problem. Maintaining a blockade of a narrow coast involves low political and economic costs; having a naval task force lingering for months on the high seas in the Gulf waiting for sanctions against Iraq to 'work' would have been unproblematic.

The problem is that, almost immediately, the Bush administration went well beyond this relatively costless option. Once it had decided to position American forces in Saudi Arabia, the Bush administration had created a considerable dilemma for itself. With American forces positioned in Saudi Arabia in large numbers, the option of sitting back and waiting for sanctions to work became too costly to contemplate. Because of the size of this force, the financial and particularly the political costs of maintaining these troops indefinitely in Saudi Arabia became exceedingly high. For their part, the Saudis did not welcome the prospect of having hundreds of thousands of American troops, and their corrupting influences, stationed in their conservative and religious kingdom for very long. For the Americans, lingering in Saudi Arabia was no more appealing: not only were the financial costs of keeping hundreds of thousands of troops supplied in temporary bases considerable, but there were concerns over the morale of so many troops kept so deep in the desert indefinitely. Finally, there was also the domestic political costs of maintaining the troops in a defensive mode: with each passing week, Bush's domestic critics would have criticized the administration for being weak and indecisive, or for squandering American military power.

At the same time, however, once in place, these American troops could not be withdrawn – at least not until Iraq had first withdrawn from Kuwait. An American withdrawal while Iraqi troops were still in Kuwait would have been unthinkable for the Bush administration, not only because the original threat that had prompted their deployment had not diminished, but also because Bush, who had publicly vowed to see the invasion reversed, would have suffered an unacceptable loss of face. In short, once the United States forces were in place, the only possibility for a peaceful resolution to the crisis would have been an Iraqi withdrawal.

In fact, both the Australian and Canadian governments came quickly to an understanding that a sanctions-only option had been ruled out by Bush's military moves. They might have joined the coalition in August in the belief that their involvement would be limited to participating in a blockade, but once they discovered that the United States was shifting the purposes of the coalition, Canberra and Ottawa had few viable options other than to stay the course. Being part of a broader international coalition put the Australian and Canadian governments in the position of queasy roller-coaster riders who discover, too late, that they have no desire to continue the ride, but have little option but to hang on tightly until the end.

There is little doubt that despite their support for the coalition's changing purposes, for Resolution 678, and for the use of force to resolve the issue, neither the Hawke government in Australia nor the Mulroney government in Canada was particularly pleased to discover that the original purposes of the coalition had changed to such a degree.

One key measure of this discomfort was that neither Australia nor Canada moved to increase its force commitments in a significant way. It is true that, at a rhetorical level, both governments remained unstinting in their commitment to the coalition and its changing purposes. For example, Mulroney was to say that Canada 'must do everything it can' to restore Iraqi respect for international law;[67] and Gareth Evans was to declare that Australia 'must remain committed to ... doing everything we can as a nation – paying whatever price is necessary.'[68] But it was clear from their behaviour that both governments were not at all convinced that 'everything' should be committed to this conflict.

For if they really had been convinced that force rather than economic strangulation should be used to drive Iraq from Kuwait, both governments would surely have embraced a more force-oriented posture, one that would have tried to match, at least in relative terms, the mounting commitments of the United States, Britain, and France. For example, if Australia and Canada had matched the British ground contribution on a per capita basis, they would have committed 12,000 and 20,000 ground troops respectively. One measure might have been the commitment of ground combat troops to Saudi Arabia at any one of six points in the conflict: at the outset, along with American and British forces; in September, when the full extent of the initial American deployment became clear; in early November when Bush doubled the United States forces and put them on the offensive; in December, in anticipation of the implementation of Resolution 678; in January, when the UN deadline expired; or in February, when the ground war began. That ground forces were not committed suggests that neither government was convinced that it was really necessary for the national interest to commit Australians or Canadians to fight a war against Iraq, a lack of conviction that stands in telling contrast to their behaviour in August, when the enthusiasm for a blockading coalition demonstrated clear conviction that such a coalition was a good idea.

At the same time, both governments recognized that the structure of the game was such that there was always a possibility that the military situation could change and that the United States might ask its coalition allies for ground troops. In Canada, the government laid the ground for such an eventuality by signalling shortly after the United States shifted its forces to an offensive posture that it would not rule out the use of Canadian ground forces. Mulroney indicated that the government would 'reflect on' a request by 'the United Nations or the allies' for 'another commitment.'[69]

In Australia, by contrast, the government moved to head off the possibility of such a request by signalling its desire to limit its involvement. Its response to Bush's 8 November announcement was to note that there were no plans to send ground troops, though Canberra promised that it would consider committing the three ships in the task force to an offensive action. Hawke clarified this position during the parliamentary debate after the passage of Resolution 678: having announced the deployment of the ships from the Gulf of Oman into the Persian Gulf and the despatch of a further two medical teams, he then stated: 'It is not proposed to make any other contribution of naval, air or ground forces.'[70]

Hawke's commitment to limit Australian involvement grew out of the multiplying divisions within the ALP on the Gulf issue. Some state ALP politicians were publicly urging their federal counterparts to bring the ships back to Australia. A meeting of the ALP's National Left (which included parliamentary and extraparliamentary members) was split between the 'hard left,' which opposed the government, and the 'pragmatic left,' which took a position of 'understanding opposition' to any escalation in Australia's role. Within the federal caucus, however, there was widespread agreement – even in Hawke's own faction, the Right – on one issue: there were to be no 'boots in the sand' (that is, no ground troops); even the medical team had to remain aboard a ship.[71]

While it can be argued that such reluctance to commit themselves to a fully offensive posture indicated that neither government was fully comfortable with the war option, it is also clear that neither government was in a position to leave the coalition at any of the points that the United States changed the operating assumptions. The option of pulling out after 10 August was, quite simply, unthinkable, in the sense that the costs of defection would have been exceedingly high: all other coalition members, and the United States in particular, had too much at stake to countenance an open crack in the unity of the coalition with equanimity. (The only viable option for those states opposed to the change in the coalition's direction was to try to make their contribution as invisible as possible – as some Muslim governments, facing strong domestic opposition, tried to do.) In the Australian and Canadian cases, moreover, there would also have been considerable domestic costs: a withdrawal would surely have brought down on both governments more trenchant criticism, and from a wider segment of the population, than they were receiving for their continued participation (indeed, the opposition Liberals in Canada discovered this when they argued for bringing the forces back to Canada in the event of hostilities).

It is important to stress, however, that in both the Australian and Canadian cases the decision to stay the course was not simply driven by a recognition of the huge costs, internationally and domestically, that would have come with a decision to defect. It is clear from their behaviour that both states wanted to remain as members of the coalition, even though they would be bit players in the larger game, and even though they might not have been comfortable with the idea of committing their own forces to battle. Evans nicely captured the mixture of resignation and willing acceptance that characterized the Australian and Canadian view when he said in September 1990 that 'the general assumption is that we are in for the long haul and we had better prepare ourselves both physically and psychologically for that.'[72] Likewise, Clark resignedly acknowledged in October that war would undoubtedly mean 'thousands of casualties.' But, he said, if war came, Canada would still be there: 'we should not rule out the possibility that young Canadian soldiers will not return to this country for celebration but will stay there for burial.'[73]

CONCLUSION

The case of the sanctions imposed against Iraq in the wake of its invasion of Kuwait in August 1990 demonstrates again the importance of coalitions in the evolution of middle-power sanctions policy. Just as coalition membership pushed and pulled the Australian and Canadian governments in the cases of sanctions against Indonesia, South Africa, and Vietnam, so too in this case did the dynamic of coalition membership have an important impact on the sanctions policies of these countries.

However, as will be clear, the coalition dynamic in this case was unusual. The governments in both Canberra and Ottawa joined what they believed was going to be a sanctioning coalition, intent on blockading what many characterized as a target that was economically weak and easy to coerce. Because of the nature of the Iraqi economy, officials in both capitals could be forgiven for believing that a wide-ranging sanctioning coalition would have a good chance of achieving instrumental effects – coercing Saddam Hussein into a reversal of the invasion.

As it turned out, sanctions were not given an opportunity to work. This is because what began as an exercise in multilateral sanctions was transformed by the coalition leader, the United States, into a war that was being driven largely unilaterally by Washington. It is clear that once the decision to join had been made on 10 August, both middle-power governments were tied tightly to the preferences of the coalition leader. And because the United States government was not interested in giving sanctions a chance, neither the Australian nor the Canadian government was in a position to embrace that option.

PART THREE: POLICY IMPLICATIONS

10

The Termination Trap in International Sanctions: Lessons from the Soviet Union and China

Despite the popularity of international sanctions in the 1980s, and for all the scholarly interest in sanctions in the last decade, our thinking about this instrument of statecraft tends to be quite partial. Those who urge the use of sanctions to achieve foreign policy goals; those whose responsibility it is to decide whether to use the measures against other states; and those who study sanctions have all tended to fix their focus on only one phase of the sanctioning process – the decision to impose these punishments – rather than to examine sanctions in a more holistic way. In other words, we tend to lose sight of the fact that sanctions have a definite life-cycle that involves more than simply a decision by the 'sender' to impose hurts on a 'target' to change its behaviour. Rather, sanctions, once in place, require an on-going calculus about their effects, and a constant series of decisions about the hurts being inflicted: should they be maintained? reduced? increased? And, of course, punishment as a purposive human behaviour requires a termination point – or a decision to bring the hurts to an end. But we tend not to look at these phases in the sanctions process: we tend to know a great deal about how sanctions are begun; we know comparatively little about how they are ended.

It is true that if sanctions achieve their nominal purpose – changing the behaviour of the target – the calculation about termination is relatively easy. And indeed there are cases where the hurts inflicted by sanctions performed precisely what the sender intended; terminating them was thus relatively unproblematic.[1] But most students of sanctions agree that such 'effectiveness' is rare: generally these measures fail to hurt enough to provoke a change in the behaviour that initially prompted the imposition of the sanctions.[2] What happens then? In that case, the sanctionist government's calculus becomes more difficult, for it is thrust into a situation not unlike that which faces the gambler in a game of five-card stud. A successful sanctionist, like the successful gambler, has to know when to hold – and when to fold. Does the sanctionist government 'hold' – maintain (or increase) the punishment in the expectation (or the hope) that the sanctions will eventually yield success? Or does it 'fold' – by lifting the sanctions? If it folds, the sanctionist state is able to cut its losses, but is forced to accept the costs of acknowledging that the measures failed to produce change, possibly losing face by such an acknowledgment and also accepting the loss of those 'sunk costs' already invested. (It should be noted that the gambling analogy has its limitations. Unlike the gambler, the international sanctionist is not limited to a mere five cards: the game, such as it is, can stretch out indefinitely, as the cases of the long-lived United States sanctions against North Korea, Vietnam, and Cuba demonstrate.)

This calculus will have important implications for the use – and duration – of sanctions. It will determine whether the sanctions will be cleanly applied (and cleanly lifted), or whether they will linger indefinitely, or whether they will disintegrate by slow, and often embarrassingly ragged, degrees.

The purpose of this chapter is to explore this problem in a preliminary way by examining the experience of Canadian sanctions against the Soviet Union in the early 1980s and Canadian and Australian sanctions against China following the Tiananmen massacre in 1989. We revisit the sanctions imposed in response to the Soviet invasion of Afghanistan in December 1979, discussed in chapter 7 above. But in this chapter, we also examine the sanctions imposed on the Soviet Union after martial law was declared in Poland in December 1981, and after Soviet fighter aircraft shot down Korean Air Lines flight 007 in September 1983. For these two sanctions episodes, following as they did the punitive measures imposed on the USSR after the Afghanistan invasion, illustrate how and why the decisions made at the time when sanctions are imposed can have a profound impact on decisions about terminating sanctions.

I will demonstrate how in the first of these cases – Afghanistan – Canadian policy-makers, and indeed Western leaders more generally, created what might be thought of as a termination trap for themselves. They structured the sanctions in a way that created a powerful dynamic of perpetuation: a logic to holding firm, and a concomitant and equally powerful disincentive to fold – even when it was clear that the Soviet leadership was not about to change its behaviour. This logic locked the sender and the target into a pattern of adversarial relations that proved difficult to break and had a not unimportant impact on deepening and extending East-West tensions. At the same time, however, there were strong disintegrative forces built into these sanctions, forces that were exacerbated by the Polish crisis of 1981–2.

The result was that the Afghanistan sanctions produced disarray in the Western camp: some of the Western allies kept the sanctions applied hard, years after the invasion; in other cases, the sanctions just withered away quietly and ignominiously; and in still others, they disintegrated noisily. All the while, the original 'wrong' that had prompted the imposition of these sanctions – the presence of Soviet troops in Afghanistan – remained. By contrast, the sanctions imposed in the wake of the shooting down of KAL 007 avoided the termination trap – in large part because they were structured very differently.

The chapter concludes by contrasting the post-Tiananmen sanctions of Australia and Canada. Canada's sanctions against China were not time-limited, with the result that lifting them became as problematic as the post-Afghanistan sanctions had been. By contrast, the Australian sanctions embraced after Tiananmen contained explicit sunset provisions that allowed the government in Canberra to lift them relatively cleanly after the passage of some time.

These cases of middle-power sanctions against the Soviet Union and China suggest somewhat unorthodox policy implications for the use of this tool of statecraft against great powers. I will argue that for all the initial attractiveness of this policy option, international sanctions should not be employed (and certainly not publicly justified) as either deterrent or compellent punishments. If sanctions are to be used against the great powers – and there are circumstances under which sanctions are an appropriate and useful policy response to actions deemed to be wrongful – they should be employed and justified publicly in a different fashion if the termination problem is to be avoided. I will argue that sanctions are most useful as retributive punishments, and should be imposed in a discrete way, and for definite and strictly limited periods of time.

THE DYNAMIC OF PERPETUATION: AFGHANISTAN

David Leyton-Brown has suggested that 'sanctions can be harder to end than to begin.'[3] Sanctions are exceedingly easy to embrace, as the various case studies in this book demonstrate, precisely because they are such a tempting 'in-between' means of punishing actions of other states that policy-makers consider wrongful or harmful to their interests.[4] Economic sanctions avoid the extremes of doing nothing, on the one hand, and using force, on the other. Sanctions are real, not just symbolic, measures: they give concrete expression to words of condemnation that can be spoken all too easily.

This is not to suggest that words alone directed at a target may not hurt as much as concrete measures. To be sure, the hurts inflicted by words are symbolic rather than material, but that does not necessarily lessen the pain. For example, one of the justifications offered for the boycott of the Moscow Olympics was the need to avoid giving the Soviet Union the kind of legitimacy that international participation at the 1936 Olympic Games in Berlin had given Hitler's regime. Such a clear and explicit equation of the Soviet Union with the Nazis, whose evilness is reviled as much in the USSR as in the West, may well have been more painful to both Soviet citizens and their government than the actual non-participation by others.

But while rhetoric *may* inflict hurt on a target, economic sanctions *will* surely do so. Economic sanctions always impose some tangible hurt on the wrong-doer, and harming a wrong-doer, even if the harms are relatively minor, is an integral component of any punishment, domestic or international.[5] First, hurting wrong-doers provides the psychological satisfaction of knowing that they have received the 'just deserts' of their wrong-doing – in other words, they do not break rules or do harm to others without incurring harmful costs. Second, hurting wrong-doers sends important signals to others about the bounds of 'acceptable' behaviour, signals that may deter by prompting others to change their behaviour through altering their calculus of costs and benefits. Moreover, to the extent that sanctions disrupt normal patterns of economic intercourse, they involve costs for the sender. This self-hurting aspect of punishment is important, for it demonstrates a resolve to rebuff wrong-doing.

But the hurts imposed by economic sanctions remain in the realm of the non-violent, and are not usually hurtful enough to prompt an escalation to war. To be sure, the economic sanctions imposed against Japan by the Western democracies in 1940 and 1941 stand as an exception. Those measures, aimed as they were at crippling Japan's military and industrial capabilities, made the decision to precipitate war in the Pacific in December 1941 an easy, if not an inevitable, one.[6]

Given the alternatives to economic sanctions, therefore, it is not difficult to see why this tool of statecraft was so frequently embraced by Canadian policy-makers as the most attractive policy response in East-West relations during the Cold War era.

But if Canadian policy-makers demonstrated some enthusiasm for economic sanctions as a means of responding to what they saw as wrong-doing by the Soviet Union or its allies, they appear to have devoted little attention to the issue of how these measures, embraced in the first flush of surprise, concern, or anger, would be brought to an end. Little attempt seemed to have been made to address the question, 'Under what conditions will these measures be lifted?' Instead, the tendency of foreign policy makers in Ottawa was to launch into sanctions, and into publicly stated justifications for those measures, as though the end point were a foregone and self-evident conclusion. Excessive attention tended to be focused on the immediate and pressing issue of how to respond appropriately to the wrong-doing in a 'credible' way. To be sure, such immediacy of focus is unavoidable given the domestic and external political imperatives to offer an immediate – and 'effective' – response to acts that disturb the international order or one's own interests (or both). Too often, however, the measures that were adopted fulfilled that need – but they were imposed and were justified publicly in a manner that ignored a longer-range, but no less critical, question: What likely outcomes would the sanctions produce once the excitement generated by the target's initial transgression had died down and the psychological satisfaction produced by the initial punitive response worn off?

The case of the sanctions invoked in response to the Soviet invasion of Afghanistan provides a good illustration of such a lack of projection. Like other Western states,[7] Canada responded to the invasion of Afghanistan with a range of punitive sanctions against the USSR, as we saw in chapter 7 above.[8] But this case illustrates how sanctions can be imposed without a clear idea of where these measures might lead in the future. In other words, the sanctions imposed in reaction to the invasion might have satisfied public demands for an 'effective response' in the first days of 1980, but the measures themselves and the justifications offered for them suggest that little thought had been given to what these sanctions would actually accomplish over even the short term of several months, much less over a period of years.

The measures themselves seem to have been taken without consideration to the longer term. The twin centrepieces of the sanctions – the grain embargo and the Olympic boycott – might have been attractive in the short term, but by their very nature had built into them longer-term problems that do not appear to have been considered in the early days of 1980. Grain was an obvious target for disruption, not only because of poor harvests and the increased importance of imported grain to the Soviet Union, but also because grain dominated the West's economic intercourse with the USSR. However, three important conditions would, as the months passed, create powerful longer-term incentives to terminate these measures, regardless of what the Soviet Union did in Afghanistan. First, because of the Soviet demand for grain, the opportunity costs of adhering to a leak-proof embargo would be considerable for all sanctioning grain producers; the temptation to defect would be high.

Second, holding the sanctioning coalition together becomes more difficult with the passage of time – unless each member of the coalition is committed to freezing *all* market relations that existed at the time the embargo was introduced. But to hope that cryogenic techniques will work better on invisible hands than on mortal ones is to ignore how the very structure of market relations militate against being able to 'freeze' the market in a static fashion over an extended period of time. It is thus not surprising that American farmers, for example, sought to compensate for the decline in Soviet grain sales by breaking into the Chinese market. Nor is it surprising that Canada should take considerable umbrage at what it saw as an 'unjustified' American intrusion into what had been 'traditionally' a Canadian market.

Third, a grain embargo ignored that the same incentives for defection existed *within* as well as *between* states, particularly in those states with the requisites of periodic elections. Even with compensation schemes, farmers had to bear the concrete costs for the grain sanctions. These costs were disproportionately heavy for them relative to other groups, the vast majority of whom had only a symbolic, not a concrete, interest in adopting punitive measures against the Soviet Union. Given these conditions, it is not surprising that the grain embargo should have been so short-lived, and should have disintegrated by the beginning of 1981.

The Olympic boycott was also a measure with short-term attractiveness but longer-term negative implications. Disrupting the Games might have been an emotionally satisfying punishment in the spring of 1980. However, no thought seems to have been given to the 'glass house' factor: measures that have a high susceptibility for comparable retaliation are merely likely to provoke that retaliation. Selecting the

Olympics as a counter-measure in 1980 was short-sighted in this respect, all the more so since the next Summer Games were due to be held in the United States itself. There is little evidence that Joe Clark considered how a rational Soviet leader would react to this symbolically hurtful act. While prediction is easy with the benefit of hindsight, it is none the less hardly surprising that the USSR took the opportunity presented by the locale of the 1984 Games to play classic tit-for-tat politics. Even if Moscow eventually had to create the flimsiest of excuses for its refusal to participate in the Los Angeles Olympics – the threat posed to Soviet athletes by crime in the Los Angeles area was cited – the Soviet leadership no doubt took some considerable satisfaction that the result in 1984 was in a sense comparable to what had been inflicted on the USSR. In both the 1980 and 1984 Games, the hosting superpower, in the absence of the traditional rival bloc, swept the field. But the boycotting superpower had the satisfaction of having made it a hollow victory by its absence. In short, because of the symbolic political importance of the Olympic Games in East-West relations in general, and Soviet-American relations in particular,[9] embracing a boycott in 1980 virtually guaranteed that this measure would aggravate – and prolong – conflict between the blocs.

But it was not only in the choice of the measures themselves that the sanctionists were not forward-looking. The public justifications for these measures also created a situation in which their termination would involve an embarrassing admission of failure. The Canadian government embraced two broad rationales for the sanctions imposed: as a deterrent against Soviet expansion elsewhere, and as a 'compellent' punishment[10] designed to secure a Soviet withdrawal from Afghanistan. Neither rationale had a logic that was forward-looking; both, ironically, favoured a perpetuation of these measures. Moreover, the rhetoric that accompanied these measures was important in creating a logic that perpetuated them.

The deterrent justification for the Afghanistan sanctions figured prominently in official statements. Like most other Western states, Ottawa pushed the deterrent rationale for sanctions – one punishes to deter future wrong-doing. In the public justifications offered by Ottawa, the sanctions were portrayed as being designed to deter the Soviet Union from invading both Iran and Pakistan. To be sure, there was, according to John Kirton,[11] a split between the ministers and their officials on the appropriate interpretation of the Soviet Union's motives – the ministers saw the invasion as a 'grab for the Gulf,' while their bureaucratic officials were more inclined to see the root cause as the situation in Afghanistan itself. However, it should be noted that we are examining here the public justifications. It may have been, as Kirton suggests, that 'Ottawa remained massively sceptical that anything the West could do would achieve such a goal [a Soviet withdrawal from Afghanistan].' This scepticism rarely manifested itself in official statements. Thus, for example, Flora MacDonald, the secretary of state for external affairs, was quoted as saying: 'We don't know where the Soviet juggernaut will move next. The entire western part of the Middle East is vulnerable ... Who knows where they will start?'[12] This theme was echoed by Canada's permanent representative to the United Nations, William Barton, on 11 January, and by Joe Clark during a press conference on 25 January.[13]

However, it could be argued that Ottawa did not think through how these sanctions would actually work in deterring the Soviet Union over the weeks or months following their imposition; or how their deterrent rhetoric, as framed, would contribute to the logic of perpetuation. For example, how would the sanctioners 'know' when the Soviet Union had been sufficiently 'deterred' so the sanctions could be lifted? If Moscow made no further expansionist moves, when would the sanctions be declared a successful 'deterrent' measure and be lifted?

In fact, the sanctions-as-deterrent rationale involves a quintessentially counterfactual condition. One cannot know whether deterrent punishments have worked until one lifts them, but the logic used to impose them as a deterrent in the first place ('We need these measures to deter further wrong-doing') would suggest that they would need to remain in place until there was sufficient evidence that the wrong-doer had in fact been deterred from further wrong-doing. One is thus left with a logical conclusion of Helleresque proportions: punishments imposed as deterrents need to be firmly applied for as long as the wrong-doer does no further wrong. In the case of the Soviet invasion of Afghanistan, a punishment imposed on the USSR as a deterrent needed to be firmly applied for as long as the Soviet Union *did not* make an expansionist move beyond Afghani borders.

In any case, the deterrent rationale for these sanctions was quickly superseded by the Carter Doctrine. As Baldwin has noted, the threat contained in the State of the Union message of 20 January – that further Soviet moves in the Gulf would be met by the use of force – was probably far more effective in cooling whatever expansionist ardour the Soviet leadership may have been harbouring.[14] Once Canada had echoed this threat of force (as Clark did explicitly on 25 January 1980), sanctions were rendered meaningless as a deterrent. However, although their rationale had suddenly disappeared, they had to remain in place, since no logic could be offered to justify lifting them and return East-West relations to the 'business as usual' footing that such termination would signal to the Soviet Union, publics in the West, and all other states.

In addition to deterrence, Canadian statements also suggested that there was a compellent rationale for these sanctions. As Clark argued, 'We are expecting that our actions and, more particularly, that the actions of a number of countries acting together may persuade the Soviet Union to withdraw from Afghanistan. That is the point of the exercise.'[15] Canadian statements linked the presence of Soviet troops in Afghanistan to the sanctions, explicitly suggesting that the sanctions would remain in place as long as the Soviets remained in Afghanistan. For example, Clark was quick to echo Carter's ultimatum on an Olympic boycott: 20 February was set as the date by which Canada would also decide whether to boycott the Olympics.

The problem for Canadian policy-makers was that by embracing compellent rhetoric for sanctions, they had laid the ground for their eventual 'failure.'[16] For the sanctions were not *designed* to compel. First, while some of them no doubt hurt the Soviet Union, as we showed in chapter 7, these measures were not hurtful enough to cause Moscow to change its calculus about the relative costs and benefits of ending the unstable regime of Hafizullah Amin by force.[17]

Second, these were measures imposed against a state that was not dependent in any sense on the West. It is doubtful, for example, that the disruption of Soviet-Canadian academic exchanges seriously affected the Soviet Union; certainly the Olympic boycott, while it deprived the USSR of much-wanted foreign currency, and deeply wounded Soviet pride, was not a measure likely to prompt a Soviet withdrawal from Afghanistan. As Robert A.D. Ford, Canada's ambassador in Moscow, suggested in his memoirs, 'Using the boycott to force Soviet troops out of Afghanistan was unrealistic and should never have been presented as its aim.'[18]

Third, while the USSR might have been hurt more by an immediate and universal grain embargo, there was neither the political will to bring all shipments to a complete halt nor the capacity to make the embargo universal. As a result, the embargo had a sieve-like quality: grains continued to flow to the USSR throughout 1980, and leakage, particularly by Argentina, was rampant.

Finally, the way in which these sanctions were imposed paradoxically made it more costly for the Soviets to comply with demands than to hold firm and suffer whatever economic harms might have been imposed by the West. The loud public condemnation of the Soviet action, the rhetorical comparisons between Soviet actions in Afghanistan and Axis expansionism in the 1930s, and the publicly announced 'deadline' for withdrawal were all designed to demonstrate the West's abhorrence and condemnation of Soviet behaviour. But policy-makers in the West either ignored, or did not care about, the impact that such rhetoric would have on the non-economic, or symbolic, cost-benefit calculus of Soviet leaders (and indeed of Soviet citizens[19]). For these methods all had the effect of virtually guaranteeing that even if the USSR had been in a position to withdraw by early January, Moscow would surely not have acted. As Paul Marantz has noted in the case of Poland, no Soviet leader was going to make it appear as though the Soviet Union was bending to Western coercion.[20]

But if the sanctions adopted were poor compellents, the rhetoric employed in their imposition left the strong impression that they would be effective means to secure a Soviet withdrawal. Little effort was made by Western leaders to communicate to their publics the limits of these measures. Instead, the tendency was to engage in the 'rain dance' explored in chapter 1 above: because it appears that something is being done, all the participants feel better – but nothing of substance is actually accomplished.

However, the dance oversold both the threat posed by the Soviet invasion and the effectiveness of sanctions as an appropriate means to counter that threat. All too often, more cautious approaches were simply drowned out by the expedient of painting the cautioner as 'soft' on Soviet expansionism. Such was the fate of Pierre Trudeau. As leader of the Opposition in January and early February 1980, he was widely criticized for arguing that the likely impact of sanctions such as the Olympic boycott 'will not by itself move one soldier or one tank out of Afghanistan.'[21]

To be sure, such tendencies were exacerbated by the Canadian election campaign that was under way as the Afghanistan crisis unfolded. The election created an additional incentive (not to mention numerous opportunities) for politicians to respond to something that in a very real sense was a crisis of their own making. In other words, what could have been painted as Soviet wrong-doing deserving of a limited and measured response was instead cast as a threat of the magnitude of the Nazi expansionism of the late 1930s, a hyperbolic interpretation that tended to be intensified by the dynamics of speechifying on the hustings.

It is hardly a novel observation, but the dynamics of speech-giving during an election will surely make a difference to what is said – and how it is said. What a politician seeking election says about the Soviet Union at a rally of thousands of cheering citizens of Eastern European origin will likely be heavily affected by the dynamics of such a setting. With the kleigs glaring and the minicams hovering, there will be a considerable temptation to engage in the kind of ad libbery that will excite the crowd and draw roars of approval. This, politicians and their spin-doctors know, is the stuff of which lead-off stories on the nightly news are made, and there are few politicians who can resist having such a positive image of thousands wildly applauding their policies communicated more widely to the electorate. Such was the situation when Flora MacDonald addressed a rally sponsored by the Canadian Committee for Captive European Nations in Nathan Phillips Square in Toronto: her rhetoric was not only designed to appeal to the strongly anti-Soviet crowd, but she appears to have become increasingly pumped up by the roars of approval her anti-Soviet statements were eliciting, with the result that her anti-Soviet rhetoric became increasingly immoderate.[22]

However, having embraced such an immoderate interpretation of Soviet actions, Canadian politicians left themselves little room for manoeuvre. Faced with publics who took the early-January declarations of their leaders about the magnitude of the Soviet threat seriously, and who were thus demanding hawkishly 'tough' action, these leaders had little choice but to demonstrate to their electorates a 'firmness' and 'decisiveness' in responding to Soviet 'expansionism.'

None the less, by publicly linking the sanctions to the Soviet occupation of Afghanistan, policy-makers were ensuring that any termination of those measures while Soviet troops remained in that country would be seen either as a 'failure' of Western statecraft or as an implicit acceptance of the 'wrong' that had been so virulently condemned. There was, in short, no good time to fold these sanctions once they had been imposed.

THE DYNAMIC OF DISINTEGRATION: AFGHANISTAN AND POLAND

I have argued that the sanctions imposed in response to the Afghanistan crisis, once in place, could not easily be lifted given their logic. By adopting short-sighted measures, and by justifying these sanctions in equally short-sighted rhetorical terms, Canadian policy-makers had built into these measures a powerful logic of perpetuation. By following the lead of the United States in casting these sanctions in compellent terms Ottawa had created the following situation: unless the Soviet Union responded in the short term by doing the non-rational – withdrawing from Afghanistan – these sanctions could not be lifted without exposing the sanctioners to charges of 'failure' or of condoning the initial offence. They were, by their own logic, destined to linger indefinitely: Western leaders had made it both too costly for the Soviet Union to withdraw its offending forces (at least in the short term) and too costly for these sanctions to be lifted or modified as long as Moscow did not withdraw. At the same time, however, equally powerful forces were at work causing a disintegration of the sanctioning coalition. These factors were accelerated by the imposition of sanctions against both the Soviet Union and Poland following the declaration of martial law in December 1981.

The first source of disintegration was the considerable incentive for members of the coalition to defect. In part, defection was driven by self-interest, primarily in the form of an economic calculus of the opportunity costs of remaining part of a sanctions effort that was clearly 'not working' as it was supposed to. The rapidity with which grain producers fell over each other to terminate the grain embargo after Ronald Reagan's election as president was eloquent testimony to the rationality of defection that is inherent in any collective effort. By the fall of 1980, grain-producing states were demonstrating a willingness to fold that was unseemly at best, and politically unwise at worst (given what signals the collapse of the grain embargo sent to the Soviet Union). By the time sanctions were imposed following the Polish crisis, the defections for economic gain were widespread and obvious.[23]

But there were also non-economic causes of defection. First, many of the allies of the United States were growing increasingly concerned with the hard-line approach towards the Soviet Union being taken by the Reagan administration, fearing that the increasing tensions between Moscow and Washington could ignite a more serious conflict between the superpowers. Second, the allies resented what they saw as the Reagan administration's propensity to act in a high-handed and unilateralist manner.[24] The furore that erupted within the Atlantic alliance in 1982 was triggered by Reagan's attempts to coerce the Europeans to impose sanctions on the construction of a natural-gas pipeline in the summer of 1982.[25]

A second disintegrative force was the continued need to engage the Soviet Union. Although Canadian politicians found it easy to assert that there would be no 'business as usual' with Moscow, the difficulty was that they could not meaningfully reduce the multidimensional East-West relationship to merely one dimension that focused on Afghanistan. However Soviet behaviour may have angered the West, this in no way could obviate the pressing need to continue to deal with the USSR on a range of other issues. While the economic interest of the Europeans in continuing trade and investment with the Soviet Union was one motivating factor, an even more pressing need stemmed from the sheer size and status of the Soviet Union in the international system. One can with ease send a small state like Vietnam to the international equivalent of Coventry, and actually follow through on promises that there will be no 'business as usual'; one simply cannot do the same with a great power (as American sanctions against the People's Republic of China in the 1950s and 1960s so clearly demonstrated). There was no way of avoiding the 'business' of international politics with the Soviet Union. Each of the sanctioning states, from the United States to the smaller powers like Canada, would discover that the logic of the sanctions enacted over Afghanistan or Poland simply could not be sustained in the face of a need to deal with Moscow.

A third factor that caused a disintegration of the commitment to sanctions was the dissipation of public hawkishness towards the Soviet Union. Marantz attributes this collapse to 'an impatient Western public opinion,' for whom 'three or four years are an eternity.'[26] He suggests that when sanctions did not 'produce results' – a Soviet withdrawal – Western publics no longer regarded sanctions as they had in early 1980.

I would not disagree with Marantz's view. However, I would argue that, in this case, the negative impact of these measures had an additional effect on the direction of public support. Once Western sanctions were in place, a deep hostility in the East-West relationship in the short and medium term was unavoidable. Both the Soviet Union and the United States had opted for stalemate on the issue of Afghanistan. First, neither side was giving the other any room for cooperative behaviour. It is true that the means chosen by the Soviet leadership to solve its acute policy problem in Afghanistan in 1979 was hardly designed to provoke a positive reaction in the West; by the same token, however, Western leaders, by responding as they did, made it impossible for the Soviet government to do anything but hang tough. But it is important to note that at that time neither side was resorting to more forceful measures. Indeed, the more forceful measures would not be adopted until 1984, when the Reagan administration began large-scale arms shipments, notably Stinger anti-aircraft missiles, to the anti-Kabul forces, thus increasing dramatically not only the military costs of Soviet occupation, but also Soviet casualties.

This stalemate proved to have an important effect on Western public opinion the longer it continued. The initial public hawkishness that had been fuelled by the hyperbolic rhetoric could not be sustained. Instead, as the hostility of the two superpowers intensified, the hawkishness was gradually replaced by a growing concern about the possibility of systemic war and a widespread feeling that such hostility-enhancing measures as economic sanctions were an inappropriate means to maintain peace.

The logic of perpetuation that had been built into the sanctions at the time of their imposition eventually began to clash with the dynamic of disintegration that manifested itself in the aftermath of the immediate response to the invasion. The result was that while the Soviet Union was still engaged in what had been characterized as wrong-doing of massive proportions, the sanctions imposed between 1980 and 1982 were dropped one by one, beginning with the grain embargo. By 1988, when the withdrawal of Soviet troops from Afghanistan began, there were few sanctions left in place. Moreover, because there had been no specific time limits set on these punishments, they were not terminated cleanly, or with any allied cohesiveness, but rather they were allowed to wither away, by slow degrees, sometimes imperceptibly.

At this point, it might be asked: So what? What are the problems associated with a withering away of sanctions? Why should we be concerned about how sanctions end? It is true that there are cases when these dynamics of perpetuation and disintegration pose few costs. The American sanctions against Cuba, North Korea, and Vietnam are illustrative examples of how sanctions can linger without it mattering very much to the international system as a whole that there is never a good or logical time to terminate these measures. Likewise, the failure of the United States to maintain a sanctioning coalition in the cases of Cuba or Nicaragua had few dramatic political consequences. But it can be argued that when sanctions are employed as an instrument of statecraft against a great power, it does matter when and how such measures are imposed – and when and how they are lifted.

One of the reasons why termination can be a problem is that squabbles over sanctions can send the wrong messages to the sanctioned states. Certainly in a historical context, economic sanctions against the Soviet Union and its allies proved to be one of the persistent sources of friction among the Western allies during the 1950s and 1960s; the sanctions imposed following the invasion of Afghanistan and the declaration of martial law in Poland were no different. But these squabbles among the Western allies over aspects of sanctions policy against the Soviet Union have wider application to future great-power rivalry. For it can be argued that such displays of disunity as we saw among Western states in the 1980s will make a difference to how foreign policy makers in the target state perceive the global correlation of forces, as well as the constraints and opportunities presented for the pursuit of their interests. As Falkenheim has suggested, the divergence within the West over both Afghanistan and Poland clearly encouraged the Soviet leadership to continue its policy of trying to drive a wedge between the Western Europeans and the United States.[27] Just as it made little sense during the Cold War for Western policy-makers to encourage hostility and tension between the blocs, so too did it make little sense to encourage adventurism and opportunism by the kind of displays of disunity among allies that seem to come so readily when economic sanctions are embraced.

But the primary problem is that sanctions can have a serious long-term effect on great-power relations. If sanctions are imposed without clear consideration of how these measures will be brought to an end, they will perforce linger, as they did after Afghanistan. Because sanctions are both an act of hostility and an act of disruption of normal intercourse, they are measures that not only enhance rather than reduce tension between great powers, but also impede rather than promote some measure of cooperation and dialogue.

THE TRAP AVOIDED: KAL 007

The difficulties surrounding the sanctions imposed in the wake of the invasion of Afghanistan and the Polish crisis were, however, avoided in the case of Western responses to the shooting down of KAL 007 by Soviet fighters in September 1983.[28] While it should be acknowledged that the destruction of KAL 007 was seen as qualitatively different from the invasion of Afghanistan or the coercion of the Polish government, we can none the less see differences in how the West responded to this case of Soviet wrong-doing. Abandoning the approach that had characterized its response to the Afghanistan case, the West instead opted for concrete punishments that were both retributive in their justification and limited in nature.

Western punishments, it should be noted, only made sense in retributive terms. It is true that Reagan asserted, 'It would be easy to think in terms of vengeance, but that is not a proper answer. We want justice and action to see that this never happens again.'[29] However, since this deed could in no way be undone, there were no grounds for compellence; and Moscow's reactions suggested that it was unlikely that such an event would recur. In these circumstances, 'justice' could only mean the justice of exacting a price for wrong-doing: retribution or vengeance.

Likewise, the punishments chosen were limited – in three ways. First, they were limited in the punitive price sought from the USSR; gone were the wide-ranging and open-ended penalties that had been imposed after Afghanistan. Regardless of the harshness of the rhetoric, there seems to have been a conscious decision not to invoke the largely negative dynamics of the post-Afghanistan and Polish sanctions. (Indeed, the price exacted for the deaths of 269 people was deemed in some quarters to be woefully inadequate: in the words of Dimitri K. Simes, the West's reaction was a 'sad mixture of jingoistic rhetoric and impotence.'[30]) Second, punitive measures were in the main limited to the issue area in which the offence had occurred – civil aviation. Punitive actions were directed against both the landing rights of Aeroflot and also other nations' flights into the Soviet Union. Finally, the measures were limited in time. Most countries followed Canada's lead in imposing time-limited bans on landing rights, or flights to the Soviet Union, ranging from two weeks to ninety days. This latter aspect allowed the West to engage in the 'rain dance' in the immediate aftermath of the incident; to impose some concrete costs on the USSR in retribution for what was portrayed as a criminal act; to remain (and appear to remain) united and determined; and, after the specified period of time, to lift the sanctions cleanly, declaring that the 'price had been paid.'

AVOIDING THE TRAP: TIANANMEN REVISITED

Did the punishments that were imposed after KAL 007 signal a change in the Canadian approach to the use of sanctions against great powers? In the case of sanctions against the Soviet Union, it is hard to know, for Canada only considered using sanctions against the USSR twice between 1983 and the Soviet Union's final disintegration in December 1991. The first occurred in January 1991, when Ottawa threatened to suspend lines of credit and other financial-assistance programs following the despatch of military forces into the Baltic republics. The second occurred in August 1991, in response to the short-lived coup d'état against Mikhail Gorbachev. Canada was in the process of suspending credit and financial-aid programs when the coup failed. In neither case can we see evidence of the termination trap in operation.

By contrast, the sanctions invoked by Australia and Canada against China in response to the Tiananmen massacre in June 1989 provide an interesting contrast in how states can structure sanctions to avoid the termination trap. As we saw in chapter 8, Canada's post-Tiananmen sanctions did not follow the more careful and time-limited approach adopted in the KAL 007 case. Instead, the sanctions tended to be more open-ended, and as a consequence revealed many of the dynamics associated with the termination of the Afghanistan and Polish sanctions. As in these earlier cases, the Tiananmen sanctions were justified by politicians in Ottawa using the 'no-business-as-usual-with-butchers' rhetoric that makes lifting sanctions cleanly a virtual impossibility: since the sanctions did not lead to the downfall of the perpetrators of the massacre, or to greater liberalization, any lifting of the sanctions was inevitably denounced as doing business with butchers. But the Canadian government soon felt the same tendencies towards disintegration that it had discovered in the case of the Soviet Union and Afghanistan: there was a need to continue dealing with China. But, as in the case of Afghanistan, Canada's approach to sanctions in the Tiananmen case meant that there was no good time to lift the sanctions. As a consequence, they tended to be lifted in a ragged fashion. By 1993, some of the sanctions imposed in 1989 had been lifted and some limited high-level contacts had been restored. But some of the other punitive measures embraced in the wake of Tiananmen, such as restrictions on the aid program and concessional financing, remained firmly in place.[31]

Australia's sanctions against China, by contrast, were carefully and purposely time-limited. When the government of Bob Hawke agreed to a set of punitive measures in July 1989, it specified quite clearly that the sanctions were only to remain in place for a limited period of time – until the end of 1989. While the Australian government did not justify its post-Tiananmen sanctions in purely retributive terms, there is little doubt that Canberra sought to structure its sanctions in such a way as to make the lifting of them easier, and in that way avoid the termination trap that had so marked the sanctions imposed after Afghanistan.

The 'sunset' provisions in Australia's Tiananmen sanctions meant that by the end of 1989 the cabinet was faced with the need to reconsider its China policies. A review by the Department of Foreign Affairs and Trade was completed by early January 1990, and Gareth Evans, the foreign minister, brought it to cabinet. The government's decision, announced on 23 January, was to confirm the policy of July 1989, but to modify it in two important respects. First, the blanket ban on ministerial visits was lifted; instead, the government proposed to consider Chinese high-level visits to Australia or Australian ministerial visits to China on a case-by-case basis. Cabinet also authorized Evans and the prime minister to make adjustments to the policy framework, depending on an on-going assessment of Australia's 'fundamental interests,' and on what other countries were doing.[32] Evans denied that this was a return to 'business as usual,' but rather argued that this policy sought to balance Australia's competing objectives. As he put it, 'Getting that balance right, and ensuring you don't send signals which can be construed as approval for what we must continue to disapprove [of] ... that's the hard part.'[33]

During an interview following the adoption of the new policy, Evans was asked if the shift in Australia's position was in any way connected to China's policy towards Cambodia – particularly the prospect that the government in Beijing might drop its support for the Khmer Rouge. Evans acknowledged that this was 'an element of the total equation.'[34] In fact, the Chinese attitude towards the peace process in Cambodia had played a most important part in the evolution of Canberra's policy. The Australians, and Gareth Evans in particular, were deeply involved in the peace process in Cambodia: following the diplomatic impasse that had emerged after the 1989 Paris International Conference on Cambodia, the Australian government had tried to break the deadlock by producing a technical blueprint for the different parties to the dispute to adopt – the so-called 'Red Book' of Working Papers prepared for the Djakarta Informal Meeting on Cambodia of 26–28 February 1990.[35] The success of the peace process depended heavily on Chinese cooperation. The government in Canberra therefore had an incentive to engage Beijing in a quid pro quo that was implicit rather than explicit: in return for continued Chinese cooperation on global issues – such as the Chinese abstention on Resolution 678 at the United Nations Security Council over the Iraqi invasion of Kuwait or Chinese cooperation over Cambodia – Australia would soften its post-Tiananmen stance. (It might be added that the same calculus was also driving the Chinese leadership: in return for a softening in Western sanctions, China would adopt a cooperative posture on international issues.)

The first high-level visit under the new policy framework occurred when Qi Yuanjing, the minister for metallurgical industry, was invited to attend the opening of the Mount Channar iron-ore mine, the Chinese-Australian joint venture in Western Australia.[36] Other visits soon followed: the deputy premier of Queensland visited China in May to press for an increase in the state's exports to China; at the end of May, one hundred members of the China-Australia Senior Executive Forum met in Shanghai.[37]

In August 1990, the Hawke government decided to send Neal Blewett, minister for trade negotiations, to visit China in early September to co-chair the fourth meeting of the Australia-China Joint Ministerial Economic Commission (JMEC) in Beijing. This visit had a number of purposes. First, the Australian government placed considerable value on the Australia-China Joint Ministerial Economic Commission. At the third meeting of the JMEC – held before the Beijing massacre – the two sides had agreed to schedule their next meeting for April 1990. While cabinet ministers in Canberra were agreed that a meeting before the first anniversary of the massacre would be inappropriate, there was none the less a concern that if the 1990 meeting were cancelled altogether, this institution would slip into disuse. Second, the government was interested in reciprocating Qi's visit to Australia in May: indeed, Blewett was scheduled to attend a symbolic opening ceremony for the Channar iron-ore project in Beijing and the opening of the China-Australia Iron and Steel Training Centre, funded by Australia's aid agency, in Wuhan. Moreover, because Blewett was a senior member of the Hawke ministry, there was some considerable symbolic significance in sending him to reciprocate the visit of a relatively junior Chinese minister for metallurgical industry.

However, Blewett was at pains to stress that his travels to China did 'not signal a return to business as usual,' but reaffirmed 'the Government's policy of preserving Australia's long-term strategic and commercial interests, encouraging modernisation and liberalisation within China and keeping open as many channels of access and communication with as many segments of Chinese society as possible.'[38] Blewett visited Beijing in early September. In a meeting with Vice Foreign Minister Liu Huaqiu, he discussed the situation in the Persian Gulf and the peace process in Cambodia. But in what was later described as a 'robust' presentation, he also raised human rights issues with Liu, reminding him that the Australian government was still concerned about those still being detained by the authorities in China, and about sixty individual

human rights cases. At the JMEC meeting, Blewett agreed to the establishment of a US$50 million export finance credit facility between Aus-
trade and the Bank of China; for their part, the Chinese side confirmed
Beijing's desire to continue importing wool and sugar, and expressed
interest in further Chinese investment in Australian resource projects.
The JMEC also agreed to explore possible projects in transport and
communication and increased cooperation in automotive components.
Finally, the two sides agreed to a further four projects under the Concessional Finance Facility that were being considered before the 13 July
1989 sanctions.[39]

Two weeks after Blewett's trip, John Hewson, leader of the Opposition, visited Beijing. Like Blewett, Hewson also raised Australia's
human rights concerns in a forceful way with Jiang Zemin, the general
secretary of the Chinese Communist Party. The meeting, described as
'very tense,' was followed by a refusal of Hewson's delegation to attend
the opening ceremonies of the Asian Games, which were occurring
during their visit.[40]

By February 1991, Evans himself was invited to visit China. In
advance of the visit, scheduled for April, Canberra lifted the last restrictions against China that had been imposed in 1989. Evans justified the
move in these terms: 'Although differences do remain between us,
mainly on our different approaches to human-rights matters, our view
is that Australia and China should look ahead to make progress on a
number of fronts where we can clearly work to the mutual benefit of
our people – trade and investment, and political and economic cooperation in areas of shared regional or multilateral concerns.'[41] A key
element in the Australian decision to lift the last barrier to the resumption of high-level visits between the two countries was the willingness
of the Chinese government to host an official Australian human rights
delegation to visit China and investigate the human rights situation
there. The idea of having such a delegation visit China emerged
through discussions in Beijing between officials of the Australian
embassy and the Chinese foreign ministry. As Peter Van Ness shows in
his study of this case,[42] both sides had good reasons to embrace this
proposal. For the Chinese government, the attempt to meet Western
criticisms of human rights abuses in such a way was impelled by a
desire to escape the isolation that had enveloped it since Tiananmen.
For the Australians, the idea of a human rights delegation provided a
useful means to make the restoration of high-level links between the
two countries more palatable to Australians.

Evans visited Beijing in late April 1991 and held wide-ranging discussions with China's foreign minister, Qian Qichen. Although it would be another two years before an Australian prime minister paid a visit to China – Paul Keating visited China from 23 to 28 June 1993[43] – and although bans remained on the sale of military equipment to China, the Evans visit marked the end of the sanctions imposed after the Beijing massacre.

CONCLUSION – TWO SUGGESTIONS FROM EXPERIENCE

There can be little doubt that imposing sanctions against great powers is fraught with difficulties, as the cases of Western sanctions against both the Soviet Union and China during the 1980s demonstrate clearly. The termination trap identified in this chapter poses one of the more serious problems, in that sanctions, as an instrument of statecraft that is essentially hostile and hurtful, inexorably get in the way of the need to continue to 'do business' with the target great power.

It is true that one way to minimize such difficulties associated with sanctions is to eschew such measures as a tool of statecraft against great powers altogether. Instead, one might reserve such punishments for smaller or weaker states who engage in wrong-doing, such as the long list of small states sanctioned by members of the international community in the 1980s and 1990s: Argentina, Burma, Cambodia, Cuba, Fiji, Haiti, Indonesia, Iraq, Laos, Libya, Nicaragua, Panama, Poland, South Africa, Sri Lanka, Syria, or Vietnam. But such a solution is both extreme and unrealistic. Sanctions are embraced because they are an attractive means of responding to wrong-doing by other states, including the wrong-doing of other great powers. They hurt, even if not enough to compel or deter, and thus satisfy what seems to be an inexorable human desire to see wrong-doers punished; they are concrete, and thus give some meaning to rhetoric that would be otherwise costless; and they are non-violent, and so do not raise the stakes to levels dangerous to systemic peace. They also satisfy domestic opinion, quieting not only fervent hawkishness, but also the kind of opinion expressed by the *New York Times* during the Polish crisis that, 'as long as the economic weapon may have some effect, it would be irresponsible not to use it.'[44] Thus, sanctions are a useful tool, even against wrong-doing by great powers.

If sanctions are not be abandoned, however, how to avoid the problems explored above? The cases of the Western sanctions imposed after the shoot-down of KAL 007 and the Australian sanctions imposed on China after Tiananmen suggest that the key is not to eschew the use of sanctions, but to refine their application.

First, while sanctions are frequently successful in compelling weak or small states, this tool of statecraft should not be imposed as a *compellent* or *deterrent* punishment against great powers, but only as *retributive* punishment. It makes little sense to try to compel or deter great powers by economic measures. As several students of the Afghanistan measures have noted, the Soviet Union's relative economic independence was too great, and the economic costs that could be imposed by the West were insufficiently hurtful. Sanctions imposed that are justified in compellent terms will merely recreate the kind of problem we saw in the Afghanistan case. Not only will the sanctions linger, perhaps longer than appropriate or desired, but compellent rhetoric in particular sets the sanctionist up for 'failure' when these costs do not have the effect of altering the cost-benefit calculus of the leadership of the offending great power.

Likewise, if deterrence of further wrong-doing elsewhere is sought, the case of Afghanistan strongly suggests that, as Baldwin has noted, the punishments imposed by economic sanctions will be of less utility in actually deterring further wrong-doing than threats of more vigorous – and potentially costly – action. As Baldwin has noted, 'punishment does not deter, threats do.'[45] Some have argued that the threats of further Western sanctions delivered to the USSR in 1981 deterred Moscow from using force against Poland.[46] However, given that there was a strong possibility that armed intervention by other Warsaw Pact countries would trigger civil war in Poland, it could be suggested that the threat of economic sanctions was of distinctly secondary importance in the Soviet calculus of how best to respond to the Polish crisis.

Rather, economic punishments meted out for acts of great-power wrong-doing should be adopted and justified in retributive terms: the great power committed an offence against the international community, and for that wrong it must itself be hurt. It must 'pay a price' for its wrong-doing.[47] In other words, sanctions should be imposed not to force a change in behaviour, but merely to exact a price for wrong-doing. It might be noted that such sanctions, when justified using a retributive formulation, cannot but 'succeed,' since alteration of wrongful behaviour is not a condition of the imposition – or the lifting – of the punishment. To the extent that punishment imposed for retribution imposes an evil for an evil, it is always remarkably 'successful' – which is probably why retributivists have been with us since the days of the ancients, the best efforts of philosophers to debunk the retributive justification for punishment notwithstanding.

It is true that there are several problems with retributive sanctions. First, such measured responses may not satisfy the hawkish clamour of public opinion for vigorous action in the face of 'wrong-doing' by other great powers; the retributive rationale does require careful and calm explication by policy-makers. Second, there will be an inexorable temptation for sanctionist leaders to slide in their public rhetoric into the idiom of compellent punishment, suggesting that the purpose of the sanctions is to effect a change in wrongful behaviour. Third, there is a significant problem in knowing what the 'price' for wrong-doing is, and when it has been paid.

Hence the second suggestion for refining the use of sanctions: that punishments for acts of great-power wrong-doing should be highly specific, involving a hurtful but limited price that can be paid in a limited period of time. The case of Afghanistan demonstrated the thorny problem of determining the appropriate time to lift the sanctions. There was never a good time to lift the measures embraced in the early days of 1980, mainly because of the vagueness with which they had been imposed. One of the ways of correcting this problem is to specify in advance what the punitive price will be, and when it will have been paid. This requires that considerable care be taken in the choice of hurtful punishments, for vague measures or sanctions without easily measurable costs will make the determination of a specific price virtually impossible. This is not to suggest that all punitive hurts have to be quantifiable in currency value, for some hurts, however appropriate, are difficult to express in dollars (or rubles). But the more quantifiable the punishment (so many dollars in economic intercourse foregone, so many months of suspended high-level official contacts, so many flights or hockey games or circus performances or academic exchanges cancelled), the more readily the punishment can be measurable.

Whatever punitive price is decided on, that price must be limited, as it is in all but exceptional cases in domestic punishment. Normally, most wrong-doers under most systems of domestic law do not face an unlimited price to be paid for their offence. To be sure, there are exceptions: indefinite incarceration imposed on 'dangerous' offenders, or disfiguring punishments, such as the amputations inflicted on offenders by some regimes, are 'limitless' in this sense. So too an international offender should not be confronted with a punishment that is limitless or indefinite.

Limiting punishment is rooted in a historical concern that the hurt imposed on an offender is in some way commensurate with the hurt of the offence – a concern evident as far back as the *lex talionis*. What restrains the imposition of limitless punishment is the recognition that hurts that are unending eventually become incommensurate with the harm of the original wrong. In international politics, there is also a pragmatic rationale for limiting punishment. Ensuring that the hurts will be limited allows the sanctioner maximum flexibility to terminate the sanctions, declaring that the punitive price has been paid, without falling into the termination trap that enthusiastic sanctionists so often set for themselves.

11

The Impact of Rhetoric:
Running Out of Steam on South Africa?

When policy-makers speak about sanctions, the rhetoric they use is not unimportant. In previous chapters, we have seen the powerful impact that the rhetoric used by politicians to explain and justify sanctions can have on policy. In the case of the Soviet invasion of Afghanistan, politicians allowed their rhetoric to ratchet up hostilities, creating an inertial attachment to sanctions and making the measures imposed against the Soviet Union difficult to lift later. Part of the reason for the 'termination trap,' I suggested, lay in the expectations about sanctions created by leaders. In the case of the Iraqi invasion of Kuwait, the rhetorical expectations attached to the sanctions option helped to obscure the shifts in coalition politics that were making sanctions largely irrelevant to the outcome of that conflict. But the expectations created by the rhetoric of political leaders can also have lingering effects on the subsequent course of their sanctions policies, creating what might be thought of as a rhetorical trap of heightened expectations.

The case of Canadian sanctions policy towards South Africa in the late 1980s demonstrates this dynamic at work. As I argued in chapter 5, one of the most dramatic changes that the Progressive Conservative government of Brian Mulroney introduced in Canadian foreign policy when it came to power in September 1984 was in Ottawa's approach to South Africa. Even staunch critics of Canada's South African policies agreed that the policies embraced by Mulroney overturned or abandoned the cautious and anti-sanctionist approach that had been the mark of each postwar government down to 1984. Instead, the Conservative government engaged in an active attempt to put pressure on the South African government, an approach that had at its core the embrace of sanctions.

However, after an initial two years of anti-apartheid diplomacy, many analysts and activists argued that the government had lost momentum: it no longer was taking the initiative; it was back-pedalling on its earlier promises to break all relations with South Africa. In short, according to many, the government's sanctionist policies towards South Africa had run out of steam.[1] Significantly, even Stephen Lewis, who as Canada's permanent representative to the United Nations had played an important part in the Mulroney government's diplomacy, would complain publicly on his retirement in August 1988 that the South African issue had lost the importance to the government that it had had in 1985.

The activism of the Mulroney government on sanctions against South Africa in the mid-1980s demonstrates the degree to which this tool of statecraft is a measure that can easily entrap a sanctionist government, snaring it in a rhetorical trap not dissimilar to the termination trap discussed in the previous chapter. For when one looks at the Mulroney government's activist policies of 1985 and 1986 and then at its policies in 1987 and 1988, it would appear at first blush that Ottawa had indeed run out of steam on the South African issue in the late 1980s. For there can be little doubt that after the Commonwealth Heads of Government Meetings in Vancouver in 1987, the pace of sanctionist measures slackened. There were few new Canadian sanctions, and the issue appeared to be of only sporadic interest to the prime minister and his secretary of state for external affairs, Joe Clark.

I argue in this chapter, however, that the Canadian government had not lost steam, nor had it lost interest in the South African issue. Rather, by 1988 the government had indeed slackened the pace of sanctions against South Africa, not for lack of interest, but because of a recognition that maintaining the logic of increasing pressure on South Africa would have led the Mulroney government into policies that would have been, for Canada, quite radical, involving implications well beyond the willingness of the prime minister to countenance.

BUILDING STEAM: CHANGES IN CANADIAN POLICY

To assess the 'loss of steam' argument, one must begin with an examination of the changes to Canadian policy introduced by the Mulroney government in the summer and autumn of 1985 and the assumptions that underlay them. As chapter 5 demonstrated, these changes, beginning with the economic and other sanctions introduced by Joe Clark on 6 July, marked a substantial shift from the traditional Canadian approach to the institutionalized racism in South Africa, which had involved rhetorical denunciation but a commitment to maintain normal diplomatic and commercial relations with Pretoria.

If previous governments had placed a premium on what T.A. Keenleyside has called a 'business as usual' approach,[2] the Mulroney government left little doubt in the summer and autumn of 1985 that it had no such commitment to maintaining ties. On the contrary: both the prime minister and his external-affairs minister had a personal, and almost visceral, antipathy for South African apartheid and an equally visceral disdain for the 'business as usual' approach that in its essence involved an acceptance of institutionalized racism. Likewise, if previous governments had been willing to let others take the lead on the South African issue in multilateral fora, the Mulroney government adopted a highly active role at the biennial Commonwealth meetings and the annual economic summit in an attempt to rally multilateral support to put pressure on Pretoria.

Thus, following the imposition of the state of emergency in South Africa in July, the government invoked further measures in September, promising that if an end to apartheid were not forthcoming, Canada would invoke 'total sanctions' and 'end our relations absolutely.' By the autumn, the prime minister would engage in what one official was later to describe to Heribert Adam and Kogila Moodley as a 'high-wire act.'[3] In his speech to the United Nations General Assembly in October, he would boldly declare that, 'if there are not fundamental changes in South Africa, we are prepared to invoke total sanctions against that country and its repressive regime. If there is no progress in the dismantling of apartheid, our relations with South Africa may have to be severed absolutely. Our purpose is not to punish or to penalize, but to hasten peaceful change.'[4] This speech, which was by all accounts delivered on the insistence of the prime minister over the objections of diplomats in External Affairs, is a good example of how the rhetoric of leaders can 'ratchet up' expectations about sanctions.

For if this approach marked a significant change in how a succession of Canadian governments before 1984 approached the South African issue, it was none the less based on a particular logic that would doom it to appear to 'lose steam' the longer that it was in place. For the Mulroney government's policies towards South Africa embraced in 1985 were premised on one key assumption: that the Republic of South Africa could be coerced, or forced by non-violent means, to abandon its commitment to the structures of apartheid – or, as the prime minister put it to the UN General Assembly, to 'come to its senses.'[5]

The attachment to the logic of coercion can be seen in the government's rejection of the primary alternative to the status quo: symbolic statecraft. However much it was dissatisfied with the cautious policies of its predecessors, the cabinet eventually rejected what might be thought of as the 'fire all your guns at once' approach to relations with South Africa. This approach, which was being advocated by many anti-apartheid activists and both opposition parties in the House of Commons, held that Canada should embrace the single grand gesture: terminate diplomatic relations and impose a unilateral and total ban on the movement between the two countries of anything that could be directly controlled by Ottawa – goods, services, capital, technology, communications, and people.

Such a single-shot blast, however satisfying emotionally, and however important it might have been in terms of the symbolic signals sent to the non-whites in South Africa and to other states, would, however, have had little instrumental value as far as apartheid was concerned. In other words, such Canadian measures would have had no concrete – or instrumental – effect on the structures of institutionalized racism. They would not have caused those in South Africa committed to the maintenance of those structures to abandon them, and would have been as unlikely to cause other governments whose concrete interests commit them to normal relations with Pretoria to adopt a sanctionist position. Moreover, the single grand gesture, eliminating as it does all the non-violent tools of coercion from one's repertoire in one stroke, would have reduced Canadian options considerably, for the only other guns left to fire would have been the real variety.

Although by all accounts Mulroney himself found the single-blast approach quite attractive, his government rejected it in 1985, and in the years afterwards. It opted instead for a coercive approach to sanctions against South Africa that was marked by a step-by-step, gradualist policy of both applying hurtful or disruptive measures and threatening to increase the hurts if South African behaviour did not change. In particular, both Mulroney and Clark kept the 'grand gestures' – terminating diplomatic relations and imposing a total trade ban – as threats that they would have no difficulty implementing at some point in the future. The government also proceeded on the assumption that Canada, acting alone, had less capacity to hurt South Africa economically than if the hurts were multilateral. Thus, emphasis was placed on trying to secure multilateral support for the threat, or imposition, of such hurtful measures, particularly in the Commonwealth and at the economic summit.

LOSING STEAM? VANCOUVER AND AFTER

However, embracing the instrumental purposes of sanctions against South Africa, and thereby rejecting the symbolic approach, carries with it a particular logic that forces sanctioners to confront the consequences of their sanctions on the behaviour of the target *ex post*. In particular, what happens when the hurtful measures imposed – and those other hurts promised for the future – do not have the intended effect of changing the target's behaviour? The logic of gradualist coercion suggests new sanctions and new threats. In other words, faced with intransigence, the logic suggests a three-fold response: (1) the maintenance of the original measures; (2) the imposition of previously threatened measures; and (3) threats of new hurtful measures that will follow if the target fails to comply. If one starts the sanctioning process with a large number of possible hurtful measures, one can go through this cycle several times against a strong or intransigent adversary whose behaviour does not change. And indeed this is precisely what the Mulroney government went through in the mid-1980s – as each attempt to use hurts, imposed or threatened, to move Pretoria was met with little but scorn and intransigence.

There are, however, limits to the gradualist cycle. The first is that one's repertoire of hurtful but non-violent measures is in fact finite. Between 1985 and 1988, Canada invoked well over twenty-five different measures designed either to hurt South Africa or to weaken the structures of apartheid, the last one being a tightening of the ban on sports contacts in August 1988.

To be sure, these measures did not empty the bag of possible hurtful sanctions. For example, Ottawa could have imposed a complete ban on travel by Canadian citizens to South Africa and a concomitant ban on the admission of South Africans to Canada; it could have embargoed all telephone, mail, and telecommunications traffic to and from South Africa over which Ottawa had control. It could have passed legislation requiring any public institution receiving federal funds, directly or indirectly, to adhere to the same internal purchasing rules applied to the federal government. Or it could have refused to engage in contract work of any sort with Canadian firms or multinationals with indirect holdings in South Africa. Or, using the well-worn Canadian technique of imposing taxes on things considered sinful, Ottawa could have instituted a special 'anti-apartheid' surtax, levied through the personal income-tax system, on dividends received from Canadian (and even foreign) firms operating directly or indirectly in South Africa, the proceeds from which would be directly added to the embassy-administered Canada Fund in Pretoria. It could also of course have made good on its promise to embrace the 'grand gestures' – the termination of diplomatic relations or total trade sanctions.

But if such measures had been invoked, and had the South African government remained steadfast in the face of these or other Canadian measures, eventually Canada would have simply run out of hurtful measures that did not involve the encouragement of violence or the use of force itself. Thus, the logic of coercion draws the sanctionist inexorably to violent measures when non-violent measures fail to coerce.

The second limit to gradualist coercion is the position taken by other states. Sanctions imposed by one middle power alone on another middle power are unlikely to have instrumental effects. However, as noted above, it is commonly supposed that if sanctions are imposed by a group of states acting together, they are likely to have a greater impact.[6] It is thus believed that what is needed for 'successful' sanctions is power, and in the case of South Africa, it was thought that if only those states with substantial economic stakes in South Africa were on side, the power to bend Pretoria to the outside world's will would be there. Thus, the Canadian government moved to gather that power by seeking the support of the world's great economic powers: Britain in the context of the Commonwealth; and the United States, Japan, Germany, France, and Britain in the context of the economic summit.

This aspect of Canadian policy was not wholly successful, though certainly not for lack of trying. For all of Canada's efforts to secure support from its G-7 partners, the economic great powers proved singularly unreceptive to Canadian entreaties. Mulroney himself was rebuffed on several occasions. At the Commonwealth Heads of Government Meetings in Nassau in 1985 and Vancouver in 1987, Margaret Thatcher, the British prime minister, openly rebuffed the efforts of Mulroney and other Commonwealth leaders seeking stiffer British sanctions against South Africa, taking great delight in doing so (much to Mulroney's scarcely concealed chagrin). Mulroney was to be no more successful at the Toronto G-7 summit in June 1988. At that meeting, the other leaders remained adamant in their refusal to embrace wholesale sanctions against South Africa. The reasons offered for their reluctance included the well-worn arguments about sanctioning South Africa: sanctions don't work; or sanctions would hurt South African blacks; or sanctions would be inappropriate in the circumstances. And from this general line, the leaders of the great powers did not move.

The logic of graduated coercion is thus increasingly blunted with the passage of time. With each new measure, the costs to the sanctioning state increase. These costs include the escalating financial costs of disrupted economy activity; the political costs of domestic opposition, particularly from those individuals or groups whose interests are affected; and the diplomatic costs of possible objections from other states that are opposed to the sanctions stakes being raised. We can see that, in the case of the initial sanctions that Canada imposed against South Africa, the costs of those measures were relatively slight. A ban on the sale of Krugerrands, for example, was easy to impose, with few external or domestic costs. Indeed, given that the Canadian government's own gold-bullion coin, the Maple Leaf, was competing directly with the Krugerrand, there was a positive incentive to embrace this sanction. The same could not be said, however, of more rigorous sanctions, such as a complete travel ban, a surtax on South African–tainted dividends, or a disruption of mail and telecommunications. Each of these measures could be expected to generate significant opposition, both within Canada and in the international community writ large.

More important, however, with each partial measure, Ottawa crept closer and closer to the penultimate policy dictated by this logic of coercion – the 'grand gestures' of a 'total break' in diplomatic and economic relations. And once those measures are embraced, and produce no result, the logic of coercion suggests that the only other option left is to threaten or use the *ultima ratio* – armed force. And while Mulroney and Clark took a line completely unlike that of all their predecessors on the use of force as a means of ending apartheid in general, it was never a realistic option for Canadian statecraft against South Africa. In short, it can be suggested that as the number of non-violent options dwindled, Ottawa's enthusiasm for proceeding at full steam diminished correspondingly.

But the second limitation – the attitudes of other states in the international community – also caused a loss of ardour. Mulroney's activism, and his government's willingness to embrace concrete sanctions, were well received by all Commonwealth countries but one, and by black African states generally. But in other circles, notably among the other members of the G-7 economic summit, Canadian activism on the South African issue was less well regarded, and indeed threatened to put the maintenance of Mulroney's influence in summit circles in some jeopardy. First, there was the general problem of keeping the South African issue alive at the G-7 summit year after year. Only very small children delight in playing the same song again and again – and yet again. Most others grow tired of repetition, particularly when they do not much like the tune in the first place. As the cases of Canadian attempts to influence American statecraft in the Korean War in the early 1950s, the Vietnam War in the mid-1960s, and the conflict in Central America in the mid-1980s all demonstrate, Canadian governments have tended to recognize that a non-great power's general influence diminishes in direct proportion to the number of times it expresses a specific objection to a greater power's policy, and that there is wisdom in not playing an unpalatable tune ad nauseam. At the economic summit, Mulroney's position on South Africa quickly became well known, and was basically rejected by the other members. There was thus little mileage for Mulroney, who had other concerns to press at these meetings, to sermonize and push Canada's position on South Africa on the other members.

Second, there was the related problem of what impact Canada's policies on South Africa have on others' perceptions of Canadian 'dependability' and 'soundness.' According to some officials in Ottawa, Mulroney's willingness in 1985 to espouse a total break with South Africa as a means of levering Pretoria into accelerating the abandonment of apartheid created the impression among other leaders that Mulroney was diplomatically immature and unrealistic. If indeed Canada had unilaterally embraced a total ban, it was commonly argued, Mulroney would merely have confirmed that suspicion, with the result that at future summits he would have been dismissed more readily as a lightweight, and would lose the capacity for exercising influence in other areas of interest to Canada. According to some officials, it was this concern, more than any other,[7] that ultimately deterred Mulroney from making the 'grand gesture' and carrying through on the threat to break all relations with South Africa.

CONCLUSION

Viewed in this way, it can be argued that what we saw after the Vancouver meetings was not a loss of steam, but rather a slowing in the pace of Canada's sanctionist policies. Such a slowing was the result neither of 'sanctions weariness,' as some have suggested, nor of a change of heart by either Mulroney or Clark about the appropriateness of the coercive approach. Indeed, there was little evidence that by 1988 the prime minister or his external-affairs minister were any less committed to sanctions as a means of bringing apartheid to an end, or any less visceral in their attitudes towards South Africa, than they were in the summer of 1985, when they launched themselves into this issue.

Rather, I have argued here that such a slowing was the result of the set of instrumental assumptions that appear to have been employed at the outset, and in particular of the expectations created by Mulroney's own rhetoric. The prime minister's 'high-wire act' at the United Nations in October 1985 was especially important, for it set a standard that proved impossible to sustain. Moreover, we can see in the slowing of the sanctionist pace the dwindling of ardour that is always likely to set in as one's potential instruments are increasingly narrowed to exceedingly costly – and eventually bloody – techniques of statecraft. Such a slowing, I have argued, was also the result of the attitudes of others, and of the importance that any Canadian prime minister must attach to how he is regarded by other leaders in the international system. In sum, given the negative effects that 'ratcheting up' Canadian sanctions would have on Mulroney's influence in summit circles, and given the increasing costs of the dwindling number of coercive measures available to the government, it is hardly surprising that the Canadian government sought to back away from its earlier rhetoric and ease the pace of sanctions at that point.

12

Conclusion:
Sanctions as Rain Dancing

The case studies of the sanctions policies of the Australian and Canadian governments presented in this book have both theoretical and policy implications. The theoretical findings focus on what these case studies tell us about the sanctions policies of smaller states in the international system, those without the capabilities of inflicting major economic hurts on targets. I argue that the generic theory of sanctions has indeed been shown to be less than useful in explaining the sanctions policies of these two middle powers. The policy implications of these case studies are more normative. I argue that sanctions are, on balance, a normatively bad policy instrument: not only are they generally ineffective in producing political change in the target nation, but they also are a violent, blunt, and gendered tool of statecraft.

THEORETICAL IMPLICATIONS

At the outset of this book, it was suggested that the generic theory of sanctions, which has informed so much of our thinking about this tool of statecraft, actually tells us very little about how and why middle powers such as Australia and Canada have used sanctions. It was hypothesized that the classic 'utilities,' or useful purposes, usually attached to sanctions in both academic and political discourse – deterrence, compellence, subversion, and symbolism – would not adequately reflect what drove the sanctions policies of these smaller states. Instead, it was suggested that non-great powers in the international system would be as likely to embrace sanctions, but their reasons for doing so would differ considerably from those employed by the system's major players, the great powers.

The case studies presented here, I would argue, do suggest that the sanctions policies of the Canadian government have been driven by factors other than the classical utilities presented by the generic theory. Importantly, the original surmise at the outset of the book that we would find a comparable pattern in the case of another middle power was also borne out. The exploration of Australian sanctions cases – particularly sanctions against the Soviet Union after its invasion of Afghanistan, against China after Tiananmen, and against Iraq after its invasion of Kuwait – suggest that the Canadian experience with sanctions is by no means unique.

However much their sanctions policies tended to be justified by Australian or Canadian politicians in the language of the orthodox theory, in fact one sees, when the sanctions decisions are analysed more closely, that other factors were more important determinants of the policies. Of the factors not mentioned by the generic theory, the most important, perhaps not surprisingly, is the constraint – and the imperative – of coalition politics. There is little place in the generic theory of sanctions for an explanation that is rooted in the desire to satisfy the expectations of other members of a coalition. But a recurring feature of the analysis of the sanctions imposed by Australia and Canada against such countries as the Soviet Union, Vietnam, China, South Africa, Iraq, and Indonesia is that they were heavily influenced by the membership of these middle powers in broader coalitions of states.

As the case of sanctions against Vietnam demonstrated, the coalition served to define the outer limits of 'acceptable' behaviour; as the case of sanctions against the Soviet Union in the early 1980s showed, the coalition also frequently determined the minimum floor of the sanctions required. As the cases of Indonesia and South Africa suggested, the coalition would be important in determining when sanctions were not welcome. The case of the post-Tiananmen sanctions likewise showed the coalition dynamic at work in presenting a common front to the leadership in Beijing. And in the Gulf case, coalition politics determined that sanctions would be but a minor part of statecraft against Iraq.

Coalition politics, in other words, was a potent determinant of Australian and Canadian sanctions policies, a potency perhaps best demonstrated by the policies that these middle powers pursued *after* the coalitions fell apart in the post–Cold War transformations following 1989. Thus, once the grand anti-Soviet coalition dominated by China and the United States withered in 1989 and 1990, both Australia and Canada were freer to pursue a less sanctionist approach towards Vietnam;

likewise, with the declining importance of strategic considerations, the governments in Canberra and Ottawa felt freer to sanction Indonesia after the Dili massacre of November 1991.

But the case studies examined here also demonstrate the importance of other factors not mentioned by the generic theory in shaping middle-power sanctions policies. One is the impact of federalism on sanctions policies. While by no means a pervasive factor, there can be little doubt that the increased willingness of non-central, or subnational, governments to engage in international activities will complicate some sanctions episodes, creating tensions between the central government and other parts of the federation. Another factor is the impact of the individual, or the degree to which a proclivity towards – or away from – sanctions is shaped by a political leader's own personal inclinations. The cases of Brian Mulroney's embrace of sanctions against South Africa or Bob Hawke's desire to punish China after Tiananmen clearly demonstrate this dynamic at work.

Moreover, even factors that do form part of the orthodox theory require some reconsideration. For example, symbolism plays a prominent part in orthodox sanctions theory; and indeed one might be tempted to explain all sanctions policies of non-great powers like Australia and Canada by reference to symbolism. However, it is clear from the analysis of the sanctions episodes in this book that a more nuanced view of the symbolic purpose of sanctions is required to explain the sanctions policies of non-great powers. For it is clear that both Australian and Canadian policy-makers themselves – not to mention their publics – firmly believed that the sanctions they embraced against a range of different countries in the 1980s would have much more than merely symbolic effects. Thus, while it is not inappropriate to characterize the sanctions of these two middle powers during this period as an elaborate 'rain dance,' intended to make it appear that a serious problem was being addressed without any possibility that the situation would actually change, it is clear that factors other than symbolism were also at work.

Likewise, it has long been recognized in orthodox sanctions theory that one of the purposes of sanctions is to satisfy domestic demands for some action against a wrong-doer. However, as the cases examined in this volume suggest, 'domestic politics' as a determining factor works itself out in substantially different ways, largely depending on the circumstances. In some cases – the Canadian sanctions against Indonesia, for example – it was not even a consideration in the government's thinking. In other cases, by contrast, the attitudes of domestic groups played an important part in shaping the sanctions policies of both governments. For example, while domestic politics was not a factor in framing the Canadian response to Indonesia in the 1970s, in the case of Australia, the domestic factor was of central importance in shaping Canberra's policies towards the Suharto regime. Likewise, the post-Afghanistan sanctions in both countries were heavily influenced by domestic politics. But all the cases suggest one clear conclusion: the concerns of domestic groups rarely impelled governments in one obvious direction. On the contrary: policy-makers were pushed and pulled in different, and often opposing, directions by the contending preferences of these groups. And, as the cases of both Vietnam and China show, when the preferences of state officials differed considerably from those of domestic groups, the state was both willing and able to manage domestic demands and pursue its own policy preferences.

From an analytical perspective, then, we are left with an important conclusion: the case studies examined in this book suggest that the sanctions policies of smaller states are best explained by factors other than those put forward by the generic theory of sanctions. In the introduction, I argued that these factors included the impact of the desire to punish; coalition membership; the different facets of domestic politics; and personal factors. I argued that these factors did not impel states in a particular direction, but instead pushed and pulled governments of smaller states, depending largely on the particularities of the case at hand. Indeed, in the introductory chapter, the factors that drive the sanctions of these non-great powers were likened to a bag of magnets, exerting force in different, and often conflicting, directions.

To be sure, such a bag-of-magnets approach to middle-power sanctions hardly qualifies as an alternative 'theory' to the well-established and orthodox generic theory. For one thing, it is far less elegant, and therefore less attractive. The generic theory postulates a tidy, understandable, rational, logical, and instrumental approach to this tool of statecraft. Both the sanctioner and the sanctioned, in the generic perspective, behave in ways that are eminently rational, and therefore eminently understandable. By contrast, the bag-of-magnets theory suggests precisely the opposite. In this view, sanctions policy is usually the result of decision-making that is invariably messy, not always forward-looking, and, most important, rarely informed by clear rationality. Policy-makers may try to ensure that their sanctions will prove 'effective' against the target – and indeed may try to convince their publics and other political leaders of their effectiveness – but, in reality, the policy-makers simply do not know what effects the measures they adopt will actually produce. As a result, the sanctions policies that emerge from this process have few of the instrumental purposes inherent in the means-end rationality of the generic theory of sanctions.

Moreover, as theory, the bag-of-magnets approach suffers considerably because of its inability to predict. While it provides us with a useful heuristic device for examining sanctions episodes ex post facto, the bag-of-magnets approach, with its intimation of relative randomness, has only limited capacity for predicting the push-and-pull of the different factors in the sanctions policies of middle powers like Australia and Canada.

SANCTIONS AND THE LOGIC OF THE RAIN DANCE

However interesting such conclusions about the utility of the generic theory of sanctions might be for the student of middle-power sanctions, they remain somewhat academic – in the pejorative sense of the word. Such conclusions might allow us to understand the disjuncture between orthodox sanctions theory and the practice we might observe, but they have little connection to the periodic debates about sanctions that take place in both Australia or Canada. On the contrary, sanctions as a preferred tool of statecraft continue to be pressed on governments in Canberra and Ottawa by citizens and groups as though the sanctions policies of their governments were in fact driven by the logic of the generic theory.

Likewise, the justificatory rhetoric of Australian and Canadian politicians continues to imbue the sanctions of their middle powers with the same means-ends rationality as that of the great powers, as though non-rational elements played little part in their policy behaviour.[1] And even if policy-makers in Canberra or Ottawa understand that the tidy and rational logic of the generic theory bears little resemblance to the evolution of their own policies, they would, quite understandably, be hesitant to admit openly that their approach to sanctions was less than rational, or that their embrace of this tool of statecraft was more symbolic than instrumental.

What implications does this deep disjuncture between the rhetoric of sanctions and their actual practice have for the foreign policy debates about sanctions of non-great powers such as Australia and Canada? On the one hand, on the basis of the case studies in this book, one could put forward a series of suggestions about the debate over sanctions in non-great powers. It might be suggested, for example, that in future instances of wrong-doing by other states, the debate over the sanctions options in countries like Canada should embrace a greater degree of realism, and more accurately reflect the lack of capabilities of a non-great power. Advocates of a sanctionist approach, both within and outside government, should adopt more moderate and modest expectations for this tool of statecraft. Policy-makers, for their part, might take more care to fashion their justifications in such a way as to avoid the termination trap explored in chapter 10, or the inflated expectations that haunted Mulroney's South African policy. They also might employ more nuanced and balanced justifications that more accurately reflect why this tool of statecraft is an attractive option for foreign policy makers despite its lack of instrumental capability.

On the other hand, it could be as readily argued that such policy prescriptions run so hard against the political current in both Australia and Canada as to render them unworkable. When sanctions are debated in these countries, the debate is impelled in a direction that in fact demands a continuation of the disjuncture exposed in this book. In short, on the issue of sanctions, both Australians and Canadians – and of course many others besides – are locked into a particularly ironic logic wherein it does not matter for the policy debate if sanctions are actually driven by means-end rationality, or by the essential untidiness of the bag-of-magnets approach.

To lay out this logic, we must begin with the recognition that sanctions will, for the foreseeable future, remain a popular policy option in both Australian and Canadian foreign policy – for at least two reasons.

The first factor is the impact of ideology. Both Australians and Canadians are steeped in an ideological and moral perspective on world affairs – a perspective, that, for example, holds dear the idea of a sovereign existence for states, as well as the idea that human beings have individual rights. They are also steeped in an ideological and moral perspective that legitimates punishment as an appropriate consequence of wrong-doing: the infliction of pain on wrong-doers as the just desert for the violation of moral norms.

Because of this, there seems to be something intuitively, even if often only inchoately, natural to both Australians and Canadians about wanting to deny those good things that trade relations, investment flows, or development assistance projects bring to governments that have done wrong, whether it be by invading another state or by abusing the rights of their own citizens.

Thus, when a government systematically mistreats, abuses, or belittles people on the basis of such attributes as gender, race, religion, or ethnic background, it seems perverse to encourage trade with that regime. When a government puts those who dissent in psychiatric hospitals, or simply 'disappears' them in the middle of the night, it seems wrong to offer concessionary terms of trade to that regime. When a government authorizes its troops to fire on a crowd of protestors, it seems only right to cancel development assistance projects to that country. When a government keeps hundreds of thousands of political prisoners in concentration camps, it seems inappropriate to approve of international development banks giving loans to that government. When a government allows its security apparatus to torture prisoners, often in the most gruesome and cruel fashion, it seems distasteful to advocate doing any business at all with that government. In short, when governments engage in what we believe to be wrong, punishing that behaviour by hurting the wrong-doers seems the most appropriate response.

Such a desire to punish international wrong-doing by imposing sanctions is, it should be noted, a peculiarly Western and liberal phenomenon. In chapter 1, I argued that the generic theory of sanctions was underwritten by essentially liberal tenets of rationality; but that same liberalism also underpins the desire to punish wrong-doing. To be sure, non-Western or non-liberal states employ sanctions in their foreign policies but it is clear that they tend to do so without the emotionalism that normally accompanies Western sanctions. Rather, non-Western states tend to use the disruptive statecraft of sanctions as a response to an injury to their national interests, not as a response to wrong-doing by other states.

Western, liberal states, by contrast, have historically tended to interweave elements of morality into the pursuit of their interests. The result is that international sanctions in a Western context tend to be marked by both sentimentality and sanctimony. The sentimentality manifests itself in an expressed concern for wrongs done against other peoples and the sense that 'something' should be done on their behalf, and that some action is better than no action at all. Sentimentality also manifests itself in a widespread belief in the West that such measures will in fact have instrumental, rather than merely symbolic, effects on the wrong-doer.

Likewise, Western sanctions are also driven by sanctimony, it being no coincidence that both words have the same root. Such sanctimony is manifested in the frequently expressed desire of Western liberals to project their own conception of moral standards beyond their borders and out into the international system, and insist that these are 'universal' standards of 'civilized' behaviour that all people should embrace. The desire to punish those who refuse to accept these projections of standards flows naturally.

The observation that liberal sentimentality and sanctimony drive Western sanctions in general has important implications for the sanctions debate in Australia and Canada. Given their widespread attachment to liberal sentiments, it could be argued that even if Australians and Canadians were to recognize explicitly that the sanctions that can be imposed by a middle power do not have the instrumental effects touted by their proponents, they could not simply turn off their concern for the wrong-doing of others – or their punishment-mindedness towards wrong-doers.

There is, however, a second reason why it is likely that sanctions as a tool of statecraft will continue to be popular in countries like Australia and Canada. The expansion of immigration to both countries in the post-1945 period has meant that large numbers of citizens in both states now have links of family, heritage, and sentiment to a much wider range of political communities in the international system than in the past. These ties mean that such individuals will rarely be indifferent to the politics of their homeland; not surprisingly, ethnic groups will frequently press the government in Canberra and Ottawa to play an activist role in the politics of their *patria*. Moreover, it is no longer expected that immigrants should properly leave the politics of their homeland behind them when they immigrate to Australia or Canada. On the contrary, one of the consequences of the institutional embedding of multiculturalism within Australian and Canadian politics in the 1980s has been to delegitimize the idea that it is not appropriate for immigrants to bring the political conflicts of their homelands with them to their newly adopted country. As a result, ethnic groups have not hesitated to press the concerns of their homeland on their new governments, a pressure to which politicians in Canberra and Ottawa are not insensitive. By the same token, Australian and Canadian politicians are eager to solicit support from these groups. And because these individuals and groups have first-hand knowledge of their homeland, as well as concrete linkages of family, language, and culture, their claims about sanctions as a policy option assume both a heightened legitimacy and a greater urgency. Moreover, as we saw in several of the sanctions cases explored in this book, these ethnic groups can have an impact on a country's sanctions, pushing governments towards or away from the sanctionist option. In short, the logic of ethnic politics in both Australia and Canada serves to entrench the prominent place of sanctions as a tool of statecraft for these middle powers.

Given these two factors, it is likely that the public in Australia and Canada will continue to press for sanctions against wrong-doing by other states – even in the face of evidence that such measures rarely change wrongful behaviour. Australians and Canadians will continue to press their governments for an 'effective' response to wrong-doing – even in the face of evidence that the government in Canberra or Ottawa lacks the capacity to inflict change-inducing damage on other states. The evidence, in short, will not matter; what will matter is the deeply held belief – absorbed largely from the debate carried on in and by the great powers – that international wrong-doing must be punished, and that sanctions are the most appropriate method of punishment.

Likewise, for their part, politicians and officials in both Australia and Canada will continue to grapple with the contradictions for foreign policy posed not only by the demands of their publics, but also by their own beliefs, sometimes only inchoate, that international wrong-doing should be punished and that sanctions are a useful tool of punishment. The insistence of their publics, and their own personal sentiments, will act as a powerful disincentive to moderate claims about the effectiveness of sanctions in their public discourse.

Moreover, policy-makers will also continue to be pushed and pulled by the imperatives of coalition politics, even if in the post–Cold War era the alliances of the post-1945 period are of diminishing importance to foreign policy makers in both Canberra and Ottawa. Both Australia and Canada remain basically multilateral in their orientation to world affairs, and despite Canada's embrace of a North American free-trade agreement in 1992, both are likely to remain so: membership in international coalitions will likely continue to be a prominent feature of foreign policy in both countries throughout the 1990s.[2] It is thus unlikely that the coalition dynamic we saw in so many of the sanctions episodes explored in this book will diminish in the future, although, as the cases of sanctions in the post–Cold War era suggest, both middle powers might have somewhat greater freedom to manoeuvre.

In short, the logic of politics in both Australia and Canada makes it unlikely that the terms of the debate about international sanctions will undergo a transformation in the near term. Publics and policy-makers alike will continue to borrow liberally from the arguments and assumptions about sanctions being advanced in the great powers, however inadequate, or downright misleading, they might be when applied in the Australian or Canadian context. But the logic of a deeply rooted belief in crime and punishment dictates why sanctions will continue to be popular in countries like Canada – and why these sanctions will continue to have all the attributes of a rain dance.

RAIN DANCING'S OTHER SIDE: THE CASE AGAINST SANCTIONS

Much of the analysis in this book focuses on the degree to which sanctions have symbolic rather than instrumental purposes and effects. The case studies examined here mirror the more general conclusion in the literature that sanctions as a tool of statecraft, for all their popularity, rarely achieve what they are supposed to. None the less, people confronted with international wrong-doing invariably reach for sanctions as the preferred policy option. And their leaders continue to embrace sanctions, partly in response to public pressure, partly because of their own beliefs, partly because of a perceived lack of alternatives, and partly because of what other leaders are doing. Moreover, I have shown above why the logic of politics in Australia and Canada suggests that this situation is unlikely to change.

I have argued throughout this book that the sanctions policies of Australia and Canada have all the attributes of a rain dance. In other words, these are measures that, generally speaking, do not have significant effects on wrong-doing; they are imposed for symbolic rather than instrumental reasons. However, they are an attractive policy tool because they are not only preferable to doing nothing, on the one hand, but are eminently preferable to taking more concrete action, such as using force, on the other. Moreover, the dance has broad and important psychological effects on the performers: when the dance is performed, it makes the participants feel good that 'something is being done' about the problem.

It would be inappropriate to leave the analysis there, however. For the rain-dance analogy might leave the impression that if sanctions are indeed like a rain dance, then one should not be overly concerned, for rain dancing is, after all, a harmless and benign activity. The conclusion that sanctions that are imposed for symbolic purposes are also harmless and benign follows inexorably.

Such an impression would be as unfortunate as it is incorrect. For sanctions may not have instrumental effects on *governments* and the *behaviour of governments*, and therefore may be likened to a rain dance.

But these measures surely do produce effects on *people*, and when one examines what impact sanctions have on human beings, it is puzzling that so many people continue to embrace this tool of statecraft as a preferred – and moral – policy option.

It is true that most people have a positive view of sanctions. They see sanctions not only as an *effective* tool of statecraft, as we have noted above, but as a *non-violent* instrument of policy, since sanctions tend to target economic and social intercourse between nations. Moreover, they see them as a *clean* policy tool, one that can readily be used to target wrong-doing governments elsewhere in the international system.

As I noted in the introduction, most studies of international sanctions argue that this tool of statecraft is generally ineffective in producing the change desired. Moreover, the larger the target state is, the harder it is to use sanctions to produce change. While sanctions have a range of uses in foreign policy, as the case studies in this book suggest, securing change in other states is by no means the most effective of their uses.

But what of the popular view that sanctions are non-violent and clean? Let me suggest that sanctions are neither non-violent nor clean, and that they produce such negative effects on human beings that they are a normatively bad policy tool, difficult to justify morally.

Given the widespread belief that sanctions are a non-violent tool of statecraft, it is easy to forget that they are always tantamount to an act of war against another state. To be sure, sanctions are rarely thought of in such terms. Indeed, enthusiasts of a sanctionist approach are wont to claim that sanctions are a preferred alternative to war – as the debate over sanctions versus the use of force in the case of the Gulf conflict in 1990–1 clearly demonstrated. In a similar vein, the oft-quoted Canadian assertion that sanctions were designed to 'bring South Africa to its senses, not to its knees' conveys well the popular idea that sanctions are a relatively mild tool of statecraft.

However, to argue that sanctions are a peaceful and mild tool of statecraft is a dubious claim at best; it is disingenuous at worst. On the one hand, it is true that sanctions do not kill human beings in the same way as a burst from an AK-47 or a 500-pound bomb dropped from a B-52. But, on the other hand, we should never lose sight of the underlying purpose of economic sanctions: they are explicitly designed to disrupt, to a greater or lesser extent, the economic life of a society. In this, they are exactly like the use of force. The disruptions to the economy are designed to *hurt* a target society, and to hurt it enough to produce political change – by prompting wrong-doers to change their behaviour, or by prompting their opponents to overthrow them in a revolution or a coup.

But however laudatory the final goals of such measures, it cannot be claimed that such disruptions to a community's economy are without consequences that involve pain and hurt for human beings. Development assistance programs that do not take place; foreign investment that does not occur; trade in goods and services that is suspended – all of this foregone economic activity produces ripple effects in the target state's economy and society. These effects include disruptions in the society's normal food distribution, health, and education systems; a rise in unemployment; rapid inflation and the appearance of a black market; and in particular an increase in social unrest.

More important, as Margaret Doxey has reminded us, sanctions tend to increase the impoverishment and marginalization of target economies, particularly in the South.[3] Such impoverishment, it must be recognized, can kill people. Disrupting an already marginalized economy can easily accelerate a collapse in infrastructure, encouraging disease and malnutrition that can easily result in death, particularly among the most susceptible group in society, infants and children. Economic dislocation can also trigger sudden and massive unemployment, with attendant increases in lethal violence, both civil and domestic.

The problem is that the causality of deaths from dehydration or starvation, or from civil or domestic violence, cannot be fingered as easily as deaths from high explosives or bullets. If children die in a bombing raid, establishing the direct causality of their deaths is easy. But if children die from starvation, or from diarrhea, or from the lack of potable water, or from being caught in the midst of a fire fight between warring factions, it is much harder to determine whether sanctions 'caused' such deaths. At the same time, however, we should acknowledge the possibility that when sanctions disrupt the economic life of a nation, that disruption can produce fatal consequences for the human beings caught in the middle. For example, in South Africa, tens of thousands of people died in the townships after 'black-on-black' violence erupted after 1985: to what extent was this surge of violence catalysed by the negative economic effects of Western sanctions? Likewise, after international sanctions were imposed following the 30 September 1991 coup in Haiti, there was a sharp deterioration in the standard of living in the Western hemisphere's most impoverished country. Moreover, there was an equally dramatic increase in civil violence and human rights abuses as the security forces began to exact revenge on the supporters of the ousted president, Jean-Bertrand Aristide, for having 'caused' Western sanctions. Indeed, one controversial study by the Center for Population and Development Studies in the School of Public Health at Harvard University claimed that sanctions were responsible for a rise in malnutrition and death among Haiti's children, alleging that 100,000 preventable deaths had been caused by sanctions, a dramatic claim that was later withdrawn.[4] It was easier to establish the relationship between sanctions and the deaths of hundreds of Haitians by drowning: as sanctions began to 'bite,' shortages grew, and human rights abuses increased, thousands of people tried to escape to the United States in boats that were frequently leaky and overcrowded; hundreds of people drowned while trying to flee Haiti.

Viewed in this light, it would be difficult to claim that deaths cannot be attributed to sanctions. Given the violent effects that economic disruptions can have, it is disingenuous to claim that, because that act of not doing business does not produce bloodshed, sanctions are a non-violent tool of statecraft. On the contrary, sanctions can – and do – produce bloodshed and the loss of life.

The observation that sanctions can produce lethal results begs a related question: Who in fact suffers when such disruptions are imposed on a target economy for the human rights violations of the government? Here we find a rather thorny contradiction, one that is frequently overlooked – or, worse, purposely fudged – by enthusiasts of the sanctionist option. The contradiction is that economic sanctions imposed for human rights violations more often than not end up punishing entirely the wrong people.

We must begin by noting that, contrary to the claims of sanctionists who claim that sanctions are a useful way of 'cleanly' targeting a wrong-doing government, in fact they are an exceedingly blunt and crude tool of statecraft. Sanctions do not differentiate: while they are imposed against a particular government for doing wrong, these measures in fact 'target' an entire national economy, and thus, obviously, all those human beings residing within that territory. Yet if you ask sanctions enthusiasts whether it is their intention to punish all those human beings, they will answer, 'Of course not, just those who have done wrong.' Yet this is not what occurs: the contradiction is that sanctions are a tool of statecraft directed against an entire state – governors and governed alike – but for the sins, as it were, of the governors alone.

Then we have to inquire into the relative capacity of the governed and the governors to withstand the hurts of economic sanctions. Here we find another paradox: sanctions may affect all the human beings residing within the boundaries of a target state, but some are more susceptible than others. Who, in other words, is able to maintain access to the diminishing supply of goods and services as economic sanctions start to 'bite'?

The answer the world over is the same: besides the tiny number of the very rich in any society, who always have the resources to buy their way around any deprivation, it is the political élites, the security apparatus, and the armed forces – the very groups that are usually responsible for the wrongs that produce the sanctions in the first place. Such groups are rarely hurt by sanctions. In virtually every sanctions episode, it is clear that the governors of a state targeted by international sanctions are much better placed to withstand the negative effects of these measures than the governed. Their access to both the necessities and the luxuries of life remains undiminished. It is the governed who must endure the shortages, the inflated prices, and the line-ups – not their governors.

For example, sanctions had devastating effects on ordinary people in Serbia. After a year and a half of international sanctions, huge damage had been done to what had been one of Eastern Europe's most prosperous countries: the official inflation rate, when annualized, had reached 1.7 billion per cent by the autumn of 1993; it was claimed that the unemployment rate was an astonishing 70 per cent; those on fixed incomes – the elderly and veterans in particular – were reported to be suffering from shortages and the negative effects of hyperinflation and bank failures. But there was little doubt that the burgeoning gangster class that had grown up with the black market and the ruling élite in Belgrade were all but immune from the negative effects that sanctions had brought.[5]

Moreover, it should be noted that the burdens of coping with the disruptive effects of sanctions fall disproportionately on women and children. While the population as a whole might be inconvenienced by international sanctions, the actual coping – lining up to get the necessities of life, dealing with the ill-effects of the collapse of health, education, and food supply systems on the children of a society – tend to be done by women. (Indeed, it is puzzling that, given the hardships imposed on women and their children by sanctions, this tool of statecraft none the less continues to be advocated enthusiastically as a 'good' measure to be imposed on rule-breaking governments by many groups in Australia, Canada, and other Western countries that otherwise tend to be sensitive to women's issues.)

This problem is compounded in those cases where the government is abusing the human rights of its citizens. In such cases, the governed are 'doubly punished' by sanctions. Not only do the people have to suffer the human rights abuses being visited on them by their own state apparatus; in addition, they have to suffer the economic deprivations visited on them by other states.

It is true that efforts have been made in some sanctions episodes to target more carefully and selectively. As we saw in chapter 8, policy-makers in Canberra and Ottawa tried to limit their sanctions against China so that the primary effect would be on the security forces and the political leadership. In the case of South Africa, sanctions might have been imposed on a range of economic activities, but efforts were also made to provide aid to the townships through such mechanisms as the Dialogue Fund, established by the Canadian government and administered by the Canadian embassy in South Africa.[6] In the case of Sri Lanka, the Canadian government's response to ethnic conflict over the Maduru Oya project was careful to avoid using development assistance in a coercive fashion.[7] In the case of Iraq, a hard sanctions net was imposed on virtually all goods and services, but medicines were generally allowed to pass through. While such provisions might have some mitigating effects, their impact on the huge dislocations otherwise produced by sanctions is limited.

Still, to recognize that sanctions tend to hurt innocent citizens more than the wrong-doers should not always and necessarily incline us away from embracing these measures. For example, what should we do if the targets of human rights violations in a country openly urge that the international community impose sanctions on them? Knowing that sanctions will generally harm the public more profoundly than the élite does not mean that one should fall into what might be called the Thatcher trap. As we have seen, Margaret Thatcher, the prime minister of Britain from 1979 to 1990, consistently opposed the imposition of sanctions against South Africa during the 1980s, even though many blacks in South Africa, including major black organizations, were advocating international sanctions as a means of catalysing political change in their country. Thatcher argued long and hard that sanctions would hurt the black population of South Africa more than the whites whose behaviour sanctions were supposed to be changing. The problem was that she was claiming to know what was in the best interests of South

African blacks, regardless of what they themselves said – ironically, the same kind of illiberal paternalism that underlay the system of apartheid.

In other words, there are occasions when it is appropriate to respond positively to the advocacy for sanctions when it comes from groups within a potential target. Thus, when Sein Win, the duly elected prime minister of Burma (or Myanmar), whose election was never recognized by the military regime, calls on the international community to impose economic sanctions against the regime in Rangoon – as, for example, he did when he visited Vancouver in June 1992 and called on the Canadian government to increase its sanctions against his country[8] – it is not inappropriate to consider embracing such measures. But in such cases, sanctions should be imposed with open eyes. In particular, one should never lose sight of the more general tendency for international economic sanctions to cause more damage to the mass than the élite; and sanctionists should express this concern to those urging such a course of action on them.

In sum, sanctions do not commend themselves as a positive measure to be embraced in the wake of international wrong-doing. Only in rare cases do they have concrete and instrumental effects on the target government; in most sanctions episodes, these measures produce little or no result at all on the governments of the target nation. Moreover, in some cases, it does not seem to matter for how long the sanctions are applied. The sanctions visited on North Korea, Cuba, and Vietnam have lingered against those countries for over three decades, producing none of the desired political change. But sanctions surely have instrumental effects on people and, I have argued, entirely the wrong people. For example, sanctions have caused economic deprivation for several generations of North Koreans, Cubans, and Vietnamese, the vast majority of whom can hardly be held responsible for the wrongs of their governors, wrongs often committed decades before they were even born. I have argued that sanctions target and hurt the wrong people, the people least capable of withstanding deprivation. I have suggested that sanctions are also a highly gendered instrument of statecraft, and inflict disproportionate burdens on women and children in a target society. In short, looked at in this way, the sanctions rain dance is hardly benign, and those who are inclined to reach for sanctions as the preferred peaceful and non-violent alternative to war might usefully ask whether there are other tools of statecraft that can produce political change more effectively without inflicting deprivations on the innocent.

Notes

CHAPTER 1: 'Generic' Theory of Sanctions

1 Jean Prévost, *For Effective and Appropriate Sanctions*, Policy Planning Staff Paper 93/04 (Ottawa: External Affairs and International Trade Canada, March 1993), 9.
2 For Doxey's full typology, see her 'International Sanctions,' in David G. Haglund and Michael K. Hawes, eds, *World Politics: Power, Interdependence and Dependence* (Toronto: Harcourt Brace Jovanovich 1990), 244, table 1.
3 Recent works would include M.S. Daoudi and M.S. Dajani, *Economic Sanctions: Ideals and Experience* (London: Routledge and Kegan Paul 1983); Gary Clyde Hufbauer and Jeffrey J. Schott, *Economic Sanctions Reconsidered: History and Current Policy* (Washington: Institute for International Economics 1985); David A. Baldwin, *Economic Statecraft* (Princeton: Princeton University Press 1985); David Leyton-Brown, ed., *The Utility of International Economic Sanctions* (London: Croom Helm 1987); Margaret P. Doxey, *International Sanctions in Contemporary Perspective* (London: Macmillan Press 1987); Philip Hanson, *Western Economic Statecraft in East-West Relations: Embargoes, Sanctions, Linkage, Economic Warfare and Detente*, Chatham Papers 40 (London: Routledge and Kegan Paul 1988); and Makio Miyagawa, *Do Economic Sanctions Work?* (New York: St Martin's Press 1992).
4 Baldwin, *Economic Statecraft*, 150–4.
5 Inverted commas seem appropriate since this word is frequently, if somewhat misleadingly, used in discussions about international sanctions as a convenient shorthand to describe commonly held assumptions about the purposes and effects of this tool of statecraft.
6 Carsten Holbraad, *Middle Powers in International Politics* (London: Macmillan 1984).

7 Makio Miyagawa, 'The Employment of Economic Strength for Foreign Policy Goals,' *Japan Review of International Affairs*, Fall 1992, 275–99.

8 For a reconsideration of the notion of middle power in assessing Australian and Canadian foreign policy, see Andrew F. Cooper, Richard A. Higgott, and Kim Richard Nossal, *Relocating Middle Powers: Australia and Canada in a Changing World Order* (Vancouver: University of British Columbia Press; Carlton: Melbourne University Press 1993), esp. chap. 1.

9 For an exploration of this contrast, see Andrew Fenton Cooper, 'Like-minded Nations and Contrasting Diplomatic Styles: Australian and Canadian Approaches to Agricultural Trade,' *Canadian Journal of Political Science* 25 (June 1992), 349–79.

10 See, for example, Baldwin, *Economic Statecraft*, 48–50; also see the argument put forward by Richard Leaver in 'Sanctions, South Africa and Australian Policy,' Working Paper 37, Peace Research Centre, Australian National University (March 1988), 5–15.

11 Again, the inverted commas seem appropriate since in international affairs, what is considered 'wrongful' is always heavily dependent on context. There is no better example of this than the relativist reactions to violations of the cardinal rule of the contemporary international states-system that one state should not send its troops uninvited into another state and overthrow the legitimate government there by force. Consider the sharply different responses of members of the international community to the cases of invasion and forcible overthrow of the existing government noted above.

12 See, for example, Leyton-Brown, 'Lessons and Policy Considerations about Economic Sanctions,' in Leyton-Brown, ed., *Utility of International Economic Sanctions*, 303–6; James M. Lindsay, 'Trade Sanctions as Policy Instruments: A Re-examination,' *International Studies Quarterly* 30 (1986), 155–6; James Barber, 'Economic Sanctions as a Policy Instrument,' *International Affairs* 55 (July 1979); and Miroslav Nincic and Peter Wallensteen, 'Economic Coercion and Foreign Policy,' in Nincic and Wallensteen, eds, *Dilemmas of Economic Coercion* (New York: Praeger 1983), 4–8.

13 Baldwin, *Economic Statecraft*, 265–6.

14 The term 'compellence' was coined by Thomas Schelling in *The Strategy of Conflict* (New York: Oxford University Press 1960), 195, to describe hurts imposed on an actor with the intention of compelling that actor to change behaviour.

15 The differences between the instrumental and expressive purposes of sanctions were originally explored by Johann Galtung, 'Pacifism from a

Sociological Point of View,' *Journal of Conflict Resolution* 3 (March 1959), esp. 69–71.

16 Prévost, *For Effective and Appropriate Sanctions*, 9.

17 Baldwin, *Economic Statecraft*, 372, for example.

18 Johann Galtung, 'On the Effects of International Economic Sanctions, with Examples from the Case of Rhodesia,' *World Politics* 19 (April 1967).

19 I have put this argument in more detail in 'International Sanctions as International Punishment,' *International Organization* 43 (Spring 1989), 301–22.

20 See the discussion in ibid., 311–13.

21 To be sure, there are considerable differences in the economies of both countries. For example, Canada's trade is overwhelmingly with the United States (approximately 80 per cent), while Australia has a more balanced trade with a more diversified set of trading partners: the United States, Japan, and the European Community. Australia has continued to rely on primary-resource exports, while in Canada there has been a slow, but persistent, shift from primary and semiprocessed to manufactured goods since 1960. See Richard A. Higgott, 'The Ascendancy of the Economic Dimension in Australian-American Relations,' in John Ravenhill, ed., *No Longer an American Lake? Alliance Problems in the South Pacific* (Berkeley: Institute of International Studies 1989), 136–9, and esp. table 1; and Lorraine Eden, 'Two Steps Forward, One Step Back: Into the 1990s,' in Maureen Appel Molot and Fen Osler Hampson, eds, *Canada Among Nations – 1989: The Challenge of Change* (Ottawa: Carleton University Press 1990), 135–62.

22 On Australia, see Hedley Bull, 'Australia and the Great Powers in Asia,' in Gordon Greenwood and Norman Harper, eds, *Australia in World Affairs, 1966–1970* (Melbourne: Cheshire 1974), 325–52; T.B. Millar, *Australia in Peace and War: External Relations since 1788*, 2d ed. (Botany, NSW: Australian National University Press, 1991), 250. On Canada, see the selections in Paul M. Evans and B. Michael Frolic, eds, *Reluctant Adversaries: Canada and the People's Republic of China, 1949–1970* (Toronto: University of Toronto Press 1991), esp. Patrick Kyba, 'Alvin Hamilton and Sino-Canadian Relations,' 168–86.

23 For discussions of the Hawke government's attitude towards Vietnam sanctions, see Philip G. O'Brien, 'The Making of Australia's Indochina Policies under the Labor Government (1983–1986): The Politics of Circumspection?' *Australia-Asia Papers* 39 (Centre for the Study of Australian-Asian Relations, Griffith University, September 1987); and Stuart Harris, 'Australian Government Perspectives and Policies,' in Colin Mackerras, Robert Cribb, and Allan Healy, eds, *Contemporary Vietnam: Perspectives*

from Australia (Wollongong, NSW: University of Wollongong Press 1988), 31–44.

24 See Walsh's speech in Australia, Parliament, *Commonwealth Parliamentary Debates* (hereafter CPD), Senate, 14 June 1989, 3964.

25 The post-ministerial conference is the annual meeting that is held between foreign ministers from Australia, Britain, Canada, Japan, New Zealand, and the United States, and the six members of ASEAN – Brunei, Indonesia, Malaysia, the Philippines, Singapore, and Thailand after ASEAN's annual meetings. The meeting was expanded in 1992 and 1993 to include as observers the foreign ministers of a number of additional Pacific rim countries.

26 For a discussion of this dynamic in the context of alliances, see Kim Richard Nossal, 'The Dilemmas of Alliancemanship: Cohesion and Disintegration in the American Alliances,' in Lauren McKinsey and Nossal, eds, *America's Alliances and the Canadian-American Relationship* (Toronto: Summerhill Press 1988), 31–54.

27 Paul Marantz, 'Economic Sanctions in the Polish Crisis,' in Leyton-Brown, ed., *Utility of International Economic Sanctions*, 131–46.

28 Kim Richard Nossal, 'Cabin'd, Cribb'd, Confin'd?: Canada's Interests in Human Rights,' in Robert O. Matthews and Cranford Pratt, eds, *Human Rights in Canadian Foreign Policy* (Montreal: McGill-Queen's University Press 1988), 54–7.

29 Hufbauer and Schott, *Economic Sanctions Reconsidered*, 211–20.

30 For an account of the CHICOM sanctions, see Paul M. Evans, 'Caging the Dragon: Post-war Economic Sanctions against the People's Republic of China,' in Leyton-Brown, ed., *Utility of International Economic Sanctions*, 59–85.

31 H. Basil Robinson, *Diefenbaker's World: A Populist in Foreign Affairs* (Toronto: University of Toronto Press 1989), 147.

32 Quoted in Robert Spencer, 'External Affairs and Defence,' in John T. Saywell, ed., *Canadian Annual Review, 1960* (Toronto: University of Toronto Press 1961), 137.

33 John G. Diefenbaker, *One Canada: The Years of Achievement, 1956 to 1962* (Toronto: Macmillan 1976), 173–4.

34 Robinson, *Diefenbaker's World*, 249.

35 Quoted in Liisa North and CAPA, eds, *Between War and Peace in Central America: Choices for Canada* (Toronto: Between the Lines 1990), 210.

36 Canada, Department of External Affairs, 'Press Release,' 5 June 1985, quoted in Peter McFarlane, *Northern Shadows: Canadians and Central America* (Toronto: Between the Lines 1989), 211.

37 Quoted in Gregory Pemberton, 'Australia and the United States,' in P.J. Boyce and J.R. Angel, eds, *Diplomacy in the Marketplace: Australia in World Affairs, 1981–90* (Melbourne: Longman Cheshire 1992), 139.

38 Australia, Department of Foreign Affairs, *Australian Foreign Affairs Record* 56 (May 1985), 464.

39 Pemberton, 'Australia and the United States,' 139.

40 See, for example, the discussion in Barber, 'Economic Sanctions as a Policy Instrument'; and Lindsay, 'Trade Sanctions as Policy Instruments,' 156. For a contrary view, see Baldwin, *Economic Statecraft*, 276–8.

41 For general discussions of the relations of these countries with the United States, see Norman Harper, *A Great and Powerful Friend: A Study of Australian-American Relations between 1900 and 1975* (St Lucia: University of Queensland Press 1987), 342; and John W. Holmes, *Life with Uncle: The Canadian-American Relationship* (Toronto: University of Toronto Press 1981).

42 For a good discussion of the compensation process in Canada, see Prévost, *For Effective and Appropriate Sanctions*, app. 2, 58–60.

43 See, for example, T.B. Millar, *Australia in Peace and War: External Relations 1788–1977* (Canberra: Australian National University Press 1978), 350 and footnote; and Elizabeth Riddell-Dixon, *The Domestic Mosaic: Domestic Groups and Canadian Foreign Policy* (Toronto: Canadian Institute of International Affairs 1985).

44 South African whites, who immigrated in large numbers to Western Australia and Queensland, would be an exception to this rule. In Canada, by contrast, South African immigrants have tended not to figure in the sanctions debate.

45 For accounts, see Howard Stanislawski, 'Domestic Interest Groups and Canadian and American Policy: The Case of the Arab Boycott,' in Robert O. Matthews, Arthur G. Rubinoff, and Janice Gross Stein, eds, *International Conflict and Conflict Management: Readings in World Politics* (Scarborough, Ont.: Prentice-Hall Canada 1984), 137–47; and David Howard Goldberg, *Foreign Policy and Ethnic Interest Groups: American and Canadian Jews Lobby for Israel* (Westport, Conn.: Greenwood Press 1990).

46 See Prévost, *For Effective and Appropriate Sanctions*, 41.

47 James Bayer, 'Sanctioning the Soviets: The Afghanistan Intervention, 1979–80,' in Don Munton and John Kirton, eds, *Canadian Foreign Policy: Selected Cases* (Scarborough, Ont.: Prentice-Hall Canada 1992), 292 no. 29.

48 A 'khaki election' is one in which the military features prominently in the campaign; likewise, green and gold being Australia's national colours, a 'green and gold election' refers to the use of nationalist appeals in electioneering.

49 See, for example, *CPD*, Representatives, 19 Feb. 1980, 28–9, 47, 52.
50 James N. Rosenau, 'Pre-theories and Theories of Foreign Policy,' in *The Scientific Study of Foreign Policy* (New York: Free Press 1971), 95–149.
51 See Philip Ayres, *Malcolm Fraser: A Biography* (Richmond, Vic.: William Heinemann Australia 1987), 394–400; Alan Renouf, *Malcolm Fraser and Australian Foreign Policy* (Sydney: Professional Publications 1986), chaps 1, 3 and 6; John Edwards, *Life Wasn't Meant to Be Easy: A Political Profile of Malcolm Fraser* (Sydney: Mayhem 1977), chap. 18; and Patrick Weller, *Malcolm Fraser* PM: *A Study in Prime Ministerial Power* (Ringwood, Vic.: Penguin 1989), 314–15.
52 J.L. Granatstein and Robert Bothwell, *Pirouette: Pierre Trudeau and Canadian Foreign Policy* (Toronto: University of Toronto Press 1990), 380.
53 United States, Senate, Committee on Foreign Relations, *Economic Relations with the Soviet Union: Hearings before the Subcommittee on International Economic Policy of the Committee on Foreign Relations* (Washington: U.S. Government Printing Office 1982), 110, quoted in Peggy L. Falkenheim, 'Post-Afghanistan Sanctions,' in Leyton-Brown, ed., *Utility of International Economic Sanctions*, 127.

CHAPTER 2: Policies towards Indonesia

1 For example, see Amnesty International, *Report 1977* (London, 1977), 186–9; and United States Congress, House of Representatives, Committee on International Relations / Senate, Committee on Foreign Affairs, *Country Reports on Human Rights Practises*, 95th Congress, 2d sess., 3 Feb. 1978, 234–44.
2 Amnesty International, *Report 1977*, 187.
3 *New York Times*, 13 Dec. 1975.
4 For an excellent survey of the linkage between Canadian aid and human rights concerns, see T.A. Keenleyside, 'Development Assistance,' in Robert O. Matthews and Cranford Pratt, eds, *Human Rights in Canadian Foreign Policy* (Montreal and Kingston: McGill-Queen's University Press 1988), 187–208.
5 Canada, Secretary of State for External Affairs, *Foreign Policy for Canadians* (Ottawa: Information Canada 1970), International Development booklet, 12.
6 *Winnipeg Free Press*, 1 Sep. 1978.
7 John W. Holmes, *Canada: A Middle-Aged Power* (Toronto: McClelland and Stewart 1976), 161–74.
8 Canada, External Aid Office, *1966–1967 Annual Review* (Ottawa 1967), 23.

9 The best account of this episode is in Theodore Cohn, 'Politics of Canadian Food Aid: The Case of South and Southeast Asia,' in Theodore
   Cohn, Geoffrey Hainsworth, and Lorne Kavic, eds, *Canada and Southeast
   Asia: Perspectives and Evolution of Public Policies* (Coquitlam, BC: Kaen
   1980).
10 These were the broad objectives outlined in the Trudeau government's
   1970 foreign policy paper, *Foreign Policy for Canadians*, Pacific booklet, esp.
   25.
11 *Foreign Policy for Canadians*, Pacific booklet, 7; also 25.
12 For example, Peyton V. Lyon, 'The Trudeau Doctrine,' *International Journal*
   26 (Winter 1970–1). The most comprehensive treatment of these changes
   may be found in J.L. Granatstein and Robert Bothwell, *Pirouette: Pierre
   Trudeau and Canadian Foreign Policy* (Toronto: University of Toronto Press
   1990).
13 Lorne Kavic, 'Canada and the Pacific: Prospects and Challenges,' *Behind
   the Headlines* 29 (May 1970), 4.
14 William Saywell, 'The Pacific,' *International Journal* 33 (Spring 1978), 411.
15 *Foreign Policy for Canadians*, Pacific booklet, 17, 20; after 1970, Indonesia
   was officially added to Canada's list of 'countries of concentration' for
   development assistance: see Canada, Canadian International Development
   Agency, *Canada and the Developing World* (Ottawa 1970), 16.
16 See, for example, Franklin B. Weinstein, 'The Uses of Foreign Policy in
   Indonesia: An Approach to the Analysis of Foreign Policy in the Less
   Developed Countries,' *World Politics* 24 (April 1972).
17 Kavic, 'Canada and the Pacific,' 5; *International Canada* (January 1971), 5–6;
   David Van Praagh, 'Canada and Southeast Asia,' in Peyton V. Lyon and
   Tariq Y. Ismael, eds, *Canada and the Third World* (Toronto: Macmillan
   1976), 334–5.
18 The most comprehensive discussion of this episode may be found in
   Douglas A. Ross, *In the Interests of Peace: Canada and Vietnam, 1954–73*
   (Toronto: University of Toronto Press 1984), chap. 11.
19 Canada, Secretary of State for External Affairs, *Viet-Nam: Canada's
   Approach to Participation in the International Commission of Control and
   Supervision* (Ottawa 1973), 28.
20 See W.M. Dobell, 'A Sow's Ear in Vietnam,' *International Journal* 29 (Summer 1974); Charles Taylor, *Snow Job: Canada, the United States and Vietnam*
   (Toronto: Anansi 1974). Three works on Canada's truce-supervisory role
   in Vietnam were published in the mid-1980s: James Eayrs, *Indochina: Roots
   of Complicity* vol. 5 of *In Defence of Canada* (Toronto: University of Toronto
   Press 1983); Ramesh Thakur, *Peacekeeping in Vietnam: Canada, India, Poland*

and the International Commission (Edmonton: University of Alberta Press 1984); and Ross, *In the Interests of Peace.*

21 For a survey of both aid and trade flows, see Geoffrey B. Hainsworth, *Innocents Abroad or Partners in Development? An Evaluation of Canada-Indonesia Aid, Trade and Investment Relations,* Field Report Series 15 (Singapore: Institute of Southeast Asian Studies 1986).

22 Canada, Department of External Affairs, *Statement 77/7,* 4 Apr. 1977. For an examination of Canadian policies towards the states of Indochina during this period, see Kim Richard Nossal, 'Retreat, Retraction and Reconstruction: Canada and Indochina in the Post-hostilities Period,' in Gordon P. Means, ed., *The Past in Southeast Asia's Present* (Ottawa: Canadian Council for Southeast Asian Studies 1977), 171–81.

23 CIDA, *Report to the Secretary of State for External Affairs on the Mission to Indonesia* (Ottawa: 10 May 1976), 20; *International Canada* (March 1976), 89.

24 *Financial Post,* 3 Apr. 1976.

25 Department of External Affairs, *Statements and Speeches 76/25,* 25 Aug. 1976, 4.

26 MacEachen's successor as SSEA, Don Jamieson, revealed the nature of the minister's quiet diplomacy in a speech on human rights in March 1977: Department of External Affairs, *Statements and Speeches 77/5,* 16 Mar. 1977, 5.

27 *International Canada* (September 1976), 228.

28 Margaret Doxey, 'Human Rights and Canadian Foreign Policy,' *Behind the Headlines* 37 (June 1979), 10.

29 T.A. Keenleyside and Patricia Taylor, 'The Impact of Human Rights Violations on the Conduct of Canadian Bilateral Relations: A Contemporary Dilemma,' *Behind the Headlines* 42 (November 1984), 25.

30 Kim Richard Nossal, 'Personal Diplomacy and National Behaviour: Trudeau's North-South Initiatives,' *Dalhousie Review* (Summer 1982), 278–91; and 'Cabin'd, Cribb'd, Confin'd?: Canada's Interests in Human Rights,' in Matthews and Pratt, eds, *Human Rights in Canadian Foreign Policy,* 46–58.

31 *International Canada* 6 (January 1977), 13.

32 Henry S. Albinski, *Australian External Policy under Labor* (Vancouver: University of British Columbia Press 1977), 106–9.

33 See Nancy Viviani, 'Australians and the Timor Issue: II,' *Australian Outlook* 32 (December 1978), for a discussion of the domestic pressures on the government in Canberra over this issue.

34 Although, at the urging of the Australian Journalists Association, the Australian embassy in Djakarta investigated the killing of the journalists,

there were conflicting stories about who was responsible for their deaths: some eyewitnesses claimed they had been killed by Fretilin forces, while others claimed they had been murdered by Indonesian troops. See Viviani, 'Australians and the Timor Issue,' 250.

35 Robert Carty and Virginia Smith, *Perpetuating Poverty: The Political Economy of Canadian Foreign Aid* (Toronto: Between the Lines 1981), 24–5.

36 See, for example, Keenleyside, 'Development Assistance,' 196–8.

37 See Carty and Smith, *Perpetuating Poverty*, chap. 1, for a selective, but none the less illustrative, survey of criticism of aid projects in the Canadian press in the late 1970s.

38 Viviani, 'Australians and the Timor Issue,' 253–4.

39 The 6+6 comprised the six ASEAN states – Brunei, Indonesia, Malaysia, the Philippines, Singapore, and Thailand – and ASEAN's six 'dialogue partners' – Australia, Canada, the European Community, Japan, New Zealand, and the United States. Canada was first invited to join ASEAN as a 'dialogue partner' in February 1977. For a discussion, see Richard Stubbs, 'ASEAN at Twenty: The Search for a New Consensus,' *Behind the Headlines* 45 (January/February 1988).

40 For the government's own account of formal Canadian reactions to the Dili massacre, see Canada, House of Commons, Standing Committee on External Affairs and International Trade, Sub-Committee on Development and Human Rights, *Minutes of Proceedings and Evidence*, issue 9, 9 Dec. 1991, especially the testimony of John Tennant, acting assistant deputy minister, Asia and Pacific Branch, External Affairs and International Trade, appendix, 9A–14ff.

41 House of Commons, *Debates*, 1991, vol. 132 unrev., 18 Nov. 1991, 4912.

42 *Globe and Mail*, 10 Dec. 1991; *Canadian International Relations Chronicle*, October–December 1991, 23.

43 Standing Committee on External Affairs and International Trade, Sub-Committee on Development and Human Rights, *Minutes of Proceedings and Evidence*, issue 9, 9 Dec. 1991: see in particular the testimony of Elaine Brière, coordinator of the East Timor Alert Network, and Li-lien Gibbons, whose step-brother had been killed in the Dili massacre.

44 For a good survey of the shifts in Canadian policy linking aid and human rights over the fall of 1991, see Gerald J. Schmitz, 'Human Rights, Democratization, and International Conflict,' in Fen Osler Hampson and Christopher J. Maule, *Canada Among Nations, 1992–93: A New World Order?* (Ottawa: Carleton University Press 1992), 235–55.

45 The fourth *Sommet des Chefs d'état et de gouvernement ayant en commun l'usage du français*, 19–21 Nov. 1991, held at Chaillot, brought together

forty-five countries, together with observers from Cambodia, Bulgaria, and Romania.

46 See, for example, House of Commons, *Debates*, 20 Nov. 1991, 5075; 5 Dec. 1991, 5858–9.

47 For a discussion of these changes, see Brian L. Job and Frank Langdon, 'Canada and the Pacific,' in Fen Osler Hampson and Christopher J. Maule, eds, *Canada Among Nations, 1993–94: Global Jeopardy* (Ottawa: Carleton University Press 1993), 280–6.

48 Herb Feith, 'East Timor after the Dili Massacre,' *Pacific Research* 5 (February 1992), 3–5.

49 As it is, some Canadian firms with operations in Indonesia complained to External Affairs that Ottawa's modest criticisms of the Suharto regime and the Canadian refusal to accept the annexation of Timor had cost them business in Indonesia: see External Affairs and International Trade Canada, *For Effective and Appropriate Sanctions*, Policy Planning Staff Paper 93/04, by Jean Prévost (Ottawa: March 1993), 56–7.

CHAPTER 3: The 'Punishment' of Vietnam

1 For a discussion of the purposely slow development of Canada's development assistance program in the immediate aftermath of the collapse of the non-Communist regimes in Indochina, see Kim Richard Nossal, 'Retreat, Retraction and Reconstruction: Canada and Indochina in the Post-hostilities Period,' in Gordon P. Means, ed., *The Past in Southeast Asia's Present* (Ottawa: Canadian Council for Southeast Asian Studies 1978), 171–81.

2 Cambodia's name was changed to Kampuchea following the victory of the Khmer Rouge forces in 1975. For much of the 1980s, 'Kampuchea' was used by all parties to the civil war; however, by the end of the decade, the old name had been restored.

3 Nancy Viviani, 'Aid Policies and Programmes,' in P.J. Boyce and J.R. Angel, eds, *Independence and Alliance: Australia in World Affairs, 1976–80* (Sydney: George Allen and Unwin 1983), 123; Hufbauer and Schott, *Economic Sanctions Reconsidered*, 615–16.

4 Gérard Hervouet, 'Vietnam at the Crossroads,' *Peace and Security* 2 (Winter 1987/8), 4–5.

5 Canada, Department of External Affairs, *Statements and Speeches* 79/1, 24 Feb. 1979.

6 Canada, Parliament, House of Commons, *Debates*, 30th Parl., 4th sess., 1979, vol. 4, 3628 and 4145.

7 *Globe and Mail*, 13 June 1979.

8 *International Canada*, July/August 1979, 184.

9 Department of External Affairs, *Communiqué* #78, 19 Oct. 1979.

10 *Globe and Mail*, 7 Nov. 1979.

11 Department of External Affairs, *Communiqué* #87, 14 Nov. 1979, 2, 3.

12 *International Canada*, December 1979, 292.

13 See UN General Assembly resolutions 34/22 (4 Nov. 1979), 35/6 (22 Oct. 1980), 36/5 (15 Oct. 1981), 37/6 (28 Oct. 1982), 38/3 (27 Oct. 1983), 39/5 (30 Oct. 1984), and 40/7 (5 Nov. 1985), which all called on unnamed 'states' to respect Cambodia's sovereignty and territorial integrity and to withdraw military forces.

14 Nossal, 'Retreat, Retraction,' 176 and n. 21.

15 *Globe and Mail*, 30 Mar. 1979.

16 Wayne Gooding and Eric Evans, 'Focus on Vietnam: Political nervousness keeps West at bay,' *Financial Post*, 15 May 1982, 28.

17 House of Commons, *Debates*, 32nd Parl., 1st sess., 1981, vol. 10, 11631.

18 Australia, Parliament, Joint Committee on Foreign Affairs and Defence, *Australia and ASEAN: Challenges and Opportunities* (Canberra: Australian Government Publishing Service 1984), 43–4; J.R. Angel, 'Australia and South-East Asia,' in Boyce and Angel, eds, *Independence and Alliance*, 226.

19 *International Canada*, June/July 1982, 15.

20 *Globe and Mail*, 6 Jan. 1983.

21 In 1986, the United States government began despatching limited military assistance to the non-Communist elements of the CGDK: see John H. Esterline, 'Vietnam in 1986: An Uncertain Tiger,' *Asian Survey* 27 (January 1987), 98. Australia provided humanitarian assistance to the non-Communist elements of the CGDK.

22 For Chrétien's announcement, see *International Canada*, July/August 1984, 7; Clark made his announcement at the post-ministerial conference of ASEAN: Department of External Affairs, *Statements and Speeches* 85/38, 11 July 1985.

23 CIDA, *Annual Reports*, 1983–6.

24 *International Canada*, February 1978, 41; Gérard Hervouet, *Le Canada face à l'Asie de l'Est* (Quebec: Nouvelle Optique 1981), 141–2.

25 Notable were the promises in the foreign policy paper of 1970 committing Ottawa to an active role in reconstruction in Indochina in the postwar period. Canada, Secretary of State for External Affairs, *Foreign Policy for Canadians* (Ottawa: Information Canada 1970), Pacific booklet, 20, 24.

26 Sheldon W. Simon, *The ASEAN States and Regional Security* (Stanford: Hoover Institution Press 1982), 50.

27 *Toronto Star*, 19 July 1986.

28 The United States extended its wartime economic sanctions against North Vietnam in 1975, 1976, and 1977 and persistently rebuffed Vietnamese efforts to normalize diplomatic relations as a prelude to greater economic aid from the West. See Esterline, 'Vietnam in 1986,' 100–2. For one account of the effects of Western responses on Vietnamese policy, see Simon, *ASEAN States*, 50–2.

29 See, for example, the discussion in chapter 5 regarding the Canadian sanctions against South Africa announced on 13 September 1985. These sanctions included the termination of all civil-aviation links with South Africa and an embargo on oil and oil products to South Africa. While Canada had neither air links nor any oil trade with South Africa, these measures had considerable symbolic importance. Imposed merely a month before the Commonwealth Heads of Government meetings in Nassau, they constituted an important signal to both Britain and other members of the Commonwealth of Canada's position on the issue. For a differing interpretation of the utility of these sanctions, see Clarence G. Redekop, 'The Mulroney Government and South Africa: Constructive Disengagement,' *Behind the Headlines* 44 (December 1986), 7.

30 Canada, Export Development Corporation, *Annual Reports* (Ottawa: 1975–86).

31 Canada, Statistics Canada, External Trade Division, *Trade of Canada: Exports by Countries* (Ottawa: December 1977–December 1980).

32 Canadian officials were able to track *entrepôt* trade through Hong Kong, but not Singapore. In 1986, well over $6 million in Vietnamese products, mainly shrimp, was exported to Canada through Hong Kong. The value of the *entrepôt* trade through Singapore was unknown, but was thought to be 'substantial.'

33 *International Canada*, April 1979, 118, and May 1979, 122.

34 See, for example, the comments in Parliament of Ian Watson (L, Châteauguay): House of Commons, *Debates*, 32nd Parl., 1st sess., 1981, 11631 (16 July 1981).

35 David Cox, 'Leadership Change and Innovation in Canadian Foreign Policy: The 1979 Progressive Conservative Government,' *International Journal* 37 (Autumn 1982), 561–2.

36 House of Commons, *Debates*, 31st Parl., 1st sess., 1979, vol. 2, 1316 (14 Nov. 1979); see also her comments later in the debate, 1323.

37 House of Commons, *Debates*, 31st Parl., 1st sess., 1979, vol. 2, 1682 (26 Nov. 1979).

38 See, for example, Stephen Orlov's argument that the 'pressure of economic sanctions should be placed on Vietnam and the Soviet Union to negotiate a settlement' after which 'extensive reconstruction aid' should

be offered by Canada and other Western states. 'Vietnam's Rule over Kampuchea Threatens Regional Stability,' *International Perspectives*, May/June 1981, 9–10.

39 See Department of External Affairs, *Statements and Speeches*: 82/18, Singapore, 17 June 1982; 83/22 Bangkok, 27 June 1983; 85/38, Kuala Lumpur, 11 July 1985.

40 Emory Swank, a former United States ambassador to Cambodia, quoted in David W.P. Elliott, 'Vietnam in Asia: Strategy and Diplomacy in a New Context,' *International Journal* 38 (Spring 1983), 315n.

41 House of Commons, *Debates*, 32nd Parl., 1st sess., 1981, vol. 10, 11631 (16 July 1981). The MP was Ian Watson (L, Châteauguay).

42 Margaret Doxey, 'Do Sanctions Work?' *International Perspectives*, July/August 1982, 14.

43 Richard Stubbs, 'ASEAN at Twenty: The Search for a New Consensus,' *Behind the Headlines* 45 (January/February 1988).

44 For an excellent examination of the international political aspects of this case, see Gérard Hervouet, *The Return of Vietnam to the International System*, Occasional Paper 6 (Ottawa: Canadian Institute for International Peace and Security 1988).

45 Michael Leifer, 'ASEAN and the Problem of Common Response,' *International Journal* 38 (Spring 1983), 325–7.

46 Joint Committee on Foreign Affairs and Defence, *Australia and ASEAN*, 45, 50.

47 *Globe and Mail*, 28 June 1980.

48 Ibid., 16 July 1981.

49 For a discussion of the MIA issue in United States–Vietnamese relations, see Esterline, 'Vietnam in 1986,' 101–2.

50 Department of External Affairs, *Statement*, Bangkok, 27 June 1983.

CHAPTER 4: Ending the Indochina Sanctions

1 For comparable impressions about the Vietnamese economy of two North American visitors to Vietnam in 1987 and 1988, see Gérard Hervouet, 'Vietnam at the Crossroads,' *Peace and Security* 2 (Winter 1987/8), and John LeBoutillier, 'Coming to Terms with Vietnam,' *New York Times Magazine*, 1 May 1988, 49ff.

2 It should be noted that even after the formal withdrawal, the Cambodian resistance based in Thailand would maintain that Vietnam had not in fact withdrawn at all. Rather, they claimed that Vietnamese troops were being 'resettled' in Cambodia as civilians.

3 Canada, Secretary of State for External Affairs, *Statement* 90/5, 25 Jan.

1990; for Clark's statement and the responses of the opposition parties, see Canada, Parliament, House of Commons, *Debates*, 1990, 25 Jan. 1990, appendix at 7494.

4 For a good discussion of DEA attitudes that distinguishes among three 'policy tendencies' within the department, see Douglas A. Ross, *In the Interests of Peace: Canada and Vietnam 1954–73* (Toronto: University of Toronto Press 1984), passim, and esp. 380.

5 This dispute frequently takes on the air of *opéra bouffe*: one of the 'islands' that were 'occupied' by China in early 1988 is in fact a reef that is submerged at high tide; the 'occupation' consisted of the Chinese sinking a large concrete dock onto the reef that would enable the PRC flag to fly above high-tide waters.

6 Quoted from *Australian Financial Review*, 29 June 1983, in Philip G. O'Brien, *The Making of Australia's Indochina Policies under the Labor Government (1983–1986): The Politics of Circumspection?* Australia-Asia Papers 39 (Nathan: Centre for the Study of Australian-Asian Relations, Griffith University 1987), 13.

7 Hervouet, 'Vietnam at the Crossroads,' 5.

8 Some Vietnamese officials to whom we spoke in May 1988, including the head of the division of the Ministry of Foreign Affairs responsible for the United States, seemed completely oblivious to the profound longer-term effects that the Vietnam War had had on American society and domestic politics.

9 One small, but not insignificant, manifestation of this is belief is the pervasive flying of the MIA/POW flag outside police stations throughout the United States.

10 See Victor Levant, *Quiet Complicity: Canadian Involvement in the Vietnam War* (Toronto: Between the Lines 1986), 1: he describes Vietnam's post-1975 behaviour as 'reprehensible'; see, however, his somewhat different rationalization in the 'Afterword,' 255. See also the preface written by Gwynne Dyer, again no fan of the United States, but who, like Levant, takes the opportunity to excoriate the Vietnamese government as 'a brutal and deceitful gang of tyrants.'

11 For a cross-Canada survey of the results of immigration from Indochina in the late 1970s, see Louis-Jacques Dorais, Kwok B. Chan, and Doreen M. Indra, eds, *Ten Years Later: Indochinese Communities in Canada* (Montreal: Canadian Asian Studies Association 1988).

12 Kenneth Rivett, 'Vietnamese Refugees in Australia,' in Colin Mackerras, Robert Cribb, and Allan Healy, eds, *Contemporary Vietnam: Perspectives from Australia* (Wollongong: University of Wollongong Press 1988), 149–50.

13 O'Brien, *Making of Australia's Indochina Policies*, 5.

14 *The Australian*, 10 May 1985.

15 *Sydney Morning Herald*, 28 June 1985.

16 Ibid., 19 Dec. 1987.

CHAPTER 5: The Impact of the Individual

1 These determinants of foreign policy formed James N. Rosenau's 'pre-theory' of foreign policy. See 'Pre-theories and Theories of Foreign Policy,' in *The Scientific Study of Foreign Policy* (New York: Free Press 1971).

2 The 'individual,' or 'idiosyncratic,' variable 'include[s] all those aspects of a decision-maker – his values, talents, and prior experiences – that distinguish his foreign policy choices or behaviour from those of every other decision-maker.' Ibid., 108; on Rosenau's decision to change the terminology, see 108 n 42.

3 T.A. Keenleyside, 'Canada–South Africa Commercial Relations, 1977–1982: Business as Usual?' *Canadian Journal of African Studies* 17 (1983), 449–68.

4 Canada, Secretary of State for External Affairs, *Foreign Policy for Canadians* (Ottawa: Information Canada 1970), United Nations booklet, 17–20.

5 See, for example, Canadians Concerned about South Africa, 'Relations between Canada and South Africa, 1948–1983,' by Joanne Naiman, Joan Bhabha, and Guy Wright, paper delivered to the United Nations North American Regional Conference for Action against Apartheid, New York, 18–21 June 1984.

6 Clarence G. Redekop, 'Commerce over Conscience: The Trudeau Government and South Africa, 1968–1984,' *Journal of Canadian Studies* 19 (Winter 1984–5), 82–105.

7 For how the Trudeau government justified its decision to 'balance' its concerns for human rights with its desire to pursue the objective of 'economic growth,' see *Foreign Policy for Canadians*, United Nations booklet, 19–20.

8 Georges Blouin, 'Canadian Policy toward South Africa: The Decision-making Process,' in Douglas Anglin, Timothy Shaw, and Carl Widstrand, eds, *Canada, Scandinavia and Southern Africa* (Uppsala: Scandinavian Institute of African Studies 1978), 159–63.

9 For an exploration of the uniqueness of the South African case, see Rhoda E. Howard, 'Black Africa and South Africa,' in Robert O. Matthews and Cranford Pratt, eds, *Human Rights in Canadian Foreign Policy* (Montreal and Kingston: McGill-Queen's University Press 1988), 265–84.

10 See the statement of the secretary of state for external affairs, Don Jamieson, to the House of Commons: Department of External Affairs, *Statements and Speeches* 77/23, 19 Dec. 1977, esp. 1–3.

11 Linda Freeman, 'Canada and Africa in the 1970s,' *International Journal* 35 (Autumn 1980), 795–6, has characterized the 1977 initiatives as 'symbolic gestures' involving 'more form than substance.' Likewise, T.A. Keenleyside and Patricia Taylor, in 'The Impact of Human Rights Violations on the Conduct of Canadian Bilateral Relations: A Contemporary Dilemma,' *Behind the Headlines* 42 (November 1984), 9–12, show empirically that there was indeed 'little substance' to the initiatives. See also Keenleyside, 'Canada–South Africa Commercial Relations,' 453–4, and Redekop, 'Commerce over Conscience,' 90ff. For a contrary interpretation, see Heribert Adam and Kogila Moodley, *Democratizing Southern Africa: Challenges for Canadian Policy*, Occasional Papers 9 (Ottawa: Canadian Institute for International Peace and Security, June 1992), chap. 1.

12 Redekop, 'Commerce over Conscience,' 83.

13 Quoted in Peyton V. Lyon, *Canada in World Affairs*, vol. 12: *1961–1963* (Toronto: Oxford University Press 1968), 294.

14 Compare, for example, the statement of R.A. MacKay, permanent delegate to the United Nations, to the Ad Hoc Political Committee on 9 November 1955, reproduced in Arthur E. Blanchette, ed., *Canadian Foreign Policy, 1955–1965: Selected Speeches and Documents* (Toronto: McClelland and Stewart 1977), 299–302, with the rhetoric in the 1970 foreign policy papers (see United Nations booklet, 17–20).

15 For a discussion of the views of officials in the early Trudeau period on the use of violent struggle in the South African context, see Garth Legge, Cranford Pratt, Richard Williams, and Hugh Winsor, 'The Black Paper: An Alternative Policy for Canada towards Southern Africa,' *Behind the Headlines* 30 (September 1970), 10, 12.

16 Robert O. Matthews and Cranford Pratt, 'Human Rights and Foreign Policy: Principles and Canadian Practice,' *Human Rights Quarterly* 7 (May 1985), 186.

17 Legge, et al., 'The Black Paper,' 9. Like weeds, such sentiments proved to be exceedingly hardy, and persistently kept popping up. They were most frequently heard in the 1980s at meetings of university boards of governors considering divestment strategies.

18 *Foreign Policy for Canadians*, United Nations booklet, 19; for a good survey of the sanguine way in which the Department of Industry, Trade and Commerce advertised the business 'opportunities' in the 'politically stable' South African environment to the Canadian corporate community in the early 1970s, see Redekop, 'Canada–South Africa Commercial Relations,' 451–2.

19 'Cabin'd, Cribb'd, Confin'd? Canada's Interests in Human Rights,' in

Matthews and Pratt, eds, *Human Rights in Canadian Foreign Policy*, 46–58.

20 For example, James Eayrs, *Canada in World Affairs*, vol. 9: *October 1955 to June 1957* (Toronto: Oxford University Press 1959), 168.

21 Department of External Affairs, *Statements and Speeches* 77/5, 16 March 1977, 3.

22 *Globe and Mail*, 31 Jan. 1987, A1–2; also Linda Freeman, 'PM has to deliver on Africa or lose face,' ibid., 5 Feb. 1987.

23 Ibid., 24 Mar. 1987.

24 Ibid., 14 Aug. 1987, A1.

25 David Taras, 'Brian Mulroney's Foreign Policy: Something for Everyone,' *The Round Table* 293 (1985), 35–46.

26 See the results of a North-South Institute poll of the three political parties on foreign policy issues during the election campaign: *International Canada*, August/September 1984, 20.

27 Department of External Affairs, *Statements and Speeches* 84/14, 20 Nov. 1984; also *International Canada*, October/November 1984, 15.

28 Canada, Parliament, House of Commons, *Debates*, 1984–85, vol. 1, 1447 (21 Dec. 1984).

29 Ibid., 1985, vol. 2, 2538.

30 Secretary of State for External Affairs, *Competitiveness and Security: Directions for Canada's International Relations* (Ottawa, May 1985), 42.

31 Clarence G. Redekop, 'The Mulroney Government and South Africa: Constructive Disengagement,' *Behind the Headlines* 44 (December 1986), 3.

32 House of Commons, *Debates*, 1985, vol. 3, 3715 (15 Apr. 1985).

33 *Globe and Mail*, 23 Mar. 1985, 5.

34 Department of External Affairs, *Statement* 85/37, Baie Comeau, PQ, 6 July 1985. This statement is reproduced in Douglas G. Anglin, ed., *Canada and South Africa: Challenge and Response* (Ottawa: Carleton International Proceedings, summer 1986), 51–5; see also the discussion in Redekop, 'Constructive Disengagement,' 5–6.

35 Department of External Affairs, *Statement* 85/37, Baie Comeau, PQ, 6 July 1985; see also Jean Prévost, *For Effective and Appropriate Sanctions*, Policy Planning Staff Paper 93/04 (Ottawa: External Affairs and International Trade Canada, March 1993), 51–2.

36 *International Canada*, August/September 1985, 5.

37 House of Commons, *Debates*, 1985, 6587–9 (13 Sept. 1985); repr. in Anglin, ed., *Canada and South Africa*, 55–60.

38 This threat had been foreshadowed in a comment by Clark to the House when it resumed on 9 September. He had claimed, 'It is the view of this government that it is now essential for us to do everything that we can to

encourage change in an offensive and unacceptable regime ... Obviously, if we have to resort to the full disruption of economic and diplomatic relations, we are prepared to do so' should other measures fail. House of Commons, *Debates*, 1985, vol. 5, 6397.

39 The text of the Commonwealth Accord on Southern Africa agreed to at Nassau is reproduced in Commonwealth Group of Eminent Persons, *Mission to South Africa: The Commonwealth Report* (Harmondsworth: Penguin Books for the Commonwealth Secretariat 1986), 142–5.

40 Ibid., 140–1.

41 Department of External Affairs, *Statement 86/35*, 12 June 1986.

42 *Globe and Mail*, 6 Aug. 1986.

43 See, for example, Timothy Shaw, 'What Canada Can Do in Africa,' *Policy Options* 8 (May 1987), 31–2.

44 See, for example, Linda Freeman's assessment of Canada's South African policy during 1986: 'What's Right with Mulroney? Canada and Sanctions, 1986,' *Southern Africa Report*, October 1986, 3. See also Steve Godfrey, 'Canada and Southern Africa: Seeing Black and White,' in The Group of 78, *Canada and the World: National Interest and Global Responsibility* (Ottawa 1985), 51–2, and 'Canadian Sanctions and Southern Africa,' *International Perspectives*, November/December 1985, 13–16; Dan O'Meara, 'Crisis of Apartheid: The Canadian Response,' *Peace and Security* 1 (Summer 1986), 2–3; and Douglas G. Anglin, 'Canadian Responses,' in Anglin, ed., *Canada and South Africa*, 41–4.

45 Richard J. Payne, 'Canada, South Africa and the Commonwealth,' *International Perspectives*, July/August 1987, 9.

46 See H. Basil Robinson, *Diefenbaker's World: A Populist in Foreign Affairs* (Toronto: University of Toronto Press 1989), chaps. 13 and 18; and Lyon, *Canada in World Affairs*, 294–5. For Diefenbaker's own assessment of this period, see *One Canada: Memoirs of the Right Honourable John G. Diefenbaker*, vol. 2: *The Years of Achievement, 1956 to 1962* (Toronto: Macmillan 1976), 173–85.

47 Godfrey, 'Canadian Sanctions and Suthern Africa,' 13.

48 Bernard Wood, 'Canada and Southern Africa: A Return to Middle Power Activism,' *The Round Table* 315 (1990), 290.

49 This argument is advanced by Robert Matthews and Cranford Pratt in 'Canadian Policy towards Southern Africa,' in Anglin, Shaw, and Witsrand, eds, *Canada, Scandinavia and Southern Africa*, 174.

50 Redekop, 'Constructive Disengagement,' 7.

51 See the Gallup poll reproduced in Don Munton and Timothy M. Shaw,

'Apartheid and Canadian Public Opinion,' *International Perspectives*, September/October 1987, 11.

52 North-South Institute, *Review '87/Outlook '88* (Ottawa 1988), 12.

53 For surveys of post-1985 opinion, see Adam and Moodley, *Democratizing Southern Africa*, 55–9.

54 See Cranford Pratt, ed., 'Canadian Policies towards South Africa: An Exchange between the Secretary of State for External Affairs and the Taskforce on the Churches and Corporate Responsibility,' *Canadian Journal of African Studies* 17 (1983), 512–13.

55 Redekop, 'Constructive Disengagement,' 3.

56 Mulroney's statement of 23 October 1985 is reproduced in Anglin, *Canada and South Africa*, 61–2.

57 For an assessment of Clark's role, see Adam and Moodley, *Democratizing Southern Africa*, 97–9.

58 *Maclean's*, 1 Dec. 1986, 11.

59 Munton and Shaw, 'Apartheid and Canadian Public Opinion,' 12.

60 *Globe and Mail*, 20 June 1986.

61 See the comments of Linda Freeman, 'Rescuing Credibility: Canadian Policy towards South Africa, 1988,' *Southern Africa Report*, December 1988, 8.

62 Parliament, Special Joint Committee of the Senate and of the House of Commons, *Independence and Internationalism* (Ottawa, June 1986), 110.

63 House of Commons, *Debates*, 1985, vol. 2, 2398 (15 Feb. 1985).

64 *Globe and Mail*, 4 July 1985; see also Clark's comments to the House of Commons, *Debates*, 1985, vol. 2, 2398 (15 Feb. 1985).

65 Department of External Affairs, UN Delegation, *Communiqué*, 31 Oct. 1985, 1. For a later indication of Lewis's views, see Michael Valpy, 'An Interview with Stephen Lewis,' *Southern Africa Report*, December 1988, 13–15.

66 Godfrey, 'Canadian Sanctions and Southern Africa,' 13.

67 Michael Valpy, 'PM's Africa policy under fire from External, caucus,' *Globe and Mail*, 14 Oct. 1987, A14; see also Freeman, 'Rescuing Credibility,' 7–8.

68 For a cogent discussion of generational differences and their impact on international politics, see Richard Ned Lebow, 'Generational Learning and Conflict Management,' *International Journal* 40 (Autumn 1985), 555–85.

69 In a July 1961 Gallup poll, fully 50 per cent of Canadians favoured not only maintaining friendly relations with South Africa but also not criticizing apartheid. Only 5 per cent supported cutting relations. Munton and Shaw, 'Apartheid and Canadian Public Opinion,' 10.

70 Ibid., 11.

CHAPTER 6: Ontario and South Africa

1 As we have noted in previous chapters, these standard variables used for the explanation of foreign policy are drawn, albeit loosely, from James N. Rosenau's work on pre-theories of foreign policy: see 'Pre-theories and Theories of Foreign Policy,' in his *The Scientific Study of Foreign Policy* (New York: Free Press 1971), 95–149.

2 For example, Ivo D. Duchacek, 'The International Dimension of Subnational Self-government'; Elliot J. Feldman and Lily Gardner Feldman, 'The Impact of Federalism on the Organization of Canadian Foreign Policy'; and John Kincaid, 'The American Governors in International Affairs,' all in *Publius: The Journal of Federalism* 14 (Fall 1984). See also Ronald G. Atkey, 'The Role of the Provinces in International Affairs,' *International Journal* 26 (Winter 1970–1); P.R. (Roff) Johannson, 'Provincial International Activities,' *International Journal* 33 (Spring 1978); and Brian Hocking, 'Regional Governments and International Affairs: Foreign Policy Problem or Deviant Behaviour,' *International Journal* 41 (Summer 1986), 477–506.

3 One exception would be John M. Kline, 'A New Federalism for the United States,' *International Journal* 41 (Summer 1986), 519–20, which provides a description of the increasing involvement of state governments in high politics.

4 R.J. Delisle, 'Treaty-making Power in Canada,' in Ontario Advisory Committee on Confederation, *Background Papers and Reports* (Toronto: Queen's Printer of Ontario 1967); Mr Justice Bora Laskin, 'The Provinces and International Agreements,' in ibid.; and Howard A. Leeson and Wilfried Vanderelst, *External Affairs and Canadian Federalism: The History of a Dilemma* (Toronto: Holt, Rinehart and Winston 1973).

5 For example, it was agreed at the premiers' conference held at St Andrew's, New Brunswick, in 1977 that 'the development of foreign policy and the conduct of international relations is the responsibility of the federal government, but it is also important to realize that the provinces have concerns in certain areas of international relations particularly in the development of their economies, ownership of their resources and transborder relations with the United States.' Quoted in Wayne Clifford, 'A Perspective on the Question [of Provincial International Activity] with Particular Reference to the Case of the Province of Alberta,' in *Choix* 14 (1981), 96.

6 On Quebec, see Jacques Brossard, André Patry, and Elisabeth Weiser,

Les pouvoirs extérieurs du Québec (Montreal: Les presses de l'Université de Montréal, 1967); Annemarie Jacomy-Millette, 'Aspects juridiques des activités internationales du Québec,' in Paul Painchaud, ed., *Le Canada et le Québec sur la Scène internationale* (Quebec: Centre québécois de relations internationales, 1977); Feldman and Feldman, 'Impact of Federalism'; and Kim Richard Nossal, *The Politics of Canadian Foreign Policy*, 2nd ed. (Scarborough, Ont.: Prentice-Hall Canada 1989), 266–75.

7 There were two critical periods during which the Quebec government attempted to assert a special place for itself in international politics. The first was in the 1960s, when, with the active support of the French government of Charles de Gaulle, a succession of governments in Quebec City sought to secure a special status for the province in international affairs. The second period extended from the election of the Parti québécois in November 1976 to the rejection of the *indépendantiste* option in the referendum of May 1980, when the government of Premier René Lévesque, this time with the support of a post-Gaullist government in Paris, attempted to have its *indépendantisme* mirrored at the international level. On the 1960s, see Charlotte S.M. Girard, *Canada in World Affairs*, vol. 13: *1963–1965* (Toronto: Canadian Institute of International Affairs 1980), esp. chap. 4.

8 Such a characterization follows standard treatments of the rational model of policy analysis. For one Canadian example, see G. Bruce Doern and Richard W. Phidd, *Canadian Public Policy: Ideas, Structure, Process* (Toronto: Methuen 1983), chap. 6.

9 One such statement can be found in Lévesque's 'Quebec Independence,' in Elliot J. Feldman and Neil Nevitte, eds, *The Future of North America: Canada, the United States and Quebec Nationalism* (Cambridge, Mass.: Center for International Affairs, Harvard University 1979), 61–70. A full statement of the PQ's foreign policy can be found in Quebec's 1979 white paper: Quebec, Conseil exécutif, *La nouvelle entente Québec-Canada: Proposition du gouvernement du Québec pour une entente d'égal à égal: La souveraineté-association* (Quebec: Editeur officiel, 1979), 62, 104–5.

10 For example, Canadians Concerned about South Africa, 'Relations between Canada and South Africa, 1948–1983' by Joanne Naiman, Joan Bhabha, and Guy Wright, paper delivered to the North American Regional Conference for Action against Apartheid, United Nations, 18-21 June 1984, 7–8.

11 For a brief discussion of Canadian private investment and apartheid, see Steven Langdon, 'Canada's Role in Africa,' in Norman Hillmer and Garth

Stevenson, eds, *Foremost Nation: Canadian Foreign Policy and a Changing World* (Toronto: McClelland and Stewart 1977), 194–5.

12 CCSA, 'Complicity in Oppression' (Toronto 1980; mimeo).

13 During his years as a member of the legislature, Lewis was a firm and outspoken critic of Canadian links with South Africa. For example, his first private member's bill introduced in the Ontario legislature was a measure to bar the Liquor Control Board of Ontario from purchasing and selling South African wines and spirits. As I noted in chapter 5, in 1984 he was appointed by the federal Progressive Conservative government of Brian Mulroney to be Canada's permanent representative to the United Nations; his rhetorical attacks on apartheid in the General Assembly played an important role in the Mulroney government's policy towards South Africa.

14 *Globe and Mail*, 20 Oct. 1973; also *International Canada*, October 1973, 271.

15 Details of this episode were revealed a year later by Donald Munro, a Progressive Conservative MP, during a federal parliamentary debate on foreign policy initiated by the Opposition: Canada, Parliament, House of Commons, *Debates*, 1982, vol. 16, 17987–8. Munro, it should be noted, was not at all pleased that the exchange had been cancelled: he criticized the Department of External Affairs for intervening in what was, in his view, a 'purely technical' interchange, 'innocuous in political terms.'

16 *Globe and Mail*, 18 Feb. 1982.

17 Figures from 'Ontario bans S. African wines,' *Toronto Star*, 15 Aug. 1985.

18 'Boycotts may undermine trade pacts,' *Globe and Mail*, 17 Aug. 1985.

19 Ibid., 10 Aug. 1985.

20 'Ontario remains satisfied with the existing situation. The federal goverment is the sole representative of Canada abroad, but it needs to make a sustained effort to ensure it gets the necessary provincial input.' Denis Massicotte, 'L'Ontario sur la scène internationale,' *Choix* 15 (1982), 90. The Feldmans make the same point: 'Impact of Federalism,' 40, 55.

21 Tareq Y. Ismael, 'Canada and the Middle East,' in Peyton V. Lyon and Tareq Y. Ismael, eds, *Canada and the Third World* (Toronto: Macmillan 1976), 265.

22 Ontario, Legislative Assembly of Ontario, *Official Report of Debates*, 32nd Parl., 4th sess., #100, (25 Oct. 1984), 3538–48.

23 Figures cited by Monte Kwinter, Ontario's minister of consumer and commercial relations: *Toronto Star*, 15 Aug. 1986.

24 See, for example, *Globe and Mail*, 30 Apr. 1986, A7.

25 Ontario, Legislative Assembly, *Official Report of Debates*, 33rd Parl., 1st sess., #15 and 17 (8 and 9 July 1985), 543 and 636–7.

26 *Globe and Mail*, 3 Aug. 1985.

27 'Ontario bans S. African wines,' *Toronto Star*, 15 Aug. 1985; *Globe and Mail*, 15 Aug. 1985.

28 *Globe and Mail*, 17 Aug. 1985.

29 Ibid., 23 Aug. 1985.

30 Ibid., 3 Aug. 1985.

31 For the reactions of key interest groups in Toronto to the decision, and the exceedingly laudatory comments about Peterson's decision, see the *Globe and Mail*, 15 Aug. 1985.

32 Henry S. Albinski, *Australian External Policy under Labor* (St Lucia, Queensland, and Vancouver: University of Queensland Press and University of British Columbia Press 1977), 274–7.

33 John M. Kline, 'Managing Intergovernmental Tensions: Shaping a State and Local Role in US Foreign Relations,' in Brian Hocking, ed., *Foreign Relations and Federal States* (London: Leicester University Press 1993) 111–13; also Duchacek, 'International Dimension,' 21–2 and n. 34.

34 Hocking, 'Regional Governments and International Affairs,' 481.

CHAPTER 7: The Invasion of Afghanistan

1 See Henry S. Bradsher, *Afghanistan and the Soviet Union*, expanded ed. (Durham: Duke University Press 1985), chaps 9 and 10.

2 Partial accounts of Australian and Canadian policies on Afghanistan can be found in Alan Renouf, *Malcolm Fraser and Australian Foreign Policy* (Sydney: Australian Professional Publications 1986), 91–103; Patrick Weller, *Malcolm Fraser PM: A Study in Prime Ministerial Power in Australia* (Ringwood, Vic.: Penguin 1989), 344–53; James Bayer, 'Sanctioning the Soviets: The Afghanistan Intervention, 1979–80,' in Don Munton and John Kirton, eds, *Canadian Foreign Policy: Selected Cases* (Scarborough, Ont.: Prentice-Hall Canada 1992), 286–98; and John Kirton, 'Economic Sanctions and Alliance Consultations: Canada, the United States and the Strains of 1979–82,' in David Leyton-Brown, *The Utility of International Economic Sanctions* (London: Croom Helm 1987), 280–6.

3 Australia, Parliament, *Commonwealth Parliamentary Debates* (hereafter *CPD*), House of Representatives, 1980, 31st Parl., 1st sess., vol. 117, 24.

4 *Globe and Mail*, 12 Jan. 1980.

5 See his 'Sanctions, South Africa and Australian Policy,' Working Paper 37, Peace Research Centre, Australian National University (March 1988), 27.

6 Kim Richard Nossal, 'International Sanctions as International Punishment,' *International Organization* 43 (Spring 1989), 301–22.

7 See, for example, *Sydney Morning Herald*, 5 Jan. 1980. It should be noted that these were the statistics for 1978, at the time the latest statistics available. For the official statistics for this period, see Australia, Australian Bureau of Statistics, *Overseas Trade Australia – Part 2: Comparative and Summary Tables 1981–82*, 25, 73; Canada, Statistics Canada, *Exports by Countries, 1981* and *Imports by Countries, 1981*.

8 John Bowan, 'Australia's Relations with the Soviet Bloc,' in Paul Dibb, ed., *Australia's External Relations in the 1980s* (Canberra: Croom Helm Australia 1983), 171.

9 *CPD*, Representatives, 28 Feb. 1980, 493–6.

10 *CPD*, Senate, 14 June 1989, 3964: Walsh was rejecting opposition calls for Australian sanctions against China in the aftermath of the Tiananmen massacre, recalling what he termed the 'hypocritical' measures adopted by the Fraser government nine years before.

11 *Sydney Morning Herald*, 11 Jan. 1980.

12 For an account of the rutile bans, see *The Age*, 28 Jan. 1980, and *Canberra Times*, 29 Jan. and 13 Feb. 1980.

13 *National Times*, 17–23 Feb. 1980; also Australia, Department of Primary Industry, *Annual Report* (Canberra: Australian Government Publishing Service 1980), 16–17.

14 See *CPD*, Senate, 19 Feb. 1980, 7.

15 *Australian Financial Review*, 9 July 1980.

16 Bayer, 'Sanctioning the Soviets,' 290–1.

17 See *Montreal Gazette*, 15 Jan. 1980.

18 See Kirton, 'Economic Sanctions and Alliance Consultations,' 284.

19 Australian Bureau of Statistics, *Overseas Trade Australia, Part 2, 1981–82*, 73; Statistics Canada, *Exports by Countries, Imports by Countries, 1979–82*.

20 Bradsher, *Afghanistan and the Soviet Union*, 189.

21 Quoted in ibid., 199.

22 *Globe and Mail*, 28 Jan. 1980.

23 Weller, *Malcolm Fraser PM*, 352–3. By the time Ellicott was interviewed by Weller, he was claiming that he had not been 'overly happy' about the Olympic boycott.

24 See the series of investigative pieces on the ONA story published by the *National Times*: 24 Feb.–1 March 1980; 2–8 March; 13–19 April; and 20–26 April.

25 Kirton, 'Economic Sanctions and Alliance Consultations,' 280–6.

26 Eric S. Morse, 'Sport and Canadian Foreign Policy,' *Behind the Headlines* 45 (December 1987), 12–13; for the sceptical view of Robert Ford, Canada's ambassador in Moscow, see Robert A.D. Ford, *Our Man in Moscow: A*

Diplomat's Reflections on the Soviet Union (Toronto: University of Toronto Press 1989), 320–1.

27 For a discussion of this dynamic, see Kim Richard Nossal, 'The Dilemmas of Alliancemanship: Cohesion and Disintegration in the American Alliances,' in Lauren McKinsey and Kim Richard Nossal, eds, *America's Alliances and the Canadian-American Relationship* (Toronto: Summerhill Press 1988), 13–51.

28 Kirton, 'Economic Sanctions and Alliance Consultations,' 280–6, and Bradsher, *Afghanistan and the Soviet Union*, 194–9.

29 See *The Australian*, 8 July 1980, and *Globe and Mail*, 17 July 1980.

30 See, for example, the discussion in James Barber, 'Economic Sanctions as a Policy Instrument,' *International Affairs* 55 (1979); and James M. Lindsay, 'Trade Sanctions as Policy Instruments: A Re-examination,' *International Studies Quaterly* 30 (1986), 156. For a contrary view, see David A. Baldwin, *Economic Statecraft* (Princeton: Princeton University Press 1985), 276–8.

31 *Globe and Mail*, 8 Jan. 1980.

32 *International Canada*, April 1980, 70.

33 Joseph A. Camilleri, *Australian-American Relations: The Web of Dependence* (Melbourne: Macmillan Australia 1980), 140, 144.

34 *CPD*, Representatives, 19 Feb. 1980, 35.

35 *National Times*, 10–16 Feb. 1980. See Peter Davies, ' "All the way with LBJ" Reconsidered,' in John McCarthy, ed., *Dependency? Essays in the History of Australian Defence and Foreign Policy*, Defence Studies Publication 1, n.d., 79–97.

36 *Financial Review*, 18 Mar. 1980.

37 *The Age*, 5 and 11 Jan. 1980.

38 Canada, Department of External Affairs, file 37-16-SU, 'Soviet trade,' 7 January 1980, cited by James Bayer, 'Electoral Politics and Canadian Sanctions: The Case of Afghanistan,' paper presented to the Conference on Canada, Sanctions and the Soviet Union: Lessons from Experience, University of Toronto, July 1988.

39 See editorial, *Evening Telegram*, St John's, 9 Jan. 1980; *Globe and Mail*, 8 Jan. 1980, cited in Bayer, 'Electoral Politics and Canadian Sanctions.'

40 *CPD*, Senate, 19 Feb. 1980, 57. Compare Lowe's criticism of the cancellation of the fisheries deal that Tasmania was bearing a 'disproportionate share of the burden.' *The Age*, 11 Jan. 1980.

41 A most sympathetic descriptive account of the Olympic boycott case, based on access to the prime minister's papers, can be found in Weller, *Malcolm Fraser PM*, 344–53; for a most unsympathetic treatment of the same issue, see Renouf, *Malcolm Fraser and Australian Foreign Policy*, 100–2.

42 See the comments of representatives of the Victorian Farmers and Graziers Association and the Australian Wheatgrowers Federation, *The Age,* 8 Jan. 1980; the Australian Wheat Board, *Canberra Times,* 8 Jan. 1980; the Wool Council of Australia, ibid., 26 Jan. and 14 Feb. 1980; and the Australian Mining Industry Council and Australian Wool Corporation, *The Age,* 30 Jan. 1980.

43 *CPD,* Representatives, 21 Feb. 1980, 229.

44 *The Age,* 8 Jan. 1980.

45 *Canberra Times,* 14, 18, and 19 Mar. 1980.

46 Weller, *Malcolm Fraser PM,* 347.

47 *National Times,* 22–28 June 1980, 3.

48 *CPD,* Representatives, 19 Feb. 1980, esp. 28, 36.

49 Ibid., 36.

50 John Armitage (ALP, Chifley, NSW): *CPD,* Representatives, 20 Feb. 1980, 98.

51 See the exchange in the House of Representatives: *CPD,* 21 Feb. 1980, 197–8.

52 See Fraser's confirmation in *The Age,* 29 Feb. 1980. However, Weller, who had access to Fraser's papers, dismisses the stories about the Nareen clip as 'unsubstantiated rumours,' but offers no other comment: *Malcolm Fraser PM,* 349.

53 *CPD,* Representatives, 21 Feb. 1980, 250.

54 *Canberra Times,* 26 Jan. 1980.

55 Weller, *Malcolm Fraser PM,* 348.

56 See *The Age,* 24 May 1980; see also *National Times,* 22–28 June 1980, 3, for the attempts by Fraser to secure a reversal of this decision.

57 *International Canada,* April 1980, 70.

58 It was not until June, when the Canadian government began formulating its plans for the new crop year beginning 1 August, that the farmers' attachment to the embargo began to slip. See Kirton, 'Economic Sanctions and Alliance Consultations,' 284–5.

59 Sandra Kereliuk, 'The Canadian Boycott of the 1980 Moscow Olympic Games,' in G. Redmond, ed., *Sport and Politics* (Champaign, Ill.: Human Kinetics Publishers 1986); *International Canada,* April 1980, 70; and Morse, 'Sport and Canadian Foreign Policy,' 12–13.

60 Bayer, 'Sanctioning the Soviets,' 292 n. 29.

61 See, for example, CPD, Representatives, 19 Feb. 1980: the comments of Hayden (28–29), Keating (47), Young (52).

62 Weller, *Malcolm Fraser PM,* 397, 403.

63 *Sydney Morning Herald,* 16 Jan. 1980.

64 *Globe and Mail,* 28 Jan. 1980. For an examination of the historical role of

this ethnic group, see Samuel J. Nesdoly, 'Changing Perspectives: The Ukrainian-Canadians' Role in Canadian-Soviet Relations,' in Aloysius Balawyder, ed., *Canadian-Soviet Relations, 1939–1980* (Oakville, Ont.: Mosaic Press 1981), 107–27.

65 *Globe and Mail*, 11 Feb. 1980.

66 Ibid., 12 Jan. 1980.

67 Ibid., 30 Jan. 1980.

68 *CPD*, Representatives, 20 Feb. 1980, 138.

69 Senator Peter Walsh's reaction in 1989 – fully six years after Fraser's departure from national politics – is instructive: the mere memory of the 1980 sanctions prompted an outpouring of invective against Fraser as 'one of the greatest humbugs and frauds of all time.' *CPD*, Senate, 14 June 1989, 3964.

70 Philip Ayres, *Malcolm Fraser: A Biography* (Richmond, Vic.: William Heinemann Australia 1987), 394–400; Renouf, *Malcolm Fraser*, chaps 1, 3, and 6; John Edwards, *Life Wasn't Meant to Be Easy: A Political Profile of Malcolm Fraser* (Sydney: Mayhem 1977), chap. 18; Weller, *Malcolm Fraser PM*, 314–15.

71 *New York Times*, 5 Jan. 1980.

72 Quoted in Weller, *Malcolm Fraser PM*, 350.

CHAPTER 8: The Tiananmen Massacre

1 For example, James Barber, 'Economic Sanctions as a Policy Instrument,' *International Affairs* 55 (1979), 371; James M. Lindsay, 'Trade Sanctions as Policy Instruments: A Re-examination,' *International Studies Quarterly* 30 (1986), 156, 166–8; Margaret Doxey, 'International Sanctions,' in David G. Haglund and Michael K. Hawes, eds, *World Politics: Power, Interdependence and Dependence* (Toronto: Harcourt Brace Jovanovich Canada 1990), 254.

2 Lindsay, 'Trade Sanctions as Policy Instruments,' 167–8.

3 For a sharp and strongly argued contrary view, however, see David A. Baldwin, *Economic Statecraft* (Princeton: Princeton University Press 1985), 276–8.

4 Lindsay, 'Trade Sanctions as Policy Instruments,' 167–8.

5 For surveys of the development of the relationships with China, see Paul Evans and Bernie Frolic, eds, *Reluctant Adversaries: Canada and the People's Republic of China, 1949–1970* (Toronto: University of Toronto Press 1991); Edmund S.K. Fung and Colin Mackerras, *From Fear to Friendship: Australia's Policies towards the People's Republic of China, 1966–1982* (St Lucia:

University of Queensland Press 1985); and E.M. Andrews, *Australia and China: The Ambiguous Relationship* (Melbourne: Melbourne University Press 1985).

6 All dollar figures are indicated in local currency; in mid-1989, A$1.00 = C$0.90.

7 See Australia, Australian Bureau of Statistics, *Foreign Trade, Australia: Comparative and Summary Tables, 1988–89* (Canberra 1990); Canada, Department of External Affairs and International Trade, *Annual Report 1988/89* (Ottawa: Supply and Services Canada 1989), 50–1.

8 *The Age*, 6 June 1989; J.T. Paltiel, 'Rude Awakening: Canada and China following Tiananmen,' in Maureen Appel Molot and Fen Osler Hampson, eds, *Canada Among Nations 1989: The Challenge of Change* (Ottawa: Carleton University Press 1990), 45.

9 See Stuart Kennedy, 'Rough Road to China,' *The Bulletin*, 18 Oct. 1988, 128; Australia, AUSSAT, *1990 Annual Report* (Canberra: Australian Government Publishing Service 1991), 14–15.

10 *Sydney Morning Herald*, 6 June 1989; *Toronto Star*, 7 June 1989.

11 For a good historical overview, see Jonathan D. Spence, *The Search for Modern China* (Sydney: Hutchinson 1990), chap. 25, 712–47. Also see George Hicks, ed., *The Broken Mirror: China after Tiananmen* (Harlow: Longman 1990); Anthony Kane, ed., *China Briefing, 1989* (Boulder: Westview Press 1989); Kevin Barry Bucknall, 'The Political Economy of the Tiananmen Massacre,' in Colin Mackerras, Kevin Bucknall, and Russell Trood, *The Beijing Tragedy: Implications for China and Australia*, Research Paper 51, Centre for the Study of Australia-Asia Relations, Griffith University, October 1989, 37–55; and Paltiel, 'Rude Awakening,' 45–50. For the Chinese government's own view of the crisis, see Chen Xitong, 'Report on Checking the Turmoil and Quelling the Counter-revolutionary Rebellion,' *Beijing Review*, 17–23 July 1989, i–xx.

12 *Globe and Mail*, 15 June 1989.

13 For a theoretical discussion of the role of ethnic groups in foreign policy, see David Howard Goldberg, *Foreign Policy and Ethnic Interest Groups: American and Canadian Jews Lobby for Israel* (Westport, Conn.: Greenwood Press 1990), esp. introduction and conclusion.

14 On Chinese Canadians, see Canada, Statistics Canada, *Canada 1986 Census: Profile of Ethnic Groups* (Ottawa: Supply and Services Canada 1989). Although the Chinese community in Canada used to be split into pro-Beijing and pro-Taiwan factions, Chinese community groups have not been active in Canadian foreign policy issues since the recognition of the People's Republic of China by Canada in October 1970. One measure of

their low profile is that no Chinese group is mentioned in Elizabeth Riddell-Dixon's survey of interest groups. See *The Domestic Mosaic: Domestic Groups and Canadian Foreign Policy* (Toronto: Canadian Institute of International Affairs 1985).

15 See Australia, Australian Bureau of Statistics, *Year Book Australia 1988* (Canberra 1988), 263, 283. Other data suggest that the postwar migration to Australia of 'ethnic Chinese' was approximately 250,000. See the discussion in Andrews, *Australia and China*, 232, 243–4.

16 *Toronto Star*, 4 June 1989.

17 See, for example, *Sydney Morning Herald*, 14 June 1989, and *The Age*, 15 June 1989.

18 *The Australian*, 15 June 1989; *Ottawa Citizen*, 16 June 1989; *Globe and Mail*, 21 June 1989.

19 *Globe and Mail*, 9 June 1989.

20 *The Australian*, 7 June 1989.

21 *Sydney Morning Herald*, 7 June 1989.

22 *The Age*, 17 June 1989.

23 For an account, see Máire O'Brien, 'Canada China Policy in the Aftermath of Tiananmen: A Bureaucratic Politics Perspective,' paper presented to the Canadian Political Science Association, Charlottetown, June 1992, 18–20; see also *Globe and Mail*, 9 and 22 June 1989; *Toronto Star*, 23 June 1989; *Ottawa Citizen*, 23 June 1989.

24 *The Age*, 5 June 1989.

25 *Canberra Times* and *Sydney Morning Herald*, 6 June 1989.

26 *Sydney Morning Herald*, 6 June 1989.

27 *The Australian*, 9 June 1989.

28 *Courier-Mail*, 25 June; also editorial, 6 June.

29 Such as Dennis Argall, a former Australian ambassador to Beijing: see his cautionary views quoted in *The Age*, 6 June 1989; *The Australian*, 7 June 1989; and *Canberra Times*, 20 June 1989.

30 *New York Times*, 5 June 1989. Winston Lord, the United States ambassador to Beijing from 1985 to 1989, was to argue later in the year that the United States needed to have a 'steadier vision' and a less emotional view of China. 'China and America: Beyond the Big Chill,' *Foreign Affairs* 68 (Fall 1989), 26.

31 See, for example, the responses of academics at the University of Sydney (*The Australian*, 6 June 1989), Flinders University (*The Advertiser*, 7 June 1989); the University of New South Wales and Murdoch University (*The Australian*, 7 June 1989); and Australian National University (*Canberra Times*, 8 June 1989).

32 Indeed, Paul M. Evans of York University would write a piece in the *Globe and Mail* urging that the government take a cautious approach to China: 'A call for caution,' *Globe and Mail*, 13 June 1989. It might be noted that no comparable view was expressed by an Australian academic in the national press.

33 *The Australian*, 7 June 1989.

34 *The Age*, 6 and 8 June 1989.

35 *Toronto Star*, 7 June 1989.

36 *Sydney Morning Herald*, 6 June 1989; *Northern Territory News*, 7 June 1989; *The Age*, 6 June 1989; *The Advertiser*, 23 June 1989.

37 *Toronto Star, Globe and Mail*, 6 June 1989.

38 Russell Trood, 'From Cooperation to Conflict,' in Mackerras, Bucknall, and Trood, *The Beijing Tragedy*, 64.

39 Department of External Affairs, *News Release* 117, 20 May 1989.

40 Evan's statement of 22 May 1989 is reproduced in Australia, *Australian Foreign Affairs and Trade – The Monthly Record* 60 (May 1989), 235; hereafter *Australian Foreign Affairs Record*.

41 A task force was created in External Affairs in Ottawa to coordinate China operations: see the account in O'Brien, 'Aftermath of Tiananmen,' 16.

42 *Australian Foreign Affairs Record*, 60 (May 1989), 233.

43 Canada, Department of External Affairs, *News Release* 099, 2 May 1989; *Globe and Mail*, 14 June 1989.

44 *Le Devoir*, 6 May 1989, A12.

45 For surveys of international reactions, see, for example, Peter Van Ness, 'Sanctions on China,' *Far Eastern Economic Review*, 21 Sept. 1989, 25–6; and William McGurn, 'The U.S. and China: Sanctioning Tiananmen Square,' in Hicks, ed., *Broken Mirror*, 233–46.

46 A brief survey appears in Paltiel, 'Rude Awakening,' 43–57.

47 *Toronto Star*, 6 June 1989.

48 *New York Times*, 4 and 5 June 1989.

49 *Toronto Star*, 5 June 1989.

50 Ibid., 4 and 5 June 1989; *Globe and Mail*, 5 June 1989. For Clark's speech in Canada, see Parliament, House of Commons, *Debates*, 5 June 1989, 2597–9 (also reproduced in Department of External Affairs, *Statements and Speeches* 89/16, Ottawa, 5 June 1989).

51 *Globe and Mail*, 8 and 9 June 1989.

52 Department of External Affairs, *Statements and Speeches* 89/16, Ottawa, 5 June 1989.

53 House of Commons, *Debates*, 5 June 1989, 2599; *Globe and Mail*, 6 June 1989.

54 Department of External Affairs, *Statements and Speeches* 89/16, Ottawa, 5 June 1989.

55 *Ottawa Citizen, Toronto Star*, 15 June 1989.

56 *Toronto Star, Globe and Mail*, 13 June 1989.

57 *Toronto Star*, 5 June 1989; *Ottawa Citizen*, 6 June 1989; House of Commons, *Debates*, 5 June 1989, 2593.

58 *Globe and Mail*, 14 June 1989.

59 Drake also provided Members of Parliament with a formal briefing on 20 June: see Canada, Parliament, House of Commons, Standing Committee on External Affairs and International Trade, *Minutes of Proceedings and Evidence*, issue 8, 20 June 1989.

60 Department of External Affairs, *Statements and Speeches* 89/18, 30 June 1989.

61 *Globe and Mail*, 7 Oct. 1989.

62 Paltiel, 'Rude Awakening,' 44–5; Department of External Affairs, *Annual Report 1986–87* (Ottawa: Supply and Services Canada 1987), 48.

63 For a discussion of COCOM sanctions against China in the postwar period, see Paul M. Evans, 'Caging the Dragon: Post-war Economic Sanctions against the People's Republic of China,' in David Leyton-Brown, ed., *The Utility of International Economic Sanctions*, (London: Croom Helm 1987), 59–85.

64 For accounts of the Australian reactions, see Stephanie Lawson, 'Problems in Australian Foreign Policy, January–June 1989,' *Australian Journal of Politics and History* 35:3 (1989); Colin Brown, 'Problems in Australian Foreign Policy, July–December 1989,' *Australian Journal of Politics and History* 36:2 (1990); Trood, 'From Cooperation to Conflict'; and Kim Richard Nossal, *The Beijing Massacre: Australian Responses* (Canberra: Australian Foreign Policy Papers 1993).

65 *The Australian*, 5 June 1989.

66 According to the embassy, Australians in Beijing included six journalists, 80 students, 300 other long-term residents and between 500 and 1500 tourists. *Canberra Times*, 6 June 1989.

67 Australia, Parliament, *Commonwealth Parliamentary Debates* (hereafter *CPD*), Senate, 5 June 1989, 3301.

68 *Canberra Times*, 17 June 1989.

69 Brown, 'Problems in Australian Foreign Policy,' 142.

70 *The Age*, 16 June 1989.

71 *CPD*, Senate, 8 June 1989, 3613–17; *CPD*, Representatives, 15 June 1989, 3523–8. It should be noted that Senator M.J. Macklin of Queensland, leader of the Australian Democrats, and Chris Schacht, an Australian Labor Party (ALP) senator from South Australia, introduced condemnatory motions on 6 and 7 June.

72 *Australian Foreign Affairs Record* 60 (June 1989), 265; *The Australian*, 15 June 1989.

73 *CPD*, Senate, 5 June 1989, 3301; Representatives, 15 June 1989, 3524; *The Australian*, 6 June 1989.

74 This general ban on contacts would also extend to minor functions: for example, members of the Department of Defence were instructed not to attend the reception given by the Chinese embassy in Canberra celebrating the 62nd anniversary of the founding of the People's Liberation Army. See Peter Van Ness, 'Analysing the Impact of International Sanctions on China,' *Working Paper* 1989/4 (Canberra: Department of International Relations, Australian National University, December 1989), 4.

75 *The Age*, 6 June 1989.

76 *CPD*, Representatives, 15 June 1989, 3526.

77 *Canberra Times*, 23 June 1989.

78 *The Age*, 6 June 1989.

79 FitzGerald, interview with *The Age*, 7 June 1989. Woodard, letter to the editor, *The Age*, 21 June 1989.

80 *Australian Financial Review*, 27 June 1989.

81 *Canberra Times*, 21 June 1989.

82 Trood, 'From Cooperation to Conflict,' 70.

83 *Canberra Times*, 22 June 1989.

84 *Australian Foreign Affairs Record* 60 (July 1989), 347.

85 Note, however, that Winston Lord has argued that one purpose of the Tiananmen sanctions was to deter not the Chinese, but the Soviet Union – in other words, to signal to the Soviet leadership that a comparable crackdown in the USSR would likely produce a very negative reaction in the West. Lord, 'China and America,' 10.

86 Lawson, 'Problems in Australian foreign policy,' 433.

87 For a less formal enunciation of the Canadian position, see the testimony of Jean McCloskey, assistant deputy minister at External Affairs responsible for Asia and the Pacific, to the House of Commons Standing Committee on External Affairs and International Trade, *Minutes of Proceedings and Evidence*, issue 8, 20 June 1989, 8:23–4.

88 Kim Richard Nossal, 'International Sanctions as International Punishments,' *International Organization* 43 (Spring 1989), 301–22.

89 This argument was made in the Australian context by Stephen FitzGerald, Australia's first ambassador to China: 'Australia's China,' *Australian Journal of Chinese Affairs* 24 (July 1990), but it is equally applicable to the Canadian situation.

90 *The Australian*, 8 June 1989.

91 Gregory Hywood in *Australian Financial Review*, 9 June 1989.

92 See the comments of Earl Drake on this issue to House of Commons, Standing Committee on External Affairs and International Trade, *Minutes of Proceedings and Evidence*, issue 8, 20 June 1989, 8:22.

93 The paper, 'China: Implications for Australian policy; a first assessment,' was obtained by *The Age*, 30 June 1989.

94 *Australian Financial Review*, 27 June 1989.

CHAPTER 9: The Gulf Conflict

1 Richard Leaver, 'Economic Sanctions and the Gulf War: The Opportunity Costs of the Military Solution,' in Michael McKinley, ed., *The Gulf War: Critical Perspectives* (Sydney: Allen and Unwin, forthcoming).

2 For accounts of the conflict, see Jean Edward Smith, *George Bush's War* (New York: Holt 1992) and Bob Woodward, *The Commanders* (New York: Simon and Schuster 1991), pt. 2, 197ff.

3 Quoted in Woodward, *The Commanders*, 260. On Thatcher's role, see Tom Mathews, 'The Road to War,' *Newsweek*, 28 Jan. 1991, 58; and Craig R. Whitney, 'The Empire Strikes Back,' *New York Times Magazine*, 10 Mar. 1991, 34.

4 Woodward, *The Commanders*, 231–73, and Mathews, 'Road to War,' 58–9, describe the intricate process by which the United States and Saudi Arabia came to an agreement on the temporary basing of foreign troops on Saudi territory.

5 *New York Times*, 9 Aug. 1990, A15.

6 *The Australian*, 3 Aug. 1990; *Globe and Mail*, 3 Aug. 1990.

7 *Globe and Mail*, 4 Aug. 1990.

8 *The Age*, 7 Aug. 1990.

9 Explicit Australian and Canadian promises of support for whatever UN sanctions were imposed may be found in the *Weekend Australian*, 4–5 Aug. 1990; *The Age*, 6 Aug. 1990; and the *Globe and Mail*, 4 Aug. 1990.

10 *Weekend Australian*, 4–5 Aug. 1990.

11 *Globe and Mail*, 8 Aug. 1990.

12 Ibid., 4 Aug. 1990.

13 Press release, cited in *Globe and Mail*, 6 Aug. 1990.

14 *The Age*, 6 Aug. 1990.

15 See the account by Greg Sheridan in *The Australian*, 10 Aug. 1990.

16 Quoted in *Australian Financial Review*, 6 Aug. 1990.

17 Australia, *Australian Foreign Affairs and Trade – The Monthly Record* 61 (August 1990), 564–5; hereafter *Australian Foreign Affairs Record*.

18 *The Age*, 7 Aug. 1990.

19 *Australian Financial Review*, 8 Aug. 1990; *Globe and Mail*, 8 Aug. 1990.

20 *Globe and Mail*, 8 Aug. 1990.
21 *The Age*, 7 Aug. 1990; *Australian Financial Review*, 8 Aug. 1990.
22 *The Age*, 9 Aug. 1990.
23 Quoted in *Sydney Morning Herald*, 1 Sept. 1990.
24 Mark Baker, 'The imperious Hawke style,' *The Age*, 7 Sept. 1990.
25 See Michelle Grattan, *The Age*, 11 Aug. 1990; Laurie Oakes, *The Bulletin*, 21 Aug. 1990; and Paul Grigson, *Sydney Morning Herald*, 1 Sept. 1990.
26 *The Age*, 10 Aug. 1990.
27 Paul Grigson, *Sydney Morning Herald*, 1 Sept. 1990.
28 *The Bulletin*, 21 Aug. 1990.
29 Laurie Oakes, *The Bulletin*, 21 Aug. 1990.
30 For treatments of ALP policies, see T.B. Millar, *Australia in Peace and War: External Relations since 1788*, 2d ed. (Canberra: Australian National University Press 1991), chaps 18 and 20; and Henry S. Albinski, *Australian External Policy under Labor* (Vancouver: University of British Columbia Press 1977).
31 On the MX crisis, see *Australian Foreign Affairs Record* 56 (February 1985), passim; also Gregory Pemberton, 'Australia and the United States,' in P.J. Boyce and J.R. Angel, eds, *Diplomacy in the Marketplace: Australia in World Affairs, 1981–90* (Melbourne: Longman Cheshire 1992), 136.
32 For accounts, see *Sydney Morning Herald*, 21 Aug. 1990; *The Australian* and *Australian Financial Review*, 22 Aug. 1990; and *Canberra Times*, 23 Aug. 1990.
33 *Globe and Mail*, 9 and 28 Aug. 1990.
34 *Sydney Morning Herald*, 1 Sept. 1990.
35 *Globe and Mail*, 9 and 28 Aug. 1990.
36 *Canberra Times*, 11 Aug. 1990.
37 *Globe and Mail*, 4 Aug. 1990.
38 Ibid., 9 Aug. 1990.
39 Ibid., 24 Aug. 1990; Charlotte Gray, 'War Games,' *Saturday Night*, March 1991, 10; Geoffrey Stevens, 'How we entered war: decision was all up to prime minister,' *Toronto Star*, 20 Jan. 1991.
40 *Globe and Mail*, 11 Aug. 1990; *The Economist*, 22 Sept. 1990, 45–6.
41 *Toronto Star*, *Globe and Mail*, 11 Aug. 1990.
42 As Martin Rudner has pointed out, relations between Canada and the Gulf region were 'fairly remote': see 'Canada, the Gulf Crisis and Collective Security,' in Fen Osler Hampson and Christopher J. Maule, eds, *Canada Among Nations 1990–91: After the Cold War* (Ottawa: Carleton University Press 1991), 268.
43 Order-in-Council PC1990–1995.

44 *Globe and Mail,* 13 Sept. 1990; Canada, Parliament, House of Commons, *Debates,* 24 Sept. 1990, 13218.

45 It should be noted that while the original Pentagon plan for the defence of Saudi Arabia had called for a deployment of 200,000 troops, the exact number had been purposely fudged in public statements in August. John Sununu, Bush's chief of staff, put out the figure of 50,000 troops to the media. And although an official at the Pentagon later leaked the real figure of 200,000 to the Associated Press, the figure of 50,000 stuck in public perceptions, making the arrival of some 100,000 troops by September seem to be a doubling of the original commitment. Woodward, *The Commanders,* 249, 279.

46 See Woodward, *The Commanders,* 312–3, 321–2; and Thomas L. Friedman and Patrick E. Tyler, 'The path to war: Bush's crucial decisions,' *New York Times,* 3 Mar. 1991, 1, 12.

47 *The Globe and Mail,* 12 Jan. 1991.

48 *The Australian,* 12 Sept. 1990; *Australian Financial Review,* 14 Sept. 1990.

49 *Australian Foreign Affairs Monthly Record* 61 (September 1990), 665.

50 Australia, Parliament,*Commonwealth Parliamentary Debates,* Representatives, 4 Dec. 1990, 4322; hereafter *CPD.*

51 *Pacific Research* 4 (February 1991), 29–30.

52 *Globe and Mail,* 15 Sept. 1990.

53 Ibid., 12 Jan. 1991.

54 Ibid., 21 Feb. 1991.

55 Kim Richard Nossal, 'Quantum Leaping: The Gulf Debate in Australia and Canada,' in Michael McKinley, ed., *The Gulf War: Critical Perspectives* (Sydney: Allen and Unwin, forthcoming).

56 J. Mohan Malik, *The Gulf War: Australia's Role and Asian-Pacific Responses,* Canberra Papers on Strategy and Defence 90 (Canberra: Strategic and Defence Studies Centre, Australian National University 1992), 4–6.

57 Denis Stairs, *The Diplomacy of Constraint: Canada, the Korean War, and the United States* (Toronto: University of Toronto Press 1974); Douglas A. Ross, *In the Interests of Peace: Canada and Vietnam, 1954–73* (Toronto: University of Toronto Press 1984).

58 Gray, 'War Games,' 13; *Globe and Mail,* 14 Aug. 1990.

59 Nossal, 'Quantum Leaping'; Cooper, Higgott, and Nossal, *Relocating Middle Powers,* 138.

60 However, it would be an oversimplification to argue, as John Kirton does, that in the Canadian case policy was determined wholly by concern over Iraqi atrocities. 'Liberating Kuwait: Canada and the Persian Gulf War, 1990–91,' in Don Munton and John Kirton, eds, *Canadian Foreign Policy:*

Selected Cases (Scarborough: Prentice-Hall Canada 1992), 383.

61 For prime-ministerial statements, see, in Australia: *CPD*, Representatives, 4 Dec. 1990, 4319–25; 21 Jan. 1991, 3–9; 22 Jan. 1991, 266–8. In Canada: House of Commons, *Debates*: 29 Nov. 1990, 15958–61; 15 Jan. 1991, 16984–91.

62 See poll results reported in the *Weekend Australian*, 1–2 Sept. 1990; *The Age*, 10 Sept. 1990; *Globe and Mail*, 30 Oct. 1990; *The PAI Report* (November 1990), 31; *Sydney Morning Herald*, 8 Dec. 1990; and Angus Reid–Southam News poll, 17–22 Dec. 1990. It should be noted that by December, fully 80 per cent of Australians supported Canberra's Gulf policies.

63 House of Commons, *Debates*, 16 Jan. 1991, 17132–4, 17165–6.

64 Once war had broken out, the NDP did feel compelled to add that they supported Canada's armed forces serving in the Gulf, but argued that the government should find a 'humanitarian' role for them. However, when the party's leader, Audrey McLaughlin, tried to verbalize this position, her speech became increasingly incomprehensible as she attempted to grapple with how one assigns a CF-18 warplane a 'humanitarian' role. See House of Commons, *Debates*, 16 Jan. 1991, 17166–7.

65 See, for example, House of Commons, *Debates*, 28 Nov. 1990: the comments of, among others, Herb Gray (L, Windsor), 15867; John Brewin (NDP, Victoria), 15869; Warren Allmand (L, Notre-Dame-de-Grace), 15888; Dan Heap (NDP, Spadina), 15899; and Stan Keyes (L, Hamilton West), 15920.

66 See *CPD*, Senate, 21 Jan. 1991: the comments of, among others, J.R. Coulter (AD, SA), 68; Margaret Reynolds (ALP, Qld), a former minister for local government, 201; and Bruce Childs (ALP, NSW), convenor of the ALP's Left faction, 238. For comments in the House, see *CPD*, Representatives, 21 Jan. 1991: Laurie Ferguson (ALP, Reid), 78–9; John Langmore (ALP, Fraser), 97–100; Frank Walker (ALP, Robertson), a former minister for the arts, 210–12; and Neville Newell (ALP, Richmond), 230–2.

67 *Toronto Star, Globe and Mail*, 11 Aug. 1990.

68 Australia, Department of Foreign Affairs and Trade, *Backgrounder* 1:25 (21 Sept. 1990), 7.

69 *Globe and Mail*, 13 Nov. 1990.

70 *CPD*, Representatives, 4 Dec. 1990, 4323.

71 For accounts of the negotiations between the cabinet and the factions, see *The Age*, 3 Dec. 1990; and *Sydney Morning Herald*, 7 Dec. 1990.

72 Department of Foreign Affairs and Trade, *Backgrounder* 1:25 (21 Sept. 1990), 4.

73 *Globe and Mail*, 27 Oct. 1990. This grim sentence was widely interpreted as

war-mongering by the Opposition – who took to calling Clark 'Rambo Joe' and 'GI Joe.' However, this speech makes more sense when read as an expression of Clark's opposition to a too-hasty embrace of the war option.

CHAPTER 10: The Termination Trap

1 For example, Canadian sanctions against Haiti, imposed in 1991 in the wake of a military coup that ousted the elected president, Jean-Bertrand Aristide, were lifted in August 1993 following the agreement of the Haitian military to restore Aristide to power, and then reimposed as quickly in October when the military reneged on the deal. For a fuller discussion of the Haitian case, Tom Farer, *Collectively Defending Democracy in a World of Sovereign States: The Western Hemisphere Prospect*, Essays on Human Rights and Democratic Development #1 (Montreal: International Centre for Human Rights and Demoncratic Development 1993), esp. 21ff.

2 M.S. Daoudi and M.S. Dajani, *Economic Sanctions: Ideals and Experience* (London: Routledge and Kegan Paul 1985), esp. app. 2, demonstrate the degree to which both students and practitioners of statecraft doubt the 'effectiveness' of sanctions. For a cogently argued revisionist view, see David A. Baldwin, *Economic Statecraft* (Princeton: Princeton University Press 1985).

3 David Leyton-Brown, 'Economic Sanctions: What They Do and How They Work,' *Peace and Security* 1 (Winter 1986–7), 5; see also External Affairs and International Trade Canada, *For Effective and Appropriate Sanctions*, Policy Planning Staff Paper 93/04, by Jean Prévost (Ottawa: March 1993).

4 This point is made, for example, by James M. Lindsay in 'Trade Sanctions as Policy Instruments: A Re-examination,' *International Studies Quarterly* 30 (1986); see also Robin Renwick, *Economic Sanctions* (Cambridge, Mass.: Center for International Affairs 1981).

5 Kim Richard Nossal, 'International Sanctions as International Punishment,' *International Organization* 43 (Spring 1989).

6 This argument is advanced by Geoffrey Blainey, *The Causes of War* (New York: Free Press 1973).

7 For good accounts of the Western response, see Peggy L. Falkenheim, 'Post-Afghanistan Sanctions,' in David Leyton-Brown, ed., *The Utility of International Economic Sanctions* (London: Croom Helm 1987), 105–30; Baldwin, *Economic Statecraft*; Gary Clyde Hufbauer and Jeffrey J. Schott, *Economic Sanctions Reconsidered: History and Current Policy* (Washington: Institute for International Economics 1985), app. C, 655–65.

8 Also see James Bayer, 'Sanctioning the Soviets: The Afghanistan Intervention, 1979–80,' in Don Munton and John Kirton, eds, *Canadian Foreign Policy: Selected Cases* (Scarborough: Prentice-Hall Canada 1992), 286–98.

9 See Allen Guttman, 'The Cold War and the Olympics,' *International Journal* 43 (Autumn 1988), 554–68.

10 As noted in the Introduction above, a 'compellent' punishment is designed to hurt the offender until he has been compelled to stop his wrong-doing. Domestic compellent punishments, for example, would include those imposed on workers for disobeying back-to-work legislation, or on witnesses for disobeying a judge's order to answer a question. The term was coined by Thomas Schelling in *The Strategy of Conflict* (New York: Oxford University Press, 1960) 195.

11 John Kirton, 'Economic Sanctions and Alliance Consultations: Canada, the United States and the Strains of 1979–82,' in Leyton-Brown, ed., *Utility of International Economic Sanctions*, 282.

12 Quoted in *Globe and Mail*, 8 Jan. 1980.

13 See *International Canada*, January 1980, 2–4.

14 Baldwin, *Economic Statecraft*, 264–5.

15 *Globe and Mail*, 12 Jan. 1980, 1.

16 Hufbauer and Shott, *Economic Sanctions Reconsidered*, 664, judge that the Afghanistan sanctions should be considered a failure; their assessment is widely shared. However, if one employs their crude analytical framework for judging 'success' and 'failure' in sanctions, one is inevitably going to end up with a plethora of failures. By contrast, as Falkenheim and Baldwin have noted, if this case is looked at through a less simplistic prism, it is not at all clear that the Afghanistan sanctions were a 'failure.'

17 See the argument Henry S. Bradsher, *Afghanistan and the Soviet Union*, expanded ed. (Durham: Duke University Press 1985), 273–4.

18 Robert A.D. Ford, *Our Man in Moscow: A Diplomat's Reflections on the Soviet Union* (Toronto: University of Toronto Press 1989), 320–1.

19 Ibid., 322.

20 Paul Marantz, 'Economic Sanctions in the Polish Crisis,' in J.L. Black and J.W. Strong, eds, *Sisyphus and Poland: Reflections on Martial Law* (Winnipeg: Ronald P. Frye 1986), 122.

21 *Globe and Mail*, 30 Jan. 1980. It might be noted that Trudeau ran into comparable problems with public opinion after both the Polish crisis and the shooting down of KAL 007. On Poland, see J.K. Fedorowicz, 'Trudeau's Views on Domestic Developments in Poland,' in Adam Bromke, Harald von Riekhoff, Jacques Lévesque, and J.K. Fedorowicz, *Canada's Response to the Polish Crisis* (Toronto: Canadian Institute of International Affairs 1982),

33–44; on KAL, see Seymour M. Hersh, 'The Target Is Destroyed': What
Really Happened to Flight 007 and What America Knew About It (New York:
Random House 1986; Vintage 1987), 347–9. On Trudeau and the USSR
more generally, J.L. Granatstein and Robert Bothwell, Pirouette: Pierre
Trudeau and Canadian Foreign Policy (Toronto: University of Toronto Press
1990), 200–1.

22 See the account of this rally in the Globe and Mail, 11 Feb. 1980, 8.
23 For discussions of the divergence between the United States and its European allies caused by different economic interests, see Bernard M. Wolf,
'Economic Impact on the United States of the Pipeline Sanctions,' in
Leyton-Brown, ed., Utility of Economic Sanctions, 207–20; Marantz, 'Economic Sanctions in the Polish Crisis'; Baldwin, Economic Statecraft, chap. 9.
24 For example, see Kirton, 'Alliance Consultations,' 269–93.
25 For an account, see Marantz, 'Economic Sanctions in the Polish Crisis.'
26 Ibid., 121.
27 Falkenheim, 'Post-Afghanistan Sanctions,' 126.
28 For discussions of this incident, see Hersh, 'The Target Is Destroyed'; and
Alexander Dallin, Black Box: KAL 007 and the Superpowers (Berkeley:
University of California Press 1985). For a discussion of the sanctions
imposed against the Soviet Union in the wake of the shoot-down, see
Hufbauer and Schott, Economic Sanctions Reconsidered, app. C, 738–43.
29 Quoted in Hufbauer and Schott, Economic Sanctions Reconsidered, 740.
30 Quoted in ibid., 94.
31 Paul M. Evans, 'Canada's Relations with China Emergent,' Canadian
Foreign Policy 1 (Spring 1993), 14.
32 The Age, Sydney Morning Herald, 24 Jan. 1990.
33 Canberra Times, 11 Jan. 1990.
34 Sydney Morning Herald, 24 Jan. 1990.
35 Australia, Department of Foreign Affairs and Trade, Cambodia: An Australian Peace Proposal (Canberra: Australian Government Publishing Service
1990). For general discussions, see Gareth Evans and Bruce Grant, Australia's Foreign Relations in the World of the 1990s (Melbourne: Melbourne
University Press 1991), 206–18; and Andrew F. Cooper, Richard A. Higgott, and Kim Richard Nossal, Relocating Middle Powers: Australia and
Canada in a Changing World Order (Melbourne: University of Melbourne
Press 1993), 149–52.
36 Australia, Australian Foreign Affairs and Trade – The Monthly Record 61
(May 1990), 315–16; hereafter Australian Foreign Affairs Record.
37 The Age, 3 May 1990; Sydney Morning Herald, 31 May 1990.
38 Australian Foreign Affairs Record 61 (August 1990), 567–8.

39 Ibid., (September 1990), 662–3.
40 *The Age*, 22 Sept. 1990.
41 Gareth Evans, 'Australia and China: Looking Back – and Forward,' *Australian Foreign Affairs Record* 62 (April 1991), 136.
42 Peter Van Ness, 'Australia's Human Rights Delegation to China, 1991: A Case Study,' in Ian Russell, Peter Van Ness, and Beng-Huat Chua, *Australian Human Rights Diplomacy*, Australian Foreign Policy Papers (Canberra: Australian Foreign Policy Publications Programme, Australian National University 1993), 49–85; and Australia, *Report of the Australian Human Rights Delegation to China, 14–26 July 1991* (Canberra: Australian Government Publishing Service 1991). A second human-rights delegation visited China in November 1992.
43 Keating met with the premier, Li Peng, and with the minister for foreign trade and investment, Wu Yi. The focus of Keating's visit was on the economic elements of the Sino-Australian relationship; Australia's concerns about human rights in China were, in the words of an *Age* editorial, 'virtually ignored.' *The Age*, 28 June 1993; see also Geoffrey Barker, 'PM bids for wool deal with China,' *The Age*, 25 June 1993.
44 Quoted in Marantz, 'Economic Sanctions in the Polish Crisis,' 110.
45 Baldwin, *Economic Statecraft*, 265.
46 See the discussion in Marantz, 'Economic Sanctions in the Polish Crisis'; and Baldwin, *Economic Statecraft*, 278–82.
47 See the argument in Nossal, 'International Sanctions as International Punishment.'

CHAPTER 11: The Impact of Rhetoric

1 For example, see Chris Brown, 'Canada and Southern Africa 1989: Autonomy, Image and Capacity in Foreign Policy,' in Maureen Appel Molot and Fen Osler Hampson, *Canada Among Nations, 1989: The Challenge of Change* (Ottawa: Carleton University Press 1990), 207–24.
2 T.A. Keenleyside, 'Canada–South Africa Commercial Relations, 1977–1982: Business as Usual?' *Canadian Journal of African Studies* 17 (1983), 449–68.
3 Quoted in Heribert Adam and Kogila Moodley, *Democratizing Southern Africa: Challenges for Canadian Policy*, Occasional Papers 9 (Ottawa: Canadian Institute for International Peace and Security, June 1992), 98.
4 Canada, Department of External Affairs, *Statements and Speeches* 85/14, 23 Oct. 1985, 3.
5 Ibid., 2.
6 In the Canadian context, see, for example, the comments of Jean Prévost,

For Effective and Appropriate Sanctions, Policy Planning Staff Paper 93/04 (Ottawa: External Affairs and International Trade Canada, March 1993), 44.

7 Such as the arguments against making a total break put to Mulroney by Robert Mugabe of Zimbabwe and Kenneth Kaunda of Zambia, both of whom were eager for the Canadian government to retain a diplomatic presence in South Africa to engage in a monitoring role. See Adam and Moodley, *Democratizing Southern Africa*, 96.

CHAPTER 12: Conclusion

1 Robert A. Frank is one economist who argues that humans are in fact not rational, self-interested calculators: see his *Passions Within Reason: The Strategic Role of the Emotions* (New York: W.W. Norton 1988).

2 Although, as Cooper, Higgott, and I have argued, Australia remained more resolutely multilateral in the 1980s and early 1990s than Canada: Andrew F. Cooper, Richard A. Higgott and Kim Richard Nossal, *Relocating Middle Powers: Australia and Canada in a Changing World Order* (Vancouver: University of British Columbia Press / Melbourne: Melbourne University Press, 1993). For an excellent historical examination of multilateralism in Canada's foreign policy, see Tom Keating, *Canada and World Order: The Multilateralist Tradition in Canadian Foreign Policy* (Toronto: McClelland and Stewart 1993).

3 Margaret Doxey, 'International Sanctions,' in David G. Haglund and Michael K. Hawes, eds, *World Politics: Power, Interdependence, and Dependence* (Toronto: Harcourt Brace Jovanovich 1990), 257.

4 See *Globe and Mail*, 12 Oct., 10 Nov., and 12 Nov. 1993: the media reported that the study showed that sanctions against Haiti were contributing to the deaths of more than 1000 children every month, and to a dramatic increase in malnutrition. However, serious questions were immediately raised about the methodology used in the study; in particular, it was noted that the figures being reported were not actual deaths, but merely extrapolations from observations of one locality. Harvard University was moved to issue a clarification shortly after the report was issued.

5 Louise Branson, 'Paying the price,' *Maclean's*, 1 Nov. 1993, 39; 'Death is the only relief for many of Belgrade's destitute elderly,' *Globe and Mail*, 22 Oct. 1993.

6 For an examination of the Dialogue Fund, see Heribert Adam and Kogila Moodley, *Democratizing South Africa: Challenges for Canadian Policy*, Occasional Papers 9 (Ottawa: Canadian Institute for International Peace and Security, June 1992), 80–8.

7 A full discussion of the Maduru Oya case is provided by David Gillies, 'Principled Intervention: Canadian Aid, Human Rights and the Sri Lankan Conflict,' in Robert Miller, ed., *Aid as Peacemaker: Canadian Development Assistance and Third World Conflict* (Ottawa: Carleton University Press 1992), 51–70.
8 *Hamilton Spectator*, 13 June 1992.

Index